Children's Testimony

27/09/05

Wiley Series in
The Psychology of Crime, Policing and Law

Series Editors

Graham Davies
University of Leicester, UK

and

Ray Bull
University of Portsmouth, UK

The Wiley series on the Psychology of Crime, Policing and the Law publishes concise and integrative reviews on important emerging areas of contemporary research. The purpose of the series is not merely to present research findings in a clear and readable form, but also to bring out their implications for both practice and policy. In this way, it is hoped the series will not only be useful to psychologists but also to all those concerned with crime detection and prevention, policing, and the judicial process.

Children's Testimony
A Handbook of Psychological Research and Forensic Practice

Edited by

Helen L. Westcott
Faculty of Social Sciences, The Open University, Milton Keynes, UK

Graham M. Davies
Department of Psychology, University of Leicester, UK

and

Ray H.C. Bull
Department of Psychology, University of Portsmouth, UK

JOHN WILEY & SO

Reprinted July 2002

Other Wiley Editorial Offices

John Wiley & Sons, Inc., 605 Third Avenue,
New York, NY 10158-0012, USA

WILEY-VCH GmbH, Pappelallee 3,
D-69469 Weinheim, Germany

John Wiley & Sons Australia Ltd, 33 Park Road, Milton,
Queensland 4064, Australia

John Wiley & Sons (Asia) Pte Ltd, 2 Clementi Loop #02-01,
Jin Xing Distripark, Singapore 129809

John Wiley & Sons (Canada) Ltd, 22 Worcester Road,
Rexdale, Ontario M9W 1L1, Canada

British Library Cataloguing in Publication Data

A catalogue record for this book is available from the British Library

ISBN 0-471-49172-1
    0-471-49173-X paperback

Project management by Originator Publishing Services, Gt Yarmouth, Norfolk
(typeset in 10/12pt Century Schoolbook)

Printed and bound in Great Britain by Antony Rowe, Chippenham, Wilts.

This book is printed on acid-free paper responsibly manufactured from sustainable
forestry, in which at least two trees are planted for each one used for paper production.

Contents

About the Editors

Helen Westcott is a Lecturer in Psychology at The Open University, Milton Keynes, England, UK and is a Chartered Forensic Psychologist. She was formerly Research Officer with the National Society for the Prevention of Cruelty to Children (NSPCC) in London, and has researched children's eyewitness testimony, and the investigative interviewing of children, for many years. Her other research interests include the abuse of disabled children, the abuse of children and young people in institutional care, and children's perceptions of social work intervention. Helen trains and presents regularly on these topics, and to date has published over 30 articles and two books, *Perspectives on the Memorandum: Policy, Practice and Research in Investigative Interviewing* (1997, edited with Jocelyn Jones) and *This Far and No Further: Towards Ending the Abuse of Disabled Children* (1996, authored with Merry Cross). She is part of the consortium working with the British Government's Home Office to revise the *Memorandum of Good Practice on Video Recorded Interviews with Child Witnesses for Criminal Proceedings* (1992).

Graham Davies is a Professor of Psychology at Leicester University, England, UK. He is a Fellow of the British Psychological Society and a Chartered Forensic Psychologist. His major research interests lie in the eyewitness testimony of children and adults, on which he has published some 100 papers and five books. Graham is regularly asked to provide training and advice to professionals working with child witnesses. He is currently chairing the consortium working with the British Government's Home Office to revise the *Memorandum of Good Practice on Video Recorded Interviews with Child Witnesses for Criminal Proceedings* (1992). His recent research has included evaluations for the Home Office of the Live Link (1991), videotape facilities for child witnesses (1995), and training procedures for police officers involved in investigative interviewing of children (1997). Graham is the immediate past Chair of the Society of Applied Research in Memory and Cognition

(SARMAC), and President-elect of the European Association of Psychology and Law.

Ray Bull is Professor of Psychology at the University of Portsmouth, England, UK. He has conducted research on witnessing since the late 1970s and on child witnesses since 1987. He regularly acts as an expert in legal cases involving child witness evidence. He has authored/co-authored over 100 papers in refereed research journals and chapters in edited books, co-authored five books, and co-edited three books. In 1991, Ray was asked by the British Government's Home Office (together with Professor Di Birch) to write the first draft of the *Memorandum of Good Practice on Video Recorded Interviews with Child Witnesses for Criminal Proceedings* (published in 1992). He is now part of the consortium working with the Home Office to revise the document. Ray is regularly asked by police forces and other organizations around the world to present on the investigative interviewing of children. In 1995, he was awarded a Higher Doctorate (Doctor of Science) in recognition of the quality and extent of his research.

About the Contributors

Kristen Weede Alexander, *Department of Psychology, University of California, Young Hall, 1 Shields Avenue, Davis, CA 95616-8686, USA*
Kristen Weede Alexander is a Doctoral Student in Human Development at the University of California, Davis. She received her Bachelor's Degree in Human Development from the University of California, Riverside, in 1995. Her research concerns children's cognitive and memory development generally and individual differences in children's eyewitness memory and suggestibility specifically. She is currently involved in several research projects related to children in the legal system.

Lynne Baker-Ward, *Department of Psychology, North Carolina State University, Raleigh, NC 27695-780, USA*
Professor Baker-Ward is Professor of Psychology and Alumni Distinguished Undergraduate Professor at North Carolina State University in Raleigh. A graduate of Wake Forest University and Emory University, she received her doctorate in developmental psychology from the University of North Carolina at Chapel Hill. She has long-standing interests in early memory development and in applied developmental psychology, which intersect in her current research on children's testimony. For over a decade, Dr Baker-Ward has collaborated in a series of investigations examining children's memory for a variety of medical experiences. Her ongoing projects continue this work by examining changes over time in children's mental representations of events.

Mark Blades, *Department of Psychology, University of Sheffield, Sheffield S10 2TP, UK*
Dr Mark Blades is a Developmental Psychologist at the University of Sheffield, UK, and has carried out studies into several aspects of young children's memory, including their recall of places, colour memory, and face recognition. He has also investigated children's source monitoring, and their ability to distinguish real and imagined events. His

books include *Understanding Children's Development* (with Peter Smith and Helen Cowie) and *Children's Source Monitoring* (with Kim Roberts).

Judy Cashmore, *Social Policy Research Centre, University of New South Wales, Australia*

Dr Cashmore has a PhD in Developmental Psychology and is currently an Honorary Research Associate at the Social Policy Research Centre, University of New South Wales, Australia, where she has been conducting a longitudinal study of young people leaving care. She has conducted and published research related to children's involvement in legal proceedings, and processes concerned with their care and protection, particularly focusing on children's perceptions of these processes. She has been actively involved in a number of government committees concerning child protection, child-death reviews and the review of child-protection legislation and policy in NSW.

Stephen J. Ceci, *Department of Human Development, Cornell University, Ithaca, NY 14853, USA*

Professor Ceci holds a Chair in Developmental Psychology at Cornell University. He studies the accuracy of children's courtroom testimony, and is the author of over 300 articles, books, and chapters. Ceci's honours include a Senior Fulbright-Hayes fellowship and a Research Career Scientist Award. In 1993, Ceci was named a Master Lecturer of the American Psychological Association. His book *Jeopardy in the Courtroom: A Scientific Analysis of Children's Testimony* (1995) (co-written with Maggie Bruck) is an American Psychological Association best-seller. Ceci is a member of the National Academy of Sciences Committee on Behavioral, Cognitive, and Sensory Sciences, and a member of the American Psychological Society's Board of Directors. Ceci has been the recipient of the American Psychological Association's (APA) Lifetime Contribution Award for Science and Society, and the American Academy of Forensic Psychology's Lifetime Distinguished Contribution Award. In addition to being past president of the Society of General Psychology, Ceci has been elected fellow of the American Association for the Advancement of Science (AAAS), the American Psychological Society (APS) and seven divisions of the APA. He currently serves on the Advisory Board of the National Science Foundation and directs the Cornell Institute for Research on Children, an NSF-funded national research center.

Brian R. Clifford, *School of Psychology, University of East London, Romford Road, London E15 4LZ, UK*

Professor Clifford is Professor of Psychology at the University of East London. He obtained an honours degree in Psychology from London University, an MSc in Artificial Intelligence from Brunel University, and a PhD in Psycholinguistics from Birkbeck College, University of London. His research falls in the field of applied memory research, especially eyewitness and earwitness testimony of both adults and children. He has published over 150 articles and chapters and has authored four books. His current research involves the relationship between witness confidence and accuracy, context reinstatement and the cognitive interview, and recall and recognition procedures. He has been consulted frequently by both police and legal personnel concerning issues of disputed eyewitness testimony.

Ingrid Cordon, *Department of Psychology, University of California, Young Hall, 1 Shields Avenue, Davis, CA 95616-8686, USA*

Ingrid Cordon is a Doctoral Student at the University of California, Davis. She received her BA in Psychology from the University of California, Los Angeles, in 1995 and her MA in Experimental Psychology from California State University, Northridge in 2000. Her primary interests are children's eyewitness memory, suggestibility, and infantile amnesia. She also has interests in child maltreatment and cultural differences in childrearing and parent–child interactions. Ms Cordon is currently conducting research on the long-term consequences of child sexual abuse and children's involvement in the legal system.

Angela M. Crossman, *Institute for the Study of Child Development, UMNDJ – Robert Wood Johnson Medical School, 97 Paterson Street, 3rd Floor, New Brunswick, NJ 08903, USA*

Dr Crossman is a Postdoctoral Fellow at the Institute for the Study of Child Development, the University of Medicine and Dentistry of New Jersey-Robert Wood Johnson Medical School. She earned a BA from Dartmouth College in 1994 and an MA in Developmental Psychology from Cornell University in 1998. Dr Crossman has completed her PhD in Developmental Psychology at Cornell University. Her research interests include children's memory and the accuracy and credibility of eyewitness testimony. Presently, she is conducting research on social and cognitive factors as predictors of individual differences in eyewitness suggestibility.

Robin Edelstein, *Department of Psychology, University of California, Young Hall, 1 Shields Avenue, Davis, CA 95616-8686, USA*

Robin Edelstein is a Doctoral Student in the Department of Psychology at the University of California, Davis. She received her bachelor's degree in Psychology from the University of California, Berkeley in 1997. Her research interests include children's experiences in the legal system, child maltreatment, and attachment in children and adults. She is currently involved in a research project investigating the long-term consequences of children's legal involvement as victims of sexual abuse.

Barbara Esam, *NSPCC National Centre, Public Policy Department, 42 Curtain Road, London EC2A 3NH, UK*

Barbara Esam is a Lawyer in the Public Policy Department of the National Society for the Prevention of Cruelty to Children (NSPCC) in London, UK. Her post is focused on campaigning for improvements in legislation and policies which affect children in the civil and criminal jurisdictions. She was a key contributor to *A Case for Balance*, a video aimed primarily at judges and lawyers which demonstrates good practice when children are witnesses. She has also contributed to the *Young Witness Pack* and the video aimed at young witnesses, *Giving Evidence: What's It Really Like?* She drafted the *Supplementary Pre-Trial Checklist for Cases Involving Child Witnesses*, which is now used in all crown courts. Barbara has previously worked as an assistant director of legal services for a local authority, prior to that as a solicitor in private practice.

Phillip W. Esplin

Dr Phillip Esplin is a licensed psychologist in the State of Arizona. He has been in private practice, specializing in Forensic Psychology, since 1978. He has been a Senior Research Consultant with the National Institute of Child Health and Human Development, the Child Witness Project, since 1989. This research is concerned with the evaluation, validation, and facilitation of children's accounts of sexual abuse. He has co-authored approximately 20 scientific articles relative to this project. He co-authored a Law Review article entitled, 'The Guessing Game: Emotional Propensity Experts in the Criminal Courts', published in the April 1997 edition of *Law and Psychology Review*, a journal published by the University of Alabama, School of Law. He has conducted numerous national and international training seminars on proper interview/investigative techniques in child molestation cases. He has consulted and/or testified in a number of major sex abuse cases such as: *State of Florida* v. *Bobby Finji*; the 'Little Rascals' daycare case in North Carolina; the Dale Akkiki case in San Diego; the Wenatchee case in Wenatchee, Washington.

Robyn Fivush, *Department of Psychology, Emory University, Atlanta, GA 30322, USA*
Professor Fivush is Professor of Psychology and Associated Faculty of Women's Studies at Emory University. She has co-edited three books on memory, co-authored a book on gender development, and published numerous journal articles and chapters. Her research focuses on autobiographical memory and its development in social context across the preschool years.

Simona Ghetti, *Department of Psychology, University of California, Young Hall, 1 Shields Avenue, Davis, CA 95616-8686, USA*
Simona Ghetti is a Doctoral Candidate in the Department of Psychology at the University of California, Davis. She received her *Laurea* in Psychology at the University of Padua, Italy, and her Master's degree in Psychology from the University of California, Davis. Her interests are in the area of memory development and psychology and law. She is currently conducting studies on false-memory formation in children and adults, as well as researching children's involvement in the legal system.

Livia L. Gilstrap, *Department of Human Development, Cornell University, Ithaca, NY 14853, USA*
Livia L. Gilstrap is an Advanced Doctoral Candidate at Cornell University. She is a recipient of the American Psychological Association Dissertation Award and has been awarded the National Research Service Award to complete her dissertation. Her work focuses on preschool children's language and memory within the context of investigative interviews.

Gail S. Goodman, *Department of Psychology, University of California, Young Hall, 1 Shields Avenue, Davis, CA 95616-8686, USA*
Professor Goodman is Professor of Psychology and Director of the Center on Social Sciences and the Law at the University of California, Davis. She has published widely in the areas of eyewitness memory, child maltreatment, and reactions to legal involvement. Dr Goodman is the recipient of numerous grants, awards, and honours. In addition, she has served as President of the American Psychology-Law Society (Division 41) and the Section on Child Maltreatment of Child, Youth and Family Services (Division 37) of the American Psychological Asso-

ciation. She obtained her PhD in Developmental Psychology from UCLA in 1977.

Emily Henderson, *Gonville and Caius College, University of Cambridge, Trinity Street, Cambridge CB2 1TA, UK*

Dr Henderson, practised as a barrister and solicitor in New Zealand for a short period while completing a Master's Thesis interviewing New Zealand barristers about their experiences and practices in cross-examining children in sexual-abuse trials. She is now completing her PhD at Cambridge Law Faculty, UK, supervised by Professor J.R. Spencer, regarding English and New Zealand barristers' understandings of the theory and limits of criminal cross-examination generally.

Irit Hershkowitz, *School of Social Work, University of Haifa, Mount Carmel, 31905 Haifa, Israel*

Dr Hershkowitz obtained BSW. and PhD degrees in Social Work from the University of Haifa, Israel, and thereafter completed postdoctoral training in the Section on Social and Emotional Development at the National Institute of Child Health and Human Development in Bethesda, Maryland. She is currently a Lecturer in the School of Social Work at the University of Haifa. Her research is focused on child witnesses and their testimony. Current studies address the effects of question types on children's testimony, the use of the Criterion Based Content Analysis for credibility assessment, false allegations made by children, and the effectiveness of interviewing children using a structured protocol.

Tiffany Hinz, *Department of Psychology, Claremont Graduate University, Claremont, CA 91711-3955, USA*

Tiffany Hinz is a PhD Candidate at Claremont Graduate University in Claremont, California. She received her MA from Claremont Graduate University in 2000. Her research has focused on eyewitness memory and forensic issues involving children's testimony in court.

Mary Lyn Huffman, *685 Watson Street, Memphis, TN 38111, USA*

Dr Huffman completed her undergraduate education at Wheaton College with a major in Psychology and a minor in Sociology. After finishing her PhD at Cornell University in Human Development and Family Studies, she continues to focus her research on children's testimony in the courtroom. Current projects analyse the mediating relationship of interview techniques and individual differences on children's memory ability.

Liz Kelly, *Child and Woman Abuse Studies Unit, University of North London, 62–66 Ladbroke House, Highbury Grove, London N5 2AD, UK*
Professor Kelly is a Feminist Researcher and Activist, who has worked in the field of violence against women and children for over 25 years. She is a founder member of a refuge and rape crisis centre, and is the author of *Surviving Sexual Violence*, and over 50 book chapters and journal articles. She is Professor and Director of the Child and Woman Abuse Studies Unit (CWASU), University of North London. The Unit has completed research projects in the areas of child sexual abuse, rape and sexual assault, domestic violence, and the links between woman and child protection. Liz was awarded a Commander of the British Empire (CBE) in 2000 for 'services combating violence against women and children'.

Günter Köhnken, *Institut für Psychologie, University of Kiel, Olshausenstr. 40, 24098 Kiel, Germany*
Professor Köhnken is currently Professor and Chair in Psychological Assessment, Personality Psychology and Psychology and Law at the Department of Psychology of the University of Kiel, Germany. From 1992 to 1994, he served as a Reader in Psychology at the Department of Psychology of the University of Portsmouth. From 1997 to 1999, he was Chair of the Division of Psychology and Law in the Germany Psychological Society. He currently is President Elect of the Division Psychology and Law of the International Association of Applied Psychology. His main areas of research are credibility assessment, interviewing, and suggestion. He is frequently called as an expert witness by German criminal courts.

Michael E. Lamb, *Section on Social and Emotional Development, National Institute of Child Health and Human Development, Rockledge One Center, Suite 8048, 6705 Rockledge Drive, Bethesda, MD 20892*
Professor Lamb has been Head of the Section on Social and Emotional Development at the National Institute of Child Health and Human Development in Bethesda, Maryland, since 1987. A developmental psychologist by training, his research is concerned with social and emotional development, the determinants and consequences of adaptive and maladaptive parental behaviour, children's testimony, and the interface of psychology and biology. Studies have been characterized by a reliance on non-experimental field and multi-cultural methodologies, longitudinal follow-up and analysis, and a concern with the application of research findings in everyday practice. Dr Lamb is the author or editor of several books, including *Investigative Interviews of Children* (APA,

1998) and has published widely in behavioural sciences and paediatrics journals.

D. Stephen Lindsay, *Department of Psychology, University of Victoria, P.O. Box 3050, Victoria V8W 3P5, Canada*

Professor Lindsay is Professor of Psychology at the University of Victoria, British Columbia, Canada. He is a cognitive psychologist who earned his PhD in 1987 from Princeton University. Much of his research has focused on memory-source monitoring (e.g. studies of conditions under which witnesses mistake memories of post-event suggestions as memories of witnessed events) in adults and children. Lindsay co-edited, with J. Don Read, a 1997 book on the recovered-memories controversy, entitled *Recollections of Trauma: Scientific Evidence and Clinical Practice.*

Thomas D. Lyon, *Law School, University of Southern California, University Park, Los Angeles, CA 90089-0071, USA*

Professor Lyon is a Professor of Law at the University of Southern California Law School. He received his JD in 1987 from Harvard Law School and a PhD in Developmental Psychology in 1994 from Stanford University. He worked as an attorney for the Children's Services Division of the Los Angeles County Counsel's Office from 1987 to 1995, representing the Department of Children's Services in dependency proceedings alleging child abuse and neglect. He was co-investigator (with Dr Karen J. Saywitz) on a grant from the National Center on Child Abuse and Neglect to determine the most sensitive means by which children can be qualified to take the oath.

Yael Orbach, *Section on Social and Emotional Development, National Institute of Child Health and Human Development, Rockledge One Center, Suite 8048, 6705 Rockledge Drive, Bethesda, MD 20892*

Dr Orbach received her PhD from the University of Natal, Durban, South Africa. Since 1993, she has been a researcher in the Section on Social and Emotional Development, National Institute of Child Health and Human Development, Bethesda, USA. Her research includes forensic interviews of children, credibility assessment using Criteria Based Content Analysis, validation of children's allegations using independent case evidence, the effects of mental-context reinstatement and of interviewing at the scene of the crime on children's recall of alleged abuse, assessing the value of structured protocols for forensic interviews, and the relationship between undesirable investigators' practices and children's retrieval of erroneous information.

Peter A. Ornstein, *Department of Psychology, University of North Carolina at Chapel Hill, NC 27515-2688, USA*

Professor Ornstein is Professor of Psychology and Chair of the Department of Psychology at the University of North Carolina at Chapel Hill, and is also Chair of the Executive Committee of the Center for Developmental Science. He received his doctorate in Experimental Psychology from the University of Wisconsin. His research on children's memory for salient personal experiences has contributed to the understanding of the major factors that influence children's memory performance. He is also currently conducting a longitudinal study of children's memory over the first six years of life. Professor Ornstein served as co-chair of the American Psychology Association's Working Group on Investigation of Memories of Childhood Abuse.

Marcus Page, *Triangle Services for Children, Unit 310, 91 Western Road, Brighton, East Sussex BN1 5DG, UK*

Marcus Page is a Co-Director of Triangle Services for Children, Brighton, UK, which provides consultancy and training around issues relating to disabled children and child protection. He is also a Group Analyst working within the National Health Service and in private practice. He worked for 11 years as a senior social-work practitioner at the Clermont Child Protection Team in Brighton, where he was a member of a multidisciplinary team involved in investigative and therapeutic work with families and children. He has published articles on child-protection work with disabled children.

Kathy Pezdek, *Department of Psychology, Claremont Graduate University, Claremont, CA 91711-3955, USA*

Professor Pezdek is Professor of Psychology at Claremont Graduate University in Claremont, California, where she has directed the PhD programme in Applied Cognitive Psychology since 1981. She is a Fellow of the American Psychological Society and has served as American Editor of the journal, *Applied Cognitive Psychology*. Her research on memory, eyewitness memory and the suggestibility of memory has appeared in numerous texts and journals. Her 1996 edited text with William Banks, *The Recovered Memory/False Memory Debate* is one of the most widely cited books on the topic.

Margaret-Ellen (Mel) Pipe, *Section on Social and Emotional Development, National Institute of Child Health and Human Development, Rockledge One Center, Suite 8048, 6705 Rockledge Drive, Bethesda, MD 20892*

Dr Pipe recently joined NICHD as a Senior Research Fellow. Previously, she was Associate Professor at the University of Otago in

Dunedin, New Zealand, where she directed a research programme on children's event memory. Her research has focused on applied questions relating to how children can be helped to provide complete and accurate accounts of their experiences and how memories change over time. She has served as Australasian Editor of the journal *Applied Cognitive Psychology*, as Editor of the *New Zealand Journal of Psychology*, and as a consultant on issues relating to memory and children's evidence for several professional and government onganizations in New Zealand.

Joyce Plotnikoff, *Consultant in Management, IT and the Law, Cheldene, Church Lane, Preston, Hitchin SG4 7TP, UK*

Joyce Plotnikoff has worked with Richard Woolfson since 1991 on research relating to criminal, civil, and family law. Co-authors of *Prosecuting Child Abuse* (1995), they were also coordinators of the *Young Witness Pack* and of three multi-agency video projects aimed at judges, local authorities, and young witnesses. Joyce has a Law Degree from Bristol University and the Diploma in Social and Administrative Studies (Distinction) from Oxford University. She worked as a probation officer in Oxford and Chicago, and as a staff attorney in the federal court system in Washington, DC. In 1981, she was awarded a Judicial Fellowship by the US Supreme Court. After returning to the UK in 1983, she became a Research Fellow at the Centre for Criminological Research, University of Oxford and the Institute of Judicial Administration, University of Birmingham.

Martine Powell, *School of Psychology, Deakin University, 221 Burwood Highway, Victoria 3125, Australia*

Dr Powell is Senior Lecturer and Co-ordinator of the Doctorate of Psychology (Forensic) in the School of Psychology, Deakin University, Australia. Prior to becoming a full-time academic, she worked as a clinical psychologist in a child-protection unit and as a schoolteacher. While she has wide interest in applied aspects of cognitive psychology, her research to date has focused primarily on the issue of children's memory of repeated events. Dr Powell is currently Australasian Editor of the journal *Applied Cognitive Psychology*, and she also conducts regular training programmes on the issue of investigative interviewing of children for police and social workers throughout Australia. Together with Clare Wilson, she recently wrote the book entitled *A Guide to Interviewing Children* (Allen & Unwin/Routledge).

Gretchen Precey, *48 Prince Edwards Road, Lewes, East Sussex BN7 1BE, UK*
Gretchen Precey is an independent social-work practitioner who specializes in training, consultation, and assessments in the field of child protection. Prior to becoming independent, she worked at the Clermont Child Protection Unit in Brighton, UK, as a senior practitioner and latterly as manager. She has worked extensively in the field of child sexual abuse as a therapist for abused children and their families, and as a trainer mainly on multi-agency courses for Memorandum of Good Practice interviewers.

Gina Priestley, *Department of Psychology, University of Auckland, Private Bag 92019, Auckland, New Zealand*
Dr Priestley is a lecturer in Developmental Psychology at the Department of Psychology, University of Auckland, New Zealand. Prior to this she was engaged as the senior researcher on a grant-funded research programme on children's eyewitness testimony, at the University of Otago (New Zealand). Dr Priestley is a clinical psychologist and an author on several publications on the use of non-verbal interview techniques, such as providing toys and models in interviews. Her current research interests include the development of symbolic and representational abilities, fantasy and imagination, and how these relate to children's event recall.

Jodi Quas, *Department of Psychology and Social Behavior, University of California, Irvine, CA 92697, USA*
Professor Quas is Assistant Professor in the Department of Psychology and Social Behavior at the University of California, Irvine. Her research focuses on two related topics: memory development and children's involvement in the legal system. She has conducted studies concerning the relationship between stress and memory in children and on individual differences in children's emotional reactions to, and later memory of, stressful experiences. She has also been collaborating on a large, federally funded study of the long-term consequences of criminal-court involvement on child victims. Much of her work has been applied to questions about children's capabilities as eyewitnesses and children's participation as victims in legal cases.

Allison D. Redlich, *Department of Psychiatry and Behavioural Sciences, Stanford University, Stanford, CA 94305, USA*
Allison Redlich is a Postdoctoral Fellow in the Department of Psychiatry and Behavioral Sciences at Stanford University. She is interested in how children, both victims and defendants, are treated and

perceived in the criminal-justice system. Of particular interest is how juveniles are interrogated by the police, and whether certain interrogation tactics lead to false confessions in juveniles. Dr Redlich has also conducted research on the effects of hearsay in legal cases involving children and attitudes towards child sexual-abuse prevention measures.

Karen Salmon, *Department of Psychology, University of New South Wales, Sydney, NSW 2052, Australia*

Dr Salmon is a Lecturer in Psychology at the University of New South Wales, Sydney, Australia. She is a clinical psychologist, and worked in both child and adult settings for 15 years prior to her academic career. In 1996, she completed a second postgraduate degree, a PhD in Developmental Psychology at the University of Otago. She has several publications in clinical and developmental journals on the use of cues and props in interviews with children. Her current research interests include children's memories of traumatic experiences, and individual differences in cognitive and social variables that impact on those memories.

Karen J. Saywitz, *Harbor, UCLA School of Medicine, UCLA Medical Center, Division of Child and Adolescent Psychiatry, Bldg D-6, 1000 West Carson Street, Torrance, CA 90509, USA*

Professor Saywitz is Professor of Psychiatry at the University of California, Los Angeles, School of Medicine. She is Director of Child and Adolescent Psychology at the Harbor-UCLA Medical Center. Dr Saywitz is the author of numerous articles regarding the capabilities, limitations, and needs of child-victim witnesses. In her research on interviewing children and preparing them for court, she develops and tests innovative interventions to enhance children's memory performance, communicative competence, emotional resilience, and their resistance to suggestive questions. Dr Saywitz is currently serving as the President of the American Psychological Association's Division of Child, Youth, and Family Services.

Jennifer M. Schaaf, *Frank Porter Graham Child Development Center, University of North Carolina at Chapel Hill, P.O. Box 2688, Chapel Hill, NC 27515-2688, USA*

Dr Schaaf is a Postdoctoral Fellow at the Frank Porter Graham Child Development Center at the University of North Carolina at Chapel Hill. She received her PhD from the University of California, Davis. Her research interests include cognitive development in normal and developmentally delayed children with a special emphasis on memory. She is also interested in children's abilities as eyewitnesses, including topics such as appropriate interviewing styles for children, individual differences in children's memory capabilities, and children's suggestibility.

Matthew H. Scullin, *Assistant Professor of Psychology at West Virginia University, WV, USA*

Matthew Scullin is currently completing his PhD in Developmental Psychology at Cornell University with Dr Stephen Ceci. He received a BA from Carleton College in 1989 and an MA from Cornell University in 1997. His research interests span cognitive and social development with a special emphasis on the interaction of individual differences, cognitive factors, and social influences. In his studies of children's memory and suggestibility, he is examining how cognitive factors, such as children's ability to encode and retrieve information, are influenced by a variety of social forces.

Christopher Spencer, *Department of Psychology, University of Sheffield, Sheffield S10 2TP, UK*

Dr Spencer is an environmental psychologist at the University of Sheffield, UK, much of whose work has been with young children's concepts of places. Together with Mark Blades and Kim Morsley, he was author of *Children and the Physical Environment* (Wiley) and was editor of *The Child's Environment* (Academic Press). Areas of interest have included children's cognitive maps, improvement of mobility in young blind children, and children's view of town centres as a resource, work conducted with planners and geographers.

Kathleen J. Sternberg, *Section on Social and Emotional Development, National Institute of Child Health and Human Development, Rockledge One Center, Suite 8048, 6705 Rockledge Drive, Bethesda, MD 20892*

Dr Sternberg is a Research Psychologist in the Section on Social and Emotional Development at the National Institute of Child Health and Human Development in Bethesda, Maryland. She has conducted research on the effects of spouse and child abuse on child development and adjustment, cross-cultural conceptions of parenting and maltreatment, and on the definition and assessment of child maltreatment. Her current research is focused on the elicitation and evaluation of children's testimony regarding their experiences of abuse. She is co-editor of *Child Care in Context* (Erlbaum, 1992), co-author of many articles, and frequently conducts workshops and seminars for investigative interviewers.

Don Thomson, *Department of Psychology, Charles Sturt University in Bathurst, Panorama Avenue, Bathurst, NSW 2795, Australia*

Professor Thomson is currently Professor of Psychology at Charles Sturt University in Bathurst, New South Wales, Australia, and adjunct Professor of Psychology at Deakin University in Victoria, Australia, and Edith Cowan University in Western Australia. He is a practising forensic psychologist and also a barrister-at-law. He was formerly a consultant to the Australian Law Reform Commission on evidence and contempt of court. In addition to his research into children as witnesses, he has been involved in research into eyewitness identification, eyewitness testimony, jury issues, and memory.

Aldert Vrij, *Department of Psychology, University of Portsmouth, King Henry Building, King Henry 1st Street, Portsmouth, Hants PO1 2DY, UK*

Professor Vrij is a Professor of Applied Social Psychology in the Department of Psychology at the University of Portsmouth, UK. He has published widely on deception, particularly the relationship between white and black suspects, and how these differences result in negative evaluations of black suspects in police interviews. His recent work has also concentrated on speech content and deception. Over the years, he has held research grants from the Dutch Ministry of Justice, the Economic and Social Research Council and the Leverhulme Trust in the UK.

Amanda Wade, *Department of Sociology and Social Policy, University of Leeds, Leeds LS2 9JT, UK*

Dr Wade is a Senior Research Fellow at the University of Leeds. Her interest in child witnesses arose from her experience as a social-work practitioner and manager, and the debates during the early 1990s on the role the criminal-justice system should play in dealing with the problem of child sexual abuse. She spent seven months observing Crown Court child-witness cases for her doctoral research, The Child Witness and the Criminal Justice Process. More recently, she has begun researching the divorce process from a children's perspective.

Amanda Waterman, *Department of Applied Psychology, University of Durham's Stockton Campus, Thornaby, Stockton-on-Tees TS17 6BH, UK*

Dr Waterman recently completed her PhD at the University of Sheffield, UK, and is now a Lecturer in Developmental and Forensic Psychology at the University of Durham, UK. She has written several articles relating to children's eyewitness testimony. Particular interests include how the phrasing of a question affects children's tendency to admit when they do not know the answer, and children's perceptions of the interview process.

Corinne Wattam, *Department of Social Work, University of Central Lancashire, RM HA337, Harrington Building, Preston PR1 2HE, UK*
Professor Wattam is Professor of Childcare at the University of Central Lancashire, UK and was previously NSPCC Reader in the Centre for Applied Childhood Studies at the University of Huddersfield and Co-ordinator of CAPCAE (Concerted Action on the Prevention of Child Abuse in Europe) at Lancaster University. She has researched and published extensively in the area of child protection, including *And Do I Abuse My Children ... No!* (with C. Woodward, a report on over 1,000 letters from survivors of childhood abuse sent to the National Commission of Inquiry into the Prevention of Child Abuse, HMSO, 1996), *Child Protection: Risk and the Moral Order* (with N. Parton and D. Thorpe, Macmillan, 1997), and *Child Sexual Abuse: Responding to the Experiences of Children* (with N. Parton, Wiley, 1999).

Richard Woolfson, *Consultant in Management, IT and the Law, Cheldene, Church Lane, Preston, Hitchin SG4 7TP, UK*
Dr Woolfson has worked with Joyce Plotnikoff since 1991 on research relating to criminal, civil, and family law. Co-authors of *Prosecuting Child Abuse* (1995), they were also coordinators of the *Young Witness Pack* and of three multi-agency video projects aimed at judges, local authorities, and young witnesses. After a first degree in Mathematics at the University of Glasgow, Scotland, Richard studied for his doctorate at Oxford and spent six years as an academic. Later, he became a consultant in the Information Systems industry, then Marketing Director of a company providing consultancy services to government and the private sector. Richard is a member of the Civil Justice Council Working Group on litigants' information needs.

Foreword

Children's Testimony: A Handbook of Psychological Research and Forensic Practice is a comprehensive summary of research findings, innovations, and vexing dilemmas in the field of child witnessing. When awareness of child abuse resurfaced in the 1970s, professionals who worked with young witnesses made decisions about emotionally charged issues in environments that offered them few standards of practice, little support, and the constant threat of criticism. The frustration that motivated research and policy change was magnified by magazine and television exposés that projected opposing images of injustice: descriptions of victimized children who were not protected by legal procedures designed for adults, and stories of adults who were falsely accused of unspeakable and often bizarre crimes against children. A decade ago, only two conclusions received widespread support: that protecting the rights of children and adults would require new information about the strengths and weaknesses of children as witnesses, and that the task of translating findings into practice could be accomplished only by unprecedented co-operation between basic researchers, child advocates, and legal professionals.

The journey to improve how the courts receive and handle evidence from children has been fraught with obstacles. Individuals who enter the child witness arena find themselves immersed in an interdisciplinary dialog that freely borrows ideas from sociology, social work, psychology, and an international legal community. This intellectual feast is both invigorating and exhausting. Newcomers often feel overwhelmed when they realize that no clear boundaries define what knowledge is necessary for analyzing witness issues and, furthermore, that critical information is scattered throughout highly technical literatures.

The current book brings order to this apparent chaos by assembling contributions from researchers and practitioners from around the world who have written extensively about children's testimony. In a rare but much appreciated effort, these authors set aside disciplinary jargon to provide readers with clear overviews of core topics, including the developmental and forensic underpinnings of children's testimony, the interplay of memory factors and interviewing strategies, legal and procedural issues, and essays that evaluate basic assumptions about how we study children's testimony.

The editors, Helen Westcott, Graham Davies, and Ray Bull, are internationally regarded as leaders in child witness research and policy. Reflecting their years of experience in the laboratory, the classroom, and the committee room, this book is a welcomed example of how to communicate across disciplines. From the thoughtful organization and insightful summaries to the glossary of specialized terms and concepts, readers will find assistance in their efforts to understand the complexities of children's testimony. By acknowledging prior accomplishments without hiding their concerns, the editors and contributors provide us with both a valuable guide for the present and a call to action for the future.

Debra Ann Poole
Central Michigan University, USA
March 2001

Preface

The new millennium offers an opportunity to step back from day-to-day involvement with child witnesses, to take stock of the changes in policy, practice, and research which have occurred over recent years, and to plot a course for the future. As editors, this opportunity was particularly highlighted for us by a series of seminars which we directed on *Understanding and Improving Children's Eyewitness Testimony*, held in Milton Keynes, England in 1998 under the auspices of The Open University, and funded by the British Psychological Society. The seminars, attended by psychologists, lawyers, policy makers, and other researchers, consisted of a series of invited presentations on different aspects of children's evidence, given both by specialists in the field and outside experts in memory and child development who were asked to bring a fresh eye to issues of child witnessing. Both the progress psychological research has made in this difficult and challenging field and the limits imposed on progress and change by the demands of the legal system and wider issues of social policy became apparent. It was also apparent that psychologists themselves have sometimes imposed their own constraints, by neglecting to take properly into account the theoretical perspectives and research of other disciplines and approaches. From these interchanges and clashing perspectives, the current book was eventually to grow.

The past decade has seen a changing agenda for psychologists studying children's testimony. In most (but not all) parts of the world, the need to establish children's ability and right to give accounts of events they have experienced is widely accepted (Bottoms & Goodman, 1996, cf. Segal, 1996). That children can, under appropriate conditions, provide compelling and accurate accounts of events they have witnessed is also widely accepted and this is reflected in the changes in law and procedure which have been implemented in many countries (see Bottoms & Goodman, 1996). In hindsight, it is apparent that although many of these changes were heavily influenced by the findings of psychological research, they were often introduced without any prior evaluation. Thus, evaluations of practice and new interviewing techniques have been prominent features of the more recent psychological agenda, together with a growing awareness among experimenters of the need for ecological realism in the design and conduct of research.

The relationship between psychological research and forensic practice is not always an easy or comfortable one, however, as some of the chapters in this volume will attest. One of the continuing challenges for the new psychological research agenda is successfully to combine the need to look 'outwards' into real forensic practice, such as interviewing and training, with the need to look 'inwards' toward more traditional concerns for developing psychological theory. The desire to make psychological research applied, or applicable to the real world of investigate interviewing and courtroom practice, can result in studies that lack a clear, discernible theoretical framework. This can sometimes lead to such research being perceived as inferior, or as having limited utility. The role of guiding theory, or theoretical concepts, is clearly important and as such is debated not only in chapters throughout this volume, but also explored in our introductory part of the book.

The principle of children's participation in various legal proceedings is enshrined in the United Nations Convention on the Rights of the Child, but the translation of that principle into practice has been far from smooth. This has led to a shift in psychological research attention beyond the narrow focus of the first disclosure by the child. One consequence of this has been innovations in investigative interviewing practice which, arguably, may represent the most successful contribution from psychological enquiry. Courtroom practice continues to vex many psychologists and practitioners, who see the undoing of many of the positive achievements wrought earlier in the investigative process by court systems which owe more to legal tradition than proven effectiveness. The growing interest of psychologists in the strengths and weaknesses of courtroom participation is reflected in Part III devoted to court issues. A further extension of the research agenda, highlighted by the emphasis on courtroom participation, is the need for more longitudinal research including evaluations of outcomes for children.

THE CURRENT VOLUME

Our desire as editors has been to provide an up-to-date and comprehensive review of children's testimony that will genuinely be of interest to practitioners and policy makers as well as to fellow psychological researchers. Thus, this volume contains contributions from psychologists, lawyers, feminists, sociologists, and social work practitioners. We have also striven to benefit from the wisdom of colleagues with differing international perspectives and experiences. These different perspectives are deliberately contrasted in a way that we hope will lead to constructive debate and enriched perspectives on issues, either through integration of ideas, or through contrasting opinions. Implications for forensic practice and psychological research are clearly highlighted by authors, and summarized by us as editors at the end of each part. A glossary of psychological terms and concepts which appear frequently in the text is also included as an aid for readers not familiar with the psychological literature.

The book is divided into four parts. In Part I, the *Introduction*, three chapters lay out the psychological and forensic considerations which underpin our discussion of children's testimony. Many of the issues raised in this part, whether of practice, cognition, or development, are returned to in greater depth in later chapters. Part II, *Memory and Interviewing*, contains nine chapters. These review what is known about different theoretical and practical aspects of memory, as well as offering a detailed critique of the state of our knowledge about interviewing practice, such as different questioning techniques and the use of props. In Part III, *Court Issues*, eight chapters discuss different aspects of court procedure in relation to child witnesses. Legal and procedural innovations to date are evaluated and recent research is described. Finally, in Part IV, three *Alternative Perspectives* on children's testimony and psychological research are presented. Each of these chapters presents a challenge to psychologists and others who may be in danger of maintaining too narrow a focus. As noted above, at the end of each part is found a brief review by the editors, which summarizes the key issues that emerge. The book concludes with an epilogue, in which we offer some concluding remarks and commentary on matters raised in the book as a whole.

ACKNOWLEDGEMENTS

Last, but by no means least, it is our pleasant duty to acknowledge the tireless efforts of two people at The Open University who have particularly assisted in the production of this volume. Anne Paynter has provided secretarial support beyond that we could have dreamed, and Sally Kynan has assisted both in proof-reading, and more importantly, in producing the glossary at the end of the book. Our grateful thanks to them both, and also to Bruce Shuttlewood at Originator for his friendly and efficient service in getting the book published. Our thanks also go to all the children who have participated in the studies mentioned in this book. As one of our friends once remarked, 'Having children is both better than I thought, and worse than I imagined.'

HELEN WESTCOTT
GRHAM DAVIES
RAY BULL

November 2001

REFERENCES

Bottoms, B.L., & Goodman, G.S. (1996) *International Perspectives on Child Abuse and Children's Testimony: Psychological Research and Law.* Thousand Oaks, California: Sage Publications.

Segal, U.A. (1996) Children as witnesses: India is not ready. In: B.L. Bottoms & G.S. Goodman (Eds) *International Perspectives on Child Abuse and Children's Testimony: Psychological Research and Law*, pp. 266–282. Thousand Oaks, California: Sage Publications.

Underpinnings

CHAPTER 1

Developmental Underpinnings of Children's Testimony

KAREN J. SAYWITZ

UCLA School of Medicine, Harbor/UCLA Medical Center, Torrance, California, USA

The legal system demands a wide array of cognitive, social, and emotional skills from its participants. Witnesses are expected to encode, store, and retrieve memories, then communicate memories through the spoken word in a foreign context. The system requires trustworthy, often detailed, reports that are not tainted by the suggestions of others. Questions often call for sophisticated reasoning skills and a fairly well-elaborated knowledge base. Often, the events that bring individuals into contact with the system are of a stressful, if not traumatic, nature, necessitating emotional maturity characterized by a facility with advanced coping strategies.

Unfortunately, children are still developing many of these capabilities. The result is a mismatch between the requirements of the legal system and the capabilities of young children. Without an understanding of developmental underpinnings of children's testimony, even a simple question easily answered by a 10-year-old, such as *'How many times did that happen?'*, creates confusion and misunderstanding when asked of a four-year-old with immature language and numerical skills. In one case, a four-year-old answered, *'one hundred times'* aloud while simultaneously raising five fingers. This child had been neglected and deprived of any pre-school experience. He had not learned to count but knew enough numbers to guess—fertile ground for misinterpretation. Awareness of developmental issues helps determine whether to ask

Children's Testimony. Edited by H.L. Westcott, G.M. Davies, and R.H.C. Bull.
© 2002 John Wiley & Sons, Ltd.

such a question of a four-year-old in the first place, and, if asked, whether to rely upon or disregard the child's answer.

A comprehensive review of the many developing processes underlying children's testimony, and the related research, is beyond the scope of this chapter. Instead, selected, but central, developmental trends are highlighted, and implications for professional practice illustrated.

COMMUNICATIVE COMPETENCE

In the legal setting, memories must be transformed into words and communicated verbally, according to unfamiliar sociolinguistic principles. Differences between children and adults are found in their intelligibility, vocabulary, grammar, conversational style, and in their ability to detect and cope with misunderstanding. Until communicative competence is fully developed, miscommunication can be an impediment to eliciting reliable information from children.

Children learn to communicate through a series of phases that unfold in a relatively unvarying order. Adult-like communicative competence is not fully developed until 10–12 years of age. In the meantime, children can have difficulty in a number of areas; for example, the pre-schooler has difficulty articulating some sounds—the 'r' sound is particularly difficult. When asked how a suspect had moved an object across the room without leaving fingerprints, a four-year-old who had been found by police at the crime site stated, '*Tom pull swing*'. The boy meant to convey that the perpetrator had pulled the object with a *string*. In the speech of the pre-schooler, 'w' is often substituted for 'r,' especially in a consonant blend.

This example also highlights another error common in the language of pre-schoolers. The inflection -*ed* is omitted from the past tense of the verb. Young children often omit endings they have not yet mastered (Brown, 1973). Knowledge about language development is important in order accurately to interpret young children's speech.

Second, children have difficulty understanding the meaning of adults' words. Even the most common legal terms can be unfamiliar to children under 10 years of age. To a young child, a *hearing* is something you do with your ears, a *court* is a place to play basketball, and *charges* are something you do with your credit card. They are unaware that adults use alternative meanings in the forensic context (Saywitz, Jaenicke, & Camparo, 1990). With adults, we assume a common vocabulary and need not choose our words so carefully.

Third, children differ in their ability to comprehend linguistically complex constructions—constructions common in the forensic context, replete with embedded clauses, conjunctives, and double negatives; for example, there are a limited number of words children can process in a sentence. Children who typically comprehend grammatical constructions five to seven words in length should not be asked lengthier questions containing complex constructions typical of adult conversation. In a representative legal case, a four-year-old was asked the following 30-word question, '*When your mom took you to your uncle's house last Sunday, did you stay the night or did you drive back to San Diego and have dinner with your dad?*' She replied, '*No.*' This question is overloaded with complex linguistic constructions, not to mention requests to verify days of the week and locations that a four-year-old is unlikely to have mastered. In reality, this question is several questions under the guise of one. Does the child's response of 'No' mean she did not visit her uncle, did not do so on Sunday, did not stay the night, did not drive to San Diego, or did not have dinner with her dad? Several short questions are required to elicit reliable information from a four-year-old.

Fourth, young children have difficulty detecting those moments when they fail to comprehend. Also, they have limited and ineffective methods of coping with instances of noncomprehension, even if detected (Saywitz, Snyder, & Nathanson, 1999). When confronted with linguistically complex questions and sophisticated vocabulary that exceed children's levels of language comprehension, even school-age children rarely ask for clarification or indicate misunderstanding. Instead, they often try to answer questions they do not fully understand. They do know that it is time for them to take their turn in the conversation. In one study, school-age children, questioned about a past classroom event with linguistically complex, open-ended, questions, gave inaccurate responses as often as accurate ones. This stands in sharp contrast to the high levels of accurate memory for the event shown when questions were phrased in simple grammar. Often, their responses were an association to a part of the question that they did understand but not the answer to the intended question (Saywitz *et al.*, 1999).

Fifth, children assume everyday rules of conversation that do not necessarily apply to the adversarial context, leading to misunderstandings on both sides of the interchange. Typically, children learn language in conversation with supportive adults who tend to structure the conversation and provide scaffolding for children's language. In everyday conversation, the adult takes responsibility for noticing and correcting miscommunications (Newhoff & Launer, 1984), but the forensic context is neither nurturant nor educational. Moreover, children may not understand the significance or consequences of their statements, something that motivates adults and older children to clarify misunderstandings, to reiterate, '*No, you misunderstood, that's not what I meant,*' comments rarely heard from younger children who do not take the listener's perspective fully into account.

Developmental limitations on children's ability to comprehend and produce language leads to miscommunication and misinterpretation when adults fail to accommodate their language to the child's developmental level. One implication is that adults will need to simplify their language in ways not necessary when conversing with other adults.

COGNITIVE DEVELOPMENT

Children differ from adults in the way they perceive, organize, and think about the world around them and about their own experiences. Such differences are found in reasoning, judgement, knowledge, and in the mastery of academic skills required by the kinds of questions witnesses encounter. Often, pre-schoolers who reason on the basis of what they see and older children who reason by trial and error are asked questions whose answers depend on an understanding of advanced, abstract principles. Sometimes, questions require hypothetical–deductive reasoning, comparisons of past and present statements, drawing inferences, and taking another's perspective. With young children, such questions can obscure the fact-finding process.

Often children are asked to describe people, places, and events using conventional systems of measurement that are only mastered gradually over the course of elementary school. Pre-schoolers are expected to answer '*How much did he weigh?*' in pounds; '*How tall was he?*' in terms of feet and inches; '*What time was it? What date was it? What month was it?*' using hours, minutes, and the calender year. In one case, a five-year-old's statement had to be relied upon to determine the location (and thus the jurisdiction) of a murder she had witnessed. She was asked, *How far was it from your home? How long was the car ride? What time did you leave? Where did he take you? What street did you turn down to get to the park? What city? Can you draw the way you went in the car?* The likelihood her answers were reliable depended upon her ability to use miles, feet, hours, minutes, her knowledge of local geography and spatial understanding, and her map-making skills. Research tells us that the average five-year-old has yet to master these skills.

Unlike questioning adults who usually have mature skills, questioning children obliges us to know or to find out the likelihood that a child of a given age possesses the skills to answer our questions before we ask them. Equipped with knowledge of developmental trends, an adult can better match questions to children's levels of functioning.

CHILDREN'S KNOWLEDGE OF THE LEGAL SYSTEM

As stated above, children possess cognitive immaturities that render the abstract systems of law, social welfare, and mental health difficult to fathom. Abstract, hypothetical–deductive, and inferential reasoning are slow to develop. In addition, children typically lack experience with and information about these systems (Saywitz, 1989). As a result, children may require a good deal of preparation and instruction in order to function optimally in the forensic setting. First, children's knowledge of the forensic context is often limited, fragmented, or distorted; for example, many children mistakenly believe that they will go to jail if they make an inadvertent mistake in the witness stand (Saywitz, 1989). Children require preparation to demystify the system, to generate accurate expectations, and to understand the consequences of their actions. Studies suggest that children can learn basic information about the operation of the legal system (Saywitz & Nathanson, 1993).

Second, young children, under about seven years of age, have difficulty putting themselves in others' shoes and anticipating their needs, expectations, and requirements. We cannot assume that young children infer the implications and constraints of the invisible (and often incomprehensible) legal rules and ethical codes that govern adult behaviour in the legal system. The implicit demands of the situation (obvious to adults) must be spelled out explicitly for children, often more than once.

Third, young children, under third or fourth grade, often fail to use the cognitive strategies that they are capable of generating because they do not know when and how to apply the strategies (Flavell, 1981). Instructions may compensate for limited metacognitive awareness. Instructions can specify the demands of the task confronting children and give suggestions for optimizing performance (e.g. giving permission to ask for a rephrase when confronted with an incomprehensible question; Saywitz et al., 1999). A number of recent studies have investigated the effects on children's testimony of various instructions and warnings (Saywitz & Lyon, 2002, for a review). Past studies have shown that instructions can improve children's and adults' performances in a host of areas, including comprehension and memory (Lovett

& Pillow, 1995; Milne & Bull, 1999). One implication of children's immaturities in cognitive functioning and lack of experience is a greater need for instructions and preparation with child witnesses than with adults.

CHILDREN'S MEMORY

There are both similarities and differences in the ways children and adults encode, store, and retrieve memories (see Lynne Baker-Ward & Peter Ornstein, Chapter 2 in this book). First, children and adults differ markedly in what they find important to notice and remember. Identifying information, such as eye and hair colour or height may be noticed and recalled by the adult but overlooked by children who instead recall something immensely more salient to them, but forensically less relevant, such as the fact that someone wore Adidas hightops (King & Yuille, 1987). As knowledge increases with maturation and experience, children's abilities to attend to, understand, encode, and store the kind of forensically relevant information required of a witness improve.

Second, older children and adults use more complex and successful retrieval strategies than younger children to increase the amount of information they retrieve independently (Pressley & Levin, 1977; Ornstein, Naus, & Liberty, 1975). Pre-schoolers show only rudimentary use of retrieval strategies on very simple tasks when experimenters suggest the strategies to the children (Ritter, Kaprove, Fitch, & Flavell, 1973). Hence, three-year-olds require a good deal of prompting, five-year-olds less so. From 4 to 12 years of age, children demonstrate increasing efficiency and flexibility in retrieval strategy usage (Kobasigawa, 1977). Still, complex heuristics resulting in exhaustive memory searches are rarely seen until the end of grade school and may not be mastered until adolescence (Salatas & Flavell, 1976).

Third, adults and children differ in their ability to narrate an event. Children's narratives begin as fairly skeletal descriptions, loosely organized, idiosyncratic, and dependent on the context to facilitate the retrieval process. Moreover, children may not understand what information is important or expected (Fivush, 1993). They have difficulty drawing inferences about the listener's perspective, often failing spontaneously and fully to orient the listener to place, time, and person. For all these reasons, young children may depend on adults for direction in order to understand what level of detail and kind of content is relevant in the forensic setting. Often, information is elicited piecemeal by questions that drive the organization of the material and guide the memory search.

Developmental research illuminates the dilemma interviewers face. Young children's spontaneous, independent reports of past events are often skeletal (Nelson, 1986) and insufficient for forensic decision-making. It can be difficult to elicit sufficient information without additional questions. However, if questions are misleading, they can distort children's reports.

Most of the recent guidelines for interviewing children in the forensic context try to address this dilemma. Beginning with open-ended questions is an oft-recommended approach based on the finding that young children's responses to free-recall instructions ('What happened?') are the most accurate in comparison to their responses to specific questions. Studies suggest that asking open-ended questions (that request a narrative multi-word response) wh- questions (who, what, where, why, how) is a better next step than launching into highly detailed, yes/no, and presumptive questions. Open-ended wh- questions can increase the completeness of children's reports without decreasing accuracy to the same extent as specific, leading questions (Hudson, 1990; Hamond & Fivush, 1991; Poole & Lindsay, 1995). Open-ended questions avoid implying that the adult prefers a particular response, and make it easier for the child to respond with 'I don't know' (Peterson, Dowden, & Tobin, 1999). One important implication from these developmental differences is the need to pay careful attention to the memory demands questions place children at different stages of development.

SUGGESTIBILITY

Although objectivity is a goal in the forensic context no matter what the age of the witness, it is worth reminding ourselves of the special circumstances surrounding young children. Recent research on children's suggestibility underscores the dangers of interviewer bias (see Stephen Ceci, Angela Crossman, Matthew Scullin, Livia Gilstrap, & Mary Lyn Huffman, Chapter 8 in this book). Strong preconceived notions about what occurred can result in a more suggestive interviewing (White, Leichtman, & Ceci, 1997). Recent studies have highlighted vulnerabilities to suggestive questioning among young children (Saywitz & Lyon, 2002, for a review).

One reason for heightened suggestibility is that young children are particularly deferential to adults' beliefs. Adults may convey their view of events to children through the questions they ask, the comments they make, and through their demeanour. At an early age children recognize adults' superior knowledge base (Taylor, Cart-wright, & Bowden, 1991). Children may assume interviewers already know the answers to the questions they are asking, which in many settings they do. Young children have a limited understanding of whether and why others know things. These limitations may increase young children's susceptibility to suggestive questioning by adults.

Moreover, a child may perceive the interviewer as an authority figure with inside knowledge, or as someone who will be disapproving if corrected. Pre-school children are more suggestible when questioned by an adult than when questioned by a child (Ceci, Ross, & Toglia, 1987; Kwock & Winer, 1986). The fact that children are deferential to adults emphasizes the special dangers of telling (rather than asking) young children what occurred, either through coaching or questions that presuppose the suggested information.

In addition, children often defer to adults' moral judgements. Studies have shown that accusatory comments by interviewers implicating individuals as 'bad' or as doing 'bad things' can influence pre-schoolers' suggestibility (Leichtman & Ceci, 1995). In one study of four-year-olds, a police officer said he thought a babysitter had done something 'bad' before he interviewed each child about a staged event with the babysitter. These children were more frequently misled by suggestive questions than a comparison group interviewed about the same babysitting incident in a neutral context (Tobey & Goodman, 1992). One implication of such studies is that objectivity is enhanced by a non-judgemental atmosphere, devoid of accusatory, stereotypic, or condescending remarks.

Another reason for heightened suggestibility with young children is that they have special difficulty in identifying the sources of their beliefs (see Stephen Lindsay, Chapter 6 in this book). A child who has experienced an event and has received false information about that event may subsequently confuse memories of the event with memories of the false information. Worse still, subsequent memory for the event might become a blend of the original perception and the false information, misleading future interviewers.

A number of researchers have found dramatic age differences in pre-school children's source-monitoring abilities as assessed through simple tasks (O'Neill & Gopnik, 1991); for example, Gopnik and Graf (1988) showed three- to five-year-olds drawers with various objects inside, and either told the child what was inside, showed the child the contents, or gave the child a clue as to the contents. Immediately afterwards, they confirmed that the child knew the contents, and then asked the child to identify how she knew. Whereas five-year-olds were almost 100% correct in identifying the correct source of their knowledge, three-year-olds were barely above chance.

Some studies have found age differences in source monitoring among older children (Lindsay, Johnson, & Kwon, 1991), although these differences can be a function of the difficulty of the task (Ackil & Zaragoza, 1995). Indeed, source-monitoring errors contribute to the suggestibility of adults as well as of children when tasks are difficult (Zaragoza & Lane, 1994). Further research is needed to clarify abilities of older children; however, young children's source-monitoring errors are the most profound.

With these underlying developmental differences in mind, a number of implications for questioning young children can be drawn. Younger children (especially 3–5-year-olds) are much more suggestive than older children and older children are much less suggestible than younger ones. Certain questioning techniques can accentuate or minimize suggestibility effects by raising or lowering a child's deference to adults and source-monitoring confusion. For example, studies suggest that when yes/no questions are repeated within an interview children make more errors because they change their answers, perhaps assuming the adult is not satisfied with the first response. Certain types of questions require children overtly to disagree with and correct an adult in order to assert the truth, such as negative term insertion questions (e.g. *Didn't they hurt you?*) and tag questions (e.g. *She stole it, didn't she?*; Cassel, Roebers, & Bjorklund, 1996). Other question types presuppose information that may create source-monitoring confusion, such as suppositional questions (e.g. *When he hit you, did you yell or cry?*). Tag, negative-term insertion and suppositional questions are more suggestive than many other question types, and should be avoided. Interviewers can consider the merits of rewording yes/no questions into a less leading form. *'Did he hit you?'* could be rephrased as *'What did he do with his hands?'* Repetition of wh- questions had not led to increased error in research studies the way that yes/no questions have (Fivush & Schwarzmueller, 1995; Poole & White, 1991).

The need for objectivity goes beyond the phrasing of individual questions. Objectivity is reflected in the way adults explore alternative explanations for children's behaviours and statements; that is, explore the possibility that a child has misconstrued an adult's behaviours or words or that a child may be minimizing, exaggerating, confabulating, or denying what happened for a host of understandable reasons, ranging from protecting a loved-one to fear of reprisal. Adults must keep in mind general principles of objectivity when listening to children's answers as well as the specific vulnerabilities of young children to certain question types.

SOCIO-EMOTIONAL MATURITY

Young children are accustomed to interacting with a limited number of familiar, predictable adults they can trust (e.g. parents, teachers, relatives). Even maltreated children have learned what to expect from caretakers. In contrast, the legal system is replete with unfamiliar people and incomprehensible rules for social interaction. Moreover, young children do not merely absorb the adult's view of reality; they create their own explanations for what they observe around them. With limited knowledge of the legal system and idiosyncratic explanations for their observations, children often generate unrealistic fears and expectations about adults' purposes. The unfamiliar interviewer, the judge, the jury can be sources of added stress.

Furthermore, most young children experience anxiety when separated from an attachment figure to accompany an unfamiliar adult to an unfamiliar place. Yet, most forensic protocols recommend interviewing children alone whenever possible to limit outside influences on testimony. When both parents and children are witnesses in a case, parents are often precluded from being in the courtroom when their children testify. Also, when children or their parents have been victims of violence, separated children are often worried about their safety and also the safety of their parents.

Unfortunately, young children have a limited repertoire of strategies for coping with the fear and anxiety they experience, and the coping strategies children do possess are rarely the most adaptive or effective; for example, avoidance is a prevalent childhood strategy for coping with people and places that generate negative feelings (Cramer, 1991). Avoiding the questioner and/or the topic can take the form of silence or oppositionality which is bound to delay or preclude a resolution to the situation. In contrast, adults rationalize the value of putting themselves through the hazards of the legal system because they hope their efforts will prevent harm to others. Unfortunately, the adult's altruistic rationalizations are not available to children who possess limited knowledge of abstract social systems beyond their immediate experience. Children can be left overwhelmed by negative feelings with little incentive to cooperate.

One implication of these developmental differences in emotional maturity is that children need time to establish rapport with the adults encountered in the legal system. Adults have a superior understanding of their own role and the roles of the various professionals in the system that facilitates productive social interaction. When the witness is a child, professionals must earn a child's trust and cooperation in the 'here and now', before an open, honest interchange can occur.

Surprisingly, the youngest children are not the only ones that require effort to establish rapport. Developments occur with age that result in greater resistance by older children. At around seven years of age, children begin to demonstrate a marked increase in selfconsciousness and embarrassment (Seidner, Stipek, & Feshbach, 1988). As they learn to draw inferences and take other people's perspectives, older children develop concerns about how others will judge them. Hence, maturity brings a new wrinkle to the rapport process.

Issues of embarrassment can be particularly acute in discussions of sexual abuse. For example, in a study of children's memories for a medical examination involving genital touch, researchers found a reverse developmental trend—younger children (five years of age) offered more complete recall than older children (seven years of age)—a trend lacking in the recall of an exam not containing genital touch (Saywitz, Goodman, Nicholas, & Moan, 1991). Older children clearly had better language and memory skills, but the authors speculated that embarrassment and a heightened sense of selfconsciousness interfered with the older children's reports.

In addition, certain developments in adolescence present new obstacles to rapport. Adolescence is a time of loosening ties to family and defining one's own identity independent of parents or other authority figures. Adolescents can present as resistant, oppositional, moody, and ready for battle. It is through this battle that they assert their autonomy and further define their identity. Of course, sometimes teens arrive ready to talk. Having felt like a helpless victim in an out-of-control situation, they perceive the legal process as an opportunity to reclaim a sense of self-agency and control. In such cases, less time may need to be spent developing rapport.

Maltreated and neglected children and children exposed to violence may require even greater attention to issues of rapport than other groups of children (Eltz, Shirk, & Sarlin, 1995). Empirical studies confirm that maltreated children are at risk for problems in interpersonal relationships (Aber, Allen, Carlson, & Cicchetti, 1989; Cicchetti, 1987; Shirk, 1988). Also, victims of violent crime are apt to feel less safe in new situations than other children. Mistrust and high levels of vigilance can predominate. One implication of children's emotional immaturity is that child witnesses may require modifications to accomodate their limited ability to cope with negative feelings that are overwhelming and otherwise interfere with their testimonial performance.

DEVELOPMENTAL TRENDS IN CONTEXT SENSITIVITY

Often, contextual cues that an adult would regard as insignificant dictate the child's response. Nowhere is this more evident than in the distractibility of the young child. Forensic interviewers who answer telephone calls during the interview may find it difficult to redirect a young child's attention back to the exacting task of detailed retrieval. The unfamiliar physical setting of the courtroom and the presence of spectators may derail a young child's ability to stay on the topic. As children mature, they develop a greater ability to resist distraction, to focus attention, and to function independently across settings of varied familiarity and complexity levels (Plude, Enns, & Brodeur, 1994).

Before a child has fully mastered a skill, such as telling the time, s/he can employ the skill in some contexts (supportive, easy) but not others (difficult, complex). Performance of a newly learned skill can be fragile and vulnerable to context effects; once the skill is mastered, its application is more robust. Thus, younger children are able to function better in certain situations than others (Revelle, Wellman, & Karabenick, 1985; Price & Goodman, 1990) resulting in greater inconsistency across statements. Older children are more resistant to contextual influences, and perform at their best across various settings more so than younger children. Thus, when the witness is a young child, consistency is not necessarily a marker of reliability and, conversely, inconsistency does not necessarily denote a false report.

In addition, individual differences interact with developmental trends to influence the effects of context on children's behaviours and statements (Forrester, Latham, & Shire, 1990); for example, personality characteristics and parental child-rearing attitudes have been shown to be related to very young children's abilities to resist interesting, attractive stimuli in the room (Silverman & Ragusa, 1991). Children with certain temperaments, cognitive styles, or certain psychiatric disorders may be more easily influenced by the context than other children. The child with Attention Deficit Disorder is one obvious example.

In sum, children are sensitive to the physical, psychological, and social context in which they find themselves. Context can affect a child's motivation, attention, retrieval of detail, resistance to suggestion, perceived credibility, and the level of stress experienced. This places a heavy responsibility upon adults in the system to control the physical surroundings of questioning, the timing of interviews and court appearances, and the psychological–social atmosphere. The goal is to create a context that facilitates, rather than undermines, children's developing abilities.

DEVELOPMENTAL TRENDS IN CHILDREN'S EXPLANATIONS

Immaturities in communication and cognition make children's statements difficult to interpret. A developmental perspective is useful to make sense of implausible statements, to generate alternative explanations, and to determine when answers should be relied upon, disregarded, or clarified. When a child in a case of alleged sexual assault describes that '*white glue came out his penis,*' the response should not be interpreted on the basis of its factual inaccuracy. It is developmentally appropriate for a child to liken an unfamiliar substance (semen) to a familiar one (glue) on the basis of its physical characteristics in order to make sense of the unfamiliar experience. Mischaracterization of semen as glue is a developmentally expected reasoning error that highlights the authenticity of the response, not its incredulity. We can avoid misinterpreting a child's response as an indicator of unreliability (or reliability) when in fact it might be a common characteristic of children at a given stage of development.

For this reason, the exact wording of the questions asked and the responses given can be crucial to unravelling a child's meaning. There are important implications for how one documents children's statements. While paraphrasing an adult's statement may not be problematic, paraphrasing children's statements leads to the loss of information whose value cannot be predicted at the time of a pre-trial interview. Paraphrasing '*He touched my pee pee*' as '*the child said she was molested*' creates confusion and impairs the pursuit of alternative explanations for the complaint. At best, it wastes limited resources and at worst it potentiates what could be false allegations. Documenting the *exact words* used by the child demonstrates a child's use of age-appropriate language, reasoning, and terminology that help evaluate credibility (Home Office & Department of Health, 1992).

Moreover, young children's vulnerability to suggestive questions necessitates the same level of scrutiny be applied to the wording of the questions used to elicit a child's statement. Documenting the question as well as the answer assists in determining whether coaching or contamination may have occurred. Detailed documentation can clarify what appear to be inconsistent statements, confabulations, denials, or recantations. Consider a situation in which an interviewer documents that '*the alleged perpetrator used a condom during the incident.*' In reality, the eight-year-old girl was asked a very leading question, '*When he did it, did he use a condom?*' and she responded, '*He put one of those hotdog balloons on his wiener before he put it in me, but he didn't blow it up*' (Elliott, pers. comm.). The child's reference to the condom as a 'hotdog balloon' demonstrates age-appropriate reasoning based on the perceptual characteristics of a novel object for which the child had no label. Verbatim documentation helps to assess her credibility in the face of a leading question.

A DEVELOPMENTAL FRAMEWORK

The goal of this chapter has been to highlight the importance of developmental trends in cognitive, communicative, social, and emotional development for eliciting and interpreting children's testimony, and formulating policies for child-witness management. Unfortunately, available research remains silent in a number of areas critical to a full understanding of the pressing issues surrounding children's testimony. Far more is known about the operation of cognitive factors, such as memory and language development, than the powerful motivational, social, and emotional factors at play in actual cases. The available research fails to address even simple social questions. Practitioners are often criticized that too little rapport heightens suggestibility out of fear of the intimidating, unfamiliar adult; too much rapport heightens suggestibility out of the desire to please the new friend. Available studies provide little guidance to identify optimal levels of rapport development.

A productive agenda for applied research will be one that acknowledges children's limitations at the same time as it seeks to promote children's abilities to the greatest extent possible. Systematic research of areas so far neglected is necessary to fully inform real-world decisions regarding risk assessment, placement, prosecution, and treatment planning. No doubt, new methodologies will need to be devised.

Intervention studies are needed to develop and test methods that optimize children's performance by reducing suggestibility effects (e.g. warning children not to speculate), overcoming anxiety and resistance (e.g. non-leading use of empathy), and/or preparing children for court. Moreover, the effects of specific question types on memory accuracy need to be further explored to develop questioning techniques that elicit sufficient information for decision making in the forensic context without distorting children's reports. In the field, interviewers weigh the merits and drawbacks of the options available to them in a given case at a given point in time, balancing the sufficiency of information obtained spontaneously with the need for additional information obtained through further questions, and the costs of additional error. To promote more informed decision-making about children in the legal system, the decision making process itself may need to become a target of systematic investigation.

In summary, reference to the existing developmental literature helps generate realistic expectations for the capabilities, limitations, and needs of children in given age ranges, while taking into account children's individual characteristics and specific circumstances. Further research of the potent developmental factors operating in children's testimony will advance sound public policies, needed practice guidelines, and the discovery of new knowledge.

REFERENCES

Aber, J., Allen, J., Carlson, V., & Cicchetti, D. (1989). The effects of maltreatment on development during early childhood: Recent studies and their theoretical, clinical, and policy implications. In: D. Cicchetti & V. Carlson (Eds), *Child maltreatment: Theory and research on the causes and consequences of child abuse and neglect* (pp. 579–619). New York: Cambridge University Press.

Ackil, J.K., & Zaragoza, M.S. (1995). Developmental differences in eyewitness suggestibility and memory for source. *Journal of Experimental Child Psychology*, **60**, 57–83.

Brown, R. (1973). *A first language: The early stages.* Cambridge: Harvard University Press.

Cassel, W.S., Roebers, C.E.M., & Bjorklund, D.F. (1996). Developmental patterns of eyewitness responses to repeated and increasingly suggestive questions. *Journal of Experimental Child Psychology*, **61**, 116–33.

Ceci, S.J., Ross, D., & Toglia, M. (1987). Age differences in suggestibility: Narrowing the uncertainties. In: S. Ceci, M. Toglia, & D. Ross (Eds), *Children's eyewitness memory* (pp. 79–91). New York: Springer-Verlag.

Cicchetti, D. (1987). Developmental psychopathology in infancy: Illustrations from the study of maltreated youngsters. *Journal of Consulting and Clinical Psychology*, **55**, 837–45.

Cramer, P. (1991). *The development of defence mechanisms: Theory, research, and assessment.* New York: Springer-Verlag.

Eltz, M.J., Shirk, S.R., & Sarlin, N. (1995). Alliance formation and treatment outcome among maltreated adolescents. *Child Abuse and Neglect*, **19**(4): 419–31.

Flavell, J. (1981). Cognitive monitoring. In: W. Dickson (Ed.), *Children's oral communication skills* (pp. 35–59). New York: Academic Press.

Fivush, R. (1993). Developmental perspectives on autobiographical recall. In: G.S. Goodman & B.L. Bottoms (Eds), *Child victims, child witnesses: Understanding and improving testimony* (pp. 1–24). New York: Guilford.

Fivush, R., & Schwarzmueller, A. (1995). Say it once again: Effects of repeated questions on children's event recall. *Journal of Traumatic Stress*, **8**, 555–80.

Forrester, M.A., Latham, J., & Shire, B. (1990). Exploring estimation in young primary school children. *Educational Psychology*, **10**(4): 283–300.

Gopnik, A., & Graf, P. (1988). Knowing how you know: Young children's ability to identify and remember the sources of their beliefs. *Child Development*, **59**, 1366–71.

Hamond, N.R., & Fivush, R. (1991). Memories of Mickey Mouse: Young children recount their trip to Disneyworld. *Cognitive Development*, **6**, 433–48.

Home Office & Department of Health. (1992). *Memorandum of good practice for video recorded interviews with child witnesses for criminal proceedings*. London: Her Majesty's Stationery Office.

Hudson, J.A. (1990). Constructive processing in children's event memory. *Developmental Psychology*, **26**, 180–7.

King, M.A., & Yuille, J.C. (1987). Suggestibility and the child witness. In: S.J. Ceci, M.P. Toglia, & D.F. Ross (Eds), *Children's eyewitness memory* (pp. 24–35). New York: Springer-Verlag.

Kobasigawa, A. (1977). Retrieval strategies in the development of memory. In: R.V. Kail & J.W. Hagen (Eds), *Perspectives on the development of memory and cognition* (pp. 177–201). Hillsdale, NJ: Erlbaum.

Kwock, M.S., & Winer, G.A. (1986). Overcoming leading questions: Effects of psychosocial task variables. *Journal of Educational Psychology*, **78**, 289–93.

Leichtman, M.D., & Ceci, S.J. (1995). The effects of stereotypes and suggestions on preschoolers' reports. *Developmental Psychology*, **31**, 568–78.

Lovett S., & Pillow, B. (1995). Development of the ability to distinguish between comprehension and memory: Evidence for strategy selection tasks. *Journal of Educational Psychology*, **87**(4), 523–36.

Lindsay, D.S., Johnson, M.K., & Kwon, P. (1991). Developmental changes in memory for source monitoring. *Journal of Experimental Child Psychology*, **52**, 297–318.

Milne, R. and Bull, R. (1999). *Investigative interviewing: Psychology and practice*. Chichester, UK: Wiley.

Nelson, K. (1986). *Event knowledge: Structure and function in development*. Hillsdale, NJ: Erlbaum.

Newhoff, N., & Launer, P. (1984). Input as interaction: Shall we dance? In: R. Naremore (Ed.), *Language science: Recent advances*. San Diego, CA: College Hill.

O'Neill, D.K, & Gopnik, A. (1991). Young children's ability to identify the sources of their beliefs. *Developmental Psychology*, **27**, 390–7.

Ornstein, P.A., Naus, M.J., & Liberty, C. (1975). Rehearsal and organizational processes in children's memory. *Child Development*, **46**, 818–30.

Peterson, C., Dowden, C., & Tobin, J. (1999). Interviewing preschoolers: Comparisons of yes/no and wh- questions. *Law & Human Behavior*, **23**(5), 539–56.

Plude, D.J., Enns, J.T., & Brodeur, D. (1994). The development of selective attention: A life-span overview. Special issue: Life-span changes in human performance. *Acta Psychologica*, **86**(2–3), 227–72.

Poole, D.A., & Lindsay, D.S. (1995). Interviewing preschoolers: Effects of non-suggestive techniques, parental coaching, and leading questions on reports of nonexperienced events. *Journal of Experimental Child Psychology*, **60**, 129–54.

Poole, D.A., & White, L.T. (1991). Effects of question repetition on the eyewitness testimony of children and adults. *Developmental Psychology*, **27**, 975–86.

Pressley, M., & Levin, J.R. (1977). Developmental differences in subjects' associative learning strategies and performance: Assessing a hypothesis. *Journal of Experimental Child Psychology*, **24**, 431–9.

Price, D. & Goodman, G. (1990). Visiting the wizard: Children's memory for a recurring event. *Child Development*, **61**, 664–80.

Revelle, G.L., Wellman, H.M., & Karabenick, J.D. (1985). Comprehension monitoring in preschool children. *Child Development*, **56**, 654–63.

Ritter, K., Kaprove, B.H., Fitch, J.P., & Flavell, J.H. (1973). The development of retrieval strategies in young children. *Cognitive Psychology*, **5**, 310–21.

Salatas, H., & Flavell, J.H. (1976). Retrieval of recently learned information: Development of strategies and control skills. *Child Development*, **47**, 941–8.

Saywitz, K.J. (1989). Children's conceptions of the legal system: Court is a place to play basketball. In: S. Ceci, M. Toglia, & D. Ross (Eds), *Perspectives on children's testimony* (pp. 131–57). New York: Springer-Verlag.

Saywitz, K.J., Goodman, G.S., Nicholas, E., & Moan, S. (1991). Children's memories of a physical examination involving genital touch: Implications for reports of child sexual abuse. *Journal of Consulting and Clinical Psychology*, **59**, 682–91.

Saywitz, K., Jaenicke, C., & Camparo, L. (1990). Children's knowledge of legal terminology. *Law and Human Behavior*, **14**(6), 523–35.

Saywitz, K.J., & Lyon, T. (2002). Coming to grips with children's suggestibility. In: M.L. Eisen, G.S. Goodman, & J.A. Quas (Eds), *Memory and suggestibility in the forensic interview*. Hillsdale, NJ: Erlbaum.

Saywitz, K., & Nathanson, R. (1993). Children's testimony and their perceptions of stress in and out of the courtroom. *Journal of Child Abuse and Neglect*, **17**, 613–22.

Saywitz, K.J., Snyder, L., & Nathanson, R. (1999). Facilitating the communicative competence of the child witness. *Applied Developmental Science*, **3**, 58–68.

Seidner, L.B., Stipek, D.M., and Feshbach, N.D. (1988). A developmental analysis of elementary school-aged children's concepts of pride and embarrassment. *Child Development*, **59**, 376–7.

Shirk, S.R. (1988). The interpersonal legacy of physical abuse in children. *Childhood and Adolescence*, 57–81.

Silverman, I.W. & Ragusa, D.M. 1991. Child and maternal correlates of impulse control in 24- month-old children. *Genetic, Social, and General Psychology Monographs*, **117**(3).

Taylor, M., Cartwright, B.S., & Bowden, T. (1991). Perspective-taking and theory of mind: Do children predict interpretive diversity as a function of differentiation in observers' knowledge? *Child Development*, **62**, 1334–51.

Tobey, A., & Goodman, G.S. (1992). Children's eyewitness memory: Effects of participation and forensic context. *Child Abuse and Neglect*, **16**, 779–96.

White, T.L., Leichtman, M.D., & Ceci, S.J. (1997). The good, the bad, and the ugly: Accuracy, inaccuracy, and elaboration in preschoolers' reports about a past event. *Applied Cognitive Psychology*, **11**, S37–S54.

Zaragoza, M.S., & Lane, S. (1994). Source misattributions and the suggestibility of eyewitness memory. *Journal of Experimental Psychology: Learning, Memory, & Cognition*, **20**, 934–45.

CHAPTER 2

Cognitive Underpinnings of Children's Testimony

LYNNE BAKER-WARD* AND PETER A. ORNSTEIN[†]

*Department of Psychology, North Carolina State University, Raleigh,
North Carolina, USA
[†]Department of Psychology, University of North Carolina, Chapel Hill,
North Carolina, USA

It is difficult to provide a simple characterization of young children's capabilities in reporting their experiences. On the one hand, young children can sometimes provide surprisingly rich accounts of past events (Bahrick, Parker, Fivush, & Levitt, 1998), and their memories can endure for years (Peterson, 1999). On the other hand, the limitations in children's remembering can be startling. Young children's accounts of their personal experiences are sometimes impoverished, even when interviewers provide extensive contextual support (Baker-Ward, Ornstein, & Principe, 1997), and can be inaccurate, even in the absence of misleading questions (Ornstein *et al.*, 1998).

In this chapter, we examine the cognitive bases for both the capabilities and the limitations that characterize young children's reports of their experiences and that determine, to a great extent, their potential competence as witnesses. From the standpoint of basic cognitive capacity, what are reasonable expectations for children's testimony? If child witnesses are effectively managed within the legal system and if interviewing is optimal, how good can children's testimony be?

Although many components are involved, memory is a basic prerequisite for children's abilities to provide accounts of their experiences (Brainerd & Ornstein, 1991). Hence, this discussion, like the literature

Children's Testimony. Edited by H.L. Westcott, G.M. Davies, and R.H.C. Bull.
© 2002 John Wiley & Sons, Ltd.

on children's testimony, emphasizes the long-term retention of events. Three different but interrelated traditions in memory research inform the present discussion. The first source of information is the 'traditional' view of memory and its development as derived primarily from laboratory-based research (for a recent overview of work conducted within this paradigm, see Schneider & Pressley, 1997). The significant differences between laboratory investigations involving neutral stimuli and children's memory for emotionally laden events notwithstanding, basic research provides important insights into the operation of the memory system (Brainerd & Ornstein, 1991).

The second important body of work examines directly children's reports of their events. Within this tradition, children's memory for routine events has been carefully examined (Nelson, 1986), children's reports of significant personal experiences have been analyzed (Fivush & Hudson, 1990), and the critical role of social interaction in the construction and maintenance of autobiographical memory has been established (see Fivush, Chapter 4 in this book). This research has led psychologists to reconceptualize their views of pre-schoolers' memory capabilities. Furthermore, the understanding of remembering as an inherently social process has led to an increased appreciation of the kinds of interactions that may maintain or alter our memories.

Finally, understanding children's testimony has been the impetus for extraordinary research activity. As a result, a voluminous literature exists, in which events that provide analogs to crimes are experienced by participants and their subsequent reports of these episodes are elicited. In many instances, the analog experiences have been medically indicated procedures involving bodily contact between the child and an adult and eliciting some degree of stress or discomfort for the child (Peterson, 1999; Steward *et al.*, 1996). The accuracy of children's memory and the course of their retention can be charted in such studies, because the details of the actual experience can be specified. The conditions under which children's reports have been obtained have enabled the examination of the effects of factors associated with increased suggestibility (Ceci & Bruck, 1995), as well as the investigation of variables hypothesized to enhance performance (Goodman & Bottoms, 1993).

Our examination of the cognitive underpinnings of children's testimony emphasizes fundamental assumptions about children's remembering. First, the nature of memory is discussed; next, some central attributes of memory development are examined. We illustrate these principles with examples from our research program. Finally, some implications of these assumptions for facilitating and interpreting children's testimony are briefly explored. The characteristics of memory and memory development that we present should by no means be considered an exhaustive inventory, and we readily admit that our selections reflect our own theoretical perspective and the results of our program of research. Nonetheless, in order to conduct effective interviews with child witnesses, examiners must understand the characteristics of children's testimony discussed in this chapter.

FUNDAMENTAL ASSUMPTIONS ABOUT MEMORY

Memory Is Not a Video Recorder

Long-term memory is sometimes seen as a permanent, veridical record of our experiences, analogous to an archive of video recordings. This popular view of memory has been fostered by media accounts of fascinating but limited experiences, including witnesses' retrieval of previously inaccessible information under hypnosis and neurosurgical patients' reliving of past events when their brains were electrically stimulated. A careful examination of accounts obtained under these circumstances, however, indicates that such reports are typically limited and sometimes inaccurate, more dream-like than veridical (Loftus, 1983). Similarly, 'flashbulb' memories for highly emotional events, which are often described as permanent and vivid impressions, turn out to decline over time and to be subject to reconstructive errors (McCloskey, Wible, & Cohen, 1988).

Psychologists have long understood that memory is a construction influenced by knowledge and beliefs (Bartlett, 1932). What we store in memory is in part the product of our subjective reality, and what we subsequently experience may alter our stored representations. The constructive nature of children's memory is illustrated by a recent investigation from our laboratory (Ornstein et al., 1998). Groups of four- and six-year-old children received a specially constructed, physical examination administered by a pediatrician in her office. The mock check-up included some typical components but omitted others that would be expected to occur on the basis of prior knowledge, and also contained some unexpected, unusual features (e.g. measuring head circumference). Subsequent interviews included questions about the typical and atypical features that were part of the mock check-up, and also incorporated probes about the typical and atypical features that were not administered ('absent features'). Although very few absent features were spontaneously reported at the initial interview, the children's expectations affected their reports of their experience at the delayed assessment. In some conditions, the children spontaneously nominated more than 20% of the expected-but-omitted features, while reporting essentially no other type of false information. Hence, children's accounts of a personal experience changed over time, as their memories tended to conform to their knowledge and expectations about the event.

Memory Exists in Interacting Layers of Representation

Psychologists have long distinguished between semantic memory, our internal reference book containing knowledge about the world, and episodic memory, our store of information about time-referenced events. Autobiographical memory, our personal life history, is an important component of episodic memory, and is of course the focus of most forensic interviews.

As indicated by the results of the Ornstein *et al.* (1998) experiment described above, these different representational systems are interacting rather than separate components of memory. Prior knowledge has been shown to be a powerful determinant of subsequent memory, as indicated by the widely documented discrepancy between experts' and novices' recall of information in a given domain (Chi, 1978). Work from our laboratory (Ornstein, Shapiro, Clubb, Follmer, & Baker-Ward, 1997) provides evidence for linkages between knowledge and the recall of personally experienced events. We established 'knowledge scores' for the individual components of a pediatric examination, based on the frequency with which they were reported by children who had not had a recent check-up. These knowledge scores predicted both the immediate and delayed recall of the components of the check-up among a group of children who had recently received a well-child examination. In addition, knowledge was predictive of different retention profiles over time. Hence, semantic memory—including background information about personal experiences and generic-event representations or scripts—can enhance autobiographical memory.

The interactions between representational systems can also decrease the accuracy with which events are reported. As illustrated by the Ornstein *et al.* (1998) study discussed above, memory is subject to distortion from expectations about the event, especially as the memory for the episode fades over time. Similarly, children as well as adults may come to rely on their 'scripts' as memory for a specific episode becomes less accessible over time (Myles-Worsley, Cromer, & Dodd, 1986). Moreover, individuals' current knowledge and beliefs influence recall. Memories that are consistent with adults' present understanding are more likely to be recalled than inconsistent information, and ambiguous memories tend to be interpreted within the context of present assumptions (Ross, 1997; Greenhoot, 2000).

Remembering Involves a Sequence of Steps

From an information-processing perspective, remembering is seen as consisting of a series of steps rather than operating as a unitary process. Recall failures can result from disruptions in the flow of information at any stage of information processing. Hence, understanding the issues involved in obtaining accurate testimony from children requires some knowledge of the encoding, storage, and retrieval of information. In our previous work, we have utilized an informal conceptual framework to facilitate our examination of the range of influences that can affect memory at each of the steps of information processing (Gordon, Schroeder, Ornstein, & Baker-Ward, 1995; Ornstein, Baker-Ward, Gordon, & Merritt, 1997). This framework includes the four general themes examined briefly below.

Not Everything Gets into Memory

The inability to report fully an experience may arise from an encoding as well as a retrieval failure; information may never have been stored in memory in the first place. A number of factors have been shown to influence the likelihood of encoding. As discussed above, the child's understanding of the details of the event is associated with the likelihood of subsequent recall. Nonetheless, a novel experience can be encoded and remembered when its component features are linked together in a causal rather than an arbitrary way (Ornstein *et al.*, 1997). Additional influences on encoding include the interest value of the to-be-remembered information, aspects of children's behavioral styles, and the degree of stress experienced at the time of the event (Gordon *et al.*, 1995). Although the relationship between stress and memory has been controversial, there is an emerging consensus that high levels of stress at the time of experience disrupt the encoding of information.

What Gets into Memory May Vary in Strength

Memory representations are not created equally. After encoding has been accomplished, the information in memory is associated with a variable degree of trace strength, a construct referring to the structure of information in memory and the ease with which it can be retrieved. Although it can only be indirectly observed, the strength of the representation is an important consideration in interviewing child witnesses, because trace strength can be assumed to affect the likelihood of forgetting. In addition, witnesses appear to be more suggestible when the strength of the relevant information is weak (Gordon *et al.*, 1995).

Several factors are associated with the strength of the memory trace. The amount of exposure to an event, in terms of both duration and frequency, is likely to increase the strength of the memory representation. In addition, prior knowledge is once again an important influence. Finally, it is likely that, other influences being equal, older children will acquire more information from a comparable exposure to an event than will younger children. This effect can be attributed to age-related changes in processing speed as well as the availability of more efficient strategies and an increased knowledge base (see Ornstein *et al.*, 1997).

The Status of Information in Memory Changes over Time

As discussed above, information in memory is not frozen, but is in contrast subject to a variety of influences. In most cases, the simple passage of time increases the probability that information will be lost. In addition, the nature of individuals' intervening experiences, both resulting from real-world events and from the 'autosuggestibility' attributable to beliefs and expectations, can affect the contents of memory. These effects can have positive as well as negative influences on the veracity of children's reports.

An investigation conducted in our laboratory illustrates the influence of experiences during the retention interval on children's recall (Principe, Ornstein, Baker-Ward, & Gordon, 2000). Groups of three- and five-year-old children all experienced a pediatric check-up and were interviewed immediately after the examination and again after a delay of 12 weeks. The children's experiences during the retention interval differed, however. The children in one condition had an additional memory interview midway through the retention period. Those in another condition viewed a video of another child's physical examination that included some components that were consistent with their own experiences, and other components that were inconsistent. Other groups of children returned to the doctors' offices where they completed an unrelated task in an examining room. Relative to control participants, the children who had the six-week interview and those who viewed the video recalled more information in response to general questions at the final interview. Moreover, the older children who saw the video or returned to their physicians' offices had relatively more difficulty in correctly rejecting misleading questions. Hence, individuals' experiences during the retention period had both positive and negative effects on memory.

Retrieval Is Not Perfect

The final step in information processing is the report of the experience. As every interviewer knows, retrieval is an imperfect process, and not every item in memory is reported. Of course, social factors such as the hesitancy to disclose embarrassing information can limit children's reports (Saywitz, Goodman, Nicholas, & Moan, 1991). But, in addition, the attributes of the context in which an interview is conducted affect the ease with which stored information is accessible. The examiner's questions, which constitute retrieval cues, are certainly among the most important components of the context. A general law of memory is the encoding specificity principle (Tulving & Thomson, 1973), which states that retrieval cues are only effective in evoking information from memory when they were present at encoding. An implication of this principle is that the more completely the interview reinstates the context present at the time of encoding, including the physical environment and the witness's internal state, the more complete retrieval is likely to be (see Fisher & McCauley, 1995, for an application of principles of cognitive psychology to the development of an interview protocol). Because children's understanding of events and reactions to their experiences may differ markedly from those of adults, interviewers face particular challenges in providing effective retrieval cues for young witnesses.

DEVELOPMENTAL CHANGES IN MEMORY

Age Affects but Does Not Determine Memory Performance

One of the most robust findings in the literature on children's testimony is the presence of age-related increases in the amount of information recalled (Ornstein *et al.*, 1997). Older children are also consistently shown to be more resistant to suggestibility than younger children (Ceci & Bruck, 1995). Nonetheless, younger pre-schoolers have better memories for personal experiences than was previously assumed to be the case. Some general expectations for event reports across the early childhood years are outlined below (see Fivush, 1998, for an engaging overview of this literature). It is emphasized that age is a proxy variable for underlying changes in the multiple domains of development which affect children's memory performance, rather than a causal factor. Hence, interviewers should view a child's age as a basis for expectations about performance rather than as a diagnosis of competence.

Very Early Memory

It appears that children must possess narrative abilities at the time of an experience in order to provide a delayed verbal account of the event. Peterson and Rideout (1998), in an investigation of one- and two-year-old children's memory for a traumatic injury and subsequent emergency medical treatment, found that children who did not have narrative skills at the time of the event provided little verbal information, even two years later when they had acquired these language skills. Moreover, the information they did provide, in response to wh- as well as yes/no questions, was of questionable accuracy. In contrast, children who were between two and three years old at the time of the accident provided more of the components of the events, and about three-quarters of their responses to wh- questions were accurate after a delay of two years.

These findings are consistent with Nelson's (1993) analysis of the origins of autobiographical memory. Nelson argues that it is the ability to engage in conversations about past events, which generally emerges between about two and a half and three years of age, that enables children to remember their experiences over long delays. Although children who do not yet have narrative skills can provide event reports, the information tends to be sparse, and memories for specific episodes become intermingled with general representations of the event or confused with other episodes (Hudson, 1990). As reviewed by Robyn Fivush (1998; see also Fivush, Chapter 4 in this book), adult–child conversations about past experiences enable young children to represent their experiences in new ways. The coherence and organization that results from such interaction can support the encoding of an experience and the subsequent retention of the experience over time.

Pre-schoolers' Memory

Although pre-school children can report their experiences after long delays, substantial improvement in memory is observed over the early childhood years. Ornstein *et al.* (1997) used hierarchical linear modeling statistical techniques to examine age-related changes in retention among groups of children from three to six and seven years old, using a dataset that pooled results from a number of investigations. The composite sample of 232 children had all been interviewed immediately following a pediatric examination, and again at a delay of either 1, 3, 6, or 12 weeks. Substantial age differences were observed, with open-ended and total recall increasing and forgetting decreasing with age.

Some evidence suggests that such changes in performance may be largely attributable to age-related increases in encoding. As noted above, encoding is likely to be enhanced by age-related changes in the speed of processing, as well as by the more extensive and coherent knowledge base that generally accompanies development. Consistent with this possibility, age differences are found in assessments conducted immediately after events, before significant forgetting can occur, as well as after delays. In addition, our attempts to minimize the impact of age differences in retrieval by using recognition protocols or dolls and other props have been unsuccessful (Baker-Ward *et al.*, 1997).

Later Childhood

After children begin formal schooling, differences associated with age appear to be less important than individual difference factors. Peterson (1999), in a large-scale investigation of 2- to 13-year-old children's memory for an accident and subsequent emergency medical treatment, reported no differences in the number of event components reported between the children in the 8- to 9-year-old group and those in the 12- to 13-year-old group. In addition, the overall accuracy of the children's reports of their experiences did not increase after age 8 to 9.

Changes in Knowledge Underlie Many Age-related Differences

In examining the nature of memory above, prior knowledge was assigned a critical role in determining recall success or failure. As we have seen, previously stored information affects the likelihood that a component of an event will be encoded, and influences the retention of the item in memory. Moreover, the characteristics of the knowledge structure in memory affect the ease with which information can be retrieved. When details about an event are integrated with previously stored information, more cues are likely to be effective in eliciting the new items. Furthermore, the structure of memory affects the likelihood that information can be retrieved. More coherent and organized knowledge structures facilitate retrieval processes.

Both the extent and the structure of the knowledge base can be expected to increase with age. Simply having lived in the world for a longer time contributes to a greater store of knowledge. As noted above, children participate in conversations about past events to an increasing degree after the early pre-school years. These social interactions improve the organization of stored information, making it subsequently more easily retrieved. When children's understanding of events increases, and previously unconnected actions are linked, the representation is less subject to forgetting and more easily accessible (Baker-Ward *et al.*, 1997). Moreover, school-aged children have developed strategies for retrieving information that enable them to actively search their memories (Brainerd & Ornstein, 1991). Effective retrieval strategies enable older children to capitalize on the organization of information in memory when they deliberately attempt to retrieve their past experiences.

Age-related changes in children's degree of reliance on the meaning rather than the exact form of information may further enhance remembering and reduce suggestibility. Brainerd and his colleagues (Brainerd, Reyna, Howe, & Kingma, 1990; Reyna & Brainerd, 1995) provide a model of recall that examines differences in memory for verbatim and gist information. According to 'fuzzy trace theory', these types of information are stored separately in memory and accessed by different retrieval processes. Furthermore, there are very significant developmental differences in memory for gist and verbatim information, with younger children being predisposed to encode and recall verbatim information, whereas older subjects rely much more extensively on memory for gist traces. Gist traces are more enduring and more easily retrieved than verbatim traces, which are more susceptible to interference and forgetting. Hence, pre-schoolers' memory may be limited by the way in which they utilize meaning, as well as by their relatively limited store of information about the world.

Recall Is Affected by Changes in Other Domains of Development

Although basic memory processes change with age, other aspects of cognitive and social development are intrinsically related to retrieval. Increased recall performance is partially explained by advances in language development, increased narrative competence, source-monitoring abilities, social cognition, and other age-related changes in children's abilities (see Karen Saywitz, Chapter 1 in this book, and Stephen Lindsay, Chapter 6 in this book).

In some instances, developmental limitations may affect perceptions of children's competence as witnesses, but not the validity of their accounts of their experiences; for example, pre-schoolers' reports of a personally experienced event lack consistency, one of the major criteria that jurors use in determining a witness' credibility. An analysis of young children's repeated accounts of a documented event, however, established that, although the children reported different components of their experience on two occasions, the information they provided was nonetheless accurate (Gordon & Follmer, 1994). In other circumstances, modification of the aspects of the interview, such as the syntax of questions directed toward very young witnesses, may compensate for developmental limitations (Imhoff & Baker-Ward, 1999).

Limitations in other domains of development, however, can also constrain the effectiveness of some techniques for assessing memory. This may explain, for example, the counter-intuitive finding that three-year-old children do not provide more information when presented with dolls to represent the self (Baker-Ward *et al.*, 1997). It would seem reasonable to expect that this practice would enhance younger pre-schoolers' reports by minimizing their reliance on verbal skills. In contrast, it appears that younger pre-schoolers' difficulties with dual representation, the capacity to represent simultaneously an object in two ways, limits the utility of the practice (see Pipe *et al.*, Chapter 11 in this book).

Because of the importance of changes in multiple domains of development on memory performance, individual differences in aspects of social and personality development can be expected to be significant influences on children's testimony. For example, in a recent investigation conducted in our laboratory, aspects of children's self-concepts, including their scores on measures of traditionalism and social avoidance, contributed to the prediction of suggestibility, even after age had been taken into account (Burgwyn-Bailes, Baker-Ward, Gordon, & Ornstein, in press). Individual difference variables should be examined within the context of their influence at each stage of information processing; for example, it is possible that stress at the time of an event may negatively affect initial encoding, but could result in increased discussion and other potential opportunities for reinstatement and continued encoding during the retention interval. At retrieval, it is possible that individual differences are relatively more important predictors of recall among younger witnesses (e.g. Greenhoot, Ornstein, Gordon, & Baker-Ward, 1999). This may be due, in part, to older children's increased experience with structured situations and their resulting skills in regulating dimensions of their own behavior.

SOME IMPLICATIONS FOR PRACTICE

Because of the characteristics of children's memory, the interviewer's performance is an integral component of any assessment of a child witness's report. Even this brief overview of the cognitive underpinnings of children's testimony establishes the role of the interviewer as complex, challenging, and multi-faceted. The examiner's task can never be reduced to simply utilizing the appropriate technique to activate a preserved experience in memory or determining when an individual is telling the truth. Our 'true' memories can include distortions arising from our beliefs and expectations, confusions among related episodes or other experiences, and additional information acquired after the fact. Hence, there cannot be a 'a Pinocchio test' (Ceci & Bruck, 1995). There are, however, skillfully conducted memory assessments that result in good evidence. Such interviews involve attention to the cognitive dimensions of the child's memory performance along with effective management of the social dynamics of the interview.

One prerequisite for an effective assessment of a child's memory is an analysis of the entire sequence of information processing. This involves an examination of the likelihood that the event was encoded, necessitating attention to the context in which the experience transpired and the child's age, level of relevant knowledge and other personal characteristics. In addition, the child's experiences during the retention interval must also be carefully assessed. The potential for reinstatement and interference, in light of the possible strength of the encoding information, must be explored. Furthermore, the child's previous reports must be evaluated with reference to the appropriateness of the retrieval supports that were present during the interview.

The developmental changes that occur in memory necessitate special considerations by the interviewer. Effective examiners must scaffold children's retrieval by controlling the elements of the recall task that exceed young witnesses' capabilities, enabling them to focus on the demands that are within their range of competence (Wood, Bruner, & Ross, 1976); for example, interviewers should be particularly careful to re-establish the context in which an event occurred and provide a variety of details about undisputed aspects of the experience when questioning young children. Such practices may help compensate in part for limitations in young children's active retrieval processes and knowledge structures.

Because memory undergoes substantial development during childhood, it is unreasonable to expect that even optimal interviewing can eliminate age differences in children's testimony. Nonetheless, in well-managed cases, even pre-schoolers can provide useful information about their personal experiences.

This work was supported in part by grant HD 32214 from the US Public Health Service.

REFERENCES

Bahrick, L.E., Parker, J.F., Fivush, R., & Levitt, M. (1998). The effects of stress on young children's memory for a natural disaster. *Journal of Experimental Psychology: Applied*, **4**, 308–31.

Baker-Ward, L., Ornstein, P.A., & Principe, G.F. (1997). Revealing the representation: Evidence from children's reports of events. In: P. van den Broek, P. Bauer, & T. Borg (Eds), *Developmental spans in event comprehension and representation: Bridging fictional and actual events* (pp. 79–107). Hillsdale, NJ: Erlbaum.

Bartlett, F.C. (1932). *Remembering: A study in experimental and social psychology*. Cambridge: Cambridge University Press.

Brainerd, C.J., & Ornstein, P.A. (1991). Children's memory for witnessed events: The developmental backdrop. In: J. Doris (Ed.), *The suggestibility of children's recollections* (pp. 10–20). Washington, DC: American Psychological Association.

Brainerd, C.J., Reyna, V.F., Howe, M.L., & Kingma, J. (1990). The development of forgetting and reminiscence. *Monographs of the Society for Research in Child Development*, **55**(3–4, Serial No. 222).

Burgwyn-Bailes, E., Baker-Ward, L., Gordon, B., & Ornstein, P. A. (in press). Children's memory for emergency medical treatment after one year: The impact of individual difference variables on recall and suggestibility. *Applied Cognitive Psychology*.

Ceci, S.J., & Bruck, M. (1995). *Jeopardy in the courtroom*. Washington, DC: American Psychological Association.

Chi, M.T.H. (1978). Knowledge structures and memory development. In R.S. Siegler (Ed.), *Children's thinking: What develops?* (pp. 73–96). Hillsdale, NJ: Erlbaum.

Fisher, R.P., & McCauley, M. (1995). Improving eyewitness testimony with the Cognitive Interview. In M.S. Zaragoza, J.R. Graham, G.C.N. Hall, R. Hirschman, & Y.S. Ben-Porath (Eds), *Memory and testimony in the child witness* (pp. 141–59). Thousand Oaks, CA: Sage.

Fivush, R. (1998). Children's recollections of traumatic and nontraumatic events. *Development and Psychopathology*, **10**, 699–716.

Fivush, R., & Hudson, J.A. (Eds) (1990). *Knowing and remembering in young children*. New York: Cambridge University Press.

Goodman, G.S., & Bottoms, B.L. (Eds.) (1993). *Child victims, child witnesses: Understanding and improving testimony*. New York: Guilford.

Gordon, B.N., & Follmer, A. (1994). Developmental issues in judging the credibility of children's testimony. *Journal of Clinical Child Psychology*, **23**, 283–94.

Gordon, B.N., Schroeder, C.S., Ornstein, P.A., & Baker-Ward, L. (1995). Clinical implications of research on memory development. In: T. Ney (Ed.), *Child sexual abuse cases: Allegations, assessment, and management* (pp. 94–124). New York: Brunner/Mazel.

Greenhoot, A.F. (2000). Remembering and understanding: The effects of changes in underlying knowledge on children's recollections. *Child Development*, **71**, 1309–28.

Greenhoot, A.F., Ornstein, P.A., Gordon, B.N., & Baker-Ward, L. (1999). Acting out the details of a pediatric check-up: The inpact of interview condition and behavioral style on children's reports. *Child Development*, **70**, 363–380.

Hudson, J.A. (1990). Constructive processing in children's event memory. *Developmental Psychology*, **26**, 180–7.

Imhoff, M.C., & Baker-Ward, L. (1999). Preschoolers' suggestibility: Effects of developmentally appropriate language and interviewer supportiveness. *Applied Developmental Psychology*, **20**, 407–29.

Loftus, E. (1983). *Memory*. Reading, MA: Addison-Wesley.

McCloskey, M., Wible, C.G., & Cohen, N.J. (1988). Is there a special flashbulb-memory mechansim? *Journal of Experimental Psychology: General*, **117**, 171–81.

Myles-Worsley, M., Cromer, C., & Dodd, D. (1986). Children's preschool script reconstruction: Reliance on general knowledge as memory fades. *Developmental Psychology*, **22**, 22–30.

Nelson, K. (1986). *Event knowledge: Structure and function in development*. Hillsdale, NJ: Erlbaum.

Nelson, K. (1993). The psychological and social origins of autobiographical memory. *Psychological Science*, **1**, 1–8.

Ornstein, P.A., Baker-Ward, L., Gordon, B.N., & Merritt, K.A. (1997). Children's memory for medical experiences: Implications for testimony. *Applied Cognitive Psychology*, **11**, S87–S104.

Ornstein, P.A., Merritt, K.A., Baker-Ward, L., Gordon, B.N., Furtado, E., & Principe, G. (1998). Children's knowledge, expectation, and long-term retention. *Applied Cognitive Psychology*, **12**, 387–405.

Ornstein, P.A., Shapiro, L.R., Clubb, P.A., Follmer, A., & Baker-Ward, L. (1997). The influence of prior knowledge on children's memory for salient medical experiences. In N. Stein, P.A. Ornstein, C.J. Brainerd, & B. Tversky (Eds), *Memory for everyday and emotional events* (pp. 83–111). Hillsdale, NJ: Erlbaum.

Peterson, C. (1999). Children's memory for medical emergencies: 2 years later. *Developmental Psychology*, **35**, 1493–506.

Peterson, C., & Rideout, R. (1998). Memory for medical emergencies experienced by 1- and 2-year-olds. *Developmental Psychology*, **34**, 1059–72.

Principe, G.F., Ornstein, P.A., Baker-Ward, L., & Gordon, B.N. (2000). The effects of intervening experiences on children's memory for a physical examination. *Applied Cognitive Psychology*, **14**, 59–80.

Reyna, V.F., & Brainerd, C.J. (1995). Fuzzy-trace theory: An interim synthesis. *Learning and Individual Differences*, **3**, 27–59.

Ross, M. (1997). Validating memories. In N. Stein, P.A. Ornstein, C.J. Brainerd, & B. Tversky (Eds), *Memory for everyday and emotional events* (pp. 49–81). Hillsdale, NJ: Erlbaum.

Saywitz, K.J., Goodman, G.S., Nicholas, E., & Moan, S. (1991). Children's memories of physical examinations involving genital touch: Implications for reports of child sexual abuse. *Journal of Consulting and Clinical Psychology*, **59**, 682–91.

Schneider, W., & Pressley, M. (1997). *Memory development between two and twenty* (2nd ed.). Mahwah, NJ: Erlbaum.

Steward, M.S., Steward, D.S., Farquhar, L., Myers, J.E.B., Reinhart, M., Welker, J., Joye, N., Driskell, J., & Morgan, J. (1996). Interviewing young children about body touch and handling. *Monographs of the Society for Research in Child Development*, **61**(4–5, Serial No. 248).

Tulving, E., & Thomson, D.M. (1973). Encoding specificity and retrieval processes in episodic memory. *Psychological Review*, **80**, 352–73.

Wood, D., Bruner, J., & Ross, G. (1976). The role of tutoring and problem solving. *Journal of Child Psychology and Psychiatry*, **17**, 89–100.

CHAPTER 3

Child Protection Concerns When Questioning Children

MARCUS PAGE AND GRETCHEN PRECEY

Triangle Services for Children, Brighton, East Sussex, UK

This chapter addresses the interviewing of children for evidential purposes from the perspective of child-protection practitioners. Both the authors have worked for many years as social workers in a multi-agency child-protection unit in the UK, which conducts over a hundred formal investigative interviews a year. The unit also has a role in assessing the risk to children of living in their current setting and working therapeutically with children and families in the aftermath of abuse investigations. Much of the thinking that informs this chapter is taken from our clinical experience of working with children within the child-protection system. We believe that this system does protect many children from harm, and can be helpful in other ways, but we are also mindful of cases in which the requirements of the system supersedes the best interests of the child and the frequency with which crimes against children are excluded from the criminal justice system.

We first describe briefly the child-protection system as it has developed in the UK. We then look more closely at the challenge it presents to professionals due to the inherent tension between keeping children's welfare paramount and adhering to official guidance about obtaining evidence for use in criminal proceedings. Case examples are used to illustrate some of the complexities involved in child-protection work and we also draw attention to the additional factors to consider for disabled children, children from ethnic or cultural minorities, and for

Children's Testimony. Edited by H.L. Westcott, G.M. Davies, and R.H.C. Bull.
© 2002 John Wiley & Sons, Ltd.

very young children. All of these groups are poorly served by the system as it currently exists and are even less likely to obtain justice than other children.

THE CHILD-PROTECTION CONTEXT AND ITS IMPLICATIONS FOR INTERVIEWING CHILDREN

The child-protection system in the UK has been subjected to significant shifts in legislation introduced in the late 1980s and early 1990s that moved the balance around between parental rights and responsibilities for the upbringing of children and the individual rights of children themselves to be protected from harm. In the past decade, major changes in the field have been brought about by the Children Act 1989 (Department of Health, 1989), that followed the Report of the Inquiry into Sexual Abuse in Cleveland (Department of Health, 1987) and the baccompanying guidelines *Working together under the children act* (Department of Health, Home Office, Department of Education and Science, & Welsh Office, 1989). These measures, which acknowledged the scale and severity of the effects of sexual abuse, also introduced the concept of partnership with parents alongside the principle that in all matters concerning children the child's welfare is paramount.

One of the central themes of the legislation and guidance is the requirement that agencies dedicated to safeguarding children must work together. The lead agencies in the investigation of abuse are the police and social services. The usual practice of these agencies is to make enquiries jointly when concerns are raised about the safety and welfare of a child and for both a social worker and a police officer to be present for the video-recorded evidential interviews of children about their experiences.

The guidance for questioning children formally about possible abuse is found in the *Memorandum of good practice* (MOGP) (Home Office & Department of Health, 1992), a document issued jointly by the Home Office, which deals with law and law enforcement, and the Department of Health, which is concerned with child welfare. The guidance is directed at child-protection professionals and concerns the conduct of interviews 'where it is intended that the result should be acceptable in criminal proceedings' (MOGP, p. 1).

The *Memorandum* describes a four-phase stepwise interview protocol in which a specially trained police officer and social worker together interview a child 'once it becomes clear that a criminal offence may have been committed' (MOGP, §1.9, p. 6). Concern that a child has been abused may have arisen from one or more sources: an account of maltreatment from the child; physical indicators such as bruising, sexually transmitted diseases or pregnancy; sexualized behaviour or emotional indicators; or a witness description by a third party.

The videotaped single interview, which normally lasts no more than an hour, is arranged as soon as the necessary preparation for it is complete, often within 24 hours of the allegation or referral. The video-tape becomes the child's evidence-in-chief should the case go to criminal prosecution. If a defendant enters a plea of not guilty, however, the child is still required to attend court to be cross-examined by the defence via a live video link between the courtroom and a separate room where the child watches the proceedings on a TV monitor. The 'special measures' provision contained in section 28 of the Youth and Criminal Justice Act 1999 (Home Office, 1999), will allow for cross-examination of the child, also to be video recorded at a preliminary hearing nearer to the time of the child's original interview (Bates, 1999).

Perceptions by professionals of the child's inability to be cross-examined in court under the current arrangements for child witnesses may result in a child not being formally interviewed in the first place. This is particularly true for some disabled children who have methods of communication other than speech (e.g. augmentative communication using a symbol system) or who have a learning diffi-culty. New guidance contained in the revised *Working together to safe-guard children* (Department of Health, Home Office, Department of Education and Science, & Welsh Office, 1999) has been introduced to address this issue, but it is not known whether this will prove effective.

There is a requirement for specially trained professionals from the social services and the police to work closely together in the investiga-tion and questioning of children, when abuse is suspected. This contains many benefits for the child: information held by each agency on the circumstances of the child and their family is shared and multiple interviewing is avoided. This encourages a more efficient, accurate investigation process. Joint agency training means that social workers become familiar with the rules of evidence and other requirements of the legal system and the police gain knowledge in aspects of child development and the psychological impact of abuse. This helps to ensure that individuals from these very different profes-sional backgrounds share a similar orientation when interviewing children.

The child-protection system nevertheless continues to have the potential for causing emotional harm to the children whose evidence is sought for a possible criminal prosecution. Joint working has made a positive contribution to how children are questioned, but some tensions are inevitable in the combining of the police and social-service agencies with their different organizational structures and objectives. This can have a negative effect on the experience of children in the interview process. At a purely practical level, police-shift patterns, social-work duty rotas, and conflicting demands on the time of child-protection professionals can result in a lack of continuity of personnel within the investigation. This can prevent the development of the necessary trust with a parent and the rapport with a child that is the foundation for effective communication in the interview.

At another level, the different aims and values of the police and social-welfare agencies may result in a child's welfare being compromised. Within the general culture of the police force, the predominant measure of success is obtaining the conviction of an alleged perpetrator. This can conflict with the specialized training of police child-protection officers that emphasizes the welfare of a child as the paramount consideration. The objective of obtaining a successful conviction can skew messages to families as to what is in a child's best interest. It can also reinforce hopes of parents that the conviction and imprisonment of the offender will be decisive in helping the child and family overcome the effects of the abuse.

The reality is that only a small minority of cases are prosecuted, fewer result in convictions and only very rarely do victims' families consider that the sentences are sufficiently severe (Davies, Wilson, Mitchell, & Milsom, 1995). If the case does not come before the court, children sometimes feel that they have not been believed or that the answers they gave to the questions at interview were not sufficiently convincing and they have failed. Our experience of working with families in the aftermath of criminal proceedings is that, even in those cases where the conviction of an abuser is achieved, it does not usually have the effect of closure and resolution that the family had been expecting. This can only be achieved through time and the family's ability to develop open communication with one another and tolerate the sometimes strongly conflicting feelings of family members during the stages of recovery.

The main problem, however, is that the current child-protection process and interviewing under the *Memorandum* guidance do not allow children the necessary time and emotional facilitation to give a full account of their experiences of abuse. We know from years of working therapeutically with children that what is revealed at the first telling is very often only a small part of what has actually happened to a child. It does not reflect the complexity of the process of the abuse and how the child feels about it. Our experience is that many children have found being questioned under these conditions as a further abusive intrusion and another event, like the abuse itself, over which they could exercise little control.

CHALLENGES TO PRACTITIONERS

The legislation and professional procedures referred to earlier in this chapter – the Children Act 1989 and MOGP – have the premise that the child's welfare should be the paramount consideration in all child-protection work. That sentiment was also famously enshrined by Lord Justice Butler-Sloss in her *Report of the Inquiry into Child Abuse in Cleveland* when she wrote 'the child is a person and not an object of concern' (Department of Health, 1987, p. 245). The fact that this principle continues to need restating is a measure of the tension that still exists between the needs of the child and the family and the child-protection system as it currently operates.

In addition, it is our experience that the children who are abused and come to the attention of the authorities are not a representative cross-section of the child population. It is often the case that children have been targeted for abuse due to pre-existing emotional vulnerabilities arising from family circumstances or other factors. It is these same vulnerabilities that are then exploited by an abuser in order to maintain the abusive relationship and that add to the difficulties presented to professionals who seek to avoid creating other forms of harm by their interventions.

The challenge for practitioners is in managing the tensions between a child's welfare and the need to secure the evidence of child witnesses in the manner prescribed by the official guidance. In considering the best interests of children, professionals need to develop an awareness of the complex combination of factors that create children's vulnerabilities but also be able to keep an open mind about their potential resilience. The factors to consider include a child's developmental stage and communication abilities, their role within their family, the overall family context, and their cultural and racial background.

The following case examples demonstrate how difficult this task for workers can be in practice when one is needing to consider a large number of elements that together constitute a particular child's world and having to make decisions about the investigation and interviewing process. Details and names in all of the following examples have been altered to protect the anonymity of the children.

The Significance of Family Context

Cases of extrafamilial abuse can appear, at first sight, to be more straightforward than abuse within the family, especially when the differences in age and power make clear who is a victim and who is the abuser. The following case example is typical however of how such scenarios take on layers of complexity when one considers the matrix of family and social relationships and sees how a child's vulnerabilities may arise from a variety of sources.

Sean, aged 9 years, was befriended over a period of months by an elderly man who became a trusted friend of the family. Sean eventually talked about 'touches he did not like' to his mother who straightaway informed the police. Non-penetrative sexual abuse had taken place on a few occasions.

At the outset of this investigation, the process of formally questioning Sean about the abuse appeared to be uncomplicated. This was because Sean had already told his mother, she believed him and acted protectively. The abuser was not a family member, the abuse had been relatively short lived and it was not accompanied by violence.

This scenario may be seen to become more complex, however, when one adds the background to this abuse. Six months previously, Sean and his elder brother had come with their mother to the area from another town in order for her to escape a violent marriage. Sean's mother remained in fear of her whereabouts being discovered by her husband and was worried about any possible publicity surrounding the investigation and prosecution that might expose her location. She therefore experienced Sean's disclosure as putting the whole family at risk.

Sean had a medical condition which necessitated a strictly controlled diet with which he was reluctant to cooperate. His mother knew that there was a risk of permanent mental impairment if the diet was not adhered to and she went to great lengths in preparing all his food herself. The elderly man had secretly given Sean sweets (candy) normally banned to him. This added to the guilt that Sean felt and to his mother's concerns about severe lasting harm to him.

Sean attributed his mother's degree of upset to his own actions and for his keeping the 'little secret' from her. Her attempts to reassure him that he was a good boy to tell and that the abuse was not his fault were belied by the distress that was visible in his mother's face. Sean's elder brother, who felt very responsible for protecting his mother, blamed Sean for upsetting her, for doing things he knew were 'dirty', and for eating the forbidden sweets.

In the formal interview, Sean experienced painfully conflicting feelings in telling about the abuse because of feeling responsible for causing his mother's distress and his brother's anger. His sense of guilt and responsibility could not be directly attended to within the structure of the evidential interview and he withheld important details because he had been manipulated by the abuser to feel that he had initiated the fondling that took place.

The case did not proceed to court as it was thought that Sean would make a poor witness. It was not until all of the issues described above could be addressed in therapy that Sean was able to feel less guilty about 'letting the abuse happen'.

Disabled Children

(*Note: We use the term 'disabled children' here to refer to children with physical or sensory impairments and children with learning difficulties but we hold to the social model of disability that describes the social processes of discrimination and prejudice that serve to disable children and adults and create barriers to opportunities afforded to their non-disabled peers [Morris, 1995].*)

Our experience is that disabled children are often unlikely even to enter the child-protection system and be questioned about their experiences. This is despite the fact that much research now exists which demonstrates that disabled children are at higher risk of abuse than other children (Westcott & Cross, 1996). When concern is raised about the possible abuse of a disabled child there is often significant delay before action is taken by protection agencies because professionals often seek to explain a child's behaviour or allegation in terms of a child's impairment and are reluctant to admit that the child may be at risk.

Child-protection police officers and social workers, who generally have little or no contact with disabled children, may also doubt that a disabled child could be a credible witness and should be considered for a formal video-recorded evidential interview. Even when an interview is clearly indicated, the needs of a disabled child may seem insurmountable to investigators unused to considering these issues. The decision whether to interview and the quality of such an interview may be influenced by factors such as: the time involved in gathering information and seeking the necessary advice from specialists; the inaccessibility of the interview suite if a child uses a wheelchair; the unavailability of a suitably qualified interpreter for a deaf child or a facilitator for a child with limited or no verbal communication.

Brenda's experience of communicating her concerns to child-protection professionals exemplifies a number of these points but also demonstrates how a disabled child may prove to be surprisingly resilient and assertive in telling about abuse.

Brenda was 12-years-old and had complex physical impairments arising from a head injury sustained in a road accident when she was six. She does not have speech and uses a communication book with pictures and symbols. Her mother's partner is a paediatric nurse, Tom, who took a special interest in Brenda during the lengthy time she spent in hospital following the accident. Tom developed a relationship with Brenda's mother and moved in with the family shortly after Brenda returned to live at home full-time. Brenda's mother became very dependent on Tom for the physical help he gave in caring for Brenda, the income he brought to the family budget, and the emotional support he provided.

Brenda indicated to the nurse at school that she was worried about the way in which Tom touched her breasts and vagina. The school nurse reported her concerns but a full child-protection investigation did not occur because it was thought that the nurse was too leading in her questions to Brenda and had made unwarranted conclusions about what Brenda was communicating. In addition, because Brenda relies on others to dress her and provide intimate care, what she was communicating about Tom was assumed to be due to her misinterpreting innocent actions by him. It was not until a second support worker, who knew nothing about the concerns of the school nurse, reported that Brenda had indicated similar worries to her that an interview was planned. This was six months after the initial concerns.

In the video-recorded interview, Brenda was able to communicate unambiguously that she was very upset by the times when Tom touched her vagina without using a babywipe. She made it clear that she experienced these occasions as different to the times that he touched her genital area in order to clean her.

This interview and Brenda's clear testimony was made possible only through the thorough preparation that preceded the interview and the specialist advice that had been sought. The interviewers had first obtained reports from the speech and language therapist about Brenda's ability to comprehend spoken language and express herself. They made themselves familiar with her communication methods and spent time with Brenda in the family home communicating with her on topics unrelated to the alleged abuse. During this time, the interviewers noted that Brenda had no word for vagina in her communication book and were able to prepare an appropriate symbol for when the substantive interview took place.

Brenda was a determined and proud child who was not prepared to be inhibited by her mother's denial that Tom could sexually abuse Brenda. Despite her physical and communication impairments, Brenda proved not to be as emotionally vulnerable as had been anticipated.

Tom was arrested and questioned by the police but a criminal prosecution was not brought. It was considered likely that prejudice about Brenda's impairments would be exploited in court and that she would be perceived as an unreliable witness. Brenda's testimony was, however, considered sufficiently convincing for the Family Court and an order was obtained to exclude Tom from the household.

Very Young Children

Very young children, especially those under five years old, are not well served by the criminal-justice system. They are perceived as being unable to give an account of what has happened to them in a way that will be usable in criminal proceedings and we know, from the accounts of abusers (Finkelhor, 1984), that for this reason they are more likely to be targeted by some abusers. In our experience, it is only the unusually assertive and more securely attached child who is sufficiently resilient to withstand the stresses involved in giving testimony at court. Child-protection workers are rightly cautious about conducting interviews with very young children in the same way as they would with older children because fantasy, imagination, and magical thinking play such an important part in the cognitive processes of children of this age. But this can lead to no other formal means of obtaining a young child's testimony being attempted by child-protection workers.

Strict adherence to the *Memorandum* guidelines is rarely appropriate when interviewing children under five years and adaptations to the usual interviewing process can sometimes assist them in giving an account of what has happened in an evidentially sound way. Our experience is that young children frequently benefit from a series of several interviews over a period of a few weeks. This allows the interviewer to become familiar with the child's world and how the child communicates about it. In order for the child to feel secure, the presence of a parent or trusted adult, at the first and sometimes subsequent sessions, can help the child to confide in the interviewer. Questions that are facilitative (e.g. 'Mummy told me that you get upset when Jimmy looks after you, can you tell me about that?'), but avoid being leading, help the child to understand what is being asked of them. While the testimony obtained in interviews like this is unlikely to be used in criminal courts, the account given by children can help to safeguard them using civil proceedings and provide supplementary information in wider child-protection investigations.

> Shortly before her fourth birthday, Rachel tearfully told her mother that she did not like the games she was being made to play with the nanny and her boyfriend. These games had been going on for a long time and now the nanny wanted Rachel to play them with her two-year-old brother as well. She was very worried about telling her mother because the nanny, who had been with the family since Rachel was born, had made her promise to keep it a secret.
>
> Rachel was a mature and articulate child for her age and had caring parents. Because of her level of development and the clear nature of her disclosure, she was interviewed under conditions as close to *Memorandum* guidelines as possible given her young age. A medical examination had been conducted before the interview took place and showed convincing physical findings of abuse for both Rachel and her brother.
>
> In interview, Rachel spent much of the time pretending to be a fairy princess waiting for the prince to come and take her away from the wicked witch who kept poking her bottom with a long stick.
>
> The interviewer concluded that the game Rachel had played with the nanny involved just such role play, but it was impossible to separate which parts of Rachel's account were fantasy and which were real and to introduce the presence of the nanny and her boyfriend into the account of what happened in a reliable way. Although the alleged abusers were questioned, there was not sufficiently strong evidence from Rachel's interview to mount a prosecution. Rachel was referred for play therapy and this led to her compulsive re-enactment of the abusive game gradually diminishing.

Children from Different Racial and Cultural Backgrounds

Sharing a similar cultural background helps to facilitate social communication. The wider the cultural disparity between people, the greater the scope for misunderstanding and communication breakdown (Hargie & Tourish, 1999). This is especially important to bear in mind for child-protection interviews when an interviewer is from a different cultural background from the child being interviewed.

Wherever possible, children also need to be given the opportunity to communicate using their first language. Being able to describe abuse in the same language in which it occurred is often the best way for the child to conceptualize what has happened to them. This requires the use of interpreters who, ideally, are not only fluent in the child's first language but who also have an understanding of the child's cultural context both in their home country, if the family has recently immigrated, and their current conditions.

The following case study illustrates several of the challenges posed to child-protection workers when investigating the abuse of children from an ethnic minority group.

Fatima was a 15-year-old girl from a Sudanese refugee family living in a tightly knit ethnic community which is socially quite separate from the rest of the mainly white population in the town. Her family had been in the UK for three years and Fatima's first language is Arabic. Her parents spoke no English. Fatima told her teacher at school that Hassan, the 25-year-old man whom her parents had arranged for her to marry, had forced her to have anal intercourse with him. She said he had told her that this was the customary practice in the Sudan in order to allow the man to achieve sexual satisfaction while still keeping his bride 'pure' for their wedding night. Fatima said that she had tried to tell her mother that Hassan was doing things she did not like, although she did not explain in detail what that was. She said her mother told her that, as she was betrothed to Hassan, she must accede to his wishes. Fatima's allegations were reported to the child-protection agencies by the teacher.

Comprehensive gathering of information and careful planning prior to the interview are especially important when questioning children from a cultural and linguistic minority group if accurate communication is to be achieved. Refugees are in an especially vulnerable position as they will have experienced persecution by the state they have fled from. They are understandably anxious about authorities in the host state due to their insecure status and are anxious about drawing attention to themselves. In this case, child-protection workers were faced with the dilemma of whether to risk trying to intervene quickly and interview Fatima before appropriate advice about the culture was obtained. To delay, in order to obtain cultural advice and maximize the chances of Fatima feeling able to repeat her allegation on videotape, ran the risk of criticism for not protecting her sooner. Premature intervention is a frequent cause, however, for adolescents retracting allegations at interview and thereby making protective action extremely difficult to achieve.

The Sudanese community in the area was small and so closed that it was difficult to find an informant whose discretion could be relied upon to help the team understand the cultural issues and to find an interpreter who was acceptable to both Fatima and her mother. The absence of a suitable foster placement and concern about Fatima's possible ostracism from the community were recognized to present large risks should the mother prove unsupportive to her daughter.

Eventually, a bilingual interpreter with knowledge of Sudanese culture was identified and assisted with the evidential interview. Fatima gave a full disclosure of what her betrothed had done and, although the family decided to send her to live with relatives in another part of the country to protect her from shame in their community, she was not blamed by her mother or father who ended the arranged betrothal. Fatima and her parents were not willing for there to be a criminal prosecution of the alleged offender because they were worried about the shame that would be brought on Fatima, the consequence of which would be that she would be unable to marry within her own community.

CONCLUSIONS

In this chapter we have drawn attention to the complexity of obtaining the testimony of a child in order to protect them from harm. When questioning children about suspected abuse, child-protection workers are often faced with the task of reconciling conflicting principles that arise from the tension between the welfare of the child and satisfying the demands of the criminal-justice system. We have argued that justice is rarely obtained for the most vulnerable groups of children because procedures designed to satisfy the rules of evidence in criminal proceedings continues to dominate the child-protection process and the interviewing of children.

Professionals often struggle with the question as to whether they can successfully promote the best interests of children within the child-protection system. This mirrors the dilemma for a child about whether or not to disclose abuse knowing that by doing so their family relationships and living situation may be irrevocably altered. Protection from the harm of physical or sexual maltreatment is a clear imperative for professionals but so is taking account of a child's wishes and feelings. The child generally wishes the abuse to stop and yet may have strong ties to the abuser that she or he does not wish to disrupt. The professional similarly wishes to prevent further abuse but imprisoning the abuser or removing children into foster care may risk other forms of harm to a child's attachments and identity.

It is important that as far as possible the operation of the child-protection system does not contribute to the child's victimization. Investigators and interviewers can play their part by developing an awareness of the complexity and unique nature of each child's world. Only then can child-protection workers sensitively address the factors that create vulnerabilities for children and build on strengths, which increase children's resilience.

REFERENCES

Bates, P, (1999). The Youth Justice and Criminal Evidence Act—the evidence of children and vulnerable adults. *Child and Family Law Quarterly*, **11**(3), pp. 289–303.

Davies, G., Wilson, C., Mitchell, R., & Milsom, J. (1995). *An evaluation of the new provisions for child witnesses.* London: Home Office.

Department of Health. (1987). *Report of the inquiry into child abuse in Cleveland.* London: Her Majesty's Stationery Office.

Department of Health. (1989). *The Children Act 1989.* London: Her Majesty's Stationery Office.

Department of Health, Home Office, Department of Education and Science, & Welsh Office. (1989). *Working together under the Children Act 1989.* London: Her Majesty's Stationery Office.

Department of Health, Home Office, & Department of Education and Science & Welsh Office (1999). *Working together to safeguard children.* London: Her Majesty's Stationery Office.

Finkelhor, D. (1984). *Child sexual abuse: New theory and research.* New York: Free Press.

Hargie, O., & Tourish, D. (1999). The psychology of interpersonal skills. In: A. Memmon & R. Bull (Eds) *Handbook of the psychology of interviewing.* Chichester, UK: Wiley.

Home Office. (1999). *Youth Justice and Criminal Evidence Act 1999.* London: Her Majesty's Stationery Office.

Home Office, & Department of Health. (1992). *Memorandum of good practice for video recorded interviews with child witnesses for criminal proceedings.* London: Her Majesty's Stationery Office.

Morris, J. (1995). *Gone missing? A research and policy review of children living away from their families.* London: The Who Cares? Trust.

Westcott, H., & Cross, M. (1996) *This far and no further.* Birmingham: Venture Press.

Review of Part I

The three chapters in Part I have highlighted a number of specific pointers for practice, as well as providing a thumbnail sketch of the different research and practice traditions from which our current knowledge stems. Both Karen Saywitz's, and Lynne Baker-Ward and Peter Ornstein's, reviews of psychological underpinnings hint at the development of different and more sophisticated research methodologies in an attempt to mimic more closely aspects of the real-world context of child-abuse investigations. Thus psychological studies are more complex, include longer delays between experience and recall, and may include naturally occurring stressful experiences such as medical examinations. Marcus Page and Gretchen Precey's chapter, however, is a useful reminder of the complexities still largely unaddressed by psychological research on witnessing, such as motivational factors, emotional factors, and individual differences arising from culture, language, and disability. The supreme difficulty of forensic practice in this field is indicated. Acknowledging this difficulty, however, what are the recommendations from Part I for interviewers? Generally, interviewers should:

- pay attention to the child's physical, psychological, and social context;
- be aware of the particular needs of very young children, children who are disabled, and children from ethnic minorities, seeking specialist advice as appropriate;
- evaluate the child's socio-emotional maturity and the implications for rapport;
- evaluate the child's production *and comprehension* of language, and use language the child is best able to understand, matching the child's level when choosing questions;
- take care when interpreting the child's statements and not make assumptions;

Children's Testimony. Edited by H.L. Westcott, G.M. Davies, and R.H.C. Bull.
© 2002 John Wiley & Sons, Ltd.

- document verbatim the child's statements;
- be open-minded and bring 'objectivity' to their investigation;
- prepare and instruct children about their participation in the legal system;
- ensure that everyone involved—child, family, and interviewers—has realistic expectations about what may happen;
- give children as much control over what happens as is possible, commensurate with their age and development.

Later Parts of this book will explore many of these issues in greater detail. When considering the child witness's memory for the alleged event, interviewers should appreciate that:

- memory is not a video recorder of experiences, and the status of information in memory changes over time;
- memory exists in interacting layers of representation, such as autobiographical memory, episodic memory, semantic memory;
- remembering involves a sequence of steps—encoding, storage, recall—and failures can occur at any stage;
- not all information enters memory, and what does may vary in its availability;
- age influences, but does not determine, memory performance;
- recall will be affected by factors such as language development, source monitoring, and styles of questioning.

Interviewers must therefore consider the entire sequence of the memory process (from encoding to retrieval) when discussing the child's ability to provide an account, and must support the child's retrieval of information through attention to other developmental considerations. In this respect, one rule of thumb seems to be that the age of seven represents a significant shift in children's abilities, and associated developmental changes, such as the increase in embarrassment or self-consciousness.

However, although research on child development of the kind reviewed in Part I provides helpful guidelines, interviewers should not over-rely on 'milestones'. They must ask themselves, 'What do we require of *this child* in *this setting*, and how can we make it easier for him or her?' The responsibility should be on the adult interviewer to facilitate the child's account, rather than on the child to provide statements in the absence of appropriate support. As Page and Precey so clearly remind us, the child's welfare is at all times paramount, and should not be negatively affected by our behaviour or intervention as interviewers. In this respect, evaluation of interventions with child witnesses has an important role to play.

CHAPTER 4

The Development of Autobiographical Memory

Robyn Fivush

Department of Psychology, Emory University, Atlanta, Georgia, USA

As growing numbers of children are brought into the legal system, there is increasing concern over their ability to provide credible testimony. As the diversity of topics covered in this volume attests, the issue of children's credibility is complex. Factors ranging from enduring aspects of children's personality, such as temperament and emotional stability, to more situationally variable characteristics, such as the social context of the interview and the form of the questions, must be considered. But at heart, all concerns about children's testimony must rely on basic memory competencies; how and what are young children able to recall about personally experienced events?

In this chapter, I focus on the development of verbal recall, both because the ability to verbally recount a past experience is the clearest evidence of an explicit, consciously accessible memory and because verbal recall is necessary for children to testify in legal settings. Moreover, I examine children's developing abilities to verbally recall their past in the absence of misleading or suggestive questions. Although we know that young children can be misled and will often acquiesce to suggestion (Ceci & Bruck, 1993), it is also the case that free recall, in response to open-ended questions, is almost always accurate. Thus, the issue I address here is the development of children's ability to give an extended, coherent verbal report of a past event.

Children's Testimony. Edited by H.L. Westcott, G.M. Davies, and R.H.C. Bull.
© 2002 John Wiley & Sons, Ltd.

THE DEVELOPMENT OF VERBAL RECALL

Somewhat surprisingly, children begin to verbally refer to their past experiences as early as 18–20 months of age, although at this early developmental point, the references are brief and almost always refer to events that occurred quite recently, only a few hours or days in the past (Eisenberg, 1985). Moreover, these early references are heavily supported or scaffolded by adults' questions; children participate by providing specific bits of information in response to specific questions. Still, that children this young are able to verbally recall some accurate details of their past raises two questions. First, what can children verbally recall of experiences that occurred before the onset of language, and, second, how long can children retain memories of events that occurred during these early years? Both questions are critical in forensic situations in which children with limited language skills are asked to report about events experienced early in life, often several years after the alleged incidents occurred.

Most adults do not spontaneously recall events that occurred before the age of about three and a half years (Pillemer & White, 1989). However, if asked specific questions about particular salient childhood experiences, such as the birth of a sibling or an overnight hospitalization, they are able to recall some details of events that occurred at age 2, but not younger (Usher & Neisser, 1993). This pattern accords with developmental findings of limited verbal recall of events beginning by age 2, with increasing ability to recall in the absence of specific prompts with age. It seems that events that occur at age 2 are verbally accessible for recall, both at the time and subsequently. However, memory of events that occurred at this early age appears quite limited in that recall must be heavily cued, and even then, seems fragmentary and sparse.

What of events that occur even earlier? Is there any evidence of verbal access to events that occurred in the first two years of life? Certainly, one-year-olds are quite able to recall specific events in their past when assessed non-verbally. Bauer (1997) has demonstrated that children this young are able to learn and remember a series of unusual actions performed on a set of toy props over delays as long as 12 months. But this kind of recall is quite context dependent; children are brought back into the same room in which they originally learned these actions, are provided with the toy props, and are able to re-enact the learned sequences of actions. While this is impressive, it is not the same as being able to verbally recall an event in the absence of physical cues and support.

Myers, Perris, and Speaker (1994) explored long-term verbal and non-verbal recall of events experienced in the first year of life. Ten-month-old infants were taught to push a hidden button on one of three presented puppets in a specially decorated play area in order to receive a prize. At 14 months of age, children still showed evidence of recall by pressing the button. At almost three years of age, children who had these early experiences spent more time playing with the puppets than children who did not previously experience this event, but they did not spontaneously press the button. Most importantly, there was almost no evidence of verbal recall of these early experiences. At five years of age, there was little evidence of explicit memory in behavior, although children with previous experience did seem to prefer playing with the puppets more than children without previous experience. Again, there was no evidence of verbal recall.

In research with somewhat older infants, Bauer and Wewerka (1997) taught 20-month-old children novel sequences of actions on sets of toy props and then asked them to recall these sequences both behaviorally and verbally one year later. Most of the children showed evidence of memory by re-enacting the sequences but verbal recall was more sporadic. Most intriguingly, it was children's language abilities at the time of the initial experiences that predicted their ability to verbally recall the event later on. Using a similar methodology, Dunisch and Stevens (1999) taught novel action sequences to 13- and 16-month-old children and then assessed their recall of these events when they were just over three-years-old. Half of the children were assessed in the original playroom context and were provided with the original toy props and half were assessed at home using only photos of the props. There was virtually no evidence of verbal recall of these events in either condition, but there was some suggestion that there was more verbalization about the events in general by children assessed in the original context than in a new context.

Several conclusions can be drawn from this research. First, events experienced in the first year of life may not remain accessible for conscious recall. These experiences may influence behavior in subtle and complex ways, but these early experiences do not seem to be retained explicitly even in behavior. Events occurring early in the second year of life seem to be transitional. Children may be able to recall these events in behavior, if placed back in the same context and given the same physical objects, but it is not clear these experiences are explicitly accessible outside of the context in which the event was initially experienced. By 20 months of age, we begin to see evidence of a more explicit, verbally accessible memory system. Children at this age, especially those children who are able to verbally describe an experience as it is occurring, demonstrate some verbal recall of the event even a year later. However, this verbal recall is limited in that children provide bits of information and recall may be dependent on being back in the same heavily contexted physical environment in which the event initially occurred.

By the time children are two and a half, they are able to provide verbal information about events experienced several months in the past in a decontextualized interview situation. Fivush, Gray, and Fromhoff (1987) asked children between two and a half and three years of age to recall events that occurred either in the recent past (up to three months ago) or the distant past (more than three months ago). All children were able to provide accurate details of events that occurred in the distant past but needed many questions and prompts from the interviewer in order to do so. Similarly, Hamond and Fivush (1990) asked children who had been on a family trip to Disneyworld when they were between two and a half and three and a half years of age to recall the event either 6 months or 18 months later. Even those children who were two and a half at time of experience were able to recall a great deal of accurate information about this experience when interviewed 18 months subsequent to the event. However, younger children needed more questions, and more specific questions in order to recall as much information as the older children. Moreover, older children's recall was more detailed than younger children's at both retention intervals. Thus, although very young children appear able to explicitly recall events of their past, they need a great deal of help from adults, in the form of questions, cues, and prompts, in order to retrieve this information and report it in verbal form.

As children progress through the pre-school years, they become increasingly able to recall their past experiences with less external support and in a more organized coherent framework; for example, Fivush and Shukat (1995) longitudinally examined children's free recall of distinctive events when they were three, four, five, and six years of age. At each age point, children were asked to recall events that they had been asked to recall at the previous time point, about one year in the past, as well as more recently experienced events. Only general, open-ended questions were asked (e.g. 'tell me about your visit to Six Flags' and general prompts such as 'Tell me more' and 'What else happened?'). Children at all time points were able to recall a good deal of information about each event and were able to recall as much information about events that occurred more than a year ago as events that occurred in the previous few months. Intriguingly, however, children recalled different, but still accurate, information about the same event at the two interviews.

In extending this research, Fivush and Schwarzmueller (1998) re-interviewed the children again when they were eight years old. Children were able to recall events that they had initially recalled at each of the previous interviews. Again, children showed an impressive amount of accurate recall, reporting as much information to open-ended questions at age 8 as they had during the previous interviews, indicating very long term retention of events experienced during the preschool years. It is particularly noteworthy that children, now aged 8, were easily able to recall events that occurred when they were barely three years old. However, again, children recalled different information during the age 8 interview than they had reported at the previous interviews. While the reasons for this inconsistency are still not clear, it is critical to point out that just because children may select different aspects of an event to report during different recall interviews, it is not necessarily the case that the newly reported information is incorrect.

Yet, at the same time, there is some evidence that information provided for the first time in a delayed interview may be less likely to be correct than information repeated across interviews. Pipe and her colleagues (Pipe, Gee, Wilson, & Egerton, 1999; Salmon & Pipe, 1997) interviewed children soon after an unusual play activity and again one or two years later. Children were highly accurate at both interviews, but there was a slight increase in error over time. Most intriguingly, children included new accurate information at the delayed interviews, but information reported in response to specific questions at the second interviews that had not been reported at the first interviews was substantially more likely to be erroneous than repeated information. Similarly, Hudson and Fivush (1991) interviewed kindergarten children about an unusual class trip to a museum of archaeology immediately after the trip, six weeks later, one year later, and again six years later. Children recalled less information, and needed more specific questions and cues, at the six year delay than at the previous interviews. Again, recall was remarkably accurate but there was a slight increase in error over time, and information reported after six years that had not been reported at previous interviews was more likely to be in error than repeated information.

Thus, in situations where only open-ended questions are asked, children appear to select different aspects of the event to recall; for example, a child might focus on the rides during one interview about Disneyworld, but on the Disney characters at another interview. In studies in which children are also asked more specific questions, there appears to be more consistency in what children recall, most likely because the questions cue them to recall information they may not have spontaneously generated. However, in this interview situation, information added to previous recalls, especially if it is provided in response to specific questions, may be more likely to be erroneous than information repeated across interviews. Thus, in assessing credibility of testimony, consistency or inconsistency of recall must be considered in light of how the child was questioned. Free recall is almost always accurate, but, as questions become more specific, there may be a trade-off between increased amount of information recalled and increased error (see Fivush, Peterson & Schwarzmueller, 2002, for a full discussion of this issue).

Overall, the research on children's memories of personally experienced events indicates remarkably detailed and enduring memories from about age 3 on. Importantly, however, these studies focus on highly distinctive, emotionally positive events. These events may be particularly memorable for several reasons. First, distinctive events may be easier to retrieve because they are easy to differentiate from other events in memory (Hudson, Fivush, & Kuebli, 1992). Events which are recurrent and familiar, such as going to fast-food restaurants or grocery shopping, are well represented even by very young children, but these memory representations are more schematic than memories of distinctive experiences (Nelson, 1986). Children, similar to adults, report recurring events as a generalized script format, reporting the actions that usually occur and omitting actions that are specific to any one experience of the event. Thus, distinctive events are more likely to be recalled in specific detail than are recurring events (see Martine Powell & Don Thomson, Chapter 5 in this book).

Distinctive events are also more likely to be the special events of our lives, the events that we talk about with others and think about on our own. Although it is unlikely that parents and children spend much time reminiscing about a routine lunch at McDonald's, they will certainly talk about events such as a first aeroplane trip or a family visit to Disneyworld. By participating in family reminiscing, children may be rehearsing and strengthening their memories. Hamond and Fivush (1990) found that maternal report of how frequently the family talked about their trip to Disneyworld was not related to the amount children recalled after six months, but was related to the amount recalled after 18 months. Perhaps, as time since the event increases, talking about it with others becomes more critical in keeping the memory alive.

Reminiscing not only aids in rehearsing specific events; a great deal of research indicates that children are learning how to organize and report their past experiences in general through participating in parent–child conversations about the past (Fivush, Haden, & Reese, 1996; Haden, Haine, & Fivush, 1997; Peterson & McCabe, 1992).

Although autobiographical memories are not necessarily represented linguistically, language is a critical tool for organizing our past in a coherent framework which can be verbally communicated to others. For young children, who are still having difficulty reporting their past experiences in an extended, coherent narrative, reminiscing with parents may play a critical role in helping them to organize these early experiences into enduring memories. Thus, the transition into language may aid in the development of autobiographical memories both by providing children the opportunity to rehearse these experiences with others in the absence of physical cues, and by providing the narrative forms through which autobiographical memories become more organized and reportable (Nelson, 1996).

In addition to reminiscing, the ways in which adults structure an event as it is occurring also influences subsequent memory. Aspects of events that mothers and children jointly discuss as the event unfolds are better recalled than aspects that either mother or child alone mention (Haden, Didow, Ornstein, & Eckerman, 1997; Tessler & Nelson, 1994). These startling findings indicate that it is not necessarily what a child notices and pays attention to that will be recalled, but rather what becomes elaborated in conversation with another.

In an experimental analogue, Pipe, Dean, Canning, and Murachver (1996) engaged five-year-old children in an interactive event, playing pirate. In one condition, the adult narrated the event as it was occurring (e.g. 'Now we are going to play pirate. First, we have to dress up in these pirate clothes ...' and so on); in a second condition, the adult used only 'empty' language (e.g. 'Now we are going to play. First, we are going to do this ...' and so on). Children in the first condition recalled more information and made fewer errors than children in the second condition.

The consistent pattern of findings across these studies indicates that the ways in which adults and children jointly construct an event through language, both as it is occurring and in retrospect, has a profound influence on what children will later recall. Young children, who are still in the process of learning how to organize and recount past experiences coherently, are dependent on the linguistic structure provided by adults to help them encode and frame their memories. In the absence of the adult-provided linguistic frame, young children's memories are more fragmentary and less accurate. Because better organized and better rehearsed memories are also more enduring (see Schwartz & Reisberg, 1991, for an overview), we can further speculate that early memories which are not discussed and structured in adult-guided conversations may be more prone to forgetting and to erroneous reconstruction over time.

This framework for understanding the development of organized and enduring autobiographical memories has several implications for memories of stressful and traumatic experiences, the kinds of experiences that are more likely to involve children in the legal system. Are stressful events recalled in the same way as more positive events? And what role do adults play in helping children organize and recall these more emotionally negative experiences?

MEMORIES OF STRESSFUL EXPERIENCES

The relationship between stress and memory has a long and controversial history. Both theory and data are mixed, suggesting that under some conditions stress can enhance memory and under other conditions stress can hinder memory. One inherent problem in this literature is the operational definition of stress. Whereas clinical descriptions of stressful memories focus on highly traumatic events, such as incestuous sexual abuse or witnessing the homicide of a parent (Terr, 1991; Malmquist, 1986), experimentally controlled studies, by necessity, focus on less stressful events such as painful medical procedures (Goodman, Quas, Batterman-Faunce, Riddlesberger, & Kuhn, 1994; Ornstein, 1995). It is quite likely that level and chronicity of stress will play an important role in mediating memory of the experience; for example, Easterbrook (1959) has proposed that memory will be enhanced at moderate levels of stress while at extreme levels of stress memory will be hindered. Alternatively, Terr (1991) has argued that a single occurrence of extreme stress will be vividly and accurately recalled, but repeated stressful experiences will lead to more fragmentary memory.

Also, problematic, different measures of stress yield different results. Depending on whether stress is measured by behavioral ratings by self or other, by hormonal measures of cortisol, or by physiological measures such as heart rate and galvanic skin response, different relationships between stress and memory are obtained. Most disconcertingly, these measures do not correlate highly with each other (Ornstein, 1995). Thus, empirical relations between stress and memory remain difficult to ascertain. Although these issues are thorny, an emerging conclusion seems to be that stress does not hinder memory overall, and may even enhance certain aspects of memory (see Fivush, 1998, and Pezdek & Taylor, 2002, for reviews); for example, Ornstein (1995) found that three- to seven-year-old children administered a voiding cystourethrogram (VCUG), an extremely stressful medical procedure involving catherterization and voiding, recalled this event quite well immediately after the procedure, and were still able to recall this event almost as well three months later.

Moreover, compared to other groups of children recalling a well-doctor visit, children recalled the VCUG more completely and more accurately. Similarly, Peterson and Bell (1996) assessed 2- to 13-year-old children's memories of an injury requiring emergency-room treatment, such as broken bones and lacerations. They found that from age 3 on, children recalled this event extremely accurately and continued to recall the event is as much detail six months later. Peterson (1999) recently reported that these children were still able to recall this event as accurately two years later. However, importantly, two-year-old children had more difficulty verbally reporting this experience immediately after it occurred, and their long-term recall was sparse and contained a great deal of error. What seems to be critical for accurate long-term retention is the ability to verbally describe the experience when it occurs.

Somewhat surprisingly, these studies found no systematic relationships between measures of individual stress and recall. But in a study of children's memories for a highly stressful natural disaster—Hurricane Andrew—Bahrick, Parker, Merritt, and Fivush (1998) found that children experiencing moderate stress (high rain and wind destroying property around the house but the house itself remaining intact) recalled more information than children experiencing severe stress (glass flying into the house, part of the roof caving in, etc.). Even children in the severe stress condition, however, recalled an enormous amount of information about the event. Children in all stress groups still recalled this event in vivid detail six years later, but children in the high-stress group needed more questions and recalled less about preparing for the storm than children experiencing moderate stress (Fivush et al., 2001). These findings accord with the clinical literature describing quite vivid and detailed memories of severely traumatic events even years later (Terr, 1991). Indeed, most children experiencing severe trauma report having difficulty not thinking about it, and often suffer from intrusive memories (Malmquist, 1986).

One limitation of the existing data is that no direct comparisons have been made between children's memories of stressful events and more emotionally positive events. Fivush, Hazzard, Brown, and Sarfati (in press) asked 5- to 12-year-old children growing up in a violent inner city neighborhood to recall both emotionally positive and emotionally negative experiences. Overall, children recalled the same amount of information about both types of events, but they focused on different kinds of information. For positive events, children recalled more about the people and the objects involved, and recalled more descriptive detail than for the negative events; in contrast, for negative events, children recalled more about their own and other people's emotions and internal states compared to positive events. This pattern suggests that emotional valence may lead to different attentional focus. For positive events, the focus is on what is happening externally in the world, but for negative events, the focus may turn inward to what one feels and thinks about the event.

THE VOICING AND SILENCING OF TRAUMA

Given the robust findings on the role of adults in guiding and structuring young children's memories, a critical question concerning memories of trauma becomes the ways in which these kinds of experiences are discussed. One of the most effective interventions for adult trauma victims is exposure therapy, during which victims repeatedly narrate their experiences, coming to a more coherent account of what occurred (Foa, Molnar, & Cashman, 1995). Even for more mundane but still stressful events, such as getting fired from one's job, the act of narrating the experience seems to lead to better physical and emotional outcome (Pennebaker, 1997). Thus, giving voice to traumatic experiences is an effective means of coping.

Very little research has examined the ways in which adults talk about stressful or traumatic experiences with young children, but a few studies suggest that, as for adults, being able to talk about and organize traumatic experiences more coherently is beneficial for young children; for example, Goodman et al. (1994) assessed young children memories for a VCUG procedure and found that children of mothers, who reported having more open and emotionally supportive conversations about this event, recalled the event more fully and more accurately than children whose mothers reported not talking about it with their children. Similarly, Principe (1996) found that when technicians spent more time explaining the VCUG procedure to their young patients, the children subsequently had better memories. Thus, similar to the more emotionally positive events discussed earlier, the opportunity to talk about negative events both as they are occurring and in retrospect appears to help young children form more accurate and more organized memories of what occurred.

Of course, unlike painful medical procedures or natural disasters, which are acknowledged and often discussed by others, many traumas, such as abuse, are private. Abuse most often occurs within family environments in which it is implicitly or explicitly silenced, if children attempt to disclose or discuss these events, they are ignored or censored. Moreover, when abuse is discussed, it is most often framed in such a way as to change its meaning or interpretation (e.g. sexual abuse is a 'special game' or physical abuse is 'punishment for bad behavior'). Because pre-school children are dependent on adults to help them form more complete and organized memories through partici-patory discussions, in abuse situations, it may be difficult for children to form coherent accounts of what has occurred. This is not to argue that young children cannot recall abuse, they most certainly can (Eisen, Goodman, Ghetti, & Qin, 1999). Rather, these memories may be more fragmented than memories of events which are openly discussed.

Furthermore, abuse is often chronic. As discussed earlier, memories for recurring events may be structurally different than memories of single occurrences. The more distinctive an event remains, the easier to access and recall. As events become more routine, the memory repre-sentation becomes more schematic, focusing on what usually happens and often losing details of specific occurrences. Thus, paradoxically, memories of chronic abuse may be less detailed than memories of a single traumatic event (see Powell & Thomson, Chapter 5 in this book).

CONCLUSIONS AND CAVEATS

By age 3, children's memories are remarkably accurate and enduring. Moreover, children seem able to recall stressful experiences at least as well as more mundane occurrences. However, we must be cautious in drawing implications for forensic settings. Not all events are recalled in the same way. The level of stress experienced, as well as its chronicity may affect how an event is remembered and recounted. Furthermore, the ways in which experiences have or have not been discussed with others will have a profound influence on children's memories. Events which are distinctive, public, and openly discussed will most likely be well recalled, but the fate of memories of private, undisclosed events is still in question.

REFERENCES

Bahrick, L., Parker, J., Merritt, K., & Fivush, R. (1998). Children's memory for Hurricane Andrew. *Journal of Experimental Psychology: Applied*, 4, 302–331.

Bauer, P. (1997). Development of memory in early childhood. In: N. Cowan (Ed.), *The development of memory in childhood* (pp. 83–112). Hove, East Sussex: Psychology Press.

Bauer, P., & Wewerka, S. (1997). Saying is revealing: Verbal expression of event memory in the transition from infancy to early childhood. In: R. van den Broek, P.J. Bauer, & T. Bourg (Eds), *Developmental spans in event comprehension and representation: Bridging fictional and actual events.* Hillsdale, NJ: Erlbaum.

Ceci, S.J., & Bruck, M. (1993). Suggestibility of the child witness: A historical review and synthesis. *Psychological Bulletin,* **113,** 403–39.

Dunisch, D.L., & Stevens, C.O. (1999, April). Something to talk about: Support in the verbal accessibility of early memories. Poster presented at the meetings of the Society for Research, in Child Development, Albuquerque, New Mexico.

Easterbrook, J.A. (1959). The effect of emotion on the utilization and organization of behavior. *Psychological Review,* **66,** 183–201.

Eisen, M., Goodman, G.S., Ghetti, S., & Qin, J. (1999, July). An examination of abuse disclosures in maltreated children. Paper presented at the meeting of the Society for Applied Research in Memory and Cognition, Boulder, Colorado.

Eisenberg, A. (1985). Learning to describe past experience in conversation. *Discourse Processes,* **8,** 177–204.

Fivush, R. (1998). Children's memories of traumatic and non-traumatic events. *Development and Psychopathology,* **10,** 699–716.

Fivush, R., Gray, J.T., & Fromhoff, F.A. (1987). Two year olds' talk about the past. *Cognitive Development,* **2,** 393–409.

Fivush, R., Haden, C., & Reese, E (1996). Remembering, recounting and reminiscing: The development of autobiographical memory in social context. In: D. Rubin (Ed.), *Reconstructing our past: An overview of autobiograhical memory* (pp. 341–59). New York: Cambridge University Press.

Fivush, R., Hazzard, A., Brown, T., & Sarfati, D. (in press). Children's memories of stressful and positive events. *Applied Cognitive Psychology.*

Fivush, R., Sales, J.M., Goldberg, A., Bahrick, L., & Parker, J. (2001). Weathering the storm: Children's long-term recall of Hurricane Andrew. Submitted manuscript.

Fivush, R., Peterson, C., & Schwarzmueller, A. (2002). Questions and answers: The credibility of child witnesses in the context of specific questioning techniques. In: M.L. Eisen, G.S. Goodman, & J.A. Quas (Eds), *Memory and suggestibility in the forensic interview,* pp. 331–354. Hillsdale, NJ: Erlbaum.

Fivush, R., & Schwarzmueller, A. (1998). Children remember childhood: Implications for childhood amnesia. *Applied Cognitive Psychology,* **12,** 455–73.

Fivush, R., & Shukat, J. (1995). Content, consistency and coherency of early autobiographical recall. In M.S. Zaragoza, J.R. Graham, G.C.N. Hall, R. Hirschman, & Y.S. Ben-Porath (Eds), *Memory and testimony in the child witness* (pp. 5–23).Thousand Oaks, CA: Sage.

Foa, E.B., Molnar, C., & Cashman, L. (1995). Change in rape narratives during exposure therapy for posttraumatic stress disorder. *Journal of Traumatic Stress,* **8,** 675–90.

Goodman, G.S., Quas, J.A., Batterman-Faunce, J.M., Riddlesberger, M.M., & Kuhn, J. (1994). Predictors of accurate and inaccurate memories of traumatic events experienced in childhood. *Consciousness and Cognition,* **3,** 269–94.

Haden, C.A., Didow, S.M., Ornstein, P.A. & Eckerman, C.O. (1997, April). Mother-child talk about the here and now: Linkages to subsequent remembering. In: E. Reese (Chair), Adult-child reminiscing: Theory and practice. Symposium paper presented at the meeting of the Society for Research in Child Development, Washington, DC.

Haden, C., Haine, R., & Fivush, R. (1997). Developing narrative structure in parent-child conversations about the past. *Developmental Psychology*, **33**, 295–307.

Hamond, N.R., & Fivush, R. (1990). Memories of Mickey Mouse: Young children recount their trip to Disneyworld. *Cognitive Development*, **6**, 433–48.

Hudson, J.A., & Fivush, R. (1991). As time goes by: Sixth graders remember a kindergarten event. *Applied Cognitive Psychology*, **5**, 346–60.

Hudson, J.A., Fivush, R., & Kuebli, J. (1992). Scripts and episodes: The development of event memory. *Applied Cognitive Psychology*, **6**, 483–505.

Malmquist, C.P (1986). Children who witness parental murder. Post-traumatic aspects. *Journal of the American Academy of Child Psychiatry*, **25**, 320–5.

Myers, N.A., Perris, E.E., & Speaker, C.J. (1994). Fifty month of memory: A longitudinal study in early childhood. *Memory*, **2**, 383–416.

Nelson, K. (1986). *Event knowledge: Structure and function in development*, Hillsdale, NJ: Erlbaum.

Nelson, K (1996). *Language in cognitive development: Emergence of the mediated mind*. New York: Cambridge University Press.

Ornstein, P.A. (1995). Children's long-term retention of salient personal experiences. *Journal of Traumatic Stress*, **8**, 581–606.

Pennebaker, J.W. (1997). *Opening up*. New York: Guilford.

Peterson, C. (1999). Children's memories for medical emergencies: Two years later. *Developmental Psychology*, **35**, 1493–506.

Peterson, C., & Bell, M. (1996). Children's memory for traumatic injury. *Child Development*, **67**, 3045–70.

Peterson, C., & McCabe, A. (1992). Parental styles of narrative elicitation: Effect on children's narrative structure and content. *First Language*, **12**, 299–321.

Pezdek, K., & Taylor, J. (2002). Memory for traumatic events. In M.L. Eisen, G.S. Goodman, & J.A. Quas (Eds), *Memory and suggestibility in the forensic interview*, pp. 165–184. Hillsdale, NJ: Eribaum.

Pillemer, D., & White, S.H. (1989). Childhood events recalled by children and adults. In H.W. Reese (Ed.), *Advances in child development and behavior* (Vol. 22) New York: Academic Press.

Pipe, M-E., Dean, J., Canning, J., & Murachver, T. (1996, July). Narrating events and telling stories. Paper presented at the second International Conference on Memory, Abano, Italy.

Pipe, M-E., Gee, S., Wilson, J.C., & Egerton, J. (1999). Children's recall 1 or 2 years after an event. *Developmental Psychology*, **35**, 781–9.

Principe, G. (1996, March). Children's memory for a stressful medical procedure. Paper presented at the Conference on Human Development, Birmingham, Alabama.

Salmon, K., & Pipe, M-E. (1997). Props and children's event reports: The impact of a one year delay. *Journal of Experimental Child Psychology*, **65**, 261–92.

Schwartz, B., & Reisberg, D. (1991). *Learning and memory*. New York: Norton.

Terr, L. (1991). Childhood traumas: An outline and overview. *American Journal of Psychiatry*, **148**, 10–20.

Tessler, M., & Nelson, K. (1994). Making memories: The influence of joint encoding on later recall by young children. *Consciousness and Cognition*, **3**, 307–26.

Usher, J., & Neisser, U. (1993). Childhood amnesia and the beginnings of memory for four early life events. *Journal of Experimental Psychology: General*, **122**, 155–65.

CHAPTER 5

Children's Memories for Repeated Events

MARTINE POWELL* AND DON THOMSON†

*School of Psychology, Deakin University, Victoria, Australia
†Charles Sturt University, New South Wales, Australia

The effect of repeated experience on memory has been an enduring topic of interest in adult memory research, particularly among the verbal-learning researchers in the 1960s and 1970s (Tulving, 1966). However, there has been relatively little empirical investigation of this issue with children, and little discussion of the implications of this research for investigative or evidential interviews. Children's ability to remember a specific occurrence of a repeated event has important implications for investigative interviewers and the courts, because in many trials in which children are required to testify, the matter involves a repeated event; for example, acts of physical or sexual abuse that occurred on more than one occasion. In most criminal proceedings (e.g. for an alleged offender to be charged and convicted of sexually abusing a child), a specific occurrence or specific occurrences of the abuse must be identified with reasonable precision with reference to time and place (see S v. R, 1989). For a witness to anchor an occurrence of an event in time, contextual factors must be recalled, such as where the incident, occurred, what clothing was worn, what the alleged perpetrator did and said during the course of the incident, and where members of the family were. Without this requirement (referred to as particularization), the accused person's capacity to respond to the allegations would be seriously eroded.

Children's Testimony. Edited by H.L. Westcott, G.M. Davies, and R.H.C. Bull.
© 2002 John Wiley & Sons, Ltd.

The issue of particularization poses a dilemma for the courts because the identification of a specific occurrence of a repeated offence is such a difficult task for witnesses, especially after a delay in time. However, even when a particular occurrence can be unambiguously identified, the witness may still experience difficulty in remembering the details that were specific to the occurrence. These difficulties are especially profound for child witnesses, whose knowledge and understanding of time is not as well developed as that of adults (Friedman, 1991). In light of this dilemma, it is important for lawyers and child-protection interviewers to consider research which indicates the factors that affect children's ability to distinguish between events.

The current chapter offers a brief review of research on the effects of event repetition on children's memory and on the factors that affect children's ability to recall an occurrence of a repeated event. These factors include the length of the time that has elapsed since the event, the question type, the age of the child, the impact of misleading suggestions from the interviewer, and the effect of non-leading intervening interviews. The implications of these findings for practitioners who conduct investigatory interviews with children about multiple offences are also discussed. While the focus of this paper is on research involving child participants, most of the effects described are not particular to children; they are generally consistent with research involving adult participants as well (Bartlett, 1932; Lindsay & Johnson, 1989; Underwood, 1957; Winograd, 1968).

DESIGN AND PROCEDURE OF RESEARCH ON CHILDREN'S MEMORY OF REPEATED EVENTS

In most empirical research on repeated events involving child participants, a unique event is created and administered by the researcher so that the child's experience of the event and the way in which details are repeated can be controlled. Furthermore, having a record of the entire event allows the precise nature of errors to be measured (i.e. it allows the researcher to determine whether an error in recalling an occurrence of the event is a reference to a detail that had occurred another time or not at all in the event). The events typically involve a series of activities which children experience at their school; for example, in work by Powell and colleagues (Powell & Thomson 1996, 1997a, 1997b; Powell, Roberts, Ceci, & Hembrooke, 1999) children participated in a repeated event in their regular classroom, each occurrence of the event involved listening to a story, doing a puzzle, having a rest, getting a surprise, and getting refreshed. In a series of studies by

Table 5.1. Examples of different types of item repetition.

Item in the event	Instantiations of items across the series of occurrences			
	Occurrence 1	Occurrence 2	Occurrence 3	Occurrence 4
Fixed				
Person who carried out event	Mary	Mary	Mary	Mary
Content of story	Cat	Cat	Cat	Cat
Variable				
Place where event occurred	Classroom	Library	Library	Library
Surprise gift given to child	Sticker	Pen	Candy	Toy

Farrar and Goodman (1990) children participated in a repeated event which consisted of four 'animal game' activities, each occurrence of the event involved the experimenter and the child using two unique toy animals to perform a unique action.

The events are typically designed so that there are unpredictable variations in the way details (memory items) make up the activities; for example, Table 5.1 displays some ways in which details may be varied across experiences. In this example, the person who carried out the activities and the story that was read are regarded as 'fixed' items because they were repeated the same way in each occurrence. The other two items are referred to as 'variable' items because the instantiations that represent these items differ across the occurrences of the event. With regard to the surprise gift, a new instantiation of the item is included in each occurrence of the event, whereas in relation to the place where the event occurred, there are only two possible instantiations (one instantiation occurred more frequently than the other). Note that in most empirical research, the assignment of items to fixed versus variable categories, and the order of particular instantiations across the series is counterbalanced to reduce the likelihood that any reported effects are due to the assignment of items rather than the experimental manipulations *per se*.

Children's memory of the event is usually examined individually using a series of general and then specific questions. The occurrence that is the focus of these questions (usually the final occurrence) is referred to as the 'target occurrence'. In order to examine the effect of repeated experience on children's memory, children's recall of the target occurrence is compared to that of a group of children who received only one occurrence of the event which is the same as the target occurrence.

THE EFFECT OF REPETITION ON CHILDREN'S MEMORY

Repetition of an event has been shown to have both beneficial and detrimental effects on children's recall. After multiple occurrences of an event, details that are common to many of the occurrences are strengthened in memory and are therefore well remembered over time compared to details that were experienced once only (Hudson, 1990; Powell & Thomson, 1996). Because fixed items are well remembered, they are highly likely to be reported by children when recalling an occurrence of a repeated event. When a fixed item is reported as being included in the target occurrence, however, it is possible that the child is referring to a different occurrence. In fact, there is no way of distinguishing which occurrence (if any) is being remembered.

With regard to children's recall of details that varied across the occurrences, repeated experience of an event decreases children's ability to remember specific details that were particular to one occurrence of the event (e.g. recalling that a toy was the surprise gift that was received in the final occurrence of the event in Table 5.1). Indeed, children, like adults, are less accurate, less certain about, and less consistent in their responses about an occurrence of a variable repeated event, compared to an event that was experienced only once (Hudson, 1990; Powell & Thomson, 1996; 1997b). This is because recalling an occurrence of a repeated event involves memory of content (i.e. remembering which details were experienced in the event) as well as the capacity to locate the temporal position of details (i.e. remembering which details were experienced in the target occurrence). The more frequently the event occurred and the greater the frequency of new instantiations of items across the series of occurrences, the more difficult it is to keep track of which details were included in a particular occurrence (Linton, 1982). Furthermore, the greater the degree of similarity across the occurrences (similarity of context or content), the greater the difficulty in discriminating between the occurrences (Lindsay, Johnson, & Kwon, 1991).

It is important to note, however, that the majority of errors children make when they are asked to remember an occurrence of an event are intrusions of details from other occurrences (e.g. recalling that candy or a pen was received in the final occurrence of the event in Table 5.1; Powell & Thomson, 1996). These errors are referred to as internal intrusion errors. Reporting of details that did not occur *at all* in the event (referred to as external intrusion errors) are uncommon and are less likely to be reported by children who have participated in a repeated event compared to a single event. One conclusion to draw from this is that the presence of errors or inconsistent responses in a child witness's account about an occurrence of a repeated event should not be regarded as evidence that the child's account has been coached or contaminated; these are merely a reflection of normal memory processes. Unfortunately, however, research has provided no clear basis for distinguishing between correct details and details intruding from other occurrences of the event, and there is also no basis for distinguishing internal intrusion errors from errors that did not occur in the event at all (Powell & Thomson, 1997a).

FACTORS THAT ARE KNOWN TO AFFECT CHILDREN'S ABILITY TO REMEMBER AN OCCURRENCE OF A REPEATED EVENT

The Length of Time between the Event and the Interview

The amount of correct information that can be recalled about a particular occurrence of the event declines rapidly as the interval between the target occurrence and the interview increases (Powell & Thomson, 1996; 1997a). While a decline in performance over time is a robust finding in almost all areas of memory research, it is particularly crucial when details of an occurrence of a repeated event need to be retrieved. As the occurrence is forgotten, the rate of errors (internal as well as external intrusion errors) increases (Powell & Thomson, 1996; Powell *et al.*, 1999; Slackman & Nelson, 1984).

The rapid decline over time in children's ability to discriminate between occurrences may be attributed to inaccessibility of content details (i.e. forgetting of details that occurred in the event) as well as the forgetting of temporal details (i.e. where in the sequence of events particular details or instantiations occurred). Studies which have examined the relative influence of these two factors on children's discrimination performance have revealed that the decline over time is more rapid for temporal details than content details (Powell & Thomson, 1997a). Indeed, children as young as four years of age have demonstrated the ability to remember various instantiations of items many months after an event even though the relative positions of these details were forgotten within a week (Powell & Thomson, 1997b). When the precise sequencing of items is forgotten, children who are required to report an occurrence of a repeated event tend to report details that were experienced frequently (Domel Baxter, Thompson, & Davis, 1998; Powell & Thomson, 1996) or details that were experienced in close temporal proximity to the target occurrence (Powell & Thomson, 1997a). The implication of these findings for the investigative process is that the timing of the interview is likely to be an important factor in determining the number and accuracy of details recalled about a specific occurrence of a repeated offence. After long delays, a child who has been abused on multiple occasions may be able to recall many details about the abuse, but his/her ability to identify features specific to the occurrence(s) of abuse in question is likely to be diminished. From an investigative point of view, the more specific details obtained, the greater the likelihood of successful prosecution.

It should be noted, however, that none of the research findings to date imply that an individual child in the courtroom setting would be unable to recall an occurrence of a repeated offence after a long delay. The likelihood of doing so would depend on numerous factors, in particular the position and the saliency of the occurrence in the series. The first and last occurrences are likely to be more easily distinguished compared to others (Berch, 1978; Dewing & Kennealy, 1974; Powell & Thomson, 1997a), as well as occurrences that are dissimilar from other occurrences in terms of context or content (Johnson, Foley, & Leach, 1988). Furthermore, research with adults has shown that a person can discriminate between competing sources of information more successfully when the total number of occurrences is small rather than large (Lindsay, 1994; Linton, 1982) and when the interval between the occurrences is long rather than short (Hintzman & Block, 1970; Slamecka, 1967).

Question Type

Research in both naturalistic and laboratory settings has shown that the amount of discriminative detail reported about a specific occurrence of an event depends largely on the type of retrieval cue that is used to access the information about the occurrence. When children are asked to freely report what happened in an occurrence of a repeated event, they provide few specific features that discriminate that occurrence from other occurrences (Powell & Thomson, 1996; Hudson, 1990; Myles-Worsley, Cromer, & Dodd 1986); for example, when freely recalling the final occurrence of the event in Table 5.1, children are likely to report the surprise gift, but they are unlikely to mention which particular gift they received without further prompting. Indeed, Hudson and Nelson (1986) demonstrated that children who are required to remember a specific occurrence of a repeated event report no more specific discriminating details compared to children who are merely asked to describe what generally occurred in the event. The use of specific questions (e.g. 'What surprise did you get?') results in a greater number of accurate specific details about the occurrence compared to general or open-ended questions (e.g. 'Tell me what else happened'). However, the number of errors also increases with the use of specific questions. This is because the detail requested, or its precise temporal location, may not be available in memory. An interviewer's decision about the number of specific questions to ask would therefore depend on the nature and purpose of the interview. In relation to the in-vestigative interview, the potential benefits of obtaining more correct details may in some cases outweigh the disadvantages of increased errors. The larger number of experienced details obtained from the child *per se* gives the investigating officers greater opportunity to follow leads and to obtain additional evidence that may be used to cor-roborate the child's account (Powell, Thomson, & Dietze, 1997).

Recently, Powell and Thomson (2001) investigated the effect of a tech-nique to maximize the amount of accurate details children recall about an occurrence of a repeated event. Specifically, children aged four and seven years of age were required to list all possible instantiations of items prior to deciding which instantiations were included in the target occurrence of the event. This technique, however, had no effect on the accuracy of the children's responses about the final occurrence. Indeed, for the younger age group, the technique appeared to create con-siderable confusion. At present, it seems that the best way to minimize errors while eliciting a report from a child about an occurrence of a repeated event is to allow the child to freely recall as much as s/he can remember about the event and any particular occurrences of the event, prior to specific questioning. This is because the interviewer's percep-tion or framework of the event may interfere with the way the event is structured in the child's memory (Tulving, 1966). Subsequently, requests for highly specific information should be minimized as much as possible throughout the interview, and the child should be informed that 'don't know' is an acceptable response to any question.

Age of the Child

It is well documented that children as young as four years of age can discriminate between memories of similar experiences (Roberts, 2000) and can provide a detailed account of an occurrence of a repeated event (Powell & Thomson, 1996). However, there are clear age differences in children's performance; younger children (i.e., four to five years of age) tend to report less specific detail in their accounts compared to older children (Farrar & Goodman, 1990), and the temporal associations that are formed between items and their positions within a series tend to be weaker and decline more rapidly over time for younger children (Powell & Thomson, 1997a). While, in absolute terms, older children may report more internal intrusion errors than younger children (because they report more details *per se*), the proportion of errors are clearly greater for younger children compared to older children. In addition, the likelihood that younger children will change their responses across repeated questions (both within and across interviews) is greater than for older children (Powell & Thomson, 1996, 1997b). In light of these findings, it is advisable that when young children (i.e. four to five years of age) are required to give evidence about an occurrence of a repeated event, they should be interviewed as soon as possible after the event. Furthermore, the interviewer should have a realistic expectation about the child's capabilities. Persistent questioning about highly specific or contextual details may only create inconsistencies in children's evidence and may thereby reduce the credibility of their accounts. As discussed earlier, a decision to avoid direct questioning about specific details would depend on the nature and purpose of the interview; the potential benefits of obtaining more correct details may in some cases outweigh the disadvantages of increased errors (Powell *et al.* 1997).

While performance typically improves with age, some studies have found no age differences in children's performance after a repeated event even though developmental differences were evident after a single experience of the event. These findings should be considered merely as artefacts of the particular experiments; for example, in a study by Powell *et al.* (1999), older children who had participated in a single event gave a greater number of correct responses and less often reported an external intrusion than did younger children. For the repeated event, however, there was no effect of age on the number of correct responses irrespective of whether the child was recalling fixed items or variable items. This finding needs to be interpreted in light of the different performance demands when remembering a single versus repeated event. After repeated experience, the questions about fixed items were so easy that all the children tended to get them correct, whereas the task of remembering which instantiations of variable items was included in the target occurrence was so difficult that most children performed near floor level. Readers should therefore be cautious when drawing generalizations about children's performance across different event groups and experimental procedures.

The Impact of Misleading Suggestions from the Interviewer

Children who are required to recall an occurrence of a repeated event may be misled by false or misleading suggestions provided by an interviewer. However, the likelihood of being misled depends primarily on the nature of the event repetition (Connolly & Lindsay, 2001, McNichol, Shute, & Tucker, 1999, Pezdek & Roe, 1995; Powell et al., 1999). When children are recalling items that were fixed across a series, they tend to be highly resistant to suggestion and more resistant to suggestion than children who participated in a single occurrence of the event (Connolly & Lindsay, 2001; Powell et al., 1999). This is a robust finding which is generally found irrespective of the retention interval, age of the child, type of suggestion, or question type. The finding is due in most part to the fact that fixed repetition reinforces or facilitates memory of details that occurred (Bartlett, 1932).

In relation to variable details, where the child has no assurance that the same detail occurred every time, the effect of repetition is more complex and differs depending on other factors such as the nature of the suggestions, the question type, and the retention interval. First, whether the child is oriented to a particular occurrence when false information is suggested influences the likelihood that the child will include the suggested details into his/her subsequent report about that occurrence; for example, Powell, Roberts, and Thomson (2000) showed that five-year-old children who were given false details that were not linked to any occurrence *per se* were less likely to intrude these false details into their subsequent recall of the target occurrence of the event compared to children who were oriented to the target occurrence when the false details were made. Interestingly, the children in the former condition were also less likely to intrude false details compared to children who participated in only a single occurrence of the event.

Second, the effect of repeated experience on suggestibility has been shown to interact with the type of question that is asked. While it is well established that yes/no questions lead to more errors than open or cued-recall questions, the detrimental impact of yes/no questions appears to be more pronounced for children who experience a repeated event. Powell and Roberts (in press) showed that when children were given false information about an occurrence of a repeated event and were subsequently asked whether the false information had been included in this occurrence using yes/no questions, they were more misled than children who participated in only a single experience of the event. The difference in suggestibility between the event groups, however, was reduced when children were asked cued-recall questions about the occurrence. Third, research has suggested that any differences in suggestibility between children who experience a single versus a repeated event are more pronounced when the interview is held a few weeks rather than a few days after the event (Powell *et al.*, 1999; Powell & Roberts, in press).

It is important to note, however, that children's recall of an occurrence can be contaminated even without suggesting false details *per se*; for example, merely asking the child whether s/he received a sticker in the event listed in Table 5.1 increases the chance that the sticker will be mentioned when the child is asked to recall one of the latter occurrences of the event (Powell *et al.*, 1999). A possible reason for this finding is that the more that experienced details are remembered, the greater the strength of these details in memory. The stronger the memory trace, the more recent the detail appears (Friedman, 1993; Johnson, Hashtroudi, & Lindsay, 1993). Overall, these findings reiterate the importance of avoiding the use of closed or leading questions, particularly when interviewing children about an occurrence of a repeated event.

The Effect of Non-leading Intervening Interviews

It is well established that an initial interview can increase children's recall of an occurrence of a repeated event in a subsequent interview; for instance, Hudson (1990) and Powell and Thomson (1997b) showed that children aged three to seven years who had an initial interview soon after an occurrence reported more correct specific details in a subsequent interview compared to children who did not have an initial interview. Importantly, this increase in correct recall was not accompanied by an increase in errors. These findings replicate similar trends in the literature relating to children's memory of single events (Tucker, Mertin, & Luszcz, 1990). The initial interview can be perceived as consolidating the event details (Poole & White, 1991) or enhancing the child's capacity to *retrieve* the information at a later test (Tulving, 1966).

Frequent consolidation is needed, however, if the details are to be maintained over a lengthy period of time (Powell & Thomson, 1997b). Offering the child the opportunity to review earlier statements may provide one way of consolidating information (Bjork & Allen, 1970). However, caution needs to be exercised; while the presentation of the original details has the potential of refreshing the child's memory of the event, research suggests that it may inhibit recall of other pertinent details (Tulving & Hastie, 1972), and it may also create the problem of determining whether the child is subsequently remembering the statement or the original event. Another way of facilitating recall of an occurrence of a repeated event after a long delay is to conduct multiple intervening interviews (Turtle & Yuille, 1994). These provide the child with further opportunities to remember details that s/he did not recall or recognize earlier. As Powell and Thomson (1996) showed, some items that are recalled in an initial interview are forgotten in subsequent interviews, whereas some new items are remembered. The implication of this finding is that fuller accounts from the child may be obtained by conducting more than one interview. However, the effective use of multiple retrieval attempts requires careful consideration of factors relating to suggestibility (Ceci & Bruck, 1993) and the added stress that these interviews may impose on the child. Furthermore, it is possible that multiple interviews could exacerbate confusion between the occurrences.

SUMMARY

Previous experimental research has demonstrated that repeated experience of an event enhances memory of fixed details (details that are common to all occurrences of the event), and increases children's resistance to misleading information about fixed details. Two detrimental effects of repetition, however, are that it reduces the ability to remember details that were included in a particular occurrence of the event and it increases the likelihood that the child will acquiesce to misleading yes/no questions about items that varied across the occurrences. When the child is required to generate a response, the detrimental effect of repetition on recall of variable details is usually manifested in confusions between the specific variable details across the occurrences (referred to as internal intrusion errors). These errors are greater among younger children than older children and increase as a function of retention interval. In light of the demands placed on child witnesses who are required to give evidence about repeated offences, practitioners need to consider research which investigates the factors that affect children's recall of an occurrence of a repeated event so that they may improve the conditions in which evidence is collected.

Research by Powell and colleagues was supported by an Oscar Rivers Schmalzbach Foundation Grant (Australian Academy of Forensic Sciences), a Lady Leitch Scholarship (Australian Federation of University Women), a Large Australian Research Council Grant (Ref#: A79924116) and two Deakin University Faculty grants.

REFERENCES

Bartlett, F.C. (1932). *Remembering: A study in experimental and social psychology*. Cambridge: Cambridge University Press.

Berch, D.B. (1978). The role of spatial cues in the probe-type serial memory task. *Child Development*, 49, 749–54.

Bjork, R.A., & Allen, T.W. (1970). The spacing effect: Consolidation or differential encoding? *Journal of Verbal Learning and Verbal Behavior*, 9, 567–72.

Ceci, S.J., & Bruck, M. (1993). The suggestibility of the child witness: A historical review and synthesis. *Psychological Bulletin*, 113, 403–39.

Connolly, D.A., & Lindsay, D.S. (2001). The influence of suggestions on children's reports of an unique event versus an instance of a repeated event. *Applied Cognitive Psychology*, 15(2), 205–224.

Dewing, K., & Kennealy, N. (1974). Age-related differences in spatial position and serial position effects in short-term memory. *Journal of Genetic Psychology*, 124, 277–86.

Domel Baxter, S., Thompson, W.O., & Davis, H.C. (1998). Accuracy of children's school lunch recalls according to how they remembered what they ate. *Topics in Clinical Nutrition*, 14, 58–66.

Farrar, M.J., & Goodman, G.S. (1990). Developmental differences in the relation between scripts and episodic memory: Do they exist? In: R. Fivush & J.A. Hudson (Eds), *Knowing and remembering in young children* (pp. 30–64). New York: Cambridge University Press.

Friedman, W.J. (1991). The development of children's memory for the time of past events. *Child Development*, 62, 139–55.

Friedman, W.J. (1993). Memory of the time of past events. *Psychological Bulletin*, 113, 44–66.

Hintzman, D.L., & Block, R.A. (1970). Memory judgments and the effects of spacing. *Journal of Verbal Learning and Verbal Behavior*, 98, 561–6.

Hudson, J.A. (1990). Constructive processing in children's event memory. *Developmental Psychology*, 26, 180–7.

Hudson, J., & Nelson, K. (1986). Repeated encounters of a similar kind: Effects of familiarity on children's autobiographical memory. *Cognitive Development*, 1, 253–71.

Johnson, M.K., Foley, M.A., & Leach, K. (1988). The consequences for memory of imagining in another person's voice. *Memory & Cognition*, 16, 337–42.

Johnson, M.K., Hashtroudi, S., & Lindsay, D.S. (1993). Source monitoring. *Psychological Bulletin*, 114, 3–28.

Lindsay, D. (1994). Memory source monitoring and eyewitness testimony. In D. Ross, J. Read, & M. Toglia (Eds), *Adult eyewitness testimony: Current trends and developments* (pp. 27–55). London: Cambridge University Press.

Lindsay, D.S., & Johnson, M.K. (1989). Eyewitness suggestibility and memory for source. *Memory & Cognition*, 17, 349–58.

Lindsay, D.S., Johnson, M.K., & Kwon, P. (1991). Developmental changes in memory source monitoring. *Journal of Experimental Child Psychology*, 52, 297–318.

Linton, M. (1982). Transformations of memory in everyday life. In U. Neisser (Ed.), *Memory observed: Remembering in natural contexts* (pp. 77–89). San Francisco: W.H. Freeman.

McNichol, S., Shute, R., & Tucker, A. (1999). Children's eyewitness memory for a repeated event. *Child Abuse & Neglect*, 23, 13.

Myles-Worsley, M., Cromer, C.C., & Dodd, D.H. (1986). Children's preschool script reconstruction: Reliance on general knowledge as memory fades. *Developmental Psychology*, **22**, 22–30.

Pezdek, K., & Roe, C. (1995). The effect of memory trace strength on suggestibility. *Journal of Experimental Child Psychology*, **60**, 116–28.

Poole, D.A., & White L.T. (1991). Effects of question repetition on eyewitness testimony of children and adults. *Developmental Psychology*, **27**, 975–86.

Powell, M.B., Roberts, K., Ceci. S.J. & Hembrooke, H.A. (1999). The effects of repeated experience on children's suggestibility. *Developmental Psychology*, **35**, 1462–77.

Powell, M.B., & Roberts, K.P. (in press). The effect of repeated experience on children's suggestibility across two question types. *Applied Cognitive Psychology*.

Powell, M.B., Roberts, K.P., & Thomson, D.M. (2000). The effect of a suggestive interview on children's memory of a repeated event: Does it matter whether suggestions are linked to a particular incident? *Psychiatry, Psychology & Law*, **7**(2), 182–191.

Powell, M.B. & Thomson, D.M. (1996). Children's recall of an occurrence of a repeated event: Effects of age, retention interval and question type. *Child Development*, **67**, 1988–2004.

Powell, M.B. & Thomson, D.M. (1997a). Contrasting memory for temporal-source and memory for content in children's discrimination of repeated events. *Applied Cognitive Psychology*, **11**, 339–60.

Powell, M.B. & Thomson, D.M. (1997b). The effect of an intervening interview on children's ability to remember an occurrence of a repeated event. *Legal and Criminological Psychology*, **2**, 247–62.

Powell, M.B. & Thomson, D.M. (2001). *The effect of question type on children's recall of an occurrence of a repeated event*. Manuscript in preparation.

Powell, M.B., Thomson, D.M. & Dietze, P.M. (1997). Children's ability to remember an occurrence of a repeated event. *Expert Evidence*, **5**, 133–9.

Roberts, K.P. (2000). An overview of theory and research on children's source monitoring. In K.P. Roberts & M. Blades (Eds), *Children's source monitoring*. Mahwah, NJ: Erlbaum.

S v. R. (1989). 89 ALR 321.

Slackman, E., & Nelson, K. (1984). Acquisition of an unfamiliar script in story form by young children. *Child Development*, **55**, 329–40.

Slamecka, N.J. (1967). Recall and recognition in list-discrimination tasks as a function of the number of alternatives. *Journal of Experimental Psychology*, **74**, 187–92.

Tucker, A., Mertin, P., & Luszcz, M. (1990). The effect of a repeated interview on young children's eyewitness memory. *Australian and New Zealand Journal of Criminology*, **23**, 117–24.

Tulving, E. (1966). Subjective organization and effects of repetition in multi-trial free-recall learning. *Journal of Verbal Learning and Verbal Behavior*, **5**, 193–7.

Tulving, E., & Hastie, R. (1972). Inhibition effects of intralist repetition in free recall. *Journal of Experimental Psychology*, **92**, 297–304.

Turtle, J.W., & Yuille, J.C. (1994). Lost but not forgotten details: Repeated eyewitness recall leads to reminiscence but not hyperamnesia. *Journal of Applied Psychology*, **79**, 260–71.

Underwood, B.J. (1957). Interference and forgetting. *Psychological Review*, **64**, 49–60.

Winograd, E. (1968). List differentiation as a function of frequency and retention interval. *Journal of Experimental Psychology*, **7**, 1–18.

CHAPTER 6

Children's Source Monitoring

D. STEPHEN LINDSAY

Department of Psychology, University of Victoria, Victoria, Canada

'Source monitoring' (SM) refers to hypothetical cognitive processes by which information from memory is attributed to particular origins or sources in our past experience. Just as each autobiographical episode is uniquely defined by the intersection of numerous dimensions (e.g. time, place, sensory modality, agent, etc.), so too the source of any given autobiographical memory is specified by the intersection of such dimensions. You may, for example, remember a prior encounter with the sentence, 'I'll get you, my pretty—and your little dog, too!' If so, was your prior experience of that sentence a fantasy or did you have a sensory encounter with it? If the latter, did you read the sentence or hear it spoken? If heard, who was the speaker and when and where did you hear the sentence? Answers to such questions converge to define a particular episode in your personal past (i.e. watching *The Wizard of Oz* at a particular place and time).

Identifying the sources of memories is an essential cognitive ability. For one thing, the meaning of a memory is closely bound up with its source (e.g. the import of a past utterance may vary dramatically depending on who said it, when and where, etc.). Furthermore, when reporting on past experiences (e.g. when testifying) it is often important to differentiate between memories of witnessing an event versus memories of imagining, inferring, or hearing about that event. Moreover, without the ability to identify the origins of memories, one would be bereft of autobiographical memory itself, because it is the quality of having a particular source in the personal past that makes a memory autobiographical.

Children's Testimony. Edited by H.L. Westcott, G.M. Davies, and R.H.C. Bull.
© 2002 John Wiley & Sons, Ltd.

This chapter provides an overview of the SM framework, followed by a review of basic research and theory on age-related changes in children's memory for source. I then describe studies in which children's SM has been examined in contexts relevant to eyewitness testimony.

THE SOURCE-MONITORING FRAMEWORK

The SM framework is grounded in Johnson's Multiple-entry Modular (MEM) model of memory (e.g. Johnson, 1983). In MEM, memory is described as a by-product of the cognitive processes that gave rise to and constituted past experiences. Rather than being separate from other cognitive processes (e.g. those involved in perceiving, thinking, feeling, etc.), memory consists of changes in those systems as a consequence of their functioning (as in connectionist models). One implication of this view is that only processes that are abstract and proposition-like (e.g. explicitly naming objects or people, consciously reflecting on relationships between events, etc.) leave memory records of an abstract, proposition-like form. Information that is tacit and implicit in ongoing experience is tacit and implicit in memory. Thus, memories rarely include abstract designations of their sources (e.g. there is no tag or label indicating 'This statement was made by the Wicked Witch of the West'), but they usually do include many clues to source.

According to the SM account, identifying objects, people, places, time, etc. when recalling a past experience is analogous in some ways to identifying such dimensions in ongoing perception. When a friend calls you on the phone, for example, you may recognize his or her voice immediately, because knowledge about your friend is evoked in the process of perceiving the auditory input in a particular context. Likewise, you may remember an utterance as having been spoken by a particular person because the activated memory records include sensory details and/or semantic content that leads you to recognize that person as the speaker. If you do not access sufficiently detailed, source-specifying memory records, you may be unable to identify the speaker of the remembered utterance (just as you may fail to recognize your friend's voice on the phone if the connection is of poor quality).

Johnson's MEM model distinguishes between cognitive processes that are largely perceptual (data driven) versus those that are more reflective (conceptual). Perceptual and reflective processes typically interact, but they operate in parallel and are independent in that processes can occur in one subsystem without reference to the other. A key assumption of the SM framework is that a test situation may cue memory records of some aspects of a past experience without cueing others (Chalfonte & Johnson, 1996). Your currently accessible memories of watching *The Wizard of Oz*, for example, may include information about the content of the witch's utterance and the sound of her voice but lack details regarding her appearance; if tested in a different context, you might recall other aspects of this episode. Test conditions also affect the stringency and appropriateness of the attribution-making processes performed when memory records are activated (e.g. SM is likely to be more conservative and systematic when testifying in court than when entertaining at a party).

According to the SM framework, most source attributions are performed rapidly and without awareness of decision making. Just as we usually recognize a friend's voice on the telephone without being conscious of any inferential process, so too we usually recognize memories of the friend's utterances as such without awareness of SM processes. Sometimes, however, these rapid, non-reflective SM processes fail to identify one or more dimensions of source. When this occurs, we have the subjective experience of recollecting some aspects of an event without fully remembering its source (e.g. we might remember a joke but not remember who told it). Often, we do not care about fully specifying the source of a recollection—in many situations it may be sufficient simply to remember the joke (provided we aren't about to tell it to the person from whom we learned it; Allen & Jacoby, 1990). When we do care about the source of a recollection and automatic SM processes fail to specify it, the source can sometimes be identified via strategic searches of memory or by reflective reasoning processes. Of course, people sometimes fail to remember aspects of the source of a memory despite arduous effort. Indeed, as Neisser (1982) pointed out, inability to remember the source of an otherwise clear recollection (as when we recall reading a particular fact but cannot remember where) is among the most common of everyday memory failures. Finally, and of central interest here, individuals sometimes misidentify the source of a recollection, attributing memory information that really came only from one source to another or to both. Such misattributions sometimes reflect errors in rapid, automatic SM processes and other times arise via more consciously mediated inferences.

Much of the empirical support for the SM framework comes from studies in which people were exposed to information from two sources and were later asked to identify the source (e.g. source *A*, source *B*, or new) of particular pieces of information (see Johnson, Hashtroudi, & Lindsay, 1993 and Johnson & Raye, 2000, for reviews). Such studies have shown that source errors are typically more frequent when potential memory sources are similar to one another in terms of their perceptual properties, semantic content, or cognitive operations (orienting tasks); for example, participants are more likely to misremember which of two people made a particular statement if the two people were similar looking or if they had both talked about the same topic (Lindsay, Johnson, & Kwon, 1991). SM also improves with the amount of time given to respond to test probes (Johnson, Kounios, & Reeder, 1994) and with full as opposed to divided attention at study (Jacoby & Kelley, 1992), and at test (Jacoby, 1991).

Biases in SM further support the hypothesis that recollections are attributed to sources via decision-making processes. For example, in a study in which participants were to discriminate between memories of their own actions and memories of a confederate's actions, participants more often misidentified distractor (new) items as actions the confederate had performed than as actions they themselves had performed (the 'it had to be you' effect) (Johnson, Raye, Foley, & Foley, 1981). Presumably, the pre-experimental familiarity of a distractor action (along with its compatibility with the sorts of actions performed and imagined in the acquisition phase of the study) sometimes led participants to mistake it as an action from the acquisition phase of the experiment, and the paucity of accessible memory information (occasioned by the fact that the action had not really occurred) led them to identify it as something they had merely seen another person do rather than as something they had done themselves. Similarly, when discriminating between memories of imagined versus actual events, participants tend to identify falsely recognized distractor items as imagined rather than as actual (the 'I must have imagined it' effect) (Bink, Marsh, & Hicks, 1999; Hoffman, 1997; Johnson & Raye, 1981).

BASIC RESEARCH ON CHILDREN'S SOURCE MEMORY

The relationship between age and SM is complex. Children as young as five years of age perform as well as adults at identifying the sources of their recollections in some situations, yet children as old as nine years perform more poorly than adults in others; for example, Foley and Johnson (1985; Foley, Johnson, & Raye, 1983) found that young children performed as well as adults when asked to remember which of two other people had done particular things, but were more likely than adults to make errors when asked to remember which things they had actually done versus which they had merely imagined themselves doing.

Findings such as these led Foley, Santini, and Sopasakis (1989) to propose that young children have special difficulty discriminating between memories of actual and imagined self-generated acts ('Realization Judgments'). Broadening this hypothesis, Lindsay *et al.* (1991) argued that young children may be more likely than adults to confuse memories from different sources when those sources give rise to memories that are highly similar to one another. Lindsay *et al.* (1991) found that the size (and in some experiments the existence) of age differences in SM interacted with source similarity; for example, in one experiment adults and eight-year-old children performed comparably and well when differentiating between memories of actual and imagined events when the actor of the imagined events differed from the actor of the actual events (act-self/imagine-other), whereas children were more likely than adults to mistake memories of actions they had merely imagined as memories of actual actions if the same actor was involved in both (act-other/imagine-other). Presumably, the fact that the same person was involved in the actual and imagined actions made memories of the two types of events relatively similar and hence confusable (but see Foley & Ratner, 1998a). Similarly, Markham, Howie, and Hlavacek (1999) found that six-year-olds performed more poorly than nine- to ten-year-olds on an auditory source-memory task that required them to differentiate between memories of words they had heard versus imagined hearing, but the two age groups performed comparably on an analogous (but easier) visual source-memory task.

Age-related changes in SM biases have also been reported. In a study by Foley *et al.* (1983), for example, six- and nine-year-old children and adults said some words and listened to the experimenter say other words; when tested, the nine-year-olds and adults showed the 'it had to be you' bias on falsely recognized items, but the six-year-old children did not. For participants in another condition, who had said some words and imagined themselves saying others, adults showed the 'I must have imagined it' bias, but neither nine- nor six-year-old children displayed this bias. Even quite young children do, however, sometimes show SM biases; for example, the six- year-old children in Foley and Ratner's (1998a) study more often mistook memories of imagined actions as memories of actual actions than vice versa, especially if instructed to imagine themselves going through the motions of performing the action, as opposed to imagining seeing themselves perform the action. Foley and Ratner (1998b) also found that young children show an 'I did it' bias when asked to remember whether they or an adult co-participant had made particular contributions to a collaborative project. The authors attributed this bias to children's tendency spontaneously to imagine themselves performing the actions they see the adult perform during the collaborative project.

A number of factors may contribute to the pattern of developmental change and invariance in SM. It may be that children's ongoing experience (and hence their memory records) differs from adults' in ways that affect some source discriminations but not others; for example, children may be better than adults at imagining themselves performing actions, such that their memories of imagined and actual self-performed actions are more similar. It may also be that the kinds of memory records that quickly and easily come to mind at test differ for children and adults, such that adults are more likely to gain access to particular kinds of source-specifying information that are especially useful in certain situations. Finally, age-related changes in SM may be due to deficiencies in children's use of retrieval strategies and reasoning processes when automatic SM processes fail to specify source; that is, when adults feel uncertain about the source of a memory they may search strategically for additional source-specifying memory information or use reflective reasoning to infer source, whereas children may fail to perform such operations or perform them less efficaciously (cf. Ackerman, 1985). Developmental differences in strategic retrieval and conscious decision-making processes could contribute to age × condition interactions because the more difficult the discrimination the more performance would require such strategies. Schacter, Kagan, & Leichtman (1995) argued that three- and four-year-olds' poor source memory may be due to immature development of the frontal lobes (which play important roles in executive control of intentional retrieval and memory judgments). In related work guided by Fuzzy Trace Theory, Brainerd and Reyna and their co-workers reported that children's memory judgments tend to be highly influenced by the extent to which the meaning of test items (especially distractors) is consistent with the gist of studied items (as opposed to relying on 'verbatim' memories of perceptual details) (Brainerd & Reyna, 1995).

According to the SM framework, memory for source is not a single skill that a child acquires at a particular age. Rather, SM involves inferences about a number of different aspects of event memories (remembering who, remembering where, remembering how, remembering when, etc.), and depends upon a number of kinds of mental activities (perceptual analysis and reflective integration during encoding, retrieval of memory records, and decision-making processes at test). Thus developmental changes in SM are gradual and situation specific rather than sudden and general. These considerations also suggest that SM development will relate to individual differences along a number of dimensions (Lorsbach & Ewing, 1995; Quas, Qin, Schaaf, & Goodman, 1997; Welch-Ross, Diecidue, & Miller, 1997).

CHILDREN'S SOURCE MEMORY IN FORENSIC RESEARCH

When individuals are asked about a past event, they sometimes include in their reports material from post-event suggestions. Such errors are more likely when witnesses are asked direct questions, but suggested information also sometimes intrudes into free-recall reports. Research indicates that some false reports reflect genuine source memory confusions, in which the witness has the subjective experience of remembering witnessing something that was actually merely suggested (with or without also accurately recollecting receiving the suggestion itself; see Higham, 1998 and Lindsay, Gonzales, & Eso, 1995). In contrast, some reports of suggestions occur because witnesses knowingly rely on memories from extra-event sources when responding to questions about an event (e.g. 'I don't remember the man wearing a hat, but I do remember that the experimenter said he did, so I'll go along with that'). False reports based on extra-event information may be confidently held (i.e. even though the person does not have an illusion of remembering witnessing the suggested event, he or she may be very confident that it occurred, due to the authority of the source of the suggestion), and such false reports may later give rise to genuine source confusions (i.e. although the witness initially was aware that the report was based solely on extra-event information, he or she may later come to 'remember' witnessing the suggested event; Bjorklund, Bjorklund, Brown, & Cassel, 1998; see also Ackil & Zaragoza, 1998). The important point is that reports of suggestions are sometimes based on aware use of extra-event information and other times reflect genuine source confusions.

Many studies have investigated age-related changes in eyewitness suggestibility (see reviews by Ceci & Bruck, 1995; Poole & Lamb, 1998; Poole & Lindsay, 1995). This research reveals that the relationship between age and suggestibility is complex. One source of this complexity is variation across experiments (and across real-life situations) in the extent to which the testing situation leads participants to assume that extra-event information is a valid source of answers. When conditions encourage participants to construe extra-event information as a valid source of answers, adult participants (who attended to suggestions in ways that promote subsequent remembering and who search memory at test in efficacious ways) may be more likely than younger participants to report suggestions (Brainerd & Poole, 1997).

This point is illustrated in a study conducted in my lab with Valerie Gonzales and Karen Eso (1995). One or three days after exposure to an illustrated story, pre-school and grade 3 children and adults listened to a narrative summary of the story that included two suggestions

Table 6.1. Mean proportion suggested details (on misinformed items) and incorrect guesses (on control items) reported in free recall.

Condition	Pre-schoolers		Third-graders		Adults	
	Misled	Control	Misled	Control	Misled	Control
High recency						
Standard	0.29	0.03	0.38	0.02	0.63	0.01
Exclusion	0.29	0.01	0.17	0.04	0.21	0.03
Low recency						
Standard	0.26	0.01	0.21	0.01	0.13	0.03
Exclusion	0.18	0.04	0.17	0.02	0.19	0.00

contradicting details in the story and two generic references to details in the story. Participants were tested by a new interviewer three days after exposure to the story (i.e. either 2 days or immediately after the misinformation) under one of two conditions. In the standard condition, participants were simply asked to 'Tell me everything you can about the Loren story that you heard that day when you saw the pictures and heard the story.' In the 'exclusion' condition, participants were informed that they had been exposed to misleading suggestions and were emphatically instructed not to base *any* of their responses on the post-event information (Jacoby, Woloshyn, & Kelley, 1989; Lindsay, 1990). Reliable misinformation effects were obtained in all conditions, but the point for present purposes is that there was a four-way interaction between age, recency of post-event information, test instructions, and target versus control items.

As shown in Table 6.1, under the standard-test instructions, suggestions were more often falsely reported when they were recent than when they had been presented two days previously, and it was the adults who most often reported recent suggestions. The exclusion instructions reduced adults' and third-graders' rates of reporting recently suggested details, but pre-schoolers did not benefit from the exclusion instructions at all. Another aspect of the interaction is that in the low-recency condition the misinformation effect was not moderated by age or test instructions, indicating that in all age groups erroneous reports of suggested details in the low recency condition were due to genuine SM confusions.

It is likely that a number of factors affect aware and unaware uses of extra-event information in the eyewitness misinformation paradigm and in real-world eyewitness situations, including:

(a) memorability of the content of the event details and of the suggestions;
(b) plausibility of the suggestions;
(c) extent to which test conditions encourage versus discourage reliance on the extra-event information as a source of answers;
(d) memorability and usefulness of source-specifying information in memories of the event details and of the suggestions; and
(e) ability to use source-specifying memory information in conjunction with automatic and consciously controlled decision-making processes to identify the sources of memories.

Inconsistent results across studies of developmental changes in suggestibility may partly be due to differences along these parameters. In the standard-test instruction conditions of the experiment described above, recently suggested details were more often reported in free recall by adults than by pre-schoolers. This may be ascribed to three factors:

(a) event details were not very memorable, because they were peripheral details in materials presented three days before the test, so the inaccuracy of the suggestions was unlikely to be detected and the event details were unlikely to pop to mind at test;
(b) the standard instructions did not discourage subjects from using the post-event information; and
(c) adults likely had better recall of the post-event suggestions than did pre-schoolers because adults are more skilled at encoding and retrieving verbal information (cf. Brainerd & Poole, 1997).

In the exclusion conditions, reports of suggestions did not reliably differ with age, perhaps because preschoolers' poorer SM was offset by their poorer memory for the content of the suggestions (cf. Coxon & Valentine, 1997).

Poole and Lindsay used source-memory tests to assess children's suggestibility in several studies using their Mr Science/parental misinformation paradigm. In this paradigm, children interact individually with an unfamiliar man named Mr Science who shows them four 'science demonstrations' (e.g. using two funnels and a rubber tube to make a telephone). Approximately three months later, parents read aloud to their children a story titled 'A Visit to Mr Science'. The story describes two demonstrations that the child had experienced and two demonstrations the child had not experienced, as well as an instance of ambiguous touching that had not actually occurred (e.g. that Mr Science had wiped the child's face with a wet-wipe that got close to the child's mouth and tasted yucky). Each child is then interviewed by a new interviewer.

Poole and Lindsay (1995) reported an initial study using the Mr Science/parental misinformation paradigm with 17 three- to four-year-old children. The most dramatic result was that even in the free-report phase of the final interview a substantial percentage of the children falsely reported events they had merely heard about in the story (e.g. 41% reported at least one suggested event during the free-report phase of the interview). Leading questions increased false reports, with 94% of the children falsely responding 'yes' to direct questions about one or more suggested event. A source-memory test—in which children were reminded of the story, explicitly told that some events in the story might not have happened to them, and asked to indicate whether they had actually experienced each event—was ineffective in reducing false reports; for example, 71% of the children erroneously answered 'yes' during the source-memory test when asked if Mr Science had really put something yucky in their mouths.

In another study using the Mr Science/parental misinformation paradigm, Poole and Lindsay (2001) examined developmental changes in 114 three- to eight-year-old children's accurate and false reports. As in the 1995 study with pre-schoolers, false reports were quite frequent in the initial free-recall portion of an interview conducted shortly after exposure to the misleading story. Consistent with arguments presented earlier, the older children described suggested events during free recall as often as the younger children. False reports of suggested events increased when children were asked direct questions about suggested events, especially among younger children. The source-memory test enabled the older children to retract some (but not all) of their prior reports of suggested events, and it did so without reducing their reports of experienced events. As in Poole and Lindsay (1995), however, the younger children did not benefit from this test.

Poole and Lindsay's (in press) most recent study using the Mr Science/parental misinformation paradigm tested a SM training procedure designed to help children avoid false reports of suggested events. Early in the final interview, the interviewer performed three 'preparation' tasks, each of which consisted of an action and a verbal description of a non-performed action (e.g. the interviewer wiped off the tape recorder and said that she usually pushed a button to reset the counter). For approximately half of the 133 three- to eight-year-old children, after each act the interviewer asked the child to report that preparation act, using both free recall and leading and misleading questions (e.g. 'Did I push the button to reset the counter?'), and provided immediate feedback on differentiating between actions that had been witnessed versus those that had merely been described ('No, I did not push the button—I only talked about pushing the button; when I ask you to tell me about things that happened to you, I want you to tell me only about things you remember really happening to you, not things that you only heard about).

During SM training, younger (three to five years) and older (six to eight years) children were equally accurate in reporting the source of witnessed actions, but the younger children were substantially less accurate in specifying the source of described actions. Both age groups improved across the three trials of the training procedure. Most importantly, among older children training reduced (but did not eliminate) false reports of suggested events in responses to direct questions, and did not reduce accurate reports of experienced events. When asked explicit SM questions in the final phase of the interview, children who had received training were no more likely than controls to reject suggested events to which they had acquiesced during leading questions. Thus, training reduced hearsay reports in older children but it did not improve ability to differentiate between memories of experienced and suggested events. The younger children did not benefit from SM training.

MEMORY FOR DATE OF OCCURRENCE AND FOR REPEATED OCCURRENCES

Date of occurrence is an important dimension of the source of an event memory, and one that poses special problems for source monitoring because the contents of event memories usually provide only very indirect cues to date. Suppose, for example, that you once had an automobile accident on your way to work; years later you might still be able to recall many details of that experience (because of its distinctiveness and salience), and those memories might enable you to specify the location of the accident, the approximate time of day (e.g., driving to versus from work, in light or darkness), and even perhaps the season (rain or snow), but the memory records of the experience are unlikely to provide direct cues to the date on which the accident occurred. The memories may provide constraints on date (e.g. if you retrieve information about geographical location and you travelled that route only during a particular period), but such constraints tend to be imprecise (except for memories of events intrinsically associated with particular dates).

Consistent with these ideas, people often have difficulty dating autobiographical events, for example, Friedman (1987) interviewed people nine months after a major earthquake. On average, respondents were correct to within one hour in their judgments of the time of day the earthquake occurred, but erred by nearly two months in their judgment of the month (Thompson, Skowronski, Larsen, & Betz, 1996; Wright, Gaskell, & O'Muircheartaigh, 1997).

Repeated experiences of very similar events compound these SM difficulties. On which birthday did you receive that blue cardigan? Such a question is likely to cue multiple birthdays, each sharing numerous features and none easily dated, such that they tend to blend together in recollection (into what Neisser, 1981, termed 'repisodes'). Powell and Thomson (1997; and Chapter 5 in this book) report evidence that young children have particular difficulty differentiating between memories of repeated episodes of similar events (cf. Brainerd & Reyna, 1995; Nelson, 1986).

Repeated experiences can also modulate the effect of misleading suggestions. In a study by Connolly and Lindsay (2001), four- to eight-year-old children experienced a complex event either once or on four successive days. In the repeated-episodes condition, some details of the event remained invariant across episodes whereas others varied across episodes. Before a final interview, children were exposed to misleading suggestions (which differed from details of all past occurrences of the event). Relative to children who had experienced the event only once, those who had experienced it repeatedly were less affected by suggestions regarding invariant details and more affected by suggestions regarding variable details (cf. Martine Powell & Don Thomson, Chapter 5 in this book).

CONCLUSIONS

Both children and adults sometimes intrude into their event reports information gained from extra-event sources. In some such cases, individuals are aware that they are drawing on extra-event sources, whereas in others they erroneously believe they are remembering the to-be- reported event itself. The extent to which conditions encourage versus discourage deliberate use of memories from extra-event sources interacts with other variables (e.g. source similarity, memorability of the event and of the suggestions) in determining suggestibility, and all of these variables may interact with age. These multi-variable interactions preclude sweeping conclusions such as 'Young children are more suggestible than adults.' Nonetheless, research indicates that young children are often especially prone to acquiescence and that they are more likely than older children or adults to confuse memories from different sources when conditions make source-monitoring difficult (e.g. when multiple sources give rise to highly similar memories).

Instructing witnesses not to use memories from a designated extra-event source ('exclusion' instructions), or asking them to differentiate between reports based on memories of the event versus memories of an extra-event source (a source-memory test), can enable adults and six- to eight-year-old children to reduce (but not necessarily eliminate) false reports of suggestions without reducing accurate reports of experienced events. This is good news for forensic interviewers. The findings indicate simple means of reducing false reports (without reducing accurate reports) in cases in which there are concerns about a particular source of misleading suggestions (e.g. a parent in a custody dispute).

Also heartening is Poole and Lindsay's (in press) recent finding that a simple and brief generic SM training procedure, which could easily be conducted by forensic interviewers, can reduce six- to eight- year-old children's rate of reporting suggestions in free recall and in response to direct (leading) questions. Compared to exclusion instructions and source-memory tests, the SM training procedure has the advantage of not being dependent upon explicit identification of a particular to-be-excluded source. This is important because in many real-world cases forensic interviewers may not be able to specify such a source.

Training has not yet been shown to enhance children's ability to discriminate memories from event versus extra-event sources, but rather merely to help them to understand that their reports should be based only on the former. Further research may yield training procedures that enhance SM skills. Perhaps even more importantly, neither exclusion instructions nor SM tests nor SM training have been found to be effective in reducing younger children's false reports of suggestions; here again, this is an important goal for future research.

The SM framework provides a useful set of metaphors and hypotheses regarding how the cognitive system differentiates between memories from different sources. Substantial additional empirical and theoretical work is required to more completely specify the cognitive processes involved in identifying the sources of memories and age-related changes in such processes (Lindsay & Johnson, 2001). Nonetheless, research inspired by the framework has already revealed much about the conditions under which children and adults are likely to confuse memories from different sources, as well as applied research on interventions designed to help witnesses avoid reports of suggestions.

REFERENCES

Ackerman, B.P. (1985). Constraints on retrieval search for episodic information in children and adults. *Journal of Experimental Child Psychology*, **40**, 152–80.

Ackil, J.K., & Zaragoza, M.S. (1998). Memorial consequences of forced confabulation: Age differences in susceptibility to false memories. *Developmental Psychology*, **34**, 1358–72.

Allen, S.W., & Jacoby, L.L. (1990). Reinstating study context produces unconscious influences of memo. *Memory & Cognition*, **18**, 270–8.

Bink, M.L., Marsh, R.L., & Hicks, J.L. (1999). An alternative conceptualization to memory 'strength' in reality monitoring. *Journal of Experimental Psychology: Learning, Memory, & Cognition*, **25**, 804–9.

Bjorklund, D.F., Bjorklund, B.R., Brown, R.D., & Cassel, W.S. (1998). Children's susceptibility to repeated questions: How misinformation changes children's answers and their minds. *Applied Developmental Science*, **2**, 99–111.

Brainerd, C.J., & Poole, D.A. (1997). Long-term survival of children's false memories: A review. *Learning & Individual Differences*, **9**, 125–51.

Brainerd, C.J., & Reyna, V.F. (1995). Autosuggestibility in memory development. *Cognitive Psychology*, **28**, 65–101.

Ceci, S.J., & Bruck, M. (1995). *Jeopardy in the courtroom: A scientific analysis of children's testimony.* Washington, DC: American Psychological Association.

Chalfonte, B.L., & Johnson, M.K. (1996). Feature memory and binding in young and older adults. *Memory & Cognition*, **24**, 403–16.

Connolly, D.A., & Lindsay, D.S. (2001). Effect of suggestions on children's reports of a unique experience vs. an instance of a repeated experience. *Applied Cognitive Psychology*, **15**, 205–223.

Coxon, P., & Valentine, T. (1997). The effects of the age of eyewitnesses on the accuracy and suggestibility of their testimony. *Applied Cognitive Psychology*, **11**, 415–30.

Foley, M.A., & Johnson, M.K. (1985). Confusions between memories for performed and imagined actions: A developmental comparison. *Child Development*, **56**, 1145–55.

Foley, M.A., Johnson, M.K., & Raye, C.L. (1983). Age-related changes in confusion between memories for thoughts and memories for speech. *Child Development*, **54**, 51–60.

Foley, M.A., & Ratner, H.H. (1998a). Children's recoding memory for collaboration: A way of learning from others. *Cognitive Development*, **13**, 91–108.

Foley, M.A., & Ratner, H.H. (1998b). Distinguishing between memories for thoughts and deeds: The role of prospective processing in children's source monitoring. *British Journal of Developmental Psychology*, **16**, 465–84.

Foley, M.A., Santini, C., & Sopasakis, M. (1989). Discriminating between memories: Evidence for children's spontaneous elaborations. *Journal of Experimental Child Psychology*, **48**, 146–69.

Friedman, W.J. (1987). A follow-up to 'Scale effects in memory for the time of events': The earthquake study. *Memory & Cognition*, **15**, 518–20.

Higham, P.A. (1998). Believing details known to have been suggested. *British Journal of Psychology*, **89**, 265–83.

Hoffman, H.G. (1997). Role of memory strength in reality monitoring decisions: Evidence from source attribution biases. *Journal of Experimental Psychology: Learning, Memory, & Cognition*, **23**, 371–83.

Jacoby, L.L. (1991). A process dissociation framework: Separating automatic from intentional uses of memory. *Journal of Memory & Language*, **30**, 513–41.

Jacoby, L.L., & Kelley, C.M. (1992). Unconscious influences of memory: Dissociations and automaticity. In: D.A. Milner & M.D. Rugg (Eds), *The neuropsychology of consciousness. Foundations of neuropsychology* (pp. 201–33). London: Academic Press.

Jacoby, L.L., Woloshyn, V., & Kelley, C. (1989). Becoming famous without being recognized: Unconscious influences of memory produced by dividing attention. *Journal of Experimental Psychology: General*, **118**, 115–25.

Johnson, M.K. (1983). The multiple-entry, modular memory system. In: G.H. Bower (Ed.), *The psychology of learning and motivation: Advances in research and theory* (Vol. 17). New York: Academic Press.

Johnson, M.K., Hashtroudi, S., & Lindsay, D.S. (1993). Source monitoring. *Psychological Bulletin*, **114**, 3–28.

Johnson, M.K., Kounios, J., & Reeder, J.A. (1994). Time-course studies of reality monitoring and recognition. *Journal of Experimental Psychology: Learning, Memory, & Cognition*, **20**, 1409–19.

Johnson, M.K., & Raye, C.L. (1981). Reality monitoring. *Psychological Review*, **88**, 67–85.

Johnson, M.K., & Raye, C.L. (2000). Cognitive and brain mechanisms of false memories and beliefs. In: D.L. Schacter & E. Scarry (Eds), *Memory and belief* (pp. 35–86). Cambridge, MA: Cambridge University Press.

Johnson, M.K., Raye, C.L., Foley, H.J., & Foley, M.A. (1981). Cognitive operations and decision bias in reality monitoring. *American Journal of Psychology*, **94**, 37–64.

Lindsay, D.S. (1990). Misleading suggestions can impair eyewitnesses' ability to remember event details. *Journal of Experimental Psychology: Learning, Memory, & Cognition*, **16**, 1077–83.

Lindsay, D.S., Gonzales, V., & Eso, K. (1995). Aware and unaware uses of memories of postevent suggestions. In: M.S. Zaragoza, J.R. Graham, G.C.N. Hall, R. Hirschman, & Y.S. Ben-Porath (Eds), *Memory and testimony in the child witness* (pp. 86–108). Thousand Oaks, CA: Sage.

Lindsay, D.S., & Johnson, M.K. (2001). False memories, fuzzy trace theory, and the source monitoring framework: Reply to Reyna and Lloyd. *Learning and Individual Differences*, **12**, 145–161.

Lindsay, D.S., Johnson, M.K., & Kwon, P. (1991). Developmental changes in memory source monitoring. *Journal of Experimental Child Psychology*, **52**, 297–318.

Lorsbach, T.C., & Ewing, R.H. (1995). Source monitoring in children with learning disabilities. *International Journal of Disability, Development & Education*, **42**, 239–41.

Markham, R., Howie, P., & Hlavacek, S. (1999). Reality monitoring in auditory and visual modalities: Developmental trends and effects of cross-modal imagery. *Journal of Experimental Child Psychology*, **72**, 51–70.

Nelson, K. (1986). *Event knowledge: Structure and function in development*. Hillside, NJ: Erlbaum.

Neisser, U. (1981). John Dean's memory: A case study. *Cognition*, **9**, 1–22.

Neisser, U. (1982). *Memory observed: Remembering in natural contexts.* San Francisco: W.H. Freeman.

Poole, D.A., & Lamb, M.E. (1998). *Investigative interviews of children: A guide for helping professionals.* Washington, DC: American Psychological Association.

Poole, D.A., & Lindsay, D.S. (1995). Interviewing preschoolers: Effects of non-suggestive techniques, parental coaching, and leading questions on reports of nonexperienced events. *Journal of Experimental Child Psychology*, **60**, 129–54.

Poole, D.A., & Lindsay, D.S. (1998). Assessing the accuracy of young children's reports: Lessons from the investigation of child sexual abuse. *Applied & Preventive Psychology*, **7**, 1–26.

Poole, D.A., & Lindsay, D.S. (1999). Children's eyewitness reports after exposure to misinformation from parents. *Journal of Experimental Psychology: Applied*, **7**, 27–50.

Poole, D.A., & Lindsay, D.S. (in press). Reducing child witnesses, false reports of misinformation from parents. *Journal of Experimental Child Psychology.*

Powell, M.B., & Thomson, D.M. (1997). Contrasting memory for temporal-source and memory for content in children's discrimination of repeated events. *Applied Cognitive Psychology*, **11**, 339–60.

Quas, J.A., Qin, J., Schaaf, J., & Goodman, G.S. (1997). Individual differences in children's and adults' suggestibility and false event memory. *Learning & Individual Differences*, **9**, 359–90.

Schacter, D.L., Kagan, J., & Leichtman, M.D. (1995). True and false memories in children and adults: A cognitive neuroscience perspective. *Psychology, Public Policy, & Law*, **1**, 411–28.

Thompson, C.P., Skowronski, J.J., Larsen, S.F., & Betz, A. (1996). *Autobiographical memory: Remembering what and remembering when.* Mahwah, NJ: Erlbaum.

Welch-Ross, M.K., Diecidue, K., & Miller, S.A. (1997). Young children's understanding of conflicting mental representation predicts suggestibility. *Developmental Psychology*, **33**, 43–53.

Wright, D.B., Gaskell, G.D., & O'Muircheartaigh, C.A. (1997). Temporal estimation of major news events: Re-examining the accessibility principle. *Applied Cognitive Psychology*, **11**, 35–46.

CHAPTER 7

The Construction of False Events in Memory

KATHY PEZDEK AND TIFFANY HINZ

Department of Psychology, Claremont Graduate University, Claremont, California, USA

In March 1992, in Philadelphia, Pamela Freyd founded the False Memory Syndrome Foundation and therein coined the phrase 'false memory'. Freyd's efforts were in response to her daughter's confrontation of her father regarding his alleged sexual abuse of her throughout her childhood. Freyd declared that the daughter's memories of sexual abuse were 'false memories', likely planted by an overzealous therapist or by one of the self-help books on the topic of sexual abuse. Thus began the False Memory Syndrome Foundation, which currently claims 2,000 members and provides legal and psychological support primarily for alleged sexual-abuse perpetrators.

The origin of the False Memory Syndrome Foundation served as a call to action for cognitive psychologists studying memory. Although in 1992 much of the accumulating research literature on memory was relevant to the suggestive planting of false events in memory, the relationship was not a very clear or direct one. Subsequently, a number of researchers have begun to explore a wide range of cognitive aspects surrounding the false memory issue (cf. Bjorklund, in press; Conway, 1997; Pezdek & Banks, 1996; Read & Lindsay, 1997).

This chapter critically reviews six programs of research in which attempts have been made to suggestively plant false events in memory. These include our own research in this area as well as that of Elizabeth Loftus, Ira Hyman, Stephen Ceci, Maryanne Garry, and Guiliana

Children's Testimony. Edited by H.L. Westcott, G.M. Davies, and R.H.C. Bull.
© 2002 John Wiley & Sons, Ltd.

Mazzoni. The purpose of this review is to elucidate the conditions under which false events are more or less likely to be planted in memory. Although research with word lists reporting false responding on recognition memory tests is also relevant to the construction of false events in memory (for a review see Roediger, McDermott, & Goff, 1997), we chose to focus on research in which false autobiographical events were suggestively planted in memory. This chapter does not focus exclusively on research with children. Because so few studies have been conducted to date on this topic, to restrict this review to the even smaller subset of studies that have tested children, would limit the findings regarding what factors influence the suggestive planting of false events in memory. Nonetheless, this research has clear implications for children and memories of childhood.

LOFTUS AND PICKRELL (1995)

One of the most widely cited studies that has sought to plant a false event in the memory of participants is that of Loftus and Pickrell (1995). In this study, 24 pairs of adults were recruited for a study on childhood memories. The majority of the pairs were parent–child pairs; the remainder were sibling pairs. Subjects were provided test booklets, mailed to them by their relative. In each booklet were descriptions of three true events (obtained from the relative) and one false event, each purported to have occurred when the subject was four to six years old. The one false event described an incident in which the subject had been lost as a child while shopping with a family member. Subjects were instructed to read each description and then to write down everything they could remember about each event. Two telephone or in-person interviews followed in which the relative 'pressed for details' of the subject's memory for each event. The first interview was a week or two after receiving the booklet; the second was a week or two later.

The major finding was that 7 out of the 24 subjects indicated in the initial test booklet that they remembered the false event 'either fully or partially'. During the subsequent interview, one of these seven subjects indicated that she did not really remember the event. Nonetheless, it is impressive that 25% of the subjects tested (6 out of 24) reported that they remembered the false event. To understand the cognitive processes underlying the planting of false events in memory, two questions regarding these results deserve attention. First, could subjects' accounts of false events be differentiated from their accounts of true events? Yes. Recalled true events ($M = 138$ words) contained more words than did recalled false events ($M = 50$ words). Also, mean clarity ratings in the second interview (on a scale of 1–10) were higher for recalled true events ($M = 6.3$) than for recalled false events ($M = 3.6$), and mean confidence ratings in the second interview (on a 1–5 scale) were higher for true events ($M = 2.2$) than for recalled false events ($M = 1.4$). At the end of the study, subjects were told that one of the events described had not really occurred. They were asked to pick which one this was. Nineteen of the 24 subjects identified the false event correctly. Clearly, the accounts of true events were discernible from the accounts of false events.

The second question concerns whether the six subjects who recalled the false event were recalling a previous true incident of being lost as a child while shopping with a family member or whether they were recalling the false event that was suggestively planted by their relative. The relatives of each subject had to verify that the subject had not been lost as a young child while shopping in a mall. However, children are so frequently lost, if only for a minute or so, that the parent's or sibling's memory for whether the subject had been lost some 13–48 years prior is of dubious value.

It is also important to note that, prior to constructing the false event, Loftus and Pickrell asked each parent or sibling to provide 'information about a plausible shopping trip to a mall or large department store in order to construct a false event where the subject could conceivably have gotten lost'. This information was then incorporated into the false event constructed for each child. It is clear, then, that the false event for each subject was constructed from information that in fact described features of true incidents from the subject's childhood. Remember that the six subjects who were considered to have recalled the false event had recalled it 'either fully or partially'. For a recalled event to be considered a 'remembered false event' in the Loftus and Pickrell study, it was not necessary for the subject to have recalled any additional information beyond that provided by the experimenters. Thus, since the described false event included much true information gathered from the parent or sibling, one interpretation of the result of Loftus and Pickrell is that the subjects who were considered to have recalled the false event simply recalled some of the true information included in the description of the false event; that is, the suggested false event was not really planted in memory.

PEZDEK, FINGER, AND HODGE (1997) AND PEZDEK AND HODGE (1999)

In two studies, we tested the hypothesis that events will be suggestively planted in memory to the degree that they are plausible and script-relevant knowledge exists in memory. This hypothesis was derived from the notion that an asserted event must first be evaluated as true before it can be incorporated into autobiographical memory and, if an event is implausible, it is not likely to be evaluated as true. Furthermore, it should be easier to form a memory trace for an event that is plausible and about which one has a well-developed generic script than to form a memory trace for an event that is implausible and about which one does not have a well-developed script.

The false event utilized by Loftus and Pickrell (1995) was clearly a plausible event. Pezdek, Finger, and Hodge (1997, Experiment 2) compared the probability of planting a false memory for a plausible event (being lost as a child in a mall while shopping) to the probability of planting a false memory for an implausible event (receiving a rectal enema as a child). In this study, 20 confederate experimenters read descriptions of one true event and two false events to a younger sibling or close relative, the subject, who was at least 15 years old (mean age = 23.5 years) at the time of the study. After each event, the subject was told by their relative, 'This is what I remember about this event. Now what do you remember about it?' One day and again about one week later, each confederate returned to test if the subject had any additional memories for the events.

The most important result involves the number of subjects who remembered the plausible versus the implausible false event. Three subjects (15%) remembered the false event about being lost and recalled additional details of this event. This figure is somewhat less than Loftus and Pickrell's (1995) report of 25% false recall for essentially the same false event. One explanation for this is that we used a stricter operational definition of what qualified as 'remembering a false event'. In our study, an event was not considered to have been recalled from memory unless the subject recalled information about the event beyond that included in the description read to them. Regarding the implausible false event, however, none of the subjects remembered the false event about receiving a rectal enema. The hypothesis was confirmed—plausible false events were more likely to be suggestively planted in memory than implausible false events.

This hypothesis was tested in a different experiment by Pezdek *et al.* (1997, Experiment 1), this time using a mixed factorial design in which each false event served as both a plausible and implausible event.

Thirty-two Jewish and 29 Catholic high-school students were read descriptions of three true events and two false events that were reported to have happened when they were eight years old and were asked what they recalled about each. One false event described a Jewish ritual; the other false event described a Catholic ritual. Catholics were significantly more likely to recognize falsely the Catholic event ($n = 7$) than the Jewish event ($n = 1$) and Jews were significantly more likely to recognize falsely the Jewish event ($n = 3$) than the Catholic event ($n = 0$). Again, the plausible false event was more likely to be planted in memory than the implausible event.

Pezdek and Hodge (1999) specifically examined developmental differences in the suggestive planting of false events in memory. In this study, the methodology used by Pezdek *et al.* (1997, Experiment 2) was used to test the vulnerability of children to suggestibility for a plausible false event (being lost as a child while shopping in a mall) versus an implausible false event (receiving a rectal enema). Developmental differences in suggestibility for plausible versus implausible events warrant investigation because young children, due to their relatively more limited world experiences, generally have less script-relevant knowledge in memory than do older children, even for events that are familiar to both age groups (Fivush & Slackman, 1986; Fivush, Kuebli, & Clubb, 1992). Thus, it might be predicted that children would not distinguish between suggestively incorporating plausible versus implausible false events into their memory.

Nineteen younger children (5–7 years old) and 20 older children (9–12 years old) were included in this study. A parent (or an experimenter with the parent sitting nearby) read descriptions of four events that they reported had happened when the child was four years old. The child was asked to recall everything he or she could remember about each event. Two events were true; the two false events were those from Pezdek *et al.* (1997, Experiment 2). Children were also prompted for recall on the next day; there were few differences in the results between days 1 and 2.

The majority of the children (54%) did not remember either false event. Three children, all in the younger age group, remembered both false events. The principal finding involves the number of children who remembered the plausible versus the implausible false event. Of the 15 children who remembered one false event on day 2, 14 remembered the plausible false event and only 1 remembered the implausible false event. The finding was consistent for both age groups. Among the younger children, all seven children who remembered one false event on day 2 also remembered the plausible event and none the implausible event. Among the eight older children who remembered one false event by day 2, seven remembered the plausible event and one the implausible event.

These results suggest that, with children as with adults, plausible false events are more likely to be suggestively planted in memory than implausible false events. Nonetheless, these results do suggest developmental differences in the general vulnerability to suggestively planting false events in memory. First, whereas 3 out of the 19 younger children (16%) reported that they remembered both false events, none of the older children did so. Also, developmental comparisons can be made based on the probability of remembering the 'lost in the mall' plausible false event scenario that has now been used in at least three different studies. Whereas 53% of the younger children and 35% of the older children in this study remembered the false event about being lost, 15% of the adults in the Pezdek *et al.* (1997) study and 25% of the adults in the Loftus and Pickrell (1995) study did so. These findings are consistent with the conclusions that age differences in the suggestibility of memory reliably occur (Ceci & Bruck, 1993).

HYMAN, HUSBAND, AND BILLINGS (1995)

The notion that false events incorporated into memory are schematic reconstructions of plausible and familiar true events receives additional support from two studies by Hyman. Hyman *et al.* (1995, Experiment 1) presented students a very brief description of one of two false events created by the experimenters, along with descriptions of two to five true events from a questionnaire completed by parents. The students were asked what they remembered about each event. The two false events described were: (a) a birthday party at age 5 and (b) an overnight visit to the hospital at age 5. A second interview followed one to seven days after the first one.

The major result was that no one recalled a false event in the first interview; four participants (4/20 = 20%) recalled a false event in the second interview. Each of these four participants had talked about related information during the first interview even though they did not recall the suggested incident. Based on this finding, Hyman *et al.* (1995) suggested that these participants constructed a memory for the false event by incorporating details suggested in the false event into an existing event schema. According to this interpretation, prior knowledge of the suggested event is a necessary condition for false recall. Accordingly, Hyman *et al.* (1995) suggested that 'it is possible that the wholesale adoption of an event when an individual has no related knowledge or when the individual does not access related information may be rare.'

In Hyman *et al.* (1995, Experiment 2), two less plausible false events were used: (a) attending a wedding reception and accidentally spilling a punch bowl and (b) having to evacuate a grocery store when the overhead sprinkler systems erroneously activated. Participants were read more detailed descriptions of the events than were provided in Experiment 1 and were asked what they remembered about each. For each participant, the descriptions included three to five true events and one false event. In addition, each subject participated in three interviews spaced one day apart, and the interviewer utilized heightened 'conformity demands' relative to Experiment 1. Participants were repeatedly told that the purpose of the experiment was to produce more complete and more accurate recall by the end of the last interview session; whenever a participant could not recall an event on the first or second trial, they were encouraged to think more about the events for the subsequent interview.

No one recalled a false event in the first interview; 9 participants (9/51 = 18%) recalled a false event in the second interview; 13 participants (13/51 = 25%) recalled a false event in the third interview. Of the 13 participants who recalled a false event by the third interview, 6 of the recall protocols reflected clear memory for the suggested false event, 5 were less clear (their recall included less of the critical information or inferential information that followed from the details in the presented description), and 2 participants recalled the false event but attributed the false recall to an image and expressed doubt about whether the image was really a memory. These findings, along with those of Loftus and Pickrell (1995), suggest that researchers should not consider false memories dichotomously as present or absent. Rather, individuals who report some memory for suggested false events nonetheless differ qualitatively in terms of the richness of their memories.

Together, Hyman's experiments along with those of Pezdek and colleagues support a consistent model of the cognitive processes underlying the suggestive planting of false events in memory. When a false event is suggested, schema-relevant information in memory is activated. Whether the event will be judged to be true is determined by the extent of the overlap between the suggested false event and the activated memory for the schema-relevant information. If the false event is judged to be true, then details of the generic script for the event as well as details from related episodes of the event can be transported to the memory for the suggested false event. Thus, memory for the false event becomes developed by this related information in memory. Memories for false events will then vary in terms of the extent to which they include: (a) elaborations of the information suggested and (b) transported information from memories for prior events. And, the more overlap there is between the distributions of these two types of information, the more likely it is that a suggested false event will be judged to be true and incorporated into memory. An interesting direction for future research would be to isolate factors that affect the relative amounts of these two types of information in false events that are judged to be true.

CECI, HUFFMAN, SMITH, AND LOFTUS (1996); CECI, LOFTUS, LEICHTMAN, AND BRUCK (1994); AND HUFFMAN, CROSSMAN, AND CECI (1997)

The results reported by Hyman *et al.* (1995) raise questions about the effect of repeated suggestion on the planting of false events in memory, and whether constructed memories for false events that were repeatedly suggested are likely to endure over time. These issues were specifically addressed in several studies by Ceci and his colleagues. Ceci *et al.* (1996) interviewed 96 three- to six-year-old children regarding the occurrence of two true events and two false events that were reported to have transpired within the prior 12 months. The two false events were: (a) getting one's hand caught in a mousetrap and having to go to the hospital to get it removed and (b) going on a hot-air balloon ride with classmates. The children were repeatedly interviewed seven to ten times over a ten week period. Each time they were interviewed, they were told to 'think really hard if it happened', and then indicate to the experimenter whether it had occurred.

The major results were that, although the effect of repeated sessions did not significantly affect the rate of assenting to false events (mean percent assents to false events in the initial session and the final session were both 34%), the age by sessions interaction approached significance ($p = 0.097$). Whereas the mean proportion of assents to false events increased (although not significantly) over sessions for children aged five to six years (from 25% in session 1 to 32% in the last session), the mean proportion of assents to false events decreased (although not significantly) over sessions for children aged three to four years (from 44% in session 1 to 36% in the last session).

These data are difficult to interpret for several reasons. First, the children were not asked what they remembered about each event, but only whether they remembered it or not. Unfortunately, the use of a dichotomous response makes it impossible to know what proportion of the 'yes' responses simply reflected a response bias to comply with authority. This issue is of particular concern given the fact that, even in the very first interview, it was reported that 44% of the false events were 'remembered' by the younger children and 25% of the false events were 'remembered' by the older children. The fact that these proportions were so high in the initial session makes it difficult to interpret what a response of 'yes' meant to these children.

Interpretation of these findings is further complicated by the fact that conflicting results were reported in a subsequent study. This study (Ceci *et al.*, 1994) was conducted similarly to the Ceci *et al.* (1996) study with the exception that in each test session the children were told that they had actually experienced each event. Children were also asked to create a visual picture of each event in their head and tell the experimenters if they remembered it. The results were that, in the initial session, younger children assented to 35% of the false events and older children assented to 25% of the false events. Furthermore, over twelve sessions, the rate of assenting increased for both age groups, to 45% for the younger children and 40% for the older children. Together, the results of these two studies suggest that children's rate of assenting to false events increases with repeated suggestion only when heightened conformity demands are imposed by the experimenter. These findings are consistent with the results summarized above by Hyman *et al.* (1995, Experiment 2) with adults. These results emphasize the importance of determining in 'false memory research', whether one is assessing a true change in memory or simply individuals' compliance with authority.

One way of determining whether children's assents to false events reflect the construction of a false event in memory is to examine the persistence of these memories over time. A test of this question was conducted by Huffman *et al.* (1997). In this study, 22 of the participants in the study by Ceci *et al.* (1996) were retested two years later when they were 71–89 months of age. Each child was re-interviewed at the site of their original interview. They were shown cards describing the same true and false events included in the original study and for each were asked to think real hard about the event and to indicate whether the event had ever happened. Of the 37 true events recalled in the original study, 29 (78%) were recalled two years later. However, of the 39 false events assented to in the original study, only 9 (23%) were assented to two years later. Seventy-seven per cent of the initial false assents were recanted two years later. This finding raises serious doubts about whether the original 'assents to false events' reflect anything more than compliance with authority.

GARRY, MANNING, LOFTUS, AND SHERMAN (1996)

Garry *et al.* (1996) investigated whether childhood events could be suggestively planted in memory by having participants simply think about the to-be-planted event (see also Heaps & Nash, 1999; Paddock *et al.*, 1998). This procedure, called 'imagination inflation', assessed the extent to which individuals' confidence that an event occurred was increased after imagining the event. Younger adults completed a 40-item Life Events Inventory (LEI) in which they rated the likelihood that each event, *or a very similar one*, had happened to them before the age of 10 on a scale from 1 (definitely did not happen) to 8 (definitely did happen). Included in this list were eight target events. Two weeks later, subjects were instructed to imagine four target events; four target events not imagined served as controls. After imagining the events, they completed the LEI a second time.

In presenting the results, Garry *et al.* (1996) selected the events to which subjects had initially responded 1–4 (low likelihood). They then examined the direction of change in these likelihood ratings in the second administration of the LEI. These results are presented in the top panel of Figure 7.1. Likelihood ratings for the majority of the target events did not change from time 1 to time 2 (57% in the imagined condition and 65% in the not-imagined condition). However, when scores did change, they were more likely to increase than decrease and there were more positive changes in the imagined condition (34%) than in the not-imagined condition (25%). From these findings the authors reported that 'imagining a self-reported counterfactual event increased confidence that the event did happen' (Garry *et al.*, 1996, p. 213).

We recently tested an alternative interpretation of these results; that is, that the results simply reflect regression toward the mean. This interpretation is suggested by two results in the Garry *et al.* (1996) study. First, likelihood ratings for events initially rated 1–4 increased from time 1 to time 2 for both imagined and not-imagined events. Second, we recently obtained from the authors the findings regarding the events initially rated 5–8; these results were not reported in the published study. These data are presented in the top panel of Figure 7.2. As can be seen, when likelihood ratings did change from time 1 to time 2 for these events, 44% decreased (32 of 73) and only 16% increased (12 of 73), and this pattern of results was consistent for both imagined and not-imagined events. These findings are exactly what would be predicted by regression toward the mean.

In the experiment we recently conducted (Pezdek & Eddy, 2001), we used a procedure very similar to that used by Garry *et al.* (1996) and

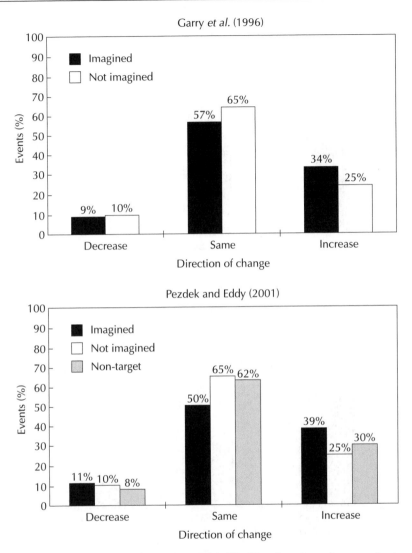

Figure 7.1. Per cent of events for which likelihood ratings decreased, stayed the same, or increased from time 1 to time 2 for participants who initially responded 1–4 in Garry *et al.* (1996) and Pezdek and Eddy (2001).

analyzed the responses to all target events, not just those with low initial likelihood rating. The data were first analyzed comparably to those of Garry *et al.* (1996) to assess whether we replicated their findings. The general pattern of results for target items initially rated 1–4 is presented in the bottom panel of Figure 7.1. When the data were

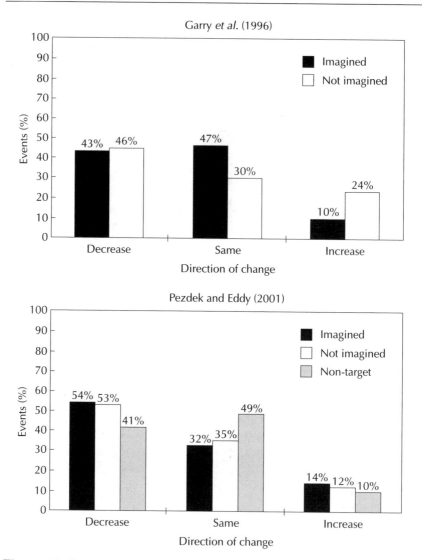

Figure 7.2. Per cent of events for which likelihood ratings decreased, stayed the same, or increased from time 1 to time 2 for participants who initially responded 5–8 in Garry *et al.* (1996) and Pezdek and Eddy (2001).

analyzed comparably to those of Garry *et al.* (1996), their findings were replicated. First, likelihood ratings for the majority of the target events initially rated 1–4 did not change from time 1 to time 2 (50% in the imagined condition and 65% in the not-imagined condition). However, when likelihood ratings did change, they were more likely to increase than decrease and there were more positive changes in the imagined condition (39%) than in the not-imagined condition (25%). In Figure 7.1, it is important to note, however, that the pattern of results was remarkably similar to the imagined target events, the target events not imagined, and the non-target events.

A very different pattern of results is revealed in the analysis of events initially rated 5–8. These results are presented in the bottom panel of Figure 7.2. As would be predicted by the regression toward the mean interpretation, likelihood ratings for the majority of the target events initially rated 5–8 decreased from time 1 to time 2; ratings for 54% of the events in the imagined condition and 53% of the events in the not-imagined condition decreased from time 1 to time 2. Furthermore, as in the bottom panel of Figure 7.1, the pattern of results was remarkably similar to the imagined target events, the target events not imagined, and the non-target events.

Additional analyses were performed on the data to assess patterns of results beyond those addressed by Garry et al. (1996). A repeated factors ANOVA (analysis of variance) was conducted to compare the effects of time and imagination condition on the magnitude of the change in likelihood ratings from time 1 to time 2. The only significant result was the main effect of time; ratings increased significantly from time 1 ($M = 2.96$) to time 2 ($M = 3.44$). The positive direction of this trend is accounted for by the fact that 75% of all target events were initially rated 1–4 and 25% were initially rated 5–8. The effect of the imagination condition was not significant ($F(1, 73) = 1.15$), nor did this condition significantly interact with time ($F(1, 73) = 0.22$).

The fact that the pattern of results was similar to the imagined target events, the target events not imagined, and the non-target events suggests that the change in results from time 1 to time 2 was not affected by the act of imagining *per se*. These results suggest that the change in likelihood ratings from time 1 to time 2 can be explained by simple regression to the mean. From the results of Garry et al. (1996) and those of Pezdek and Eddy (2001), it is clear that simply imagining a fictitious childhood event does not increase the probability that the event will be planted in autobiographical memory.

Results similar to those of Garry et al. (1996) were reported in two recent studies by Heaps and Nash (1999) and Paddock et al. (1998), using procedures similar to those of Garry et al. (1996). In the first of these studies, results were not reported separately for events initially rated 1–4 versus 5–8, and 90% of the target events were initially rated 1–4. The results of Paddock et al. also focused on analyses of events initially rated 1–4. They did include some analyses of all target events initially rated 1–7, but they did not separately examine events with high versus low initial likelihood ratings. Because in most imagination inflation studies only the minority of events receive initial high likelihood ratings, analyses that combine results for all events are not sensitive to the direction of the effect for events with initial high likelihood ratings. Furthermore, in their Experiment 2, Paddock *et al.* tested subjects who were not from a college population and reported no evidence of imagination inflation; imagining the target events did not inflate likelihood ratings from time 1 to time 2.

MAZZONI, LOFTUS, SEITZ, AND LYNN (1999)

Mazzoni *et al.* (1999) introduced a variation in the procedure of Garry *et al.* (1996) to test if individuals' beliefs about the occurrence of a suggested childhood event can be altered by having their dreams interpreted to indicate that they had experienced the event in their childhood. Participants were administered a 20-item LEI similar to that used by Garry *et al.* (1996). After reading each event, they indicated, on a scale from 1 (definitely did not happen) to 8 (definitely did happen), how likely it was that they had experienced the event, *or a similar one*, before the age of three. The critical target event was either 'was harassed by a bully' or 'was lost in a public place for more than one hour'. All subjects completed the LEI in session 1 and three to four weeks later in session 2. All subjects selected to participate in the complete experiment had initially specified a rating of 1–3 for the critical target event.

One and a half to two weeks after session 1, subjects in the dream interpretation condition participated in what they were led to believe was an unrelated session. They were asked to bring two of their dreams to this session to be interpreted by a clinical psychologist with extensive experience in dream interpretation. During the session, the psychologist interpreted one of their dreams to suggest that a difficult childhood experience such as being bullied/lost appeared to have happened to them before the age of three. The control subjects did not have a session that intervened between LEI sessions 1 and 2.

Mazzoni *et al.* (1999) reported that in the dream interpretation condition from time 1 to time 2 for the critical target item, likelihood ratings of 46% of the participants stayed the same, 50% increased, and 4% decreased. In the control condition, however, from time 1 to time 2 for the critical target item, ratings of 58% of the participants stayed the same, 11% increased, and 31% decreased. These results reflect that subjects were more likely to change their likelihood ratings if they were in the dream interpretation condition than the control condition and, when a change in ratings occurred, it was more likely an increase in the dream condition and a decline in the control condition.

This pattern of results, unlike that reported Garry *et al.* (1996), cannot be explained by simple regression to the mean; performance differed between the control and experimental conditions. On the other hand, these results do not appear to reflect a change in *memory* for the target event; the false target event was not actually planted in memory. In the dream interpretation session, the subjects were provided with a reason why it was likely or plausible that they had been bullied/lost as a child. When they later rated how likely it was that they had been bullied or lost as a child, their likelihood ratings increased.

Mazzoni *et al.* (1999) provided in their article the memory reports of the eight subjects in the dream condition whose likelihood scores increased from time 1 to time 2. Four of these subjects included in their description, time references significantly older than the age of three that was included in the false target event. Two additional children included in their descriptions indications that they had *inferred* that the event occurred, although they may not have a specific memory of it ('I was walking beside my mother in a public place, so there is a chance I got lost in a public place' and 'Probably when I was playing outside the house'). Also, because being bullied and being lost are not uncommon childhood experiences, it is possible that subjects were recalling details of true autobiographical experiences rather than details of the specific false event tested. Without additional evidence indicating that these individuals were recalling the specific event suggested, it does not appear that their memory for the target event was changed through dream interpretation.

CONCLUSIONS

The research on the construction of false events in memory is clearly in its infancy. Although it is evident that some false events can be planted in memory under some conditions, it is not yet clear what the full range of these conditions is. It does appear that plausible false events are more likely to be planted in memory than implausible false events (Pezdek *et al.*, 1997; Pezdek & Hodge, 1999) and that prior knowledge of the suggested event increases the probability that the false event will be incorporated into memory (Hyman *et al.*, 1995). It has also been demonstrated that false events are more likely to be planted with young children (5–7 years of age) than with older children (9–12 years of age), and both of these age groups are more suggestible than adults

(Pezdek & Hodge, 1999). Beyond this, we have more questions than answers because the research in this area is riddled with methodological problems.

The finding that false events are more likely to be planted with young children than with older children or adults has obvious implications for courts trying to assess the veracity of children's testimony. This concern is further complicated by that fact that Criterion Based Content Analysis (CBCA), a commonly used technique for differentiating between accounts of true and false events, is far less effective with accounts of young children than with those of older children and adults (Esplin, Boychuk, & Raskin, 1988). This is not surprising given that the general characteristics of the CBCA are the most discriminating factors (i.e. the logical structure and amount of detail in the account), and pre-schoolers' narratives are less well structured than those of older children (Fivush & Slackman, 1986; Fivush et al., 1992).

Research on the construction of false autobiographical memories is methodologically challenging, and we have several suggestions to reduce methodological problems. First, that researchers use a clear operational definition of when a false event is 'remembered'. Such a definition should be sensitive to the extent to which a subject is retrieving information about the supposed false event from their own autobiographical memory versus simply complying with the experimenter's suggestion that the false event did occur. This is an especially important consideration when testing children, given that children are more compliant with authority than are adults. The operational definition of when a false event is 'remembered' should also be sensitive to the extent to which a 'memory' for a false event is truly an enduring episodic autobiographical memory for the suggested event versus the retrieval of information from memory for a true event that the subject was reminded of by the false event. In the majority of the false memory studies reviewed here, this distinction has not been made.

The second suggestion is that if an experimenter includes, in the description of a false event, details gathered from family members regarding actual events in the subject's past, the experimenter must have some way of distinguishing in the recall protocols between whether the subject is recalling details of the suggested false event or details of similar true events.

The call to action to cognitive psychologists provided by the False Memory Syndrome Foundation continues. This is an area of research that has significant and immediate application. It is important to understand which memories are more likely to be falsely planted in which people under what conditions. This research is being used in courts of law to influence decisions regarding whether accounts of childhood abuse by adults and children are true or false. It is thus critical that research in this area adheres to the highest scientific standards.

We are grateful to the Fletcher Jones Foundation for supporting Kathy Pezdek research during the period in which this chapter was written. We thank Maryanne Garry, Ira Hyman, Elizabeth Loftus, and Guiliana Mazzoni and for their comments on this chapter.

REFERENCES

Bjorklund, D.F. (Ed.). (In press). *Research and theory in false-memory creation in children and adults.* Mahwah, NJ: Erlbaum.

Ceci, S.J., & Bruck, M. (1993). Suggestibility of the child witness: A historical review and synthesis. *Psychological Bulletin*, **113**, 403–39.

Ceci, S.J., Huffman, M.L. C., Smith, E., & Loftus, E.F. (1996). Repeatedly thinking about a non-event: Source misattributions among preschoolers. In: K. Pezdek & W. Banks (Eds), *The recovered memory/false memory debate* (pp. 225–44). San Diego, CA: Academic Press.

Ceci, S.J., Loftus, E.F., Leichtman, M.D., & Bruck, M. (1994). The possible role of source misattributions in the creation of false beliefs among preschoolers. *International Journal of Clinical & Experimental Hypnosis*, **42**, 304–20.

Conway, M.A. (Ed.). (1997). *Recovered memories and false memories.* Oxford: Oxford University Press.

Esplin, P.W., Boychuk, T., & Raskin, D.C. (1988, June). A field study of criteria-based content analysis of children's statements in sexual abuse cases. Paper presented at the NATO Advanced Study Institute on Credibility Assessment, Maratea, Italy.

Fivush, R., Kuebli, J., & Clubb, P.A. (1992). The structure of events and event representations: A developmental analysis. *Child Development*, **63**, 188–201.

Fivush, R., & Slackman, E. (1986). The acquisition and development of scripts. In: K. Nelson (Eds), *Event knowledge: Structure and function in development* (pp. 71–96). Hillsdale, NJ: Erlbaum.

Garry, M., Manning, C.G., Loftus, E.F., & Sherman, S.J. (1996). Imagination inflation: Imagining a childhood event inflates confidence that it occurred. *Psychonomic Bulletin & Review*, **3**, 208–14.

Heaps, C., & Nash, M. (1999). Individual differences in imagination inflation. *Psychonomic Bulletin & Review*, **6**, 313–18.

Huffman, M.L., Crossman, A.M., & Ceci, S.J. (1997). 'Are false memories permanent?': An investigation of the long-term effects of source misattributions. *Consciousness & Cognition*, **6**, 482–90.

Hyman, I.E., Husband, T.H., & Billings, F.J. (1995). False memories of childhood experiences. *Applied Cognitive Psychology*, **9**, 181–97.

Loftus, E.F., & Pickrell, J.E. (1995). The formation of false memories. *Psychiatric Annals*, **25**, 720–5.

Mazzoni, G.A.L., Loftus, E.F., Seitz, A., & Lynn, S.J. (1999). Changing beliefs and memories through dream interpretation. *Applied Cognitive Psychology*, **13**, 125–44.

Paddock, J.R., Joseph, A.L., Chan, F.M., Terranova, S., Manning, C., & Loftus, E.F. (1998). When guided visualization procedures may backfire: Imagination inflation and predicting individual differences in suggestibility. *Applied Cognitive Psychology*, **12**, S63–S75.

Pezdek, K., & Banks, B. (Eds). (1996). *The recovered memory/false memory debate*. San Diego, CA: Academic Press.

Pezdek, K., & Eddy, R.M. (2001). Imagination inflation: A statistical artifact of regression toward the mean. *Memory & Cognition*, **29**, 707–718.

Pezdek, K., Finger, K., & Hodge, D. (1997). Planting false childhood memories: The role of event plausibility. *Psychological Science*, **8**, 437–41.

Pezdek, K., & Hodge, D. (1999). Planting false childhood memories in children: The role of event plausibility. *Child Development*, **70**, 887–95.

Read, J.D. & Lindsay, D.S. (Eds). (1997). Recollections of trauma: Scientific evidence and clinical practice. *The NATO ASI series: Series A: Life sciences* (Vol. 291). New York: Plenum Press.

Roediger, H.L., McDermott, K.B., & Goff, L.M. (1997). Recovery of true and false memories: Paradoxical effects of repeated testing. In: M. Conway (Ed.), *Recovered memories and false memories* (pp. 118–49). Oxford: Oxford University Press.

CHAPTER 8

Children's Suggestibility Research: Implications for the Courtroom and the Forensic Interview

STEPHEN J. CECI, ANGELA M. CROSSMAN, MATTHEW H. SCULLIN,
LIVIA GILSTRAP, AND MARY LYN HUFFMAN

*Department of Human Development, Cornell University, Ithaca,
New York, USA*

There is substantial debate about what researchers can and should say when reporting in academic outlets, when testifying in court, and when consulting and training (Ceci & Hembrooke, 1998; Lyon, 1999). In the area of children's testimonial competence, there is no caveat more important than informing the court about the various reliability risks inherent in research, pointing out the qualifications that may limit the application of findings to a particular case at bar. One concern is that while research findings are applicable to samples at the aggregate level, they may not be applicable to specific individuals. Group trends are always accompanied by within-group variability. The particularities present in any specific case make individual predictions difficult.

This caveat is often not appreciated by participants in legal proceedings. The difficulty predicting an individual's behavior from the behavior of a group is frequently lost when an expert witness testifies about aggregate age-related differences in memory, suggestibility, and

Children's Testimony. Edited by H.L. Westcott, G.M. Davies, and R.H.C. Bull.
© 2002 John Wiley & Sons, Ltd.

testimonial competence; for example, in this chapter we will review research that has established that, under the following conditions, young children *can* be suggestible:

(a) when they experience repeated erroneous suggestions and hold pre-existing stereotypes (Leichtman & Ceci, 1995);
(b) when they are repeatedly asked to visualize fictitious events (Ceci, Loftus, Leichtman, & Bruck, 1994);
(c) when they are asked about personal events that happened a substantial period of time ago and there has been no 'refresher' in the interim (Bruck, Ceci, Francoeur, & Barr, 1995a);
(d) when they are suggestively asked to use anatomical dolls to re-enact an alleged event (Bruck, Ceci, Francoeur, & Renick, 1995b); and
(e) when they are questioned by a biased interviewer who pursues a hypothesis single-mindedly (White, Leichtman, & Ceci, 1997).

We emphasize the word 'can' because these same studies also demonstrate that not all children succumb to the baleful effects of these conditions; some are quite resistant to suggestive interviews, and, as yet, we have not been successful at identifying who these children are, at least not with any confidence. This can be problematic for courts, given their interest in a particular child as opposed to children in general.

Hence, not all children are equally vulnerable to suggestive influence, and we have no sure method of knowing whether the children involved in a given case are the rule or the exception. Researchers are capable of providing courts with useful information *if* they are allowed to report *all* of what they have learned, including the shortcomings, exceptions, ecological constraints, and potential confounds of their findings. But the exigencies inherent in an adversarial legal system sometimes make such scholarly discourse unlikely.

Even when research cannot provide the courts with concrete predictions about individual children, however, findings about children's aggregate behavior can still be useful for frontline interviewers. Much of this chapter focuses on the relationship between research on children's memory and its application to forensic interviews with children. We discuss strengths and weaknesses of children's memories, counterintuitive findings in the current research, and individual differences underpinning children's suggestibility. Each section presents a practical question, discusses some relevant research, and the current 'best answers.'

QUESTION: WHAT HAPPENS WHEN CHILDREN ARE QUESTIONED SUGGESTIVELY AND ENCOURAGED TO FORM A STEREOTYPE ABOUT SOMEONE?

One highly suggestive interviewing procedure is repeated interviews, particularly when they are suggestive and accompanied by a stereotype induction (Ceci & Bruck, 1995). This is especially important, given the likelihood that during some investigations child witnesses may be repeatedly interviewed over extended periods of time by adults who inadvertently inculcate a negative stereotype about theof a defendant. It was against this backdrop that Leichtman and Ceci (1995) designed a situation in which a child witness was repeatedly, suggestively interviewed, with or without an accompanying stereotype.

In their study, a stranger named Sam Stone visited three- to six-year-olds. Later, they were asked to describe his visit on four separate occasions over a 10-week period. Children in the control condition received no stereotyping information about Sam Stone prior to his visit, and during the four subsequent interviews they were asked only non-suggestive questions about what Sam Stone had done during his visit. One month later, children were interviewed a fifth time by a new interviewer who asked about two 'non-events' which involved Sam Stone doing something to a teddy bear and a book. In reality, he never touched either item.

Only 10% of the control group of the three- to four-year-olds, in response to the question about the non-events, 'Did Sam Stone do anything to a book or a teddy bear?' claimed Sam Stone did anything to a teddy bear or book. And when asked if they actually *saw* these misdeeds, only 5% claimed they did. Finally, when gently challenged ('You didn't really see him do anything to the book/the teddy bear, did you?'), only 2.5% of these children insisted that the fictitious misdeeds had occurred. None of the five- to six-year-old children claimed that they saw Sam Stone do anything with either object. *Thus, when not misled or supplied with negative stereotypes, even the youngest children were quite accurate in their reports, despite being subjected to repeated interviews.*

Another group of children received stereotypical information about Sam Stone's prior to his visit. They were told 12 stories that depicted Sam Stone as a very clumsy person.

These children were also interviewed four times over a 10-week period. However, each interview contained erroneous suggestions, such as 'When Sam Stone ripped that book, was he being silly or was he angry?' During the fifth interview (which was identical to the interview of the control group), 46% of the youngest and 30% of the oldest pre-schoolers spontaneously reported that Sam Stone had committed one or both misdeeds. In response to specific questions, 72% of the youngest children claimed that Sam Stone did one of the misdeeds and 44% stated they actually saw him do these things, while 21% continued to insist that he did them, despite challenges. Although they were more accurate, 11% of older pre-schoolers also insisted they saw Sam Stone perform the misdeeds.

Obviously, then, even the youngest children are capable of accurately reporting if they are allowed to deliver their reports without misdirection from adult interviewers. However, when faced with both suggestive questioning and a negative stereotype about an individual, pre-schoolers are more susceptible to misleading information. Importantly, several large-scale studies show that a sizable proportion of front-line interviewers in Israel and the United States engage in highly problematic behaviors with children (Lamb *et al.*, 1996).

QUESTION: WHAT HAPPENS WHEN CHILDREN ARE ASKED TO VISUALIZE IMAGINARY EVENTS?

The conventional wisdom has been that, while children may be suggestible about other people's actions, their own personal experiences may be too salient to be susceptible to suggestion. In addition, there has been resistance to the proposition that children will believe things that they had only been asked to imagine (e.g. by a therapist who asked the child to engage in pretense). To test these assumptions, Ceci, Huffman, Smith, and Loftus (1994) asked pre-schoolers to think about events repeatedly. Events were both actual (i.e. an accident that resulted in stitches) and fictitious (i.e. getting a finger caught in a mousetrap and having to go to hospital to have the mousetrap removed).

For 10 consecutive weeks, pre-schoolers were asked if each of the real and fictitious events had ever happened to them (e.g. 'Think real hard, and tell me if this ever happened to you: Can you remember going to the hospital with the mousetrap on your finger?')

After 10 weeks of thinking about both real and fictitious personal experiences, 58% of the children produced false accounts of one or more of the fictitious events, with 25% producing false accounts of the majority of the false events. Thus, the mere act of repeatedly imagining participation in an event caused these pre-schoolers to falsely report that they had engaged in the fictitious events.

Ceci, Loftus *et al.* (1994) found that children were shown to have the highest false assent rates to neutral, non-participant events (an increase from 42% to 68% mean assent rate between the 1st and 11th interviews) and the lowest to negative events (from 13% to 30%). Assent rates to imagined positive and neutral participant events fell in the middle. This supports the claim that negative events are more resistant to false suggestions than neutral events. However, it also shows that 'although abusive events may be more resistant to suggestive interviewing methods than other types of events, [they] are by no means immune to the deleterious effects of suggestive interviewing techniques' (Ceci, Loftus et al., 1994, p. 316). (In subsequent research Bruck and her colleagues (Ref.) found that negative events were no less likely to be contaminated by suggestive interviewing than neutral or positive events.)

Huffman, Crossman, and Ceci (1996) decided to follow up the children in the above study two years later, to see whether they recalled their former reports. They found that, although they remembered 91% of the true events, they only assented to 13% of the false events (as opposed to 34% found originally by Ceci, Huffman et al., 1994). Their high rate of remembering true events makes it unlikely that their 'recanting' of false events was due to forgetting. In combination with previous research, this finding raises important, yet unanswered questions about the fate of children's false beliefs and the potential social ramifications of their existence (see Kathy Pezdek & Tiffany Hinz, Chapter 7 in this book).

QUESTION: ARE CHILDREN SUGGESTIBLE ABOUT HIGHLY SALIENT EVENTS SUCH AS BODILY TOUCHING?

The studies above detailed ways in which children can seemingly come to believe they witnessed events that never occurred. However, they were questioned about minor, peripheral events that bore no resemblance to sexual abuse (Goodman, Aman, & Hirschman, 1987).

To examine memory for a more forensically relevant situation, Bruck et al. (1995a) examined children's memories for a visit to a pediatrician. We looked at the effects of suggestions on children's memories for an inoculation, an event that involves some degree of stress as well as pain and discomfort. One might expect children's memories for such a painful event to be resistant to suggestions. They were not, however.

The study was conducted in two phases. In the first phase, children were given a routine examination by their pediatrician and then led to an 'inoculation room' where an assistant discussed a poster on the wall. Five minutes later, the pediatrician entered the room and administered an oral polio vaccine and a DPT (diphtheria, pertussis, tetanus) shot. The assistant remained present and coded the child's level of distress and how long it took the child to stop crying. The child was then taken to another room by the assistant and randomly assigned to one of three feedback conditions in which the child was told how s/he had acted while receiving the inoculation.

Children in the pain-denying group were told that the inoculation did not seem to hurt them (no-hurt condition). Other children were given pain-affirming feedback and told that the inoculation seemed to hurt them (hurt condition). The final group was simply told that the inoculation was over (neutral condition).

After giving the child feedback, the assistant gave the child a treat sweet and read a story about a child who gets injured after falling from a tree. The mother in the story gave the fictional child the same feedback that the child subject had received from the research assistant. One week later, a second assistant interviewed the children in their homes, and it was found that the children were not rendered less accurate by suggestive feedback given immediately following the event.

In the second phase of the study, children were suggestively interviewed three additional times approximately one year later. They were repeatedly given either 'no hurt' feedback (i.e. told that they had been brave and had not cried at the time of the inoculation) or 'neutral' feedback (i.e. not told how they acted). For ethical reasons, the pain-affirming 'hurt' condition was discontinued to avoid inducing in the children a phobia of doctors. During a fourth interview, the children were again asked to rate how much the shot had hurt and how much they cried. This time there were large suggestibility effects, with children in the 'no hurt' condition reporting significantly less hurt and crying than children who were not given feedback.

These findings are at odds with the conventional wisdom regarding children's resistance to suggestion about such personally salient events. It is important to note, however, that, even when given misleading information, the children were fairly accurate during initial questioning one week after the inoculation. Unfortunately, it is very common in many countries for child witnesses to be questioned repeatedly over extended periods of time and our results indicate that caution is necessary to avoid biasing children's memories for an event over the course of multiple interviews.

QUESTION: DO ANATOMICALLY CORRECT DOLLS HELP CHILDREN REPORT ABOUT ABUSE?

Investigations of child sexual abuse often focus on where and in what manner a child was touched. However, it is commonly assumed that children may either be embarrassed about events that involve sexual bodily touching or lack the vocabulary for describing what happened to them, especially when the touching may have involved the anal or genital area.

In order to facilitate discussion with young children about these issues, many investigators and clinicians make use of anatomically detailed dolls. The belief is that the use of the dolls with young children, along with skillfully worded interview questions, can bring about more accurate recollections about personally experienced bodily events (Boat & Everson, 1993). This is problematic because if non-abused children can be led to use the dolls in a manner suggesting physical or sexual abuse then use of dolls in the interviewing process could cause investigators to mistakenly conclude that abuse had occurred when it had not. In fact, recent empirical research on the use of the dolls during the questioning of young children has failed to demonstrate the dolls' benefits as interview aids (Bruck *et al.*, 1995b).

In order to approach this issue in an ethically acceptable manner, visits by 40 three-year-old children for a routine pediatric examination were studied. The children were assigned to either a genital-examination condition, in which they received a genital examination before being interviewed, or to a no-genital-examination condition, in which they received a general physical examination before their interview and their genital examination after the interview.

Five minutes after the initial pediatric examination, in an interview with the children's mothers present, children were asked to describe where the doctor touched them. They were then presented with anatomical dolls and asked to tell and demonstrate where the pediatrician had touched them.

Consistent with research that has found that very young children have difficulty understanding that scale models can symbolically represent real objects (DeLoache & Marzolf, 1995), three-year-olds were generally confused by questions about their bodies and about symbolically representing them with anatomical dolls. Approximately 50% of the children who *were* touched in the genital region did not indicate that they were touched there when questioned either with or without dolls (errors of omission). However, a sizable number of children in both groups made errors of commission when questioned with the dolls. In all, nearly 60% of the total sample indicated genital insertions, used the props in a sexualized manner, or committed other aggressive acts that would otherwise be cause for concern. This is contrary to a commonly held belief that children who have not been sexually touched will not indicate sexual events with dolls (Goodman & Aman, 1990). In recent research, Bruck and her colleagues replicated this finding with four-year-olds (Bruck, Ceci, and & Francoeur, in press).

In sum, the studies discussed thus far have shown that, contrary to widely held public opinion, young children can have difficulty accurately reporting events that involve their bodies, when questioned either with or without anatomically correct dolls. Hence, on the basis of this research, it would seem best not to use anatomical dolls when interviewing three- and four-year-olds unless the dolls' incremental validity as a forensic tool can be demonstrated and unless it can be established that the dolls were not used suggestively as in the Bruck *et al.* studies. Among children five and older, the use of anatomical dolls appears to be less problematic and results in fewer false reports than among younger children (Goodman, Quas, Batterman-Faunce, Riddlesberger, & Kuhn, 1997).

QUESTION: DO INTERVIEWERS' PRECONCEPTIONS ALTER CHILDREN'S REPORTS?

In the experiments discussed thus far, interviewers intentionally asked questions that they knew were misleading. However, in many forensic interviews, the interviewer suspects that some event has happened and probes for information about that event, often using misleading questions without realizing. One of the most prevalent findings in the study of human reasoning is that people have a 'confirmation bias'. They pay more attention to favored hypotheses, preferentially treat evidence supporting existing beliefs, look primarily for positive cases, overweight confirmatory instances, and generally see what they are looking for in the data (Nickerson, 1998).

White *et al.* (1997) decided to simulate a forensic situation by leading an experienced interviewer to form inaccurate hypotheses about an event and then asking this interviewer to question child witnesses about the event.

Children aged three to six years played a game of Simon Says and were interviewed one month later. The interviewer, a trained social worker, received a one-page sheet containing events that *might* have occurred during the game. This sheet contained both factual and erroneous information; for example, if child *A* had touched child *B*'s nose and patted her own head, the interviewer might have been told that child *A* had touched child *B*'s toe (inaccurate) and patted her own head (accurate). We instructed the interviewer to determine what the child was still able to remember about the event. After soliciting a child's free recall, the interviewer could use any strategies she felt prudent to elicit the most factually accurate recall.

When accurately informed, the interviewer elicited the correct information from the children nearly 100% of the time. However, when misinformed the interviewer was misinformed, 34% of the three- to four-year-olds and 18% of the five- to six-year olds corroborated one or more of the false events. As the interview progressed, children who had accommodated false information became more credible in their affect and speech patterns when describing the false event.

One month later, we gave the first interviewer's notes to a second interviewer and asked her to re-interview the children. Just as the first interviewer had used our information to form biases about the event, the second interviewer imitated the biases of the first. Not only did the children's confidence levels about the false claims increase but the number of false events that they accepted as true also increased. We should note that our findings were based on only two interviews, while in real forensic situations children may be repeatedly interviewed. Thus, we find that another important source of potential variability in children's susceptibility to suggestion is the bias of the adult interviewing the child.

QUESTION: ARE SOME CHILDREN MORE SUGGESTIBLE THAN OTHERS?

Although the previously cited research has established a developmental pattern in the suggestibility of pre-school children on the aggregate level, researchers have begun examining the cognitive and social differences that may lead some individuals to be highly suggestible and other individuals to be highly resistant to suggestions (Bruck, Ceci, & Melnyk, 1997).

Intelligence

It has long been established that adults with low intelligence are more suggestible than others (Gudjonsson, 1992). Among children, the relationship between suggestibility and IQ has been relatively little studied. Recent results have been mixed, with some studies finding no relationship between IQ and suggestibility (Bruck et al., 1995b), while others studies have found the expected negative relationship between intelligence and suggestibility (Endres, Poggenpohl, & Erben, 1999). There is not enough research to draw firm conclusions, one surmise is that the relationship is non-linear; very low-IQ children may indeed be more suggestible than average and above average IQ children, who may not differ from each other.

Memory

There is a fairly strong body of evidence that better memory is linked to diminished suggestibility. In a study that examined the effect of increasing the trace strength of a memory by repeating the presentation of a stimulus, Pezdek and Roe (1995) found that when four- to ten-year-olds viewed a slide sequence twice (i.e. increased memory strength), they were more resistant to misinformation about the slides. In some studies discussed earlier where children were interviewed about their behavior during an inoculation both a week after and a year after the event, it was easier to mislead the children about their pain after the one-year interval (Bruck *et al.*, 1995a), as the original memory was weakened by the passage of time.

Knowledge Base

Research has found that the more children know about a topic, the more resistant to suggestion they are likely to be if the suggestions are at odds with their knowledge. When three- to ten-year olds were interviewed one to three weeks after undergoing a voiding cysto-urethrogram (VCUG), the accuracy of children's reports was positively related to children's memory accuracy (Goodman *et al.*, 1997). However, when suggestions are congruent with their knowledge, their ability to resist suggestions may be reduced, as discussed earlier in the Sam Stone study (Leichtman & Ceci, 1995).

Source Monitoring

Confusions about the sources of a memory have been linked to suggestibility in a number of studies (see Stephen Lindsay, Chapter 6 in this book). As discussed earlier, when children were repeatedly asked to 'think really hard' about an event that never took place such as getting a finger caught in a mousetrap, over time many of them produced detailed accounts about these imaginary (Ceci, Loftus *et al.* 1994).

Theory of Mind

Theory of mind (TOM) refers to ability to understand that the process of creating mental representations is subjective and related to the information available to a person. TOM undergoes a striking period of development between the ages of three and five. Welch-Ross, Diecidue, and Miller (1997) noted similarities between young children's poor performances on TOM tasks and the apparent 'overwriting' effect that occurs when some children are given misleading information. Differences in children's ability to handle conflicting mental representations (i.e. comprehend that another person's understanding of reality may differ from their own depending upon the information available to that person) accounted for a significant proportion of the differences in misinformation acceptance in three- to five-year-old children, even when memory for the event and age differences were taken into consideration.

Temperament

While there has been a fair amount of speculation about temperamental factors that may be related to suggestibility, little research has been done in this area. Kagan has found that high reactive, easily irritable children often become behaviorally inhibited 'shy' young children who are easily intimidated by adults (Schacter, Kagan, & Leichtman, 1995). Schacter *et al.* (1995) speculated that the high reactive-inhibited children might be more likely to accept suggestions than low reactive-uninhibited children, although research has not tested this claim yet.

Compliance, Self-Esteem, and Overall Functioning

While a number of studies have been conducted with adults linking suggestibility to compliance and self-esteem, few such studies have been conducted with children. It is well established that children try to answer questions posed to them by adult authority figures even when asked a nonsensical question like 'Is red heavier than yellow?' (Hughes & Grieve, 1980; but see Amanda Waterman & Mark Blades, Chapter 10 in this book). In a study analyzing self-confidence and suggestibility in five- to six-year olds and ten- to eleven-year olds, Vrij and Bush (1998) found that self confident children incorrectly answered a substantially lower percentage of misleading questions.

Bruck *et al.* (1997) pointed out that it may be difficult to disentangle the effects of compliance, self-esteem, temperament, and overall level of adjustment because they may be highly intercorrelated and may have different effects on encoding, storage, and retrieval. There may also be age effects in these measures (Eisen, Goodman, & Qin, 1995).

SOME GENERAL GUIDELINES FOR FORENSIC INTERVIEWERS

There is no group of signs or symptoms that unambiguously diagnose sexual abuse, and there is a good deal of overlap in the behavior of children who have been sexually abused with those who have not, with about a third of abused children showing no symptoms (Kendall-Tackett, Williams, & Finkelhor, 1993). Our studies have shown that investigators must conduct fact-finding interviews in a careful, non-biased manner to avoid pressuring children to behave in a manner consistent with a preconceived profile of an abused child.

The amount of detail and expressiveness displayed by a child when telling a narrative may enhance the child's believability, even though the account may have resulted from suggestions. As an illustration, we showed videotapes of children who participated in the Sam Stone study to hundreds of professionals who specialize in interviewing children. They performed no better than chance at divining which children were providing accurate accounts of what happened when Sam Stone visited the classroom (Leichtman & Ceci, 1995). Nonetheless, children can provide highly accurate information when they are interviewed in a proper manner.

The use of one or more suggestive techniques in a single interview may not cause irreparable harm to a child's accuracy, especially if they are done by an unbiased interviewer. However, when these techniques are used repeatedly over a lengthy period of time they can have detrimental effects on a child's memory. Bear in mind also that there are substantial age differences in suggestibility, with pre-schoolers generally being more suggestible than older children. Pre-schoolers are more likely to make mistakes about events involving actions upon their own bodies and are less likely to understand what is being asked for when called upon to represent their bodies with anatomical dolls.

It is important for therapists working with child witnesses to avoid techniques, such as guided imagery and play enactments, where a child is asked to visualize past events or imagine certain scenarios. If a defendant is innocent, these techniques could promote and reinforce false allegations. If a defendant is guilty, these techniques can be challenged by the defense and used to discredit the child's testimony. Ideally, therapy should consist of helping the child develop everyday coping strategies which will not be challenged by the defendant's attorney lawyer as being a source of false memories (see Kathy Pezdek & Tiffany Hinz, Chapter 7 in this book), while helping the child obtain a positive mental-health outcome.

With knowledge comes responsibility. Since our studies have helped illuminate some of the ways in which children can be affected by suggestion, we hope that they will aid those responsible for protecting the welfare of children by helping ensure children's testimony is as accurate and as fact based as possible.

REFERENCES

Boat, B.W., & Everson, M.D. (1993). The use of anatomical dolls in sexual abuse evaluations: Current research and practice. In: G.S. Goodman & B.L. Bottoms (Eds), *Child victims, child witnesses* (pp. 47–69). Chicago: University of Chicago Press.

Bruck, M., Ceci, S.J., & Francoeur, E. (in press). Children's use of anatomically detailed dolls to report on genital touching in a medical examination: Developmental and gender comparisons. *Journal of Experimental Psychology: Applied.*

Bruck, M., Ceci, S.J., Francoeur, E., & Barr, R.J. (1995a). 'I hardly cried when I got my shot!' Influencing children's reports about a visit to their pediatrician. *Child Development,* **66**, 193–208.

Bruck, M., Ceci, S.J., Francoeur, E., & Renick, A. (1995b). Anatomically detailed dolls do not facilitate preschoolers' reports of a pediatric examination involving genital touching. *Journal of Experimental Psychology: Applied,* **1**, 95–109.

Bruck, M., Ceci, S.J., & Melnyk, L. (1997). External and internal sources of variation in the creation of false reports in children. *Learning and Individual Differences,* **9**, 289–316.

Ceci, S.J., & Bruck, M. (1995) *Jeopardy in the courtroom: A scientific analysis of children's testimony.* Washington, DC: American Psychological Association.

Ceci, S.J., & Hembrooke, H. (1998). *Expert witnesses in child abuse cases.* Washington, DC: American Psychological Association.

Ceci, S.J., Huffman, M.L.C., Smith, E., & Loftus, E. (1994). Repeatedly thinking about a non-event: Source misattributions among preschoolers. *Consciousness and Cognition,* **3**, 388–407.

Ceci, S.J., Loftus, E.F., Leichtman, M.D., & Bruck, M. (1994). The possible role of source misattributions in the creation of false beliefs among preschoolers. *International Journal of Clinical and Experimental Hypnosis,* **42**, 304–20.

DeLoache, J.S., & Marzolf, D.P. (1995). The use of dolls to interview young children: Issues of symbolic representation. *Journal of Experimental Child Psychology,* **60**, 155–73.

Eisen, M. L., Goodman, G. S., & Qin, J. (1995, August). The impact of dissociation, trauma, and stress arousal on memory and suggestibility in the assessment of abused and neglected children. Paper presented at the Meeting of the American Psychological Association, New York, NY.

Endres, J., Poggenpohl, C., & Erben, C. (1999). Repetitions, warnings, and video: Cognitive and motivational components in children's suggestibility. *Legal and Criminological Psychology,* **4**, 129–46.

Goodman, G.S., & Aman, C. (1990). Children's use of anatomically detailed dolls to recount an event. *Child Development,* **61**, 1859–71.

Goodman, G.S., Aman, C., & Hirschman, J. E. (1987). Child sexual and physical abuse: Children's testimony. In: S.J. Ceci, M.P. Toglia, & D.F. Ross (Eds), *Children's eyewitness memory* (pp. 1–23). New York: Springer-Verlag.

Goodman, G.S., Quas, J.A., Batterman-Faunce, J.M., Riddlesberger, M.M., & Kuhn, G. (1997). Children's reactions to and memory for a stressful event: Influences of age, anatomical dolls, knowledge, and parental attachment. *Applied Developmental Science,* **1**, 54–75.

Gudjonsson, G.H. (1992). *The psychology of interrogations, confessions and testimony.* Chichester, UK: Wiley.

Huffman, M.L.C., Crossman, A.M., & Ceci, S.J. (1996). *An investigation of the long-term effects of source misattribution error: Are false memories permanent?* Presentation at the Biennial Meeting of the American Psychology-Law Society, Hilton Head, SC.

Hughes, M., & Grieve, R. (1980). On asking children bizarre questions. *First Language*, 1, 149–60.

Kendall-Tackett, K.A., Williams, L.M., & Finkelhor, D. (1993). Impact of sexual abuse on children: A review and synthesis of recent empirical studies. *Psychological Bulletin*, 113, 164–80.

Lamb, M.E., Hershkowitz, I., Sternberg, K.J., Esplin, P.W., Hovav, M., Manor, T., & Yudilevitch, L. (1996). Effects of investigative utterance types on Israeli children's responses. *International Journal of Behavioral Development*, 19, 627–37.

Leichtman, M.D., & Ceci, S.J. (1995). The effect of stereotypes and suggestions on preschoolers' reports. *Developmental Psychology*, 31, 568–96.

Lyon, T.D. (1999). The new wave in children's suggestibility research: A critique. *Cornell Law Review*, 84, 1004.

Nickerson, R.S. (1998). Confirmation bias: A ubiquitous phenomenon in many guises. *Review of General Psychology*, 2, 175–220.

Pezdek, K., & Roe, C. (1995). The effect of memory trace strength on suggestibility. *Journal of Experimental Child Psychology*, 60, 116–28.

Schacter, D.S., Kagan, J., & Leichtman, M.D. (1995) True and false memories in children and adult: A cognitive neuroscience perspective. *Psychology, Public Policy, and Law*, 1, 411–28.

Vrij, A., & Bush, N. (1998, April). Differences in suggestibility between 5–6 and 10–11 year olds: A matter of differences in self confidence? Paper presented at the Meeting of the American Psychology-Law Society, Redondo Beach, CA.

Welch-Ross, M.K., Diecidue, K., & Miller, S.A. (1997). Young children's understanding of conflicting mental representation predicts suggestibility. *Developmental Psychology*, 33, 43–53.

White, T.L., Leichtman, M.D. and Ceci, S.J. (1997). The good, the bad, and the ugly: Accuracy, inaccuracy, and elaboration in preschoolers' reports about a past event. *Applied Cognitive Psychology*, 11, S37–S54.

CHAPTER 9

The Effects of Forensic Interview Practices on the Quality of Information Provided by Alleged Victims of Child Abuse

MICHAEL E. LAMB,* YAEL ORBACH,* KATHLEEN J. STERNBERG,*
PHILLIP W. ESPLIN,† AND IRIT HERSHKOWITZ‡

* National Institute of Child Health and Human Development, Bethesda,
Maryland, USA
† Private Practitioner, Phoenix, Arizona, USA
‡ University of Haifa, Israel

Sex crimes against children have been alleged with alarming frequency in the last two decades (American Association for Protecting Children, 1986; National Society for the Prevention of Cruelty to Children, 1989; Sedlak & Broadhurst, 1996). Unfortunately, such crimes are extremely difficult to investigate because the evidence often consists only of the victims' and suspects' accounts of the alleged events, and this has increased the importance of obtaining and evaluating information provided by children. Recognizing this, many researchers have studied the capacity of young children to provide reliable and valid information about their experiences, with a noteworthy flood of books and papers published in the last decade (Ceci & Bruck, 1995; Doris, 1991; Lamb, Sternberg, & Esplin, 1998; Lamb, Sternberg, Orbach, Hershkowitz, &

Children's Testimony. Edited by H.L. Westcott, G.M. Davies, and R.H.C. Bull.
© 2002 John Wiley & Sons, Ltd.

Esplin, 1999; McGough, 1994; Memon & Bull, 1999; Milne & Bull, 1999; Poole & Lamb, 1998; Spencer & Flin, 1993). As summarized in this chapter, our own research has been designed to explore and describe the practices of forensic investigators in the field and to evaluate attempts to improve the quality of interviewing.

Because of the way children have been socialized to communicate with adults, children rarely 'volunteer' detailed and complete accounts of abusive events. Interviewers face the task of eliciting additional information about sexual events, the temporal and spatial context in which they occurred, and the people involved. In the first section of the chapter, we summarize descriptive research on the actual practices of forensic interviewers and contrast these practices with widespread professional and expert recommendations. In the second section, we briefly review the empirical and experimental rationale for these recommendations before showing, in the final section, how changes in the behavior and practices of interviewers can indeed affect the quality of information obtained from alleged victims.

RESEARCH ON INVESTIGATIVE INTERVIEWS

Our research in this area has been conducted using verbatim transcriptions of forensic interviews conducted in Israel, the United States, the United Kingdom, and Sweden by social workers, sheriffs or police officers. For purposes of the analyses summarized here, we focused on the portion of each interview concerned with substantive issues by having coders review the transcripts, counting the number of words in each utterance and tabulating the number of new details conveyed by the child. By definition, details involve the identification and description of individuals, objects, events, or actions relevant to the alleged incident. Coders also categorized each interviewer utterance, defined as 'turns' in the discourse. In this chapter, we focus on the five types of utterances that consistently comprise around 90% of interviewer utterances:

1. *Facilitators* like 'OK', restatements of the child's previous utterance, and non-suggestive words of encouragement that are designed to prompt continuation of the child's narrative.
2. *Invitations* (using questions, statements, or imperatives) for an open-ended response from the child. Such utterances do not delimit the child's focus except in the most general way (e.g. 'And then what happened?')
3. *Directive utterances* focus the child's attention on details or aspects

of the event that the child mentioned previously. Most of these are WH-questions (e.g. 'What colour was that shirt?').

4. *Option-posing utterances* which focus the child's attention on aspects of the event that the child had not previously mentioned (e.g. 'Did you see a knife?' or 'Were his clothes on or off?'). These were called 'leading' in some of our earlier reports, but have been re-labelled to avoid confusion with those questions described as leading by other professionals.

5. *Suggestive utterances* stated in such a way that the interviewer strongly communicates what response is expected or assumes details that have not been revealed by the child. Most of these utterances would be called leading by lawyers, jurists, and researchers.

Directive, option-posing, and suggestive utterances are sometimes grouped as focused questions, though they lie along a continuum of risk, varying with respect to the degree of suggestive influence they exert on children's responses.

When used in forensic interviews, invitations consistently yield responses that are three to four times longer and three times richer in relevant details than responses to focused interviewer utterances (Lamb, Hershkowitz, Sternberg, Boat, & Everson, 1996; Lamb, Hershkowitz, Sternberg, Esplin *et al.*, 1996; Sternberg, Lamb, Hershkowitz *et al.*, 1996). The superiority of open-ended utterances is apparent regardless of the age of the child being interviewed, but unfortunately focused utterances are much more common in the field than open-ended questions; for example, in the field sites we studied initially around 80% of the interviewer utterances were focused whereas only 6% or fewer were invitations, and the over-reliance on focused questions is evident regardless of the children's age, the nature of the offenses, the professional background of the interviewers, or the utilization of props and tools like anatomical dolls (Craig, Sheibe, Kircher, Raskin, & Dodd, 1999; Davies, Westcott & Horan, 2000; Lamb, Hershkowitz, Sternberg, Boat *et al.*, 1996; Lamb, Hershkowitz, Sternberg, Esplin *et al.*, 1996; Sternberg *et al.*, 1996; Walker & Hunt, 1998).

Despite warnings concerning the risks of asking option-posing and suggestive questions, analyses of investigative interviews conducted at sites in the USA, UK, Sweden, and Israel all reveal that over half of the information is typically elicited from children using focused questions (Aldridge & Cameron, 1999; Cederborg, Orbach, Sternberg, & Lamb, 2000; Craig, Sheibe, Kircher, Raskin, & Dodd, 1999; Davies & Wilson, 1997; Davies *et al.*, 2000; Lamb, Hershkowitz, Sternberg, Boat *et al.*, 1996; Lamb, Hershkowitz, Sternberg, Esplin *et al.*, 1996;

Lamb, Sternberg, & Esplin, 2000; Sternberg *et al.*, 1996; Walker & Hunt, 1998; Warren, Woodall, Hunt, & Perry, 1996). Davies and Wilson (1997) described problems with interviews conducted in the UK following implementation of the *Memorandum of Good Practice* (1992). In 28% of the cases they reviewed, interviewers did not attempt to elicit free-narrative responses from children, and, in an additional 43% of the cases, interviewers allowed less than two minutes to obtain information from free-recall. The interviewers also asked many option-posing questions.

These descriptive data are noteworthy because they reveal wide-spread similarities across countries and cultures in forensic interview practices. Furthermore, the documented practices are at considerable variance with the practices recommended by experts and professional advisory groups from around the world (American Professional Society on the Abuse of Children [APSAC], 1997; Bull, 1995, 1996; Fisher & Geiselman, 1992; Jones, 1992; Lamb *et al.*, 1998; Lamb, Sternberg, Orbach *et al.*, 1999; *Memorandum of Good Practice*, 1992; Poole & Lamb, 1998; Raskin & Esplin, 1991; Sattler, 1998). As Poole and Lamb (1998) pointed out, these books and papers reveal a substantial degree of consensus regarding the ways in which investigative interviews should be conducted. Clearly, it is possible to obtain valuable information from children, but doing so requires careful investigative procedures as well as a realistic awareness of their capacities and tendencies. In particular, experts recommend that questions and statements be worded carefully, with due consideration for the child's age and communicative abilities. As much information as possible should be obtained using open-ended invitations. When more focused questions, especially option-posing questions, are necessary, they should be used as sparingly as possible, and only after open-ended prompts have been exhausted. Suggestive and coercive practices should be avoided completely. In the next section, we review the empirical evidence supporting these recommendations.

FACTORS INFLUENCING CHILDREN'S INFORMATIVENESS

Language and Communicative Abilities

Few interviewers seem to recognize and understand the gradual pace of communicative development and it is thus common for interviewers to misunderstand children's speech and to overestimate their linguistic capacities. Young children—especially pre-schoolers—frequently use words before they know their conventional adult meaning, use words that they do not understand at all, and misunderstand some apparently simple concepts, such as 'any', 'some', 'touch', 'yesterday', and 'before' (Walker, 1999). In addition, the accuracy of children's accounts is greatly influenced by the linguistic style and the complexity of the language addressed to them by investigators. A particularly widespread problem involves compound questions, responses to which are inherently uninterpretable (Walker & Hunt, 1998).

Children's accounts of abusive experiences are also influenced by social or pragmatic aspects of communication. Young witnesses are typically unaware of the amount and type of information needed, so interviewers need to communicate their needs and expectations clearly, motivating children to provide as much information as they can. Both Saywitz, Snyder, and Nathanson (1999) and Sternberg *et al.* (1997) have shown that young witnesses can be trained to provide detailed narrative responses before starting to discuss the substantive issues under investigation. In addition, open-ended prompts such as 'Tell me everything about that' encourage children to provide full accounts of their experiences.

Memory

Experimental research in the last two decades makes clear that the distinction between recall and recognition testing is crucial (Dale, Loftus, & Rathbun, 1978; Dent, 1986; Dent & Stephenson, 1979; Goodman & Aman, 1990; Goodman, Hirschman, Hepps, & Rudy, 1991; Hutcheson, Baxter, Telfer, & Warden, 1995; Oates & Shrimpton, 1991; Peterson & Bell, 1996). If adults and children are asked to describe events from free recall ('Tell me everything you remember ...'), their accounts may be incomplete and sketchy, but are more likely to be accurate. If prompted for more details using open-ended prompts like 'Tell me more about that', children often recall additional details. If interviewers prompt with focused questions—especially option-posing questions such as 'Did he touch you with his private?'—however, they shift from recall to recognition testing, and the probability of error rises dramatically. Open-ended prompts encourage respondents to provide as much relevant information as they 'remember', whereas focused questions focus children on domains of interest to investigators and exert greater pressure to respond, whether or not the children are sure of the response. Recognition probes are also more likely to elicit erroneous responses in eyewitness contexts because of response biases and the false recognition of details mentioned in previous interviews or inferred from the gist of the experienced events (Brainerd & Reyna,

1996). Effective interviewers must thus maximize the opportunities for recall by offering open-ended prompts so as to minimize the risk of eliciting erroneous information. Recall memories are not always accurate, of course, especially when the events occurred long before the interview or there have been opportunities for either pre- or post-event contamination (Leichtman & Ceci, 1995; Poole & Lindsay, 1995, 1996; Poole & White, 1993), but accounts based on recall memory are much more likely to be accurate than those elicited using recognition cues or prompts, regardless of the informant's age. Children clearly *can* remember incidents they have experienced, but a variety of factors influence the quality of information provided. Most importantly, the interviewer's ability to *elicit* information and the child's willingness and ability to *express* it may obscure the child's ability to *remember* it.

Suggestibility

Whatever the vagaries and strengths of children's memories, the competency of child witnesses is often doubted on the grounds that children are too susceptible to influence by misleading questions or other sources of misinformation. Most researchers agree that the manner in which children are questioned can have profound implications for what is 'remembered', and this increases the importance of careful interviewing (Lamb *et al.*, 1998; Lamb, Sternberg, Orbach *et al.*, 1999; Poole & Lamb, 1998). Suggestive interviewing is most likely to be influential when the memory is not rich or recent, when the content was imagined rather than experienced, when the questions themselves are so complicated that the witness is confused, and when the interviewer appears to have such authority or status that the witness feels compelled to accept his or her implied construction of the events. Whatever the processes involved, there is general agreement that preschoolers are more susceptible to suggestion than older children and adults (Ceci & Bruck, 1993). In a series of studies, Goodman and her colleagues (Goodman & Aman, 1990; Goodman, Bottoms, Schwartz-Kenney, & Rudy, 1991; Goodman, Wilson, Hazan, & Reed, 1989) showed that three- to four-year-olds falsely assented to 'abuse-related' questions such as 'Did he keep his clothes on?' and 'He took your clothes off, didn't he?' between 20% and 35% of the time, even when the questions implied actions quite different from those that were witnessed or experienced. Levels of acquiescence to suggestion also vary depending on the circumstances: children are more resistant to suggestion when misleading questions are not repeated, children are not exposed to misleading stereotypes about target individuals or given incentives to respond falsely, and children are not encouraged to 'pretend,' or 'guess' (Bruck, Ceci, Francouer, & Barr, 1995; Bruck, Ceci, Francouer, & Renick, 1995; Cassel, Roebers, & Bjorklund, 1996; Ceci, Huffman, Smith, & Loftus, 1994; Eisen, Goodman, Qin, & Davis, 1998; Garven, Wood, Malpass, & Shaw, 1998; Goodman *et al.*, 1989; Leichtman & Ceci, 1995; Poole & White, 1991; Siegal, Waters, & Dinwiddy, 1988; Thompson, Clarke-Stewart, & Lepore, 1997).

Because acquiescence is likely to misdirect further questioning and lead to mistaken conclusions, it can have serious implications. Investigators have thus been urged to probe recall memories using open-ended prompts as extensively as possible and to avoid strings of focused questions in which the risks of compounded errors are especially serious.

ENHANCING CHILDREN'S INFORMATIVENESS

Recent research demonstrates that forensic interviewers can be trained to conduct 'better interviews'—interviews in which fewer suggestive questions are asked and in which greater proportions of the information is elicited using open-ended prompts, ideally before any focused or leading questions are asked. In the first such study, which was conducted in Israel, Sternberg *et al.* (1997) showed that children who had been 'trained' by forensic interviewers to give narrative responses provided responses that were two and one-half times more detailed than did children who were (like children in most forensic interviews) 'trained' to respond to focused questions. Similar findings were obtained when such 'training' was given to alleged victims in the United States (Sternberg, Lamb, Esplin, & Baradaran, 1999).

These findings prompted the development of a fully structured investigative protocol designed to translate empirically based research guidelines into a practical interview tool that can be used by investigators conducting forensic interviews (Lamb, Sternberg, Esplin, Hershkowitz, & Orbach, 1999). The NICHD investigative protocol covers all phases of the investigative interview and is designed to translate research-based recommendations into operational guidelines in order to enhance the retrieval of informative, complete, and accurate accounts of alleged incidents of abuse by young victim/witnesses. This is accomplished by creating a supportive interview environment (pre-substantive rapport building), adapting interview practices to children's developmental levels and capabilities (e.g. minimizing linguistic complexity and avoiding interruptions), preparing children for their tasks as information providers (clarifying communication rules, training children to report event-specific episodic memories), maximizing the interviewers' reliance on utterance types which tap children's free-recall memory, using option-posing questions only to obtain essential information at the end of the interview, and eliminating suggestive practices.

The pre-substantive phase of the structured interview is used to prepare children for tasks they will have to perform during the substantive phase of the interview (Saywitz & Goodman, 1996; Saywitz *et al.*, 1999; Sternberg *et al.*, 1997, 1999) by providing practice responding to open-ended prompts about neutral experienced events and introducing them to detail-enhancing investigative techniques, including open-ended refocusing probes.

Following the pre-substantive phase, the interviewer attempts to shift the child's focus to the substantive issues as non-suggestively as possible so that the recollection process can commence. Only if the child fails to identify the target event/s in response to the first completely open prompt ('Tell me why you came to talk to me today') does the interviewer employ progressively more focused prompts to identify the alleged abuse.

Once the allegation has been mentioned, the free-recall phase begins with the first substantive invitation ('Tell me everything that happened from the beginning to the end as best you can remember'), followed by open-ended prompts aimed at eliciting spontaneous recall accounts of the alleged incident/s. Open-ended questions and prompts are used exhaustively, with focused questions only used at the end of the questioning phase to elicit essential information that is still missing. Contextual cueing (references to events, people, places, or things mentioned by the child) and time segmentation techniques (requests for information about blocks of time demarcated by events mentioned by the child) are used to refocus children on material they have disclosed before requesting elaboration using open-ended 'invitations' (i.e. utterances requesting that the interviewees report everything they remember about something). In essence, the protocol is thus designed to maximize the amount of information elicited using recall memory prompts, since information elicited in this way is more likely to be accurate. In addition, the structured interview minimizes opportunities for contamination of the children's accounts.

Analyses revealed drastic improvements in the organization of the interview, the quality of questions asked by interviewers, and the quality of information provided by children when youth investigators followed the protocol in Israel (Orbach, Hershkowitz, Lamb, Sternberg, Esplin, & Horowitz, 2000). Fifty-three of 55 children aged 4 to 13, interviewed using the structured protocol, made a disclosure in response to the first transitional utterance ('Do you know why you came here today'), one disclosed in response to the next prompt ('I understand you told x that something may have happened to you'), and one disclosed in response to a suggestive prompt. Children provided an average of 51 spontaneous details in their first narrative response, and the interviewers asked more than five times as many open-ended invitations ($M = 30\%$) as they did in comparable interviews conducted before the structured protocol was introduced. The number of option-posing questions dropped by almost 50% as well (from an average of 33% to 18% of the total number), and much more of the information was obtained using free recall rather than investigator-directed recognition probes. Children in the protocol condition provided proportionally more of the total number of details in their first narrative response than did children in the non-protocol condition, and they also provided significantly more information before being asked the first option-posing question. More of the details they provided were elicited by open-ended prompts, whereas fewer were elicited by directive, option-posing, and suggestive utterances.

Similar results were obtained when we studied investigative interviews conducted by police officers in the western United States (Sternberg, Lamb, Esplin, Orbach, & Hershkowitz, 2002; Sternberg, Lamb, Orbach, Esplin, & Mitchell, 2001). Preliminary analyses suggested a substantial improvement in the quality of interviews being conducted using the structured protocol. In addition to being better organized, interviewers used more open-ended prompts and fewer option-posing and suggestive questions than in the comparison (baseline) interviews. In the baseline condition, only 10% of the interviewers' questions were invitations; whereas in the protocol interviews, 35% of the interviewers' questions were invitations. The total amount of information elicited from free-recall memory also increased dramatically; whereas only 16% of the information was elicited using free recall in the pre-protocol interviews, 49% of the information was obtained using free recall in the protocol interviews. Use of the protocol also reduced the use of directive, option-posing, and suggestive prompts. In the baseline interviews, 41% of the information was obtained using option-posing and suggestive questions compared with 24% in the protocol interviews. Interestingly and importantly, this pattern of results was similar regardless of the children's age. Although younger children provided shorter and less detailed responses than older children, analyses of interviews with four- to six-year-old children revealed that the interviewers relied heavily on invitations (34% of their questions) and succeeded in eliciting a substantial amount of information (49% of the total) using free-recall prompts.

These findings are particularly encouraging in light of the difficulties interviewers frequently encounter when interviewing young children.

Success clearly depended on extended and intensive training, monitoring, and feedback, however. Whereas most training provided to forensic interviewers is brief and intensive, the training received by the interviewers we have studied was both intensive and extended over several months. It involved repeated practice using feedback-monitored simulations and the systematic analysis of both simulated and (later) actual forensic interviews, all of which were recorded. In addition, research staff continued to provide detailed feedback even after the investigators began using the protocol in the field. Similarly intense, prolonged, and quality-controlled practice in forensic settings may be a necessary component of successful training. None of the studies documenting the ineffectiveness of training (Aldridge & Cameron, 1999; Craig et al., 1999; Davies & Wilson, 1997; Memon, Bull, & Smith, 1995; Stevenson, Leung, & Cheung, 1992; Warren et al., 1999) have involved such intense and prolonged practice and supervision in the field.

CONCLUSION

The results of the two studies reviewed above suggest that a structured interview protocol, supplemented by detailed feedback and intensive training sessions can enhance the quality of forensic interviews with 4- to 14-year-old alleged victims of abuse. When guided by the protocol, interviewers retrieved more information using open-ended questions, conducted better organized interviews, introduced option-posing questions later in the interview, and were more likely to follow focused questions with open-ended probes (pairing). Because all of these practices are supported by empirical research on children's memory and communication, the structured protocol clearly provided investigative interviewers with an effective tool for interviewing children and obtaining information of the highest possible quality. In our experience, the more structured the protocol, the higher the quality of the interviews. As a result, the guidelines we developed have been made mandatory throughout Israel and are being field-tested with success in several parts of the United States. A demonstration project in the United Kingdom began in 1999 and another is scheduled to begin in Sweden in 2002.

REFERENCES

Aldridge, J., & Cameron, S. (1999). Interviewing child witnesses: Questioning strategies and the effectiveness of training. *Applied Developmental Science*, 3, 136–47.

American Association for Protecting Children. (1986). *Highlights of official child neglect and abuse reporting*, 1984. Denver, CO: AAPC.

American Professional Society on the Abuse of Children. (1997). *Guidelines for psychosocial evaluation of suspected sexual abuse in young children (Revised)*. Chicago: APSAC.

Brainerd, C.J., & Reyna, V.F. (1996). Mere testing creates false memories in children. *Developmental Psychology*, 32, 467–76.

Bruck, M., Ceci, S.J., Francouer, E., & Barr, R. (1995). 'I hardly cried when I got my shot!' Influencing children's reports about a visit to their pediatrician. *Child Development*, 66, 193–208.

Bruck, M., Ceci, S.J., Francouer, E., & Renick, A. (1995). Anatomically detailed dolls do not facilitate preschoolers' reports of a pediatric examination involving genital touching. *Journal of Experimental Psychology: Applied*, 1, 95–109.

Bull, R. (1995). Innovative techniques for the questioning of child witnesses, especially those who are young and those with a learning disability. In: M. Zaragoza, J.R. Graham, G.C.N. Hall, R. Hirschman, & Y.S. Ben-Porath (Eds), *Memory and testimony in the child witness* (pp. 179–94). Thousand Oaks, CA: Sage.

Bull, R. (1996). Good practice for video recorded interviews with child witnesses for use in criminal proceedings. In: G. Davies, S. Lloyd-Bostock, M. McMarran, & C. Wilson (Eds), *Psychology, law, and criminal justice: International developments in research and practice* (pp. 100–17). New York: Walter de Gruyter.

Cassel, W.S., Roebers, C.E.M., & Bjorklund, D.F. (1996). Developmental patterns of eyewitness responses to repeated and increasingly suggested questions. *Journal of Experimental Child Psychology*, 61, 116–33.

Ceci, S.J., & Bruck, M. (1993). Suggestibility of the child witness: A historical review and synthesis. *Psychological Bulletin*, 113, 403–39.

Ceci, S.J., & Bruck, M. (1995). *Jeopardy in the courtroom: A scientific analysis of children's testimony*. Washington, DC: American Psychological Association.

Ceci, S.J., Huffman, M.L.C., Smith, E., & Loftus, E.F. (1994). Repeatedly thinking about a non-event: Source misattributions among preschoolers. *Consciousness and Cognition*, 3, 388–407.

Cederborg, A-C., Orbach, Y., Sternberg, K.J., & Lamb, M. (2000). Investigative interviews of child witnesses in Sweden. *Child Abuse and Neglect*, 24, 1355–1361.

Craig, R.A., Sheibe, R., Kircher, J., Raskin, D.C., & Dodd, D. (1999). Effects of interviewer questions on children's statements of sexual abuse. *Applied Developmental Science*, 3, 77–85.

Dale, P.S., Loftus, E.F., & Rathbun, L. (1978). The influence of the form of the question on the eyewitness testimony of preschool children. *Journal of Psycholinguistic Research*, 7, 269–77.

Davies, G.M., Westcott, H.L., & Horan, N. (2000). The impact of questioning style on the content of investigative interviews with suspected child sexual abuse victims. *Psychology, Crime and Law*, **6**, 81–97.

Davies, G., & Wilson, C. (1997). Implementation of the *Memorandum*: An overview. In: H. Westcott & J. Jones (Eds), *Perspectives on the Memorandum: Policy, practice and research in investigative interviewing* (pp. 1–12). Aldershot, UK: Arena Publishers.

Dent, H.R. (1986). Experimental study of the effectiveness of different techniques of questioning mentally handicapped child witnesses. *British Journal of Clinical Psychology*, **25**, 13–17.

Dent, H.R., & Stephenson, G.M. (1979). An experimental study of the effectiveness of different techniques of questioning child witnesses. *British Journal of Social and Clinical Psychology*, **18**, 41–51.

Doris, J. (Ed.) (1991). *The suggestibility of children's recollections: Implications for eyewitness testimony*. Washington, DC: American Psychological Association.

Eisen, M.L., Goodman, G.S., Qin, J.J., & Davis, S. (1998). Memory and suggestibility in maltreated children: New research relevant to evaluating allegations of abuse. In: S.J. Lynn & K.M. McConkey (Eds), *Truth in memory*. New York: Guilford Press.

Fisher, R.P., & Geiselman, R.E. (1992). *Memory-enhancing techniques for investigating interviewing: The cognitive interview*. Springfield, IL: Charles C. Thomas.

Garven, S., Wood, J.M., Malpass, R.S., & Shaw, J.S. (1998). More than suggestion: The effect of interviewing techniques from the McMartin Preschool case. *Journal of Applied Psychology*, **83**, 347–59.

Goodman, G.S., & Aman, C. (1990). Children's use of anatomically detailed dolls to recount an event. *Child Development*, **61**, 1859–71.

Goodman, G.S., Bottoms, B.L., Schwartz-Kenney, B.M., & Rudy, L. (1991). Children's testimony about a stressful event: Improving children's reports. *Journal of Narrative and Life History*, **1**, 69–99.

Goodman, G.S., Hirschman, J., Hepps, D., & Rudy, L. (1991). Children's memory for stressful events. *Merrill-Palmer Quarterly*, **37**, 109–58.

Goodman, G.S., Wilson, M.E., Hazan, C., & Reed, R.S. (April, 1989). Children's testimony nearly four years after an event. Paper presented to the Eastern Psychological Association, Boston, MA.

Home Office & Department of Health. (1992). *Memorandum of Good Practice*. London: Her Majesty's Stationery Office.

Hutcheson, G.D., Baxter, J.S., Telfer, K., & Warden, D. (1995). Child witness statement quality: Question type and errors of omission. *Law & Human Behavior*, **19**, 631–48.

Jones, D.P.H. (1992). *Interviewing the sexually abused child*. Oxford: Gaskell.

Lamb, M.E., Hershkowitz, I., Sternberg, K.J., Boat, B., & Everson, M.D. (1996). Investigative interviews of alleged sexual abuse victims with and without anatomical dolls. *Child Abuse and Neglect*, **20**, 1239–47.

Lamb, M.E., Hershkowitz, I., Sternberg, K.J., Esplin, P.W., Hovav, M. Manor, T., & Yudilevitch, L. (1996). Effects of investigative style on Israeli children's responses. *International Journal of Behavioral Development*, **19**, 627–37.

Lamb, M.E., Sternberg, K.J., & Esplin, P.W. (1998). Conducting investigative interviews of alleged sexual abuse victims. *Child Abuse and Neglect*, 22, 813–23.

Lamb, M.E., Sternberg, K.J., & Esplin, P.W. (2000). Effect of age and length of delay on the amount of information provided by alleged abuse victims in investigative interviews. *Child Development*, 71, 1586–1596.

Lamb, M.E., Sternberg, K.J., Esplin, P.W., Hershkowitz, I., & Orbach, Y. (1999). The NICHD protocol for investigative interviews of alleged sexabuse victims. Unpublished manuscript, NICHD, Bethesda, MD.

Lamb, M.E., Sternberg, K.J., Orbach, Y., Hershkowitz, I., & Esplin, P.W. (1999). Forensic interviews of children. In: A. Memon & R. A. Bull (Eds), *Handbook of the psychology of interviewing* (pp. 253–77). New York: Wiley.

Leichtman, M.D., & Ceci, S.J. (1995). The effects of stereotypes and suggestions on preschoolers' reports. *Developmental Psychology*, 31, 568–78.

McGough, L. (1994). Child witnesses. New Haven, CT: Yale University Press.

Memon, A., & Bull, R. (Eds) (1999). *Handbook of the psychology of interviewing*. Chichester, UK: Wiley.

Memon, A., Bull, R., & Smith, M. (1995). Improving the quality of police interviews: Can training in the use of cognitive techniques help? *Policing and Society*, 5, 53–68.

Milne, R., & Bull, R. (1999). *Investigative interviewing: Psychology and practice*. Chichester, UK: Wiley.

National Society for the Prevention of Cruelty to Children. (1989). *Child abuse trends in England and Wales, 1983–1987*. London: NSPCC.

Oates, K., & Shrimpton, S. (1991). Children's memories for stressful and nonstressful events. *Medical Science and Law*, 31, 4–10.

Orbach, Y., Hershkowitz, I., Lamb, M.E., Sternberg, K.J., Esplin, P.W., & Horowitz, D. (2000). Assessing the value of structured protocols for forensic interviews of alleged child abuse victims. *Child Abuse and Neglect*, 24, 733–752.

Peterson, C., & Bell, M. (1996). Children's memory for traumatic injury. *Child Development*, 67, 3045–70.

Poole, D.A., & Lamb, M.E. (1998). *Investigative interviews of children: A guide for helping professionals*. Washington, DC: American Psychological Association.

Poole, D.A., & Lindsay, D.S. (1995). Interviewing preschoolers: Effects of nonsuggestive techniques, parental coaching, and leading questions on reports of nonexperienced events. *Journal of Experimental Child Psychology*, 60, 129–54.

Poole, D.A., & Lindsay, D.S. (1996, June). Effects of parental suggestions, interviewing techniques, and age on young children's event reports. Paper presented to the NATO Advanced Study Institute on Recollections of Trauma, Port de Bourgenay, France.

Poole, D.A., & White, L.T. (1991). Effects of question repetition on the eyewitness testimony of children and adults. *Developmental Psychology*, 27, 975–86.

Poole, D.A., & White, L.T. (1993). Two years later: Effects of question repetition and retention intervals on the eyewitness testimony of children and adults. *Developmental Psychology*, 29, 844–53.

Raskin, D.C., & Esplin, P.W. (1991). Statement validity assessments: Interview procedures and content analyses of children's statements of sexual abuse. *Behavioral Assessment*, 13, 265–91.

Sattler, J. (1998). *Clinical and forensic interviewing of children and families*. San Diego, CA: Author.

Saywitz, K.J., & Goodman, G.S. (1996). Interviewing children in and out of court: Current research and practice implications. In: J. Briere, L. Berliner, J.A. Bulkley, C. Jenny, & T. Reid (Eds), *The APSAC handbook on child maltreatment* (pp. 297–318). Thousand Oaks, CA: Sage.

Saywitz, K.J., Snyder, L., & Nathanson, R. (1999). Facilitating the communicative competence of the child witness. *Applied Developmental Science*, **3**, 58–68.

Sedlak, A.J., & Broadhurst, D.D. (1996). *Third national incidence study of child abuse and neglect: Final report*. Washington, DC: US Department of Health and Human Resources, Administration for Children and Families.

Siegal, M., Waters, L., & Dinwiddy, L. (1988). Misleading children: Causal attributions for inconsistency under repeated questioning. *Journal of Experimental Child Psychology*, **45**, 438–56.

Spencer, J., & Flin, R. (1993). *The evidence of children* (2nd ed.). London: Blackstone Press.

Sternberg, K., Lamb, M.E., Esplin, P.W., & Baradaran, L. (1999). Using a scripted protocol to guide investigative interviews: A pilot study. *Applied Developmental Science*, **3**, 70–6.

Sternberg, K.J., Lamb, M.E., Esplin, P.W., Orbach, Y., & Hershkowitz, I. (2002). Using a scripted protocol to improve the quality of investigative interviews. In M. Eisen, J. Quas & G. Goodman (Eds), *Memory and suggestibility in the forensic interview* (pp. 409–436). Mahwah, NJ: Erlbaum.

Sternberg, K.J., Lamb, M.E., Hershkowitz, I., Esplin, P.W., Redlich, A., & Sunshine, N. (1996). The relationship between investigative utterance types and the informativeness of child witnesses. *Journal of Applied Developmental Psychology*, **17**, 439–51.

Sternberg, K.J., Lamb, M.E., Hershkowitz, I., Yudilevitch, L., Orbach, Y., Esplin, P.W., & Hovav, M. (1997). Effects of introductory style on children's abilities to describe experiences of sexual abuse. *Child Abuse and Neglect*, **21**, 1133–46.

Sternberg, K.J., Lamb, M.E., Orbach, Y., Esplin, P.W., & Mitchell, S. (2001). Use of a structured investigative protocol enhances young children's responses to free recall prompts in the course of forensic interviews. *Journal of Applied Psychology*, **86**, 997–1005.

Stevenson, K.M., Leung, P., & Cheung, K.M. (1992). Competency-based evaluation of interviewing skills in child sexual abuse cases. *Social Work Research & Abstracts*, **28**, 11–16.

Thompson, W.C., Clarke-Stewart, K.A., & Lepore, S.J. (1997). What did the janitor do? Suggestive interviewing and the accuracy of children's accounts. *Law and Human Behavior*, **21**, 405–26.

Walker, A.G. (1999). *Handbook on questioning children. A linguistic perspective* (2nd ed.). Washington, DC: American Bar Association Center on Children and the Law.

Walker, N., & Hunt, J.S. (1998). Interviewing child victim-witnesses: How you ask is what you get. In C.R. Thompson, D. Herrman, J.D. Read, D. Bruce, D. Payne, & M.P. Toglia (Eds), *Eyewitness memory: Theoretical and applied perspectives* (pp. 55–87). Mahwah, NJ: Erlbaum.

Warren, A.R., & Lane, P. (1995). Effects of timing and type of questioning on eyewitness accuracy and suggestibility. In: M.S. Zaragoza, J.R. Graham, G.C.N. Hall, R. Hirschman, & Y.S. Ben-Porath (Eds), *Memory and testimony in the child witness* (pp. 44–60). Thousand Oaks, CA: Sage.

Warren, A.R., Woodall, C.C., Hunt, J.S., & Perry, N.W. (1996). 'It sounds good in theory, but': Do investigative interviewers follow guidelines based on memory research? *Child Maltreatment*, **1**, 231–45.

Warren, A.R., Woodall, C.E., Thomas, M., Nunno, M., Keeney, J., Larson, S., & Stadfeld, J. (1999). Assessing the effectiveness of a training program for interviewing child witnesses. *Applied Developmental Science*, **3**, 128–35.

CHAPTER 10

How and Why Do Children Respond to Nonsensical Questions?

AMANDA WATERMAN,* MARK BLADES,† AND CHRISTOPHER SPENCER†

*Department of Applied Psychology, University of Durham,
Stockton-on-Tees, UK
†Department of Psychology, University of Sheffield, Sheffield, UK

If a child becomes involved in the legal setting, as the result of witnessing a crime or being the victim of a crime, s/he will usually participate in one or more interviews. In fact, children are often interviewed on several occasions and by different people. Given the centrality of the interview in the legal process, it is important to investigate factors affecting how children understand and respond to different types of question.

When children are interviewed about an alleged crime, it is essential that they are able to provide accurate and reliable answers (see Michael Lamb, Yael Orbach, Kathleen J. Sternberg, Phillip W. Esplin, & Irit Hershkowitz, Chapter 9 in this book). This includes being able to indicate when they do not understand a question or do not know the answer to a question. However, research carried out by Hughes and Grieve (1980) and Pratt (1990) showed that children may not necessarily indicate when a question does not make sense. They found that children attempted to answer 'bizarre' questions rather than saying they did not understand the question or that the question was silly.

Hughes and Grieve (1980) asked five- and seven-year-olds four 'bizarre' questions. Two of the questions were phrased in a closed

Children's Testimony. Edited by H.L. Westcott, G.M. Davies, and R.H.C. Bull.
© 2002 John Wiley & Sons, Ltd.

format; that is, they only required a 'yes' or 'no' answer (e.g. 'Is red heavier than yellow?'). The other two questions required a more extensive answer, and we will refer to these as 'open' questions (e.g. 'One day there were two people standing at a bus stop. When the bus came along, who got on first?'). Despite the nonsensical nature of these questions, they found that virtually all the children answered all of the questions.

In a similar study, Pratt (1990) asked five-, six-, and seven-year-olds and adults three sensible and six nonsensical questions. The latter were all similar to the closed questions used by Hughes and Grieve (e.g. 'Is a cup sadder than an orange?'). Pratt found that the children tried to answer about 90% of these questions and the adults provided answers to about three-quarters of the questions. This result supported Hughes and Grieve (1980) and indicated that young children were willing to answer nonsensical questions, rather than indicate that they did not understand or that the question was silly. These studies have been cited frequently to show that children's willingness to answer a question cannot be taken as evidence that they understand the question (Siegal, 1997), and that when children are asked to give evidence they may answer questions without any understanding of what they are being asked (Moston, 1990; Poole & White, 1991; Ceci & Bruck, 1995; Warren & McGough, 1996; Carter, Bottoms, & Levine, 1996).

However, there are problems with both the Hughes and Grieve (1980) and the Pratt (1990) studies, and these problems merit further investigation into children's tendency to answer nonsensical questions. In the Hughes and Grieve (1980), study, children were asked two open questions and two closed questions, but all of the questions used by Pratt (1990) only required a 'yes' or 'no' answer. Therefore, the findings to date are based largely on children's responses to closed questions. Other researchers have demonstrated that children's responses to sensible questions can be influenced by whether the question is phrased in a closed or an open format (Ceci & Bruck, 1995; Davies, Westcott, & Horan, 2000; Dent, 1992; Lamb, Sternberg, & Esplin, 1998; Memon & Vartoukian, 1996; Peterson & Biggs, 1997; Peterson, Dowden, & Tobin, 1999; Poole & White, 1991; Sternberg et al., 1996).

For example, in Peterson et al.'s (1999) study, young children witnessed a staged event and were subsequently questioned about the event. Some of the questions were phrased in a closed format and therefore only required a 'yes' or 'no' answer (e.g. 'Was there a poster of dogs in the room?'). Other questions asked for particular details of the event to be reported and were therefore more open in format (e.g.

'What was on the table?' They found that the children were less accurate in responding to the closed questions compared with the open questions. Therefore, there may also be differences in the way that children respond to closed nonsensical questions and open nonsensical questions.

Although Hughes and Grieve (1980) found that children did try to answer both open and closed questions, children's responses to the open questions are worth examining; for example, in response to the question 'One day there were two people standing at a bus stop. When the bus came along, who got on first?', some children responded with, 'The one there first' or 'The one at the front of the line' (Hughes and Grieve, 1980, p. 157). Although such responses might be thought to be reasonable replies, they were counted as examples of children giving answers to 'bizarre' questions. The only way that children could avoid answering the questions in Hughes and Grieve's study was to say 'I don't know'. However, if children responded 'I don't know' the question was repeated, and this may have resulted in children thinking that they had to give a different answer. Furthermore, we do not know whether children were answering the nonsensical questions, despite realizing they were silly, or because they thought that the questions were reasonable.

In Pratt's (1990) study, participants were asked to judge the questions as sensible or silly. However, the participants who were asked the questions were different from those who were asked to rate each individual question as silly or sensible. Also, a quarter of the adults judged the silly questions to be sensible. From the adults' responses, we infer that the participants in Pratt's study thought that at least some of the nonsensical questions were ones that could be answered reasonably.

This chapter presents a series of studies we conducted that expanded on previous research and investigated children's responses to, and understanding of, nonsensical questions. In the first experiment, 73 five- to eight-year-olds were asked a series of both sensible and nonsensical questions (Waterman, Blades & Spencer, 2000). The sensible questions were included to ensure that children would be able to answer some of the questions. Half of each type of question was phrased in a closed format (i.e. the question only required a 'yes' or 'no' answer), and half was phrased in an open format (i.e. an answer had to be generated). Selection of the questions was based on a questionnaire completed by adults who were asked to judge whether questions were sensible or nonsensical. The questions used in the experiments were all ones that the adults' unanimously judged as sensible (for the sensible questions) or as silly (for the nonsensical questions). Examples of each type of question are shown in Table 10.1.

Table 10.1. Examples of each question type used in the first experiment.

Sensible questions	Nonsensical questions
Open question · What colour is a banana?	*Open question* What do bricks eat?
Closed question Is a bus longer than a car?	*Closed question* Is a jumper angrier than a tree?

In this experiment, there were two tasks separated by three weeks. In the first task, all the children were simply asked to answer the questions. Three weeks later, in task two, the same children were given the same questions again. They were not asked to answer them, but were only asked to say whether they thought the questions were silly (i.e. did not make sense) or OK (i.e. did make sense). The tasks were separated in order to make the children's judgement of the questions as independent as possible from their original responses to the questions. In contrast to previous studies, at the beginning of both tasks children were explicitly told that it was OK to say 'don't know' if they did not know the answer. This was in line with guidelines for interviewing children involved in criminal proceedings given in the *Memorandum of Good Practice* (Home Office & Department of Health, 1992; Milne & Bull, 1999).

For task 1, children's responses to sensible questions were scored as correct if they gave an appropriate response, and incorrect if they gave an inappropriate response or said 'don't know'. For the nonsensical questions, a response was scored as correct if the child said 'don't know', 'don't understand', indicated that the question was silly, or could not be answered. Certain other responses to nonsensical questions were also scored as correct; for example, for the question 'What do feet have for breakfast', the response 'nothing' was scored as correct. There were 10% of such answers to the nonsensical questions. All other responses to nonsensical questions were scored as incorrect.

With the sensible questions, we found that all the children were able to provide appropriate answers. Therefore, children were not so confused by the task that they were unable to answer any questions at all. With the nonsensical questions an interesting pattern emerged. The majority of children responded 'don't know' or said that they did not understand when the nonsensical questions were phrased in an open format (i.e. an answer had to be generated). However, few children indicated that they did not understand when the nonsensical questions were phrased in a closed format. Instead, most children

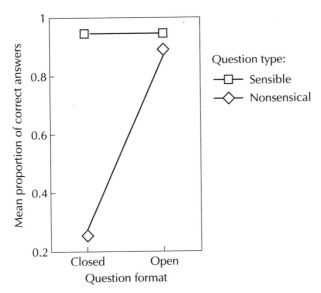

Figure 10.1. Effect of interaction between question type and question format on the mean proportion of correct answers.

provided a response (i.e. 'yes' or 'no') to this type of questions (see Figure 10.1). This pattern was consistent across all the age groups.

In task 2, almost all the children judged the sensible questions to be OK, and the nonsensical questions to be silly. Therefore, children agreed with the adults' judgements about the nature of the questions. When children judged the sensible questions to be OK, the most common justification was to affirm the reality of the question; for example, 'Is a bus longer than a car?' was judged to be OK because a bus is longer than a car. For the very few children who judged the sensible questions to be silly, the most common justification was that it was silly because you already knew the answer.

When children judged the nonsensical questions to be silly, the most common reason was to deny the reality of the question; for example, 'Is a jumper angrier than a tree?' was thought to be silly because a jumper and a tree could not be angry and 'Where do circles live?' was judged to be silly because circles do not live anywhere. For the very few children who judged the nonsensical questions to be OK, the most common reason they gave was to offer an explanation; for example, 'Where do circles live?' was judged OK because circle shapes were kept in the classroom cupboard at school.

We also examined the relationship between children's willingness to answer a nonsensical question in task 1, and how they judged it in task

2. For those children who did answer particular nonsensical questions, the majority judged the questions to be silly: over 90% of the nonsensical questions that elicited a response in task 1 were later judged to be silly in task 2.

Therefore, in contrast to previous research (e.g. Hughes & Grieve, 1980), we found that children did not try to answer all the nonsensical questions. Most children did not attempt to answer open nonsensical questions, but most children did answer nonsensical questions in a closed format. Also, when children did answer the nonsensical questions, it was not because they thought the questions were sensible, as almost all the children subsequently judged the nonsensical questions to be silly.

However, there was one limitation with the first experiment that required further investigation. In this study, all the closed questions happened to involve a comparison between two items, whereas all the open questions did not involve a comparison. Therefore, the difference in children's tendency to answer closed and open questions could have been as a consequence of the format of the questions, whether the questions involved a comparison, or a combination of the two factors. A second experiment was therefore run with a similar number of five- to eight-year-olds using a wider range of questions (Waterman *et al.*, 2000). For both the open and the closed questions, half involved a comparison and half did not (see Table 10.2 for examples of each additional question type).

The results of this second experiment confirmed the original findings. Most children gave appropriate responses to open nonsensical questions, whether or not they involved a comparison (mean percentage appropriate responses, 87%). However, most children gave inappropriate answers to closed nonsensical questions, both comparative and non-comparative (mean percentage inappropriate responses, 26%).

An important issue to consider is *why* children answer nonsensical

Table 10.2. Examples of each additional question type used in the second experiment.

Sensible questions	Nonsensical questions
Open comparative Why is night-time darker than daytime?	*Open comparative* Why is a banana happier than a leaf?
Closed non-comparative Is the sun very hot?	*Closed non-comparative* Should lights eat potatoes with clouds?

closed questions, but not open nonsensical questions. Previous researchers have found that children can be misled by suggestive questions or change answers to repeated questions, and they have argued that children may be responding to the demand characteristics of the task (Goodman & Reed, 1986; Siegal, 1997); for example, if an adult asks a child a question, the child may feel that an answer is required. But in our experiments, the nonsensical closed questions that the children usually tried to answer were asked in exactly the same context as the nonsensical open questions which the children avoided answering. It is therefore unlikely that demand characteristics *per se* can account for children's willingness to answer nonsensical closed questions.

Children may not monitor their comprehension of a situation as well as older children and adults (Markman, 1977; 1979; Snyder & Lindstedt, 1995; Ruffman, 1996), and it is therefore possible that the children in these experiments were not monitoring their comprehension of the questions effectively. The answer to a closed question only needs to be 'yes' or 'no' and is readily accessible, but the answer to an open question has to be generated and the additional processing required may focus children more on the question's comprehensibility. We decided to investigate this possibility in a third experiment by eliminating any differences in the time children took to consider an open question and a closed question.

We therefore decided to prevent children from answering the question immediately and to give them more time in which they might focus on any uncertainty about, or problems with, the questions. One option was simply to get the children to pause before answering the question. However, during the pause children may not necessarily have focused on the question; they may have been distracted or may have found it difficult to remember the question. Therefore, we asked the children to repeat the question before they were allowed to answer it. The children were told that the experimenter wanted them to repeat the question to check that the child had heard it properly. We used the shorter question set from the first experiment in order to prevent the task from becoming too long, and 75 five- to eight-year-olds participated.

We found exactly the same pattern of results as for the first experiment. For task 1, all the children were able to answer the sensible questions. Most children responded appropriately to the nonsensical open questions, whereas most children tried to answer the nonsensical closed questions. In task 2, children again judged the sensible questions to be OK, and the nonsensical questions to be silly.

Providing children with extra time, which hopefully enabled them to focus on any uncertainty they might have had about the nonsensical closed questions, did not decrease children's tendency to answer such questions. Therefore, the difference between children's tendency to answer nonsensical open and nonsensical closed questions in our earlier experiments did not appear to be due to children potentially having extra time to focus on the nonsensical nature of the open questions. So, the question remains as to why children did not attempt to provide an answer to nonsensical open questions but did provide answers to nonsensical closed questions.

One possibility is that children's use of the answer 'no' for the nonsensical closed questions may not have been meant to communicate that they had considered the proposition seriously and decided to reject it, but rather that they were denying the proposition itself; for example, for the question 'Is a jumper angrier than a tree?' the answer 'no' might mean 'no, because trees are angrier than jumpers' or it might mean 'no, because jumpers aren't angry at all'. This cannot be true for the answer 'yes' which necessarily accepts the nonsensical nature of the question.

Potential misunderstanding of a child's response when they do not elaborate on an answer can also be a problem in a court situation. Walker (1993) gave examples of this type of problem in her analysis of a five-year-old girl's testimony about witnessing a murder. The following is a question–answer exchange between the child and one of the lawyers (Walker, 1993, p. 70):

Adult: Do you remember Martha asking you, 'Do you know who Mark is?'
Child: Yeah.

An adult is likely to interpret this as meaning 'Yes, I remember'. However, another exchange highlighted the problem with this interpretation (Walker, 1993, p. 71):

Adult: Do you remember when Don asked you, 'What colour was their skin, like mine or like Martha's?'
Child: Like yours.

Here, it is obvious that the child is only responding to the second part of the question—the question embedded within the question. Therefore, in the first example, the child's response of 'yeah' could mean 'yeah, I know who Mark is'. So, when children give 'yes' or 'no' answers and do not elaborate on these answers, adults might misinterpret what a child means by that response.

In Pratt's (1990) study, children were asked to justify their answers if they gave a 'yes' or 'no' response (all of Pratt's questions were closed and involved a comparison between two items). Pratt (1990) categorized in four types the justifications given by children of their answers to non-sensical questions. Two involved accepting the nonsensical nature of the question; one was a 'residual' category for responses such as 'don't know'; and the final category was for children who indicated that the question asked for an inappropriate comparison to be made. Therefore, children in the final category were indicating that the question did not make sense. Fifty per cent of the five-year-olds' explanations were classified as residual, perhaps indicating their difficulty with justifying their answers. In contrast, only 14% of the six- and seven-year-olds' explanations were classified as residual. Across all age groups, the mean percentage of children indicating that the question was inappropriate was 16%. Therefore, the majority of children were either giving justifications that accepted the nonsensical proposition contained within the question or were unable to explain their answers.

In our fourth experiment, we again asked children a series of nonsensical and sensible questions, and their initial responses were noted and scored as before. In addition, we also asked the children to explain their answers. We were particularly interested in children's explanations when they responded 'no' to a nonsensical closed question. However, unlike in the Pratt (1990) study, children were asked to explain all their answers to avoid creating a response bias. The questions used were based on the larger question set from the second experiment, and 91 five- to nine-year-olds participated.

Children's explanations of their answers when they responded 'no' to a nonsensical closed question in task 1 were divided into two categories. The first category was for explanations where the child indicated that the question was inappropriate or silly and the second category was for any other type of response, including 'don't know' or explanations that accepted the nonsensical nature of the question. On the basis of the children's explanations, the children's original 'no' responses to nonsensical closed questions were re-coded. If a child had tried to answer a nonsensical closed question, but then gave an explanation that indicated the question was inappropriate or silly, the response was re-scored as correct. If a child had tried to answer a nonsensical closed question and had then explained the answer by accepting the nonsensical proposition or had been unable to explain their answer, the response was not re-coded and therefore remained as incorrect.

For children's initial responses to the questions, we found a very similar result to the previous experiments. With the nonsensical questions, the majority of children gave inappropriate responses to the closed questions, but most indicated they did not understand or did not know the answer with the open questions. When children's explanations of their 'no' responses to nonsensical closed questions were divided into the two categories discussed above, we found that three-quarters of the children indicated that the question was inappropriate or silly. The remaining children either could not explain their answer or explained their answer by elaborating on the nonsensical nature of the question.

Therefore, different children giving the same response to the same question could mean different things by that response; for example, to the question 'Is a jumper angrier than a tree?', one child who responded 'no' went on to explain their answer by saying, ''cos trees and jumpers don't get angry'. Another child, who had also responded 'no', explained their answer very differently; 'a tree's got to be angrier 'cos it just sits there being bored all day'.

If children's initial 'no' responses were re-coded on the basis of these explanations then the difference between the number of appropriate answers to open and closed nonsensical questions virtually disappeared. For the three older age groups the difference in the number of correct answers to the nonsensical closed and nonsensical open questions was eliminated. For the five- to six-year-olds, although the number of correct answers to nonsensical closed questions increased, the re-coded percentage was still lower than the number of correct answers to the nonsensical open questions.

There are thus two main findings from the fourth experiment. First, it replicated the results from previous experiments: children were initially more likely to respond inappropriately to a nonsensical question if it was phrased in a closed format and were more likely to indicate that they did not know the answer or did not understand the question, if the question was phrased in an open format. Second, if children were asked to explain what they meant when they responded 'no' to a nonsensical closed question, then the difference between closed and open questions was eliminated for the older children and substantially reduced for the five- to six-year-olds.

These results show that it is important to ask children to clarify what they mean when they are asked a closed question that is complicated or difficult to understand in an interview situation. When a child answers an ambiguous or complicated closed question, adult interviewers may assume they know what the child is trying to communicate. However, the child may have meant to communicate something else and be unaware of the need to clarify the response. Such misunderstandings could have serious consequences when children are interviewed as witnesses and potentially in other interview contexts (e.g. the medical setting).

SUMMARY AND CONCLUSION

Our experiments showed that, in contrast to previous research (Hughes & Grieve, 1980; Pratt, 1990), children do *not* answer all nonsensical questions. If a question only required a 'yes' or 'no' response, then children tended to give inappropriate responses. However, if the question was phrased in an open format, the majority of children indicated that they did not understand or did not know the answer. Therefore, the way a question was phrased had a significant effect on whether or not children indicated when they did not know the answer.

Giving children more time potentially to consider the questions before answering them did not affect the pattern of responses (i.e. children still gave inappropriate responses to nonsensical closed questions). However, asking children to explain their answers when they responded to this type of question provided interesting results. We found that different children giving the same response to the same question could mean different things by that response. Three-quarters of the children who responded 'no' to nonsensical closed questions justified their answer by explaining that the question was silly; the remainder either could not explain their answer or justified it by elaborating on the nonsensical proposition. Therefore, the majority of children appeared to mean to communicate that the nonsensical questions were silly when they gave their initial 'no' response.

This has important implications in more 'real-world' contexts when children are questioned or formally interviewed. First, we would suggest that open questions are used wherever possible, and if closed questions are necessary that they are kept as simple and unambiguous as possible. Second, if a child is asked an ambiguous or difficult closed question, then the child should be asked to clarify their response: what the interviewer thinks the child means and what the child actually means may be very different. Third, this highlights the importance of training for forensic interviewers. Adult interviewers need to be aware of the most effective ways of questioning children and the potential effects of question format on children's responses.

The findings from these studies highlight the need for continuing research into how children understand questions and how they respond in an interview situation, particularly those that more closely mirror the forensic interview context. For children to be given the best opportunity to provide reliable information, interviewers need to be aware of how to question children effectively and sensitively and to phrase the questions in such a way as to help children to communicate to the best of their ability.

REFERENCES

Carter, C.A., Bottoms, B.L., & Levine, M. (1996). Linguistic and socio-emotional influences on the accuracy of children's reports. *Law and Human Behavior*, **20**, 335–58.

 Ceci, S.J., & Bruck, M. (1995). *Jeopardy in the courtroom: A scientific analysis of children's testimony*. Washington, DC: American Psychological Association.

Davies, G.M., Westcott, H., & Horan, N. (2000). The impact of questioning style on the content of investigative interviews with suspected child sexual abuse victims. *Psychology, Crime and Law*, **6**, 81–97.

Dent, H.R. (1992). The effects of age and intelligence on eyewitness ability. In: H. Dent & R. Flin (Eds), *Children as witnesses* (pp. 1–13). Chichester, UK: Wiley.

 Goodman, G.S., & Reed, R.S. (1986). Age differences in eyewitness testimony. *Law and Human Behavior*, **10**, 317–32.

Home Office, & Department of Health (1992). *Memorandum of good practice on video recorded interviews with child witnesses for criminal proceedings*. London: Her Majesty's Stationery Office.

Hughes, M., & Grieve, R. (1980). On asking children bizarre questions. *First Language*, **1**, 149–60.

Lamb, M.E., Sternberg, K.J., & Esplin, P.W. (1998). Conducting investigative interviews of alleged sexual abuse victims. *Child Abuse and Neglect*, **22**, 813–23.

Markman, E.M. (1977). Realising that you don't understand: A preliminary investigation. *Child Development*, **48**, 986–92.

Markman, E.M. (1979). Realising that you don't understand: Elementary school children's awareness of inconsistencies. *Child Development*, **50**, 643–55.

Memon, A., & Vartoukian, R. (1996). The effects of repeated questioning on young children's eyewitness testimony. *British Journal of Psychology*, **87**, 403–15.

Milne, R., & Bull, R. (1999). *Investigative interviewing: Psychology and practice*. Chichester, UK: Wiley.

Moston, S. (1990). How children interpret and respond to questions: Situational sources of suggestibility in eyewitness interviews. *Social Behaviour*, **5**, 155–67.

Peterson, C., & Biggs, M. (1997). Interviewing children about trauma: Problems with 'specific' questions. *Journal of Traumatic Stress*, **10**, 279–90.

Peterson, C., Dowden, C., & Tobin, J. (1999). Interviewing preschoolers: Comparisons of yes/no and wh- questions. *Law and Human Behavior*, **23**, 539–55.

Poole, D.A. & White L.T. (1991). Effects of question repetition on the eyewitness testimony of children and adults. *Developmental Psychology*, **27**, 975–86.

Pratt, C. (1990). On asking children—and adults—bizarre questions. *First Language*, **10**, 167–75.

Ruffman, T. (1996). Reassessing children's comprehension-monitoring skills. In: T.O. Nelson (Ed.), *Reading comprehension difficulties: Processes and intervention* (pp. 33–67). Mahwah, NJ: Erlbaum.

Siegal, M. (1997). *Knowing children. Experiments in conversation and cognition*. Hove, UK: Psychology Press.

Snyder, L.S., & Lindstedt, D.E. (1995). Children's courtroom narratives: Competence, credibility, and the communicative contract. *Topics in Language Disorders*, **15**, 16–29.

Sternberg, K.J., Lamb, M.E., Hershkowitz, I., Esplin, P.W., Redlich, A., & Sunshine, N. (1996). The relation between investigative utterance types and the informativeness of child witnesses. *Journal of Applied Developmental Psychology*, **17**, 439–51.

Warren, A.R., & McGough, L.S. (1996). Research on children's suggestibility: Implications for the investigative interview. *Criminal Justice and Behavior*, **23**, 269–303.

Walker, A.G. (1993). Questioning young children in court—A linguistic case study. *Law and Human Behavior*, **17**, 59–81.

Waterman, A.H., Blades, M., & Spencer, C.P. (2000). Do children try to answer nonsensical questions? *British Journal of Developmental Psychology*, **18**, 211–225.

CHAPTER 11

Enhancing Children's Accounts: How Useful Are Non-verbal Techniques?

MARGARET-ELLEN PIPE,* KAREN SALMON,† AND GINA K. PRIESTLEY‡

*Section on Social and Emotional Development, NICHD, Bethesda, Maryland, USA
†University of New South Wales, Sydney, Australia
‡University of Auckland, New Zealand

When young children are simply asked to recount a past experience, to 'tell what happened when . . .', the descriptions they provide are typically very brief and, on their own, contain too little information to be of use in forensic contexts. Yet, it is clear that even very young children remember and can report much more information when appropriate interview techniques are introduced. In clinical contexts, and more recently in laboratory-based research, a variety of non-verbal interview techniques, such as providing props or encouraging children to draw, have been shown to help children talk about their experiences.

One way in which non-verbal techniques are potentially useful in interviews is by helping children to communicate information. Allowing the child to 'show' or 'draw' as well as to 'tell' reduces reliance on language ability, a particularly important consideration for very young children (Bentovim, Bentovim, Vizard, & Wiseman, 1995; Boat & Everson, 1994; Fivush, Kuebli, & Clubb, 1992; Price & Goodman, 1990). Prop-based interview techniques may also help children comprehend what adults are asking them, directing and guiding their recall.

Children's Testimony. Edited by H.L. Westcott, G.M. Davies, and R.H.C. Bull.
© 2002 John Wiley & Sons, Ltd.

Importantly, from a forensic perspective, they can reduce the social and emotional demands of the interview and generally reduce 'the intrusion of the interviewer into the child's world' (Steward et al., 1996, p. 33). These considerations are likely to be particularly important if, for example, the information to be conveyed is embarrassing or very personal (Koocher et al., 1995; Saywitz, Goodman, Nicholas, and Moan, 1991).

A second way in which these techniques can be useful is by facilitating memory retrieval processes. Young children tend to be reliant on external retrieval cues when recalling past events and, unlike older children and adults, have difficulty generating and using strategies to search memory efficiently and flexibly (Brown, Bransford, Ferrara, & Campione, 1983; Flavell, Miller, & Miller, 1993). Props potentially provide the kind of concrete, external retrieval cues likely to be of benefit to them (Bentovim et al., 1995; Pipe, Gee, & Wilson, 1993; Price & Goodman, 1990). Props are also likely to help by extending the memory search process, compared to a standard verbal interview, because they typically remain present for a period of time during the interview (Butler, Gross, & Hayne, 1995; Steward et al., 1996).

In theory, then, there is good reason to expect that non-verbal interview techniques will enhance children's accounts of their past experiences. From a forensic perspective, of course, a critical question is whether such techniques affect the accuracy of children's accounts; more is better only if it is accurate. In the remainder of this chapter, we review research studies that examine the impact of non-verbal techniques on children's reports, paying particular attention to whether these techniques compromise the accuracy of the information reported.

REINSTATING REAL PROPS DURING INTERVIEWS

Providing actual items from an event should be an extremely effective means of supporting children's accounts; not only do real props offer children the opportunity to show what happened, they potentially provide excellent retrieval cues. According to Tulving's principal of encoding specificity, retrieval cues are effective to the extent that their attributes match attributes specific to the stored memory trace (Tulving & Thomson, 1973), and real items are likely to provide a good match. The evidence supports these predictions. When prop items that were part of an event are provided at the time of interview to help children show and/or tell what happened, children typically report more information than in a standard verbal interview. Real props enhance reports not only when children have the opportunity to re-enact the activities (Salmon & Pipe, 1997; Smith, Ratner, & Hobart,

1987) but also when the prop items are simply present as visual cues and the child cannot interact with them (Gee & Pipe, 1995; Goodman & Aman, 1990; Pipe & Wilson, 1994). This latter finding clearly demonstrates their function as retrieval cues. Nonetheless, the opportunity to show as well as tell using the props often results in information over and above that described in verbal reports.

What of the effects on the *accuracy* of children's accounts? The answer here depends on how the prop items are used. In open-ended verbal reports, accuracy (the proportion of correct to total information) is typically not compromised (Gee & Pipe, 1995; Pipe & Wilson, 1994; Salmon, Bidrose, & Pipe, 1995); that is, although errors may increase slightly, the increase in errors is proportional to the increase in accurate information. Even if distracter items (items not from the event) are present, there is little effect on the accuracy of verbal accounts if the child is not specifically asked about the distracters and cannot interact with them (Pipe & Wilson, 1994; Pipe, Gee, Wilson, & Egerton, 1999). However, when children are specifically asked about prop items or use them to show what happened, error rates are likely to increase significantly (Gee & Pipe, 1995; Pipe *et al.*, 1999; Salmon *et al.*, 1995; Salmon & Pipe, 1997). Increased numbers of errors (and decreased accuracy) are particularly marked when distracters are introduced (Salmon *et al.*, 1995; Salmon & Pipe, 1997; Steward *et al.*, 1996), when props are introduced after several years and children are asked to re-enact what happened (Pipe, Woolcock, Jones, Fivush, & Murachver, 2001), or when there is free access to a large number of real props, including attractive distracters (Steward *et al.*, 1996). Steward *et al.* suggest that when young children have the opportunity to manipulate real props, the assigned task shifts from one of remembering to one of play, exploring, or demonstrating knowledge. Clearly, this is not appropriate when children are being interviewed about a specific past experience for forensic purposes.

Reinstating Environmental Context

In many of the studies involving real items, environmental context has also been reinstated, and only a few studies have attempted to sort out the separate effects of the context and prop items involved in the event; for example, Wilkinson (1988) found that when pre-school children were interviewed about a school outing after a 1-day delay, those who were interviewed while walking the same route taken the day before reported significantly more than children interviewed back in the pre-school setting. In this study, everything associated with the event, including items involved in activities, was reinstated, although children did not interact with the items. Hershkowitz *et al.* (1998) examined the effects of context reinstatement with children between the ages of four and thirteen, undergoing investigative interviews in a real-world context. They found that children were able to provide additional details about alleged sexual abuse when re-interviewed at the scene of the alleged incident. Pipe and Wilson (1994), however, found no significant positive (or negative) effects of environmental context only (location, distinctive furnishings) on the reports of six- and ten-year-old children in an analogue study (see also Pipe *et al.*, 1999), although event context together with relevant props did enhance recall. Context reinstatement has not increased error rates in those studies in which it has been assessed (Wilkinson, 1988; Pipe & Wilson, 1994). However, the effects of changing aspects of the environmental context or including distracter context items have not yet been addressed.

Asking children to *think about* the event context may also benefit children's subsequent reports. Mental reinstatement of an event context is one of several techniques comprising the cognitive interview, which has been shown to significantly increase the amount of information adults report (for a review, see Fisher & Geiselman, 1992). Instructions to mentally reinstate the event context combined with the instruction to report everything (both components of the cognitive interview) can enhance recall for children as young as five and six years old over short delays (Dietze & Thompson, 1993; Hayes & Delamothe, 1997; McCauley & Fisher, 1995; Memon, Wark, Holley, Bull, & Köhnken, 1996; Memon, Wark, Bull, & Köhnken, 1997), although over longer delays results have been mixed (McCauley & Fisher, 1995; Memon *et al.*, 1996; Memon *et al.*, 1997). Memon *et al.* (1997), for example, found the cognitive interview, including mental-context reinstatement, led to more correct information (and errors) in open-ended recall when children were interviewed two days after the event, but not when they were interviewed following a longer (twelve day) delay. They raise the possibility that components of the cognitive interview, in particular asking children to report everything they can remember, could lead to less accurate accounts.

Reinstating Prop Items Prior to the Interview

The usual way of thinking about using prop items is to have them present during the interview, but children may also benefit from the provision of prop items *prior* to an interview (e.g. a day before or even immediately before). Studies with infants show that memories, that might otherwise be presumed to have been forgotten, can be reactivated by reinstating the original context of the event prior to memory testing

(Rovee-Collier & Hayne, 1987; Rovee-Collier & Shyi, 1992). With older children, too, it seems that memories can be made more accessible if children are given a 'reminder' prior to being interviewed about an experience (Hudson & Sheffield, 1998). Priestley, Roberts, and Pipe (1999) found that when five and six-year-old children were interviewed six months after an event, a brief (five minute) re-exposure to the event context the day before the interview significantly enhanced recall. Reminder procedures may be even more effective following very long delays (e.g. of two years) when the memory has faded (Daniels & Pipe, 2000). No negative effects of reminders on recall accuracy have been reported, perhaps because children do not interact with the prop items. However, as was noted for context reinstatement, above, the inclusion of distracter items as part of the procedure has not yet been examined.

Real Props Evaluated

Reinstating aspects of an event can be an effective means of enhancing children's recall. Items and objects central to the event are likely to be the most effective retrieval cues, although environmental context—returning to the scene of the crime—may also have positive effects under some circumstances. From a forensic perspective, the role of many prop-based procedures, whether having the props present during interviews, presenting them prior to interviews, or reinstating them mentally, is one of making the memory more accessible for reporting rather than facilitating communication directly. When children are asked to use the items to show what happened, accuracy is at risk. As a result, in forensic contexts, interactions with prop items should be minimized. Nonetheless, real props clearly can enhance children's reports, without decreasing accuracy, if used appropriately.

TOYS, DOLLS, SCALE MODELS

Relatively few empirical studies have examined the effects of different kinds of toys on children's reports. It is clear from the few studies that do exist, however, that the extent to which toys facilitate children's reports is influenced significantly by the age of the child, the type of toy provided, and the way in which the toys are used in the interview.

Dolls, alone or in combination with other toys, have been the focus of several studies, because of their obvious forensic relevance (e.g. as a means for conveying information about where the child was touched. Dolls are least effective as interview aids with very young children. When used with children aged five years or younger, dolls fail to substantially increase the correct information that children report (DeLoache, Anderson, & Smith, 1995; Goodman & Aman, 1990; Gordon *et al.*, 1993; Samra & Yuille, 1996) and increase errors (DeLoache *et al.*, 1995; Goodman, Quas, Batterman-Faunce, Riddlesberger, & Kuhn, 1997). Moreover, very young children have a poor ability to use a doll to show where they were touched (DeLoache & Marzolf, 1995). Indeed, DeLoache *et al.* (1995) concluded, on the basis of a series of studies, that whether they are used to show where children had been touched or to recount a past experience '. . . dolls do not assist young children's testimony' (p. 8). Bruck, Ceci, Francouer, and Renick (1995) also reported that anatomically detailed dolls and toys markedly compromised the accuracy of two-and-half to four-year-old children's responses when they were asked direct, leading, and misleading questions about genital and anal touch. Other studies have, however, failed to find any impact of dolls on children's ability to respond to specific and misleading questions (Goodman & Aman, 1990; Gordon *et al.*, 1993).

With older children (between the ages of five and ten), dolls and other toys may help children produce more complete reports (Goodman *et al.*, 1997; Gordon *et al.*, 1993; Saywitz *et al.*, 1991). Anatomically detailed dolls, particularly in conjunction with direct questions, may also help children report sensitive information about touch, including genital contact (Goodman *et al.*, 1997; Saywitz *et al.*, 1991; Steward *et al.*, 1996). As was found for younger children, however, dolls with other toys introduce additional errors when children use them to demonstrate what happened (Goodman *et al.*, 1997; Saywitz *et al.*, 1991), although they do not necessarily decrease accuracy in a relative sense (Goodman *et al.*, 1997).

Toys other than dolls, and scale models of items from the event, may also lead to increases in the amount of information that children report (Price & Goodman, 1990; Priestley & Pipe, 1997, 1999; Salmon *et al.*, 1995; Salmon & Pipe, 1997), particularly if they are very similar to corresponding items from the event (Priestley & Pipe, 1997). However, as with dolls, the cost to accuracy of providing these other toys can be significant, particularly with younger children (DeLoache *et al.*, 1995; Goodman & Aman, 1990; Goodman *et al.*, 1997; Greenhoot, Ornstein, Gordon, & Baker-Ward, 1999; Priestley & Pipe, 1997; Priestley & Pipe, 1999; Salmon *et al.*, 1995; Salmon & Pipe, 1997; Saywitz *et al.*, 1991). Toys typically introduce significantly more errors than do real props (Salmon *et al.*, 1995; Salmon & Pipe, 1997) and even verbal recall may become less accurate, especially over long delays (Salmon & Pipe, 1997). Distracter toys, in particular, are likely to introduce a disproportionate number of errors into children's accounts (Salmon *et al.*, 1995; Salmon & Pipe, 1997; Saywitz *et al.*, 1991).

Dolls, Toys and Scale Models Evaluated

Dolls and toys in interviews with children are associated with a significant increase in the number of errors in children's reports, particularly in the case of children five years and younger. Why might this be so? First, toys and dolls usually have a relatively low level of similarity to the items that were involved in the event and, therefore, are not likely to be very effective retrieval cues. Scale models that convey highly specific information about an event are likely to provide the most effective retrieval cues without a cost to accuracy, but they are unlikely to be available in clinical and forensic contexts very often.

Second, the more familiar role of toys and dolls as playthings may interfere with children's recognition of their representational function; that is, young children have difficulty understanding that the toy can be both an object in its own right and also stand for something else (e.g. that a doll is a toy and also represents the child him or herself, DeLoache, 1990). Even where there is a high level of similarity between the toy and the items in the event, their salience as play objects may become paramount (DeLoache & Marzolf, 1995; Salmon *et al.*, 1995), with the result that children are diverted from the central tasks of remembering and recounting a specific past event to play, exploration, or demonstrating general knowledge. Toys must be used extremely cautiously when it is important to obtain an accurate account of what happened on a particular occasion (see Poole & Lamb, 1998, for further discussion).

PHOTOGRAPHS

Children as young as two-and-a-half years understand the relationship between a photo and the items depicted, and this symbolic understanding appears to develop earlier for pictures than for models and toys (DeLoache & Burns, 1993). Photographs could potentially, therefore, act as retrieval cues in much the same way as the actual items they depict. Moreover, because children do not interact with the objects themselves, photographs minimize the risk of introducing errors.

Five studies examining the role of photos in event recall have been reported to date. Hudson and Fivush (1991) used photographs to elicit five-year-old children's memories of an event (a museum visit) after delays of six weeks, one year, and six years. The photographs were introduced only after questioning failed to elicit information and were highly specific to that unique event. Hudson and Fivush (1991) reported that these specific cues were increasingly necessary over the four interviews that took place over the delay and very few errors were made overall. Paterson and Bull (1999) also found photos to be effective in aiding recall after a long delay. Five- and six-year-old children's verbal recall of a magic show was substantially assisted one year later by showing them a few photographs of objects used in the event. Ascher-mann, Dannenberg, and Schulz (1998) interviewed three- to seven-year-old children about an event after a 10-day delay, with black and white photographs of items from the event as well as distracters. Children were asked to select the item they recognized and were asked specific questions relating to the object. Children interviewed with photos provided more correct answers and made fewer errors than those inter-viewed without photographs. Priestley and Pipe (1999) showed three- to four-year-old children photographs of real props from an event together with distracter items. The photographs elicited more correct information than did verbal prompts alone, as well as errors, although accuracy (correct recall as a proportion of total) was not compromised relative to a standard verbal interview. Most of the errors related to items in the distracter photographs. Finally, Salmon and colleagues have recently reported that photographs of distinctive items of medical equipment did not help children recount a painful medical pro-cedure six months later (Salmon, Price, & Pereira, 2000).

Photographs Evaluated

These preliminary studies suggest that this is a promising area of research and that photos can be effective retrieval cues following short and long delays. Further work is needed regarding the effects of distracter photos or of distracter items in photos on accuracy and whether photos are more likely to assist recall of some events than others.

DRAWING IN INTERVIEWS

Drawing has been used extensively in clinical contexts for a range of purposes; for example, to facilitate communication about traumatic ex-periences (Bentovim et al., 1995; Pynoos & Eth, 1986) and to trigger memories of specific experiences (Bentovim et al., 1995; see Gross & Hayne, 1998, for a review). Recent research has focused on the impact of drawing on children's verbal reports of an event rather than on inter-pretation of the drawing itself.

Compared to a standard verbal interview, asking children to draw and tell about the event increases the correct information reported by children aged between the ages of five and ten years without compromising accuracy, although it is less effective for younger (three- to five-year-old) children (Brennan & Fisher, 1998; Butler *et al.*, 1995; Gross & Hayne, 1999). Drawing appears to be most effective when it is used in combination with relatively specific but non-leading prompts such as 'draw and tell me everything you saw' (Butler *et al.*, 1995; Gross & Hayne, 1999), rather than direct and probing follow-up questions or free recall (Brennan & Fisher, 1998; Butler *et al.*, 1995; Gross & Hayne, 1999).

There are mixed findings concerning the extent to which drawing facilitates children's reports after very long (one or two year) delays (Gross & Hayne, 1999; Salmon & Pipe, 2000). The inconsistent findings may relate to the different kinds of event in the studies. In particular, drawing may be effective after a long delay only when the event is relatively well retained in memory, for example, when the event is distinctive, unique, and logically structured as was the case in the visit to a chocolate factory in the Gross and Hayne (1999) study. When the event is not particularly salient or does not involve remarkable or distinctive features, as in the medical examination in the Salmon and Pipe study, drawing may provide insufficient support for memory to help the child to retrieve the event in question. Indeed, the interaction between the nature of the event and techniques useful for enhancing recall clearly requires further consideration.

Drawing evaluated

Drawing shows promise as a means of facilitating children's accounts of their experiences. Further research is needed to establish the conditions under which drawing is most likely to facilitate children's reports, as well as those under which it does not, and may even lead to errors, for example, where the interviewer provides leading or misleading prompts or when the child does not remember the particular target event but nonetheless has relevant general knowledge (Gross & Hayne, 1999). Several factors have been identified that may underlie the effectiveness of drawing; for example, children whose drawings are ranked by independent adults as being of better representational quality also report more correct information than is the case for children whose drawings are of lesser quality (Butler *et al.*, 1995; Gross & Hayne, 1999). It may be that the better drawings provide children with more effective retrieval cues. Furthermore, drawing extends the duration of the interview relative to a verbal interview (Brennan & Fisher, 1998; Butler *et al.*, 1995; Edwards & Forman, 1989), raising the possibility that the length of the interview is one factor influencing the effectiveness of drawing.

CONCLUDING COMMENTS

Asking children to recall and recount experiences that happened months or years earlier, in a way that adults who have little or no knowledge of the events in question understand, can be a tall order. The research reviewed here suggests that it is possible to make the child's task easier. Several techniques, such as providing props, reinstating event context (physically or mentally) and drawing, have all been shown to help children remember and recount much more information than they otherwise would provide in (unaided) verbal recall. However, careful consideration must be given to how, when, and with whom specific techniques are used if the accuracy of children's accounts is not to be compromised.

We believe that the most important function of non-verbal techniques from a forensic perspective is that they aid memory retrieval processes and, in turn, make the memory more accessible for verbal reporting. Simply having prop items present, without the child interacting with them, is often sufficient to enhance recall and even a relatively brief exposure to the props prior to interview can significantly enhance children's open-ended accounts. It is also likely that retrieval-related processes underlie the effectiveness of drawing, from a forensic perspective. When used to facilitate memory, these techniques can enhance children's accounts without putting accuracy at risk.

In contrast, when props are used to help children communicate information, and children are invited to show as well as tell what happened, all too frequently accuracy is compromised. Interpreting what children do (or draw) is considerably more risky than listening to what they say, when the objective is an accurate description of a specific past event. Moreover, when invited to show what happened, for young (pre-school) children especially, it is very easy for the perceived task to change from one of talking about the past to that of exploring, playing, or demonstrating general knowledge with the prop items. The negative effects of interacting with props, whether toys or actual items and objects, are likely to be exacerbated over long delays when memories have faded and are less readily available for report. Only a few studies have addressed the question of how to effectively enhance children's reports over such very long delays, although this is frequently a very relevant issue for forensic interviewers.

The non-verbal techniques examined here will not, of course, be appropriate for all interview situations or, indeed, even the majority. Reinstating an event context or prop items may not be practical and, furthermore, it may be highly traumatic to a witness to return to the scene of an event or to be presented with vivid reminders of it. Similarly, children may not be able (or willing) to draw aspects of their experience or to mentally reinstate the event context. Nonetheless, children's eye-witness accounts are a function of both the child's abilities and the support or obstacles that the interview context presents. These non-verbal techniques add to the range of strategies available to help inter-viewers help children to tell their stories most effectively.

Preparation of this chapter was supported by a grant from the New Zealand Public Good Science Fund.

REFERENCES

Aschermann, E., Dannenberg, U., & Schulz, A.-P. (1998). Photographs as retrieval cues for children. *Applied Cognitive Psychology*, 12, 55–66.

Bentovim, A., Bentovim, M., Vizard, E., & Wiseman, M. (1995). Facilitating interviews with children who may have been sexually abused. *Child Abuse Review*, 4, 246–62.

Boat, B.W., & Everson, M.D. (1994). Exploration of anatomical dolls by non-referred preschool-aged children: Comparisons by age, gender, race, and socioeconomic status. *Child Abuse and Neglect*, 18, 139–53.

Brennan, K.H., & Fisher, R.P. (1998). Drawing as a technique to facilitate children's recall. Unpublished manuscript.

Brown, A.L., Bransford, J.D., Ferrara, R.A., & Campione, J.C. (1983). Learning, remembering, and understanding. In: P.H. Mussen (Series Ed.), J.H. Flavell & E.M. Markman (Vol. Eds). *Handbook of child psychology: Vol. 3. Cognitive development* (4th ed., pp. 77–166). New York: Wiley.

Bruck, M., Ceci, S.J., Francouer, E., & Renick, A. (1995). Anatomically detailed dolls do not facilitate preschoolers' reports of a pediatric examination involving genital touching. *Journal of Experimental Psychology: Applied*, 1, 95–109.

Butler, S., Gross, J., & Hayne, H. (1995). The effect of drawing on memory performance in young children. *Developmental Psychology*, 31, 597–608.

Daniels, K., & Pipe, M.-E. (2000, March). Helping children to remember a novel event after a 2-year delay. Poster presented at the University of Otago Memory Theme Symposium on Memory Development, Dunedin, New Zealand.

DeLoache, J.S. (1990). Young children's understanding of models. In: R. Fivush and J.A. Hudson (eds), *Knowing and remembering in young children* (pp. 94–126). New York: Cambridge University Press.

DeLoache, J.S., Anderson, K., & Smith, C.M. (1995, March). Interviewing children about real-life events. Paper presented at the biennial meeting of the Society for Research in Child Development, Indianapolis, IN.

DeLoache, J.S., & Burns, N.M. (1993). Symbolic development in young children: Understanding models and pictures. In: C. Pratt & A.F. Garton (Eds). *Systems of representation in children: Development and use* (pp. 91–112). Chichester, UK: Wiley.

DeLoache, J.S., & Marzolf, D.P. (1995). The use of dolls to interview young children: Issues of symbolic representation. *Journal of Experimental Child Psychology*, **60**, 155–173.

Dietze, P.M., & Thomson, D.M. (1993). Mental reinstatement of context: A technique for interviewing child witnesses. *Applied Cognitive Psychology*, **7**, 97–108.

Edwards, C.A., & Forman, B.D. (1989). Effects of child interview method on accuracy and completeness of sexual abuse information recall. *Social Behavior and Personality*, **17**, 237–47.

Fisher, R.P., & Geiselman, R.E. (1992). Memory-enhancing techniques for investigative interviewing. *The Cognitive Interview*. Springfield, IL: Charles C. Thomas.

Fivush, R., Kuebli, J., & Clubb, P. (1992). The structure of events and event representations: A developmental analysis. *Child Development*, **63**, 188–201.

Flavell, J.H., Miller, P.H., & Miller, S.A. (1993). *Cognitive development* (3rd ed.). Englewood Cliffs, NJ: Prentice Hall.

Gee, S., & Pipe, M.-E. (1995). Helping children to remember: The influence of object cues on children's accounts of a real event. *Developmental Psychology*, **31**, 746–58.

Goodman, G.S., & Aman, C. (1990). Children's use of anatomically detailed dolls to recount an event. *Child Development*, **61**, 1859–1871.

Goodman, G.S., Quas, J.A., Batterman-Faunce, J.M., Riddlesberger, M., & Kuhn, J. (1997). Children's reactions to and memory for a stressful event: Influences of age, anatomical dolls, knowledge, and parental attachment. *Applied Developmental Science*, **1**, 54–75.

Gordon, B.N., Ornstein, P.A., Nida, R.E., Follmer, A., Crenshaw, M.C., & Albert, G. (1993). Does the use of dolls facilitate children's memory of visits to the doctor? *Applied Cognitive Psychology*, **7**, 459–74.

Greenhoot, A.F., Ornstein, P.A., Gordon, B.N., & Baker-Ward, L. (1999). Acting out the details of a pediatric check-up: The impact of interview condition and behavioral style on children's memory reports. *Child Development*, **70**, 363–80.

Gross, J., & Hayne, H. (1998). Drawing facilitates children's verbal reports of emotionally laden events. *Journal of Experimental Psychology: Applied*, **4**, 163–79.

Gross, J., & Hayne, H. (1999). Drawing facilitates children's verbal reports after long delays. *Journal of Experimental Psychology: Applied*, **5**, 265–83.

Hayes, B.K., & Delamothe, K. (1997). Cognitive interviewing procedures and suggestibility in children's recall. *Journal of Applied Psychology*, **82**, 562–77.

Hershkowitz, I., Orbach, Y., Lamb, M.E., Sternberg, K.J., Horowitz, D., & Hovav, M. (1998). Visiting the scene of the crime: Effects on children's recall of alleged abuse. *Legal and Criminological Psychology*, **3**, 195–207.

Hudson, J.A., & Fivush, R. (1991). As time goes by: Sixth grade children remember a kindergarten experience. *Applied Cognitive Psychology*, **5**, 347–60.

Hudson, J.A., & Sheffield, E.G. (1998). Deja vu all over again: Effects of reenactment on toddlers' event memory. *Child Development*, **69**, 51–67.

Koocher, G.P., Goodman, G.S., White, C.S., Friedrich, W.N., Sivan, A.B., & Reynolds, C.R. (1995). Psychological science and the use of anatomically detailed dolls in child sexual-abuse assessments. *Psychological Bulletin*, **118**, 199–222.

McCauley, M.R., & Fisher, R.P. (1995). Facilitating children's eyewitness recall with the revised cognitive interview. *Journal of Applied Psychology*, **80**, 510–16.

Memon, A., Wark, L., Bull, R., & Köhnken, G. (1997). Isolating the effects of the cognitive interview techniques. *British Journal of Psychology*, **88**, 179–97.

Memon, A., Wark, L., Holley, A., Bull, R., & Köhnken, G. (1996). Interviewer behaviour in investigative interviews. *Psychology, Crime and Law*, **3**, 135–55.

Paterson, B., & Bull, R. (1999). Young children's recall after long delays. Paper presented at the Annual Conference of the European Psychology and Law Association, Dublin.

Pipe, M.-E., Gee, S., & Wilson, J.C. (1993). Cues, props, and context: Do they facilitate children's event reports? In: G.S. Goodman & B.L. Bottoms (Eds), *Child Victims, Child Witnesses: Understanding And Improving Testimony* (pp. 25–45). New York: Guilford Press.

Pipe, M.-E., Gee, S., Wilson, C., & Egerton, J.M. (1999). Children's recall one and two years after an event. *Developmental Psychology*, **35**, 781–9.

Pipe, M.-E., & Wilson, J.C. (1994). Cues and secrets: Influences on children's event reports. *Developmental Psychology*, **30**, 515–25.

Pipe, M.-E., Woolcock, C., Jones, C., Fivush, R., & Murachver, T. (2001). *Event and story recall 4 years later*. Submitted for publication.

Poole, D.A., & Lamb, M.E. (1998). *Investigative interviews of children*. Washington, DC: American Psychological Association.

Price, D.W.W., & Goodman, G.S. (1990). Visiting the wizard: Children's memory for a recurring event. *Child Development*, **61**, 664–80.

Priestley, G., & Pipe, M.-E. (1997). Using toys and models in interviews with young children. *Journal of Applied Cognitive Psychology*, **11**, 69–87.

Priestley, G., & Pipe, M.-E. (1999, September). *Representation, imagination, and young children's event reports*. Paper presented at the New Zealand Psychological Society Conference, Dunedin, New Zealand.

Priestley, G., Roberts, S., & Pipe, M.-E. (1999). Returning to the scene: Reminders and context reinstatement enhance children's recall. *Developmental Psychology*, **35**, 1006–19.

Pynoos, R.S., & Eth, S. (1986). Witness to violence: The child interview. *Journal of the American Academy of Child Psychiatry*, **25**, 306–19.

Rovee-Collier, C., & Hayne, H. (1987). Reactivation of infant memory: Implications for cognitive development. In: H.W. Reese (Ed.), *Advances in child development and behavior* (Vol. 20, pp. 185–238). New York: Academic Press.

Rovee-Collier, C., & Shyi, G.C.W. (1992). 'A functional and cognitive analysis of infant long-term retention. In: M.L. Howe, C.J. Brainerd, & V.F. Reyna (Eds), *Development of long-term retention* (pp. 3–55). New York: Springer-Verlag.

Salmon, K., Bidrose, S., & Pipe, M.-E. (1995). Providing props to facilitate children's event reports: A comparison of toys and real items. *Journal of Experimental Child Psychology*, **60**, 174–94.

Salmon, K., & Pipe, M.-E. (1997). Props and children's event reports: The impact of a 1-year delay. *Journal of Experimental Child Psychology*, **65**, 261–92.

Salmon, K., & Pipe, M.E. (2000). Recalling an event one year later: The impact of props, drawings, and a prior interview. *Applied Cognitive Psychology*, **14**, 99–120.

Salmon, K., Price, M., & Pereira, J. (2000). *Effortful control, distress and children's long-term recall of an aversive medical procedure.* Unpublished manuscript.

Samra, J., & Yuille, J.C. (1996). Anatomically-neutral dolls: Their effects on the memory and suggestibility of 4- to 6-year-old eyewitnesses. *Child Abuse and Neglect*, **20**, 126–172.

Saywitz, K.J., Goodman, G.S., Nicholas, E., & Moan, S.F. (1991). Children's memories of a physical examination involving genital touch: Implications for reports of child sexual abuse. *Journal of Consulting and Clinical Psychology*, **59**, 682–91.

Smith, B.S., Ratner, H.H., & Hobart, C.J. (1987). The role of cuing and the organization in children's memory for events. *Journal of Experimental Child Psychology*, **44**, 1–24.

Steward, M.S., Steward, D.S., Farquhar, L., Myers, J.E.B., Reinhart, M., Welker, J., Joye, N., Driskill, J., & Morgan, J. (1996). Interviewing young children about body touch and handling. *Monographs of the Society for Research in Child Development*, **61**(4–5), 1–186.

Tulving, E., & Thomson, D.M. (1973). Encoding specificity and retrieval processes in episodic memory. *Psychological Review*, **80**, 352–73.

Wilkinson, J. (1988). Context effects in children's event memory. In: M.M. Gruneberg, P.E. Morris, & R.N. Sykes (Eds), *Practical aspects of memory: Current research and issues* (Vol. 1, pp. 107–11). Chichester, UK: Wiley.

CHAPTER 12

Deception in Children: A Literature Review and Implications for Children's Testimony

ALDERT VRIJ

Department of Psychology, University of Portsmouth, UK

A popular statement, sometimes expressed in the media, is that 'children never lie' (Ceci & DeSimone Leichtman, 1992). Child-deception research has convincingly demonstrated that this statement is incorrect, however, it may well have influenced the direction of child-deception research. Adult-deception research mainly focuses on two questions: 'What are the differences between liars and truth-tellers in behaviour, speech content, and physiological responses?' and 'How good are people at detecting behavioural, verbal, and physiological cues to deceit?' Although some of these aspects have also been investigated in child-deception research, studies mainly focus on whether children lie, why they lie, and when they lie (Frank, 1992). The first part of this chapter addresses these latter issues. I then review the literature about which verbal cues and which behavioural cues emerge in children when they lie, followed by how good adults and children are at detecting these verbal and behavioural cues to deceit. Finally, I discuss the implications for children's testimony, together with directions for new research.

Children's Testimony. Edited by H.L. Westcott, G.M. Davies, and R.H.C. Bull.
© 2002 John Wiley & Sons, Ltd.

FEATURES OF A LIE

Elsewhere (Vrij, 2000), I have defined a lie as 'A successful or unsuccessful deliberate attempt, without forewarning, to create in another a belief which the communicator considers to be untrue.' Several aspects of this definition merit attention. First, the word 'deliberate'. Lying is an intentional act. Someone who makes an erroneous statement by mistake is not lying. A woman who mistakenly believes that she was sexually abused in her childhood, and therefore goes to the police to report this abuse, gives a false report but is not lying. This is an important issue. As discussed later in this chapter, liars may experience several emotions. The three most common types of emotion associated with deceit are fear, guilt, and excitement (Ekman, 1992). These emotions may be reflected in someone's behaviour, and lies could be detected by spotting such emotional behavioural cues to deceit. However, these emotions will not be felt when someone makes an erroneous statement by mistake, and behavioural emotional cues are therefore unlikely to be present in this type of false statement.

Second, 'without forewarning' means that people are only lying when they do not inform others in advance of their intention to lie (Ekman, 1992). Magicians are therefore not lying during their performance, as people in the audience expect to be deceived. Third, 'a belief which the communicator considers to be untrue' indicates that even a true statement could be a lie. Suppose that a child intends to eat the bar of chocolate which he thinks is left in the cupboard but that, unknowingly to the child, the chocolate has already been eaten by his mother. In order to prevent his sister from looking in the cupboard, the child might therefore tell her that there is no chocolate left in the cupboard. The child is then lying to his sister although his statement is actually true. The emotional behavioural cues which are likely to be absent when someone makes an erroneous statement by mistake are possibly present when someone makes this type of truthful statement.

Several factors may increase the likelihood of an erroneous statement occurring when the child speaker believes it to be true. First, a number of people might interview the child about the same event which allegedly occurred. This repeated interviewing sometimes results in the child starting to believe that s/he has witnessed an event which actually never occurred (Ceci, Loftus, Leichtman, & Bruck, 1994). Second, asking the same question twice in one interview (because, for example, the interviewer wants to be sure of the child's reply or did not believe the answer the child initially gave) sometimes results in children giving a different answer the second time, particularly if these repeated interviews are conducted by interviewers who ask leading questions and have preconceived notions about what might have occurred (Ceci, Bruck, & Loftus, 1998; Moston, 1987; Poole & White, 1991). Third, the wording of a question may affect people's memory about the event (Loftus & Palmer, 1974). Dale, Loftus, and Rathbun (1976) found that when questions are asked about entities which did not occur, a question such as 'Did you see *the* ...' were answered yes more frequently than a question such as 'Did you see *a* ...' Hence, the latter form of question is the form of question most likely to produce a correct response. Finally, young children, under some circumstances, can confuse memories for experienced events with similar events which they have seen on television (Roberts & Blades, 1999).

TYPES OF LIE

DePaulo, Kashy, Kirkendol, Wyer, and Epstein (1996) made a distinction between three types of lie: outright lies, exaggerations, and subtle lies. Outright lies (or falsifications) are total falsehoods: lies in which the information conveyed is completely different from, or contradictory to, the truth. Falsifications may be multiword statements (a child who tells her parents that she went to the zoo although she actually went to the cinema) or may be one word responses ('Do you know who ate that chocolate bar?' 'No') or may be gestures (pointing in the wrong direction). Exaggerations are lies in which liars overstate the facts. A boy who claims to have 50 compact discs (CDs) although he actually possesses 10 CDs is exaggerating. As in fabrications, exaggerations can be multiword statements, one word responses, or gestures. Concealing information (i.e. not volunteering relevant information) is an example of a subtle lie. The child who knows who broke the toy but remains silent when her mum asks her who broke it is concealing information.

THE FIRST LIE

There is a debate in the literature regarding the age at which children start telling lies. There is agreement that children are capable of telling deliberate lies at the age of four (Bussey, 1992; Leekam, 1992; Newton, Reddy, & Bull, 2000). However, even before the age of four, children are able to misinform others. In their experiment, Lewis, Stanger, and Sullivan (1989) instructed children aged between 33 and 37 months not to peek at a toy while the experimenter left the room. Most children transgressed and did look at the toy. When asked, the great majority of children either denied that they peeked or would not answer the question. Nigro and Snow (1992), who replicated this study with children as young as 32 months, obtained similar results. Ceci and DeSimone Leichtman (1992) found that three-year-olds, each of whom believed that the interviewer was unaware that the child's mother broke a toy, frequently claimed that it was broken by another or that she did not know who broke it. Chandler, Fritz, and Hala (1989), utilizing a hide-and-seek board game, have shown that even two-year-olds withheld information by 'erasing footprints', 'laying false trails', and pointing to the wrong place in order to prevent another person from finding a treasure. Naturalistic studies revealed similar results. Newton, Reddy, and Bull (2000) found that a two-and-a-half-year-old boy provided wrong information in an effort to put his mother on the wrong track.

The discussion in the literature focuses on the question as to whether these examples are forms of genuine deception; that is, deliberate attempts by children to get someone to believe something that the children know to be false, or forms of 'practical deception', deceptive acts where the 'liars' want to achieve a goal by saying or doing something that they know or believe to be false without actually trying to affect the belief of the person who is duped (Sinclair, 1996). However, what is important in this context is that as soon as children consider the listener's mental state (as they will do by the age of four, Bussey, 1992) they will become better liars (Leekam, 1992). From that stage, they will realize that in order to lie successfully they must convince another of the veracity of a false statement (Oldershaw & Bagby, 1997). A girl who has broken a toy may simply accuse her brother of this transgression. However, she may also actually try to let her mother believe that her brother has broken the toy (e.g. by arguing that she is not strong enough to do this).

Research has demonstrated that, as they get older, children become better at influencing other people's mental states. In a hiding game in which children had to deceive a competitor, Sodian (1991) found that three-year-olds used acts of 'sabotage' (physically preventing the competitor from gaining a reward) whereas most four-year-olds fooled the other person (pointing in the wrong direction) to prevent that person from stealing the object. In another hiding game, in which children had to point to an empty box in order to deceive another, Russell, Mauthner, Sharpe, and Tidswell (1991) found that four-year-olds performed remarkably better than three-year-olds. In Peskin's (1992) study, three- to five-year-olds were confronted with a competitor who always chose the object for which the children themselves had previously stated a preference. The children were asked to 'think of what to do or to say so that the competitor won't get what you want.' More five-year-olds (87%) than three-year-olds (29%) tried to influence the competitor's mental state by pointing to an object they did not like or by concealing information. Unfortunately, all these experimental studies only required easy lies (pointing at an object, one word statements, concealments) and none required the children to engage in complicated verbal deception. Observational data in daily life settings has revealed that four-year-olds' lies typically take the form of one word responses rather than the more sophisticated elaborations of older children and adults (Bussey, 1992).

WHY DO CHILDREN LIE?

There are at least five reasons why children lie (DePaulo & Jordan, 1982; Saarni & von Salisch, 1993): to avoid negative outcomes (punishment); to obtain a reward; to protect their self-esteem; to regulate relationship dynamics ('I didn't want to make him feel bad, that's why I didn't show my disappointment'); and to conform to norms and conventions. There is empirical evidence to suggest that the earliest lies are those that are meant to escape punishment (Bussey, 1992; Lewis, 1993; Saarni, 1979; Stouthamer-Loeber, 1986). Lies generated to obtain rewards probably appear later (DePaulo & Jordan, 1982), followed by lies to protect one's self-esteem (Bussey, 1992). Saarni's (1979) research with six-, eight-, and ten-year-olds showed that the latter were the only children who lied to maintain norms.

Children lie for other reasons as well; for example, Ceci and DeSimone Leichtman (1992) found that children as young as three years old will lie to protect a loved one. Children also lie when they are asked to do so. Tate, Warren, and Hess (1992) conducted an experiment in which a 'coach', who was on friendly terms with the children, asked them to 'trick' someone else in a subsequent interview and to pretend that they had played with a certain toy. The children varied in age from two and a half to eight years. They found that 60% of the children participated in the lie (more older than younger children) and that 35% maintained the ruse throughout. They further found that most of these 'lying throughout' children knew the coach well. In another coaching study, Bussey (1992) found, as did Tate et al. (1992), that younger children (three-year-olds) were less likely to lie than older children (5-year-olds). However, 24% of the three-year-olds were willing to lie when instructed to do so, a percentage that rose to 50% when they were instructed in a very stern manner.

Children do seem to realize that they are lying when they are told to lie by an adult. Haugaard, Reppucci, Laird, & Nauful, (1991) showed children (four- to six-year-olds) a videotaped event in which a girl lies to a policeman about a neighbour hitting her. The vast majority (94%) of the children understood that the girl was lying, even though she was instructed by her mother to do so. In Haugaard's (1993) study, children (four- to twelve-year-olds) were shown a videotape in which a mother makes a false statement and a boy corroborates it. None of the children classified the corroboration as the truth. Hence, children of these ages who are asked to lie do realize that they are lying.

CHILDREN'S LYING SKILLS

People's lying skills can be measured in two different ways. The first method is to count the frequency of occurrence of verbal and non-verbal behaviour of truth-tellers and liars (count the number of details they mention, count the number of seconds they look away from the conversation partner, and so on) and then compare the scores of liars and truth-tellers. The second method is to show observers videoclips of a number of liars and truth-tellers and ask them to indicate whether they think that each person is lying or telling the truth. The fewer correct answers the judges give, the better liars the people in the videoclips are. The first method is better than the second, as the second method is confounded. It does not only investigate how good liars are at lying but also how good observers are at lie detecting. This section presents the research findings derived from the first method. Unfortunately, there are very few studies conducted with children using this approach.

Non-verbal Behaviour

Research has revealed that there is no typical deceptive behaviour, but some behaviours are more likely to occur than others during deception, depending on emotions experienced by the liar, the complexity of the lie, and the amount of effort the liar exerts in controlling his or her behaviour (Vrij, 2000).

Telling a lie might evoke three different emotions: fear, guilt, or duping delight (Ekman, 1992) (and all three processes may occur at the same time). Liars may be afraid of getting caught, feel guilty when they lie, or feel excited to have the opportunity to fool somebody. The expression of such emotions (e.g. nervous behaviours such as facial emotional expressions, gaze aversion, smiling, fidgeting, and stuttering) could betray a lie. Alternatively, sometimes liars find it difficult to lie, as it is not always easy to give an answer which sounds plausible and convincing. They then have to think hard while lying, which might result in indicators of hard thinking, such as stuttering, waiting before giving an answer, including pauses in speech, slower speech, or a decrease in movements. Finally, in order to make an honest impression, liars may try to suppress cues which they think will give their lies away; for example, they may try to avoid stuttering, fidgeting, looking away, and so on. Research has shown that, when people attempt to control their behaviour, the result often appears planned, rigid, and not spontaneous (DePaulo & Kirkendol, 1989).

The best liars are probably those who manage to suppress signs of nervousness and hard thinking and exhibit, even under difficult circumstances, behaviour that looks natural. In order to show natural behaviour, three aspects are important (Vrij, 2000). First, liars should realize that observers watch their behaviour to detect deceit; second, liars should know which behaviours make an honest impression on others, and, third, liars should be able to control their behaviour. The first two issues imply that the effective liar should be able to 'take the role of the other', an ability which is largely lacking in children under six years old (Flavell, Botkin, Fry, Wright, & Jarvis, 1968). This suggests that more cues of nervousness and more cues of hard thinking can be expected in younger children when lying than in older children, simply because younger children will not try so hard to suppress these cues.

Children's muscular control ability increases with age as well (Ekman, Roper, & Hager, 1980; Feldman & Phillipot, 1993); for example, Saarni (1984) observed, in a naturalistic study, six- to ten-year-olds' reactions when they received a disappointing gift. Younger children (and particularly boys) were more likely than older children to show their true reaction (negative faces). Ekman *et al.* (1980) studied five-, nine-, and thirteen-year-olds and found that older children have greater ability deliberately to produce the component actions involved in facial expression. These findings suggest, again, that with increased age fewer cues to deceit are likely to occur.

DePaulo and Jordan (1982), however, have argued that younger children may experience less emotion when lying; for example, because of their young age they might be less affected by feelings of guilt, might overlook the consequences of getting caught more often and so experience less fear of getting caught. Also, with increasing age, children show more spontaneous facial emotional expressions, which they need to suppress in order to conceal deceit (Morency & Krauss, 1982). Therefore, older children's role-taking skills, and increased muscular control that improves their skills in deception, may well be counteracted in part by an increase in emotions and an increase in emotional expression while lying.

Behavioural cues to deceit are least likely to occur when the stakes are low, the lie is easy, and the liar is not really motivated. Only four studies have been published presenting data concerning children's behaviour during deception (Lewis, 1993; Lewis *et al.*, 1989; Feldman, Devin-Sheehan, & Allen, 1978; Vrij & Winkel, 1995), and, unfortunately, all these studies fell into the latter category (i.e. the stakes were low, the lies were easy, and there was no effort to motivate the children to lie). In both Lewis's studies, children (two- and three-year-olds) were instructed not to peek. However, some of them did peek and denied that they peeked (thus lied) when asked. Their responses were compared with those children who did not peek and therefore truthfully responded not to have peeked. The analyses of facial and bodily behaviour (smiling, gaze aversion, sober mouth, relaxed-interest mouth, nervous touching) only revealed one (small) difference: truth-tellers smiled less than liars. In the study conducted by Feldman and colleagues, eight-year-olds were asked to praise a confederate who conducted a task. In the truthful condition, the confederate performed well and the praise was therefore honest. In the deception condition, the confederate performed poorly and the praise was therefore deceptive. Twenty-six different behaviours were scored and the results revealed only three behavioural differences: liars smiled less, showed less pleasant mouth expressions, and paused more than truth-tellers. Vrij and Winkel asked children (five- and nine-year olds) to taste two drinks, one the children liked and one they disliked. After each drink, they were requested to convince the interviewer that both drinks tasted good, regardless of how the drinks actually tasted. Vrij and Winkel scored ten behaviours and found four significant deception by age interaction effects. In younger children, false statements resulted in an increase in hand/arm movements, self-manipulations, and leg/foot movements as well as a longer latency period (pause between question and answer). In older children, there was a decrease in hand/arm movements, self-manipulations, leg/foot movements, and a shorter latency period. In explaining these age differences, Vrij and Winkel speculated that the behavioural cues exhibited by younger children were signs of nervousness and hard thinking, whereas the cues displayed by older children were signs of attempted behavioural control.

Verbal Behaviour

Criteria-Based Content Analysis (CBCA) is the most popular technique for measuring the veracity of verbal statements to date. The technique was initially developed in Germany to determine the credibility of child witnesses' testimonies in trials for sexual offences, as part of Statement Validity Assessment (SVA, Steller & Köhnken, 1989; Vrij & Akehurst 1998). SVA assessments are accepted as evidence in court in several European countries, including Germany and the Netherlands. CBCA is the systematic assessment, by trained examiners, of the presence or absence of 19 criteria compiled by Steller and Köhnken (1989). The presence of each criterion in the statement enhances the judged quality of the statement and strengthens the hypothesis that the account is based on genuine personal experience. Some of the criteria, such as 'reproduction of speech', 'description of interactions', 'unexpected complications', and 'unusual details' are understood to be cognitively too difficult for young children to include in a fabricated report. Other criteria, such as 'admitting lack of memory', 'raising doubts about one's own memory', and 'pardoning the perpetrator' are less likely to occur in fabricated reports for motivational reasons. Liars (although perhaps not the very young ones) might believe that these characteristics will make their stories less credible and convincing.

Several field studies in which children's statements in sexual abuse cases were examined have shown that reports believed to be truthful obtained higher CBCA scores than reports believed to be fabricated, although the differences were sometimes small (Boychuk, 1991; Lamb et al., 1997; Lamers-Winkelman & Buffing, 1996; Vrij, 2000). To date, only three laboratory CBCA studies have examined children's statements (Akehurst, Köhnken, & Höfer, 1995; Steller, Wellershaus, & Wolf, 1988; Winkel & Vrij, 1995), although none of these studies examined the statements of very young children (children participating in these studies were aged from six to eleven years old). Several differences between truth-tellers and liars emerged; however, the studies did not find the same criteria to be discriminating. A 100% overlap only occurred with regard to the criterion 'number of details'. In all three studies, truth-tellers included more details in their reports than did fabricators.

PEOPLE'S ABILITY TO DETECT CHILDREN'S LIES

Table 12.1 provides an overview of laboratory studies examining people's ability to detect children's lies. In most studies, observers watched videoclips of a number of people (mostly children) who were either lying or telling the truth. The observers had to indicate for each clip whether the person was lying or not.

Lewis' studies are perhaps particularly interesting because, unlike any other study mentioned in Table 12.1, participants in his

Table 12.1. People's ability to detect children's lies.

Author	Objective difference	What was visible	Age of senders	Age of judges	Number of judges	Deception task	Choice to lie	Dependent variable	Scale	Outcomes
Akehurst et al. (1995)	Yes	Written transcripts	7–8 10–11, adults	CBCA experts	3	Pretend to have your photo taken	No	Veracity of the statement	CBCA	Hit rates: truth, 73%; lie, 67%. No age differences were found
Allen and Atkinson (1978)	Not reported	Total image without sound	9–10	Adults	40	Trick a teacher and make her think that you understood the difficult lesson and did not understand the easy lesson	No	Understanding of the lecture	10-point	Observers actually differentiated between understanding and not understanding the lessons
Chahal and Cassidy (1995)	Not reported	Face or total image	8	Students, teachers, social workers	60	Falsify major excerpts of a film you had just seen	No	Lie detection	Yes/No	Hit rates, social workers: truth, 63%; lie, 70%; teachers: truth, 75%; lie, 65%; students: truth, 70%; lie, 63%; people having children: truth, 69%; lie, 82%; people not having children: 70%; lie, 52%. No differences between two channels were found
DePaulo, Jordan, Irvine and Laser (1982)	Yes	Total image	Adults	11, 13, 15, 17, and 18	176	Pretend to like someone you actually dislike and pretend to dislike someone you actually like	No	Lie detection + Ratings of liking	9-point	Observers at all ages were able to discriminate truth from deception by liking ratings. Detection deception accuracy was significantly worse than chance for 11-year-olds, at level of chance for 13, 15, and 17-year-olds and greater than chance for 18-year-olds
Feldman (1979)	Not reported	Face	8, 14, 22	Adults	23	Pretend to like a drink you actually dislike and pretend to dislike a drink you actually like	No	Ratings of liking	7-point	Males at all age levels and 8-year-old girls were rated as liking the drinks most while lying, 14-year-old girls were rated as liking the drink most while truth telling, no difference for 22-year-old women

Study		Channel	Age	Sample	N	Task		Measure	Scale	Findings
Feldman et al. (1978)	Yes	Face	8	8	55	Praise someone who performs poorly on a task	No	Ratings of happiness	6-point	Observers rated targets happier when they told the truth
Feldman et al. (1979)	Not reported	Face	6, 13, 19	Adults	15	Pretend to like a drink you actually dislike	No	Ratings of liking	7-point	Observers could only detect truths and lies in 6-year-olds.
Feldman and White (1980)	Not reported	Face or body	5–6, 7–8, 9–10, 11–12	Adults	13	As Feldman (1979)	No	Lie detection	7-point	The degree to which the face revealed deception *decreased* with increasing age for the girls and *increased* with increasing age for the boys. No age effects were found with regard to body movements
Feldman et al. (1982)	Not reported	Face without sound	5–12	5–12	39	As Feldman (1979)	No	Lie detection	Yes/No	Positive correlation between role-taking ability and ability to detect lies
Jackson (1996)	Not reported	Total image	11–12	Students, solicitors	200	Pretend to have seen a film	No	Lie detection	3-point	Hit rates, solicitors: truth, 54%; lie, 32%; students: truth, 71%; lie, 25%
Lewis (1993)	No	Total image	3–6	Adults	—	Deny to have peeked	Yes	Lie detection	Yes/No	Detection deception accuracy was at a level of chance
Lewis et al. (1989)	Yes	Total image	3	Adults	60	Deny to have peeked	Yes	Lie detection	3-point	Detection deception accuracy was at a level of chance
Morency and Krauss (1982)	Not reported	Face	6, 10	6, 10, adults, parents	130	Watch pleasant and unpleasant slides and feign opposite	No	Lie detection	Yes/No	Adults could detect deception in 6 and 10-year-olds on pleasant stimuli and in 6-year-olds on unpleasant stimuli. Parents were better than other adults at detecting their child's deception. Six- and 10-year-olds could only detect deception in 6-year-olds on pleasant stimuli

(continued)

Table 12.1 (*cont.*)

Author	Objective difference	What was visible	Age of senders	Age of judges	Number of judges	Deception task	Choice to lie	Dependent variable	Scale	Outcomes
Rotenberg et al. (1989)	Yes	Face	Actors	5, 7, and 9	60	NA	NA	The use of a verbal–non-verbal consistency principle	3-point	The use of a verbal–non-verbal consistency principle to infer truth or lying increased with age
Shennum and Bugental (1982)	Not reported	Vocal or face + upper body	6–7, 8–9, 10–12	Adults	10	Pretend to like something you dislike; pretend to dislike something you like; pretend to be neutral about something you like; pretend to be neutral about something you dislike	No	Lie detection	9-point	Successful control of facial expression increased with age for boys and girls when attempting to pretend to like something they disliked, but boys improved with age more than girls to pretend to be neutral about something they disliked; children of all ages failed to control positive affect through facial channel; children of all ages failed to control negative and positive affect through vocal channel
Steller et al. (1988)	Yes	Written transcripts	6, 9, experts	CBCA	3	Produce a story about a fictitious event	No	CBCA		Hit rates: truth, 78%; lie, 62%
Vrij and Van Wijngaarden (1994)	Yes	Total image	5, 9	Adults	82	Pretend to like a drink you actually dislike	No	Lie detection	Yes/No	Hit rates, total, 57%: truth, 51%; lie, 63%. No effect for age
Westcott et al. (1991)	Not reported	Total image	7–8, 10–11	Experts	32	Pretend to have visited a museum	No	Lie detection	Yes/No	Hit rate, total, 59%: truths better detected than lies, younger targets better detected than older
Winkel and Vrij (1995)	Yes	Written transcripts	8, 9 experts	CBCA	2	Produce a story about having a cat	No	CBCA		Higher scores for truth-tellers than for liars on several CBCA criteria

experiments could choose whether to lie. Obviously, this improves the ecological validity of the findings. In real life, people are not *forced* to lie but make the *choice* to lie. Those who consider themselves to be poor liars often choose not to lie (Vrij, 2000). Lewis's judges had great difficulty in detecting deceit: in both studies, they performed at the level of chance. The results, (slightly) above the level of chance, obtained in the other four studies might be due to the fact that some children who do not lie or rarely lie in daily life were now forced to lie for the sake of the experiment. These inexperienced liars were perhaps easy prey. The table further shows that the CBCA studies obtained higher accuracy rates than the non-verbal studies.

In several studies, judges gave their answers on 5- or 9-point Likert scales (e.g. 'Is the person lying?'—definitely not 1 … 5 definitely). As well as lie detection in this 'direct way', lie detection was sometimes measured in an indirect way (e.g. 'Did the person really like the other person?'). Results suggest that judges perform better using this indirect way of lie detection than using the direct way. This phenomenon has also been found in research on adult deception (Hurd & Noller, 1988). The reason for this finding is not clear. It might be caused by conversation rules which regulate politeness. Observers are often unsure as to whether someone is lying to them. In these cases, it will be impolite or for other reasons undesirable to accuse someone of being a liar, but it might be possible to challenge the words of a speaker more subtly. In other words, it is more difficult to say 'I don't believe you' than it is to say 'Do you really like that person so much?'

One might suggest that 'experts', people who deal with children in their daily work, could be better at detecting children's lies than lay people. Only one study considered this issue. Chahal and Cassidy (1995) compared the lie detection skills of college students with those of teachers and social workers. They did not find a difference in lie detection ability between lay persons and the professional groups. However, when comparing participants who had children with those who did not, they found that parents were better lie detectors than were non-parents, suggesting that experience in dealing with children does benefit lie detection, although 'experience with children at home' seems to be more important than 'work experience'. Morency and Krauss (1982) found that, in general, parents were better than other adults at detecting their own child's deception.

In seven studies, observers tried to detect lies in children of differing ages, providing an opportunity to test whether children's lies are more difficult to spot (children become better liars as they get older). The results show general support for this assumption (Feldman, 1979; Feldman, Jenkins, & Popoola, 1979; Feldman & White, 1980; Morency

& Krauss, 1982; Shennum & Bugental, 1982; Westcott, Davies, & Clifford, 1991), although gender differences emerged. Feldman and White (1980) found that for girls, but not for boys, the face revealed less about deception with increasing age, making older girls the best liars. Girls are generally more rewarded for being expressive than boys and thus may have greater opportunity to practise non-verbal displays of emotion. Shennum and Bugental (1982) found that with increasing age boys became better than girls in their ability to neutralize negative affect (pretend to be neutral about something they disliked). Boys are taught not to show negative emotions, so may be particularly well trained in neutralizing negative emotions.

Three studies (Chahal & Cassidy, 1995; Feldman & White, 1980; Shennum & Bugental, 1982) investigated whether it is more difficult to detect deceit by observing children's faces than other 'channels' such as observation of the body or listening to the voice. The literature on adult deception has revealed that lie detection is most difficult when paying attention to the face, because people are more practised and more skilled in controlling their face than other channels (Vrij, 2000). The children's results only partially support this; for example, Chahal and Cassidy (1995) found no difference in the ability to detect deceit after exposure to children's body or face. Shennum and Bugental (1982) found that children, to some extent, could deceive observers via controlling their facial expressions. Observers, however, were able to detect lies when they listened to the children.

Finally, Vrij and Van Wijngaarden (1994) examined the effect of young liars' personality on judges' decision making in their experiment. Their findings demonstrated that introverted and socially anxious children were more often judged to be deceptive than were the other children.

CHILDREN'S TESTIMONY

What do all these findings tell us about children's testimony in a judicial context? First of all, it shows that children will lie, even young children, when they have motives to do so. Initially, children will lie when they anticipate punishment, perhaps when they are threatened by someone not to disclose the truth. Older children may also lie to gain reward. Children are also willing to lie when someone else (especially someone they like) asks them to lie.

It remains unclear how skilful children are at lying, given the sparsity of literature in this area; for example, studies in which elaborate statements were required have rarely been conducted. However, it seems

doubtful whether children at a very young age are capable of spontaneously telling elaborate lies which sound plausible and convincing. It
is more likely that they will conceal information or that their lies will
contain only a few words. The fact that children at a very young age
are already capable of telling one word lies renders a style of interviewing requiring only one word answers undesirable. By the age of
entering school, children should be capable of telling plausible and convincing elaborate lies. Whether this is indeed the case needs to be investigated in future research.

Children's lies may become more sophisticated when someone
(perhaps a parent) helps them prepare their lies. Perhaps even young
children might be capable of telling an elaborate, convincing lie with
the help of others. In the study conducted by Tate *et al.* (1992), a limited
form of coaching took place. However, the coached children were not
very successful at lying. More extensive coaching might achieve better
results. This issue seems worthy of further investigation.

Whether children's lies reveal behavioural cues to deceit is virtually
unknown. To date, only a few studies have been conducted in this area
and all of them lacked ecological validity. It sounds plausible (and
there is some evidence to support this) that younger children will show
clearer non-verbal indicators of deceit (signs of nervousness or signs of
hard thinking) than older children, perhaps because they yet do not
realize that they should try to suppress these cues in order to be a successful liar or because they may not yet have the muscular control to
control themselves. Further research is needed in this area.

Experimental studies of the detection of deception have shown that it
is difficult to detect deceit even in very young children. It is, however,
problematic to generalize these findings to real-life situations. First, in
these studies, the lies were not difficult to tell and the stakes (consequences of getting caught) were low. Second, in several studies, observers did not have a total picture of the liars but could only see their
face or body or could only hear their voices. This might have impaired
their lie detection skills. Third, observers only had access to the
messages provided to them on the videotape or audiotape. Unlike in
real life, they did not have the opportunity to check whether the information the children gave was correct.

However, the research reviewed above and summarized in Table 5
leads to the following tentative conclusions. First, with increasing
age, children become better liars. Second, parents are better lie detectors than non-parents. Third, children's lies are easier to detect when
listening to their voices than when looking at their faces. Fourth, lies
are easier to detect when one uses an 'indirect method' of lie detection.
Fifth, introverted children and socially anxious children seem less

likely to be believed by observers. Sixth, judges are better at detecting lies when analysing speech content with the CBCA method than by paying attention to children's non-verbal behaviour. However, one issue here merits attention. Analyses of speech content are always conducted by trained experts, whereas analyses of non-verbal behaviour are usually carried out by lay persons. It could be that hit rates in deception studies will improve if experts in the relationship between non-verbal behaviour and deception are used as observers instead of lay persons.

It is unknown where people look when they try to detect deceit in children, as hardly any studies have been conducted in this area. In my view, this type of research is needed. First, it gives insight into why some children make a suspicious impression on observers. Second, insight into the strategies used by good lie detectors might be used to improve the lie detecting skills of poor lie detectors. Third, the few studies conducted in this area suggest that observers look at different cues when attempting to detect lies in children as against detecting lies in adults.

In conclusion, a clear picture about children's ability to lie (in court) and people's ability to detect such lies does not exist. More research is needed and this chapter provides several ideas for further research. However, research findings to date suggest that people are probably engaged in some form of self-deception if they believe that children never lie and that it is easy to detect their lies in case children do lie.

REFERENCES

Akehurst, L., Köhnken, G., & Höfer, E. (1995). The analysis and application of Statement Validity Assessment. Paper presented at the Fifth European Conference on Psychology and Law, Budapest, Hungary.

Allen, V.L., & Atkinson, M.L. (1978). Encoding of nonverbal behaviour by high-achieving and low-achieving children. *Journal of Educational Psychology*, **70**, 298–305.

Boychuk, T. (1991). Criteria-Based Content Analysis of children's statements about sexual abuse: A field-based validation study. Unpublished doctoral dissertation, Arizona State University.

Bussey, K. (1992). Children's lying and truthfulness: Implications for children's testimony. In: S.J. Ceci, M. DeSimone Leichtman, & M. Putnick (Eds), *Cognitive and social factors in early deception* (pp. 89–110). Hillsdale, NJ: Erlbaum.

Ceci, S.J., Bruck, M., & Loftus, E.F. (1998). On the ethics of memory implanting research. *Applied Cognitive Psychology*, **12**, 230–40.

Ceci, S.J., & DeSimone Leichtman, M. (1992). 'I know that you know that I know that you broke the toy': A brief report of recursive awareness among 3-year-olds. In: S.J. Ceci, M. DeSimone Leichtman, & M. Putnick (Eds), *Cognitive and social factors in early deception* (pp. 1–9). Hillsdale, NJ: Erlbaum.

Ceci, S.J., Loftus, E.F., Leichtman, M.D., & Bruck, M. (1994). The possible role of source misattributions in the creation of false beliefs among preschoolers. *The International Journal of Clinical and Experimental Hypnosis*, **17**, 304–20.

Chahal, K., & Cassidy, T. (1995). Deception and its detection in children: A study of adult accuracy. *Psychology, Crime, & Law*, **1**, 237–45.

Chandler, M., Fritz, A.S., & Hala, S. (1989). Small-scale deceit: Deception as a marker of two-, three-, and four-year-olds' early theories of mind. *Child Development*, **60**, 1263–77.

Dale, P.S., Loftus, E.F., & Rathbun, L. (1976). The influence of the form of the question on the eyewitness testimony of preschool children. *Journal of Paralinguistic Research*, **7**, 269–77.

DePaulo, B.M. & Jordan, A. (1982). Age changes in deceiving and detecting deceit. In: R.S. Feldman (Ed.), *Development of nonverbal behaviour in children* (pp. 151–80). New York: Springer-Verlag.

DePaulo, B.M., Jordan, A., Irvine, A., & Laser, P.S. (1982). Age changes in the detection of deception. *Child Development*, **53**, 701–709.

DePaulo, B.M., Kashy, D.A., Kirkendol, S.E., Wyer, M.M., & Epstein, J.A. (1996). Lying in everyday life. *Journal of Personality and Social Psychology*, **70**, 979–95.

DePaulo, B.M., & Kirkendol, S.E. (1989). The motivational impairment effect in the communication of deception. In: J.C. Yuille (Ed.), *Credibility assessment* (pp. 51–70). Dordrecht: Kluwer.

Ekman, P. (1992). *Telling lies: Clues to deceit in the marketplace, politics and marriage*. New York: W.W. Norton.

Ekman, P., Roper, G., & Hager, J.C. (1980). Deliberate facial movement. *Child development*, **51**, 886–91.

Feldman, R.S. (1979). Nonverbal disclosure of deception in urban Koreans. *Journal of Cross-Cultural Psychology*, **10**, 73–83.

Feldman, R.S., Devin-Sheehan, L., & Allen, V.L. (1978). Nonverbal cues as indicators of verbal dissembling. *American Educational Research Journal*, **15**, 217–31.

Feldman, R.S., Jenkins, L., & Popoola, O. (1979). Detection of deception in adults and children via facial expressions. *Child Development*, **50**, 350–5.

Feldman, R.S., & Phillipot, P. (1993). Children's deception skills and social competence. In: G. Goodman & B. Bottoms (Eds), *Child victims, child witnesses* (pp. 80–99). New York: Guilford Press.

Feldman, R.S., & White, J.B. (1980). Detecting deception in children. *Journal of Communication*, 121–8.

Feldman, R.S., White, J.B., & Lobato, D. (1982). Social skills and nonverbal behaviour. In R. S. Feldman (Ed.), *Development of nonverbal behaviour in children*. New York: Springer-Verlag.

Flavell, J.H., Botkin, P.T., Fry, C.L., Wright, J.C., & Jarvis, P.T. (1968). *The development of role-taking and communication skills in children*. New York: Wiley.

Frank, M.G. (1992). Commentary: On the structure of lies and deception experiments. In: S.J. Ceci, M. DeSimone Leichtman, & M. Putnick (Eds), *Cognitive and social factors in early deception* (pp. 127–46). Hillsdale, NJ: Erlbaum.

Haugaard, J. (1993). Young children's classification of the corroboration of a false statement as the truth or a lie. *Law and Human Behaviour*, **17**, 645–59.

Haugaard, J.J., Reppucci, N.D., Laird, J., & Nauful, T. (1991). Children's definitions of the truth and their competency as witnesses in legal proceedings. *Law and Human Behaviour*, **15**, 253–71.

Hurd, K., & Noller, P. (1988). Decoding deception: A look at the process. *Journal of Nonverbal Behaviour*, **12**, 217–33.

Jackson, J.L. (1996). Truth or fantasy: The ability of barristers and laypersons to detect deception in children's testimony. Paper presented at the AP-LS Biennial Conference, Hilton Head Island, South Carolina.

Lamb, M.E., Sternberg, K.J., Esplin, P.W. Hershkowitz, I., Orbach, Y., & Hovav, M. (1997). Criterion-based content analysis: A field validation study. *Child Abuse and Neglect*, **21**, 255–64.

Lamers-Winkelman, F., & Buffing, F. (1996). Children's testimony in the Netherlands: A study of Statement Validity Analysis. In: B.L. Bottoms & G.S. Goodman (Eds), *International perspectives on child abuse and children's testimony* (pp. 45–62). Thousand Oaks, CA: Sage.

Leekam, S.R. (1992). Believing and deceiving: Steps to becoming a good liar. In: S.J. Ceci, M. DeSimone Leichtman, & M. Putnick (Eds), *Cognitive and social factors in early deception* (pp. 47–62). Hillsdale, NJ: Erlbaum.

Lewis, M. (1993). The development of deception. In: M. Lewis & C. Saarni (Eds), *Lying and deception in everyday life* (pp. 90–105). New York: Guilford Press.

Lewis, M., Stanger, C., & Sullivan, M.W. (1989). Deception in three-year-olds. *Developmental Psychology*, **25**, 439–43.

Loftus, E.F., & Palmer, J.C. (1974). Reconstructions of automobile destruction: An example of the interaction between language and memory. *Journal of Verbal Learning and Verbal Behaviour*, **13**, 585–9.

Morency, N.L., & Krauss, R.M. (1982). Children's nonverbal encoding and decoding of affect. In: R.S. Feldman (Ed.), *Development of nonverbal behaviour in children* (pp. 181–99). New York: Springer-Verlag.

Moston, S. (1987). The suggestibility of children in interview studies. *Child Language*, **7**, 67–78.

Newton, P., Reddy, V., & Bull, R. (2000). Children's everyday deception and performance on false-belief tasks. *British Journal of Developmental Psychology*, **18**, 297–317.

Nigro, G.N., & Snow, A.L. (1992). Sex, lies, and smiling faces: A brief report on gender differences in 3-year-olds' deceptions. In: S.J. Ceci, M. DeSimone Leichtman, & M. Putnick (Eds), *Cognitive and social factors in early deception* (pp. 63–8). Hillsdale, NJ: Erlbaum.

Oldershaw, L., & Bagby, R.M. (1997). Children and deception. In: R. Rogers (Ed.), *Clinical assessment of malingering and deception* (pp. 153–66). New York: Guilford Press.

Peskin, J. (1992). Ruse and representations: On children's ability to conceal infomation. *Developmental Psychology*, **28**, 84–9.

Poole, D.A., & White, L.T. (1991). Effects of question repetition and retention interval on the eyewitness testimony of children and adults. *Developmental Psychology*, **27**, 975–86.

Roberts, K.P., & Blades, M. (1999). Children's memory and source-monitoring of real-life and televised events. *Journal of Applied Developmental Psychology*, **20**, 575–96.

Rotenberg, K.J., Simourd, L., & Moore, D. (1989). Children's use of a verbal-nonverbal consistency principle to infer truth from lying. *Child Development*, **60**, 309–22.

Russell, J., Mauthner, N., Sharpe, S., & Tidswell, T. (1991). The 'windows task' as a measure of strategic deception in preschoolers and autistic subjects. *British Journal of Developmental Psychology*, **9**, 331–49.

Saarni, C. (1979). Children's understanding of display rules for expressive behaviour. *Developmental Psychology*, **15**, 424–9.

Saarni, C. (1984). An observational study of children's attempts to monitor their expressive behavior. *Child Development*, **55**, 1504–13.

Saarni, C., & von Salisch, M. (1993). The socialization of emotional dissemblance. In: M. Lewis & C. Saarni (Eds), *Lying and deception in everyday life* (pp. 106–25). New York: Guilford Press.

Shennum, W.A., & Bugental, D.B. (1982). The development of control over affective expression in nonverbal behaviour. In: R.S. Feldman (Ed.), *Development of nonverbal behaviour in children* (pp. 101–21). New York: Springer-Verlag.

Sinclair, A. (1996). Young children's practical deceptions and their understanding of false belief. *New Ideas in Psychology*, **4**, 157–73.

Sodian, B. (1991). The development of deception in young children. *British Journal of Developmental Psychology*, **9**, 173–88.

Steller, M., & Köhnken, G. (1989). Criteria-Based Content Analysis. In: D.C. Raskin (Ed.), *Psychological methods in criminal investigation and evidence* (pp. 217–45). New York: Springer-Verlag.

Steller, M., Wellershaus, P., & Wolf, T. (1988, June). Empirical validation of Criteria-Based Content Analysis. Paper presented at the NATO Advanced Study Institute on Credibility Assessment in Maratea, Italy.

Stouthamer-Loeber, M. (1986). Lying as a problem behaviour in children: A review. *Clinical Psychology Review*, **6**, 267–89.

Tate, C.S., Warren, A.R., & Hess, T.H. (1992). Adults' liability for children's 'Lie-Ability': Can adults coach children to lie successfully? In: S.J. Ceci, M. DeSimone Leichtman, & M. Putnick (Eds), *Cognitive and social factors in early deception* (pp. 69–88). Hillsdale, NJ: Erlbaum.

Vrij, A. (2000). *Detecting lies and deceit: Psychology of lying and the implications for professional practice*. Chichester, UK: Wiley.

Vrij, A., & Akehurst, L. (1998). Verbal communication and credibility: Statement Validity Assessment. In: A. Memon, A. Vrij, & R. Bull (Eds), *Psychology and law: Truthfulness, accuracy, and credibility* (pp. 3–26). New York: McGraw-Hill.

Vrij, A., & Van Wijngaarden, J.J. (1994). Will truth come out? Two studies about the detection of false statements expressed by children. *Expert evidence: The International Digest of Human Behaviour, Science and Law*, **3**, 78–84.

Vrij, A., & Winkel, F.W. (1995). Detection of false statements in first and third graders: The development of a nonverbal detection instrument. In: G.

Davies, S. Lloyd-Bostock, M. McMurran, & C. Wilson (Eds), *Psychology, law and criminal justice: International developments in research and practice* (pp. 221–30). Berlin: Walter de Gruyter.

Westcott, H.L., Davies, G.M., & Clifford, B.R. (1991). Adults' perceptions of children's videotaped truthful and deceptive statements. *Children & Society*, **5**, 123–35.

Winkel, F.W., & Vrij, A. (1995). Verklaringen van kinderen in interviews: Een experimenteel onderzoek naar de diagnostische waarde van Criteria Based Content Analysis. *Tijdschrift voor Ontwikkelingspsychologie*, **22**, 61–74.

Review of Part II

Part II has provided a wide-ranging discussion of research and practice relating to the intertwined issues of children's memory and interviewing children, since, as Fivush so eloquently remarks, 'at heart, all concerns about children's testimony must rely on basic memory competencies'. In the field of forensic interviewing, the manner in which social influences, such as the behaviour of the interviewer, can affect such memory competencies becomes crucial. A host of implications for investigative interviewers have been raised by contributors to this part of our book; some of these points will be familiar to readers and others less so. As we noted at the very outset to this book, it is all too easy to become wrapped up in our own area of specialism and to start taking our own practice for granted. For this reason, we hope a restatement of familiar conclusions alongside more novel material will be a valuable exercise for all who are charged with the difficult task of talking to children in investigative contexts.

POINTS TO REMEMBER ABOUT CHILDREN'S MEMORY

- With appropriate 'scaffolding' or support from adults, from the age of two, children will have limited verbal recall of events.
- Inconsistency in accounts from children does not equate to inaccuracy, especially in repeated recalls that follow open-ended questioning.
- Repeated events lead to good script memory, but poorer memory for specific details.
- Distinctive (and 'one-off') events are more likely to be recalled in specific detail than recurring or repeated events.
- Repeated events are especially susceptible to delays in recall, both

in terms of details provided and in terms of the temporal sequence of activities.

- Young children do not know how to report past experiences in an extended, coherent narrative. Their reports will therefore be more fragmented and less accurate.
- The precise effects of stress on children's memories are not fully understood. It may be that the opportunity to talk about negative events as they are occurring, and in retrospect, helps young children to form more accurate and more organized memories.
- Younger children (especially pre-schoolers) are usually more suggestible than older children and adults, but a number of factors— many of which are in the control of the interviewer—will influence how suggestible any particular child may be.
- Children are less suggestible about personally salient events, such as body touch, but are not immune if subjected to repeated leading questions.
- Children are less suggestible about fixed or repeated aspects of repeated events.
- Young children may be more likely than adults to confuse memories from different sources (e.g. from real experience or from information suggested by another person), when those sources give rise to memories that are highly similar to one another.
- Children may have less developed retrieval strategies and reasoning processes to enable them to specify the source of their memory (e.g. from real experience or from information suggested by another person) when their source-monitoring processes fail.
- Children over six years of age can be taught (with practice) to reduce their false reports of suggested (rather than experienced) events with source-monitoring instructions which explicitly instruct them only to rely on memories of the event itself. This could be incorporated into discussions at the rapport phase of an interview.
- Plausible false events are more likely to be suggestively 'implanted' in the memory of children and adults than implausible false events.
- The 'wholesale adoption' of an event into memory when the individual concerned has no related knowledge of that event or access to information related to the event is likely to be rare.
- False memories are not dichotomously 'present' or 'absent': children may incorporate false (i.e. not experienced) details into an otherwise true account of an experience or true details of a similar experience into an otherwise false account.
- When considering children's accounts, it is important to identify what may be a false memory from what may be a compliant

response in the face of authority (e.g. agreeing with an adult authority figure such as an interviewer).

- The amount of detail a child provides, their expressiveness and their confidence in reporting are not necessarily indicators of accuracy.
- The presence of non-verbal aids such as props, photos, and drawings is beneficial to the degree that such aids assist retrieval processes and make memory more accessible for verbal reporting; however, *physical interactions* with such aids (rather than simply their presence) should be minimized in a forensic context.

POINTS TO REMEMBER WHEN INTERVIEWING CHILDREN

- Interviewers must communicate their appropriate needs and expectations of the child clearly (e.g. about the amount and type of detail required in responses).
- Interviewers should use the rapport phase to establish such expectations (e.g. through ground rules, practising open-ended questioning and responding, minimizing interviewer speaking time, permitting 'don't know' or 'don't understand' responses).
- Interviewers should resist interrupting the child at all times, as this can signal a lack of control to the child, as well as disrupting his or her memory framework for the experience.
- Open-ended-question forms yield three to four times longer responses from children with more detailed replies than focused questions, regardless of age.
- Interviewers are very poor at asking open-ended questions, these typically contribute less than 6% of questions in investigative interviews.
- If specific or closed questions need to be asked, they should be followed by an open question to restore the initiative to the child.
- Closed questions and leading questions should be avoided as far as possible and reserved till the very end of the interview; for some children, however (e.g. those who are disabled), such questions may be the only type that can be responded to.
- Reasons to avoid asking closed questions that require single-word responses from children (especially 'Yes/No' questions) include the following:
  1   children answer them less accurately (but more consistently);
  2   children are more suggestible to closed questions;
  3   they are especially problematic for children recalling repeated experiences;

4   children are less able to answer nonsensical questions correctly in closed format;

5   children are less likely to volunteer that they do not know the answer to closed questions;

6   it is easier for children to be deceptive in response to closed questions.

- A 'one-off' suggestive technique or question in a single interview will probably not cause irreparable harm to a child's account, especially if the interviewer returns immediately to open questioning.

- Children should not be questioned in a suggestive manner (e.g. by the use of leading questions, about details the child has not previously mentioned, or by suggesting an interpretation of what has happened to the child).

- Children's language should not be taken for granted, nor children's linguistic capacities overestimated.

- Interviewers should be discouraged from fostering any stereotype of the alleged perpetrator (e.g. by maligning the character of the alleged perpetrator or suggesting he was 'naughty' or 'bad').

- Children should not be encouraged to visualize imaginary events (e.g. hypothetical situations) which may be related to the alleged abuse.

- Some non-verbal techniques (e.g. the presence of props or reinstatement of context) may add to the range of interviewing strategies available, but will not be appropriate for all children (e.g. they may not be readily available or may upset the child).

- Dolls and toys used in conjunction with questions about events (i.e. not in rapport) are associated with a significant increase in errors and inaccuracies, especially for children under five.

- Anatomical dolls should not be used with under-fives and used with caution when questioning older children, such that the interviewer knows precisely what role the doll(s) will fulfil (e.g. as a communication aid).

- Asking children to identify specific occurrences (e.g. the first and/or last time, most memorable occasion) can help children to provide more specific details about repeated events.

- Biases or preconceived ideas about what may have happened to the child should not be maintained. If a 'hypothesis' about events seems likely, a sensitive way of challenging or disproving it in the interview should be explored—this will prevent narrow-mindedness.

Vrij's chapter provides a helpful reminder of a major area largely unaddressed by memory research—motivation. Many of the suggestibility effects referred to above, and cognitive deficits such as those in source-monitoring processes, occur without any conscious effort on the part of the child. Yet, as Vrij has shown, children will lie when they are motivated to do so. The concealment of information by children in interviews is perhaps particularly relevant to debates about interviews for suspected abuse, since we know from child witnesses that there are many reasons why they do not tell everything in investigative interviews; for example, they have been threatened or they are fearful of the ramifications of disclosure, such as upsetting loved ones.

Another step forward in research would be the examination of individual differences, including how psychologists can help practitioners move from guidelines based on group level data to the assessment of a child in a specific case. As Ceci *et al.* have noted in their chapter, we still do not know why some children are more resistant to suggestion than others and how to predict the best performers. We should not overlook the contribution self-reports from children can make to our awareness of relevant issues. Waterman *et al.* clearly show how a greater understanding of the child's viewpoint can be obtained by unpicking their responses to bizarre or confusing questions. Asking children to clarify their meaning in investigative interviews is a very practical implication of this research.

Another instinctive research development would be further evaluation of why it is that interviewers do not follow interviewing guidelines that are founded on well-established psychological principles. At an individual level, interviewers should reflect on their own practice and become more aware of the different types of questions or utterances that they rely on. At a macro-level, the pressures placed upon interviewers by the criminal justice system can be considered. Intensive training, with ongoing monitoring, supervision, and refresher courses, seems an inevitable requirement.

Finally, it is worth restating that the perceived credibility of children is not necessarily a reflection of the accuracy of their memories. Some children, such as those who are introverted or socially anxious, can appear to be less honest or credible when interviewed. Unfortunately, these are the very children who may perhaps be among the most vulnerable to improper advances from adults.

PART III

Court Issues

CHAPTER 13

Innovative Procedures for Child Witnesses

JUDY CASHMORE

Social Policy Research Centre, University of New South Wales, Australia

Over the last two decades, increasing numbers of children have given
evidence about crimes against them, most frequently child sexual
assault (Cashmore, 1995; Cashmore & Horsky, 1988; Myers, 1996). This
is a result of the increasing recognition of child sexual assault and the
easing of the restrictions on children's evidence in most common law
jurisdictions (McGough, 1997; Spencer & Flin, 1993). As more children
and younger children have come before the courts as witnesses, the
problems they face in an adversarial adult-oriented system have
become increasingly evident. These problems include being required
to tell a number of different people what happened, waiting months
and perhaps even years before the case gets to court, having to face the
alleged abuser, and answer difficult questions asked by lawyers generally unused to speaking to children in age-appropriate language
(Spencer & Flin, 1993).

Concerns about the stressful and potentially harmful effects on
children, and the possibly detrimental effect on the reliability and completeness of their evidence, have led to a number of changes in investigative and court procedures to try to accommodate the needs of child
witnesses while still protecting the rights of the accused. These
changes fall into three categories: modifications to the court environment and innovative procedures to alleviate the main stressors for
children in court, empowering children by preparing them for the

Children's Testimony. Edited by H.L. Westcott, G.M. Davies, and R.H.C. Bull.
© 2002 John Wiley & Sons, Ltd.

court experience, and increasing the skills of the professionals involved in the investigative and court process.

The focus of this chapter is on the innovative use of video-technology which allows children's evidence either to be recorded beforehand (videotaped interviews and pre-trial depositions) or to be transmitted contemporaneously from another place (closed-circuit television or 'live link'). The aim of these procedures (videotaped interviews, pre-trial depositions, and closed-circuit television) is, in various ways, to reduce the stress on the child and to improve (and preserve) the quality and completeness of the child's evidence. The following sections outline the available research evidence about the extent to which these aims have been achieved for each of the three forms of video-technology. The focus is on the following questions: What is the effect of using these procedures on child witnesses? On the quality of the child's evidence? On the process? What evidence is there that the use of these innovative procedures affects the credibility of child witnesses or the likelihood of a conviction? Closed-circuit television (CCTV) is dealt with first, and the research about the likely impact of children's 'televised' evidence on the court process, also relevant to the other procedures, is discussed in this section.

CLOSED-CIRCUIT TELEVISION ('LIVE LINK')

Using CCTV or the live video link, child witnesses are able to testify from a separate room or remote location which means that they do not need to be either in the formal environment of the courtroom or in the presence of the accused, so accommodating two of the main concerns child witnesses have about testifying (Sas, Hurley, Austin & Wolfe, 1991; Spencer & Flin, 1993).

The way that CCTV is used and the conditions on its use vary, however, from one jurisdiction to another. In Canada and in some US states, for example, the prosecution and defence lawyers are also in the separate room with the child, and in several US states, the accused may also be present because of the interpretation of the Sixth Amendment right of the accused to confront witnesses. This of course defeats one of the primary reasons for using CCTV—to prevent the child from having to testify in the presence of the accused. There are also differences in the court's discretion as to its use, with the prosecution in some jurisdictions required to satisfy the court that the child would suffer 'mental or emotional harm' or that their evidence would be impaired if they were required to give evidence in the traditional manner in open court. In some US states, this may require the child to be 'technically unavailable' or to face a further examination of the child in court, with the child exposed to the accused to test the 'need' (Montoya, 1995). In England and Wales, and in several Australian states (New South Wales, Western Australia, Tasmania, and the Australian Capital Territory), however, there is a rebuttable presumption that a child giving evidence in a sexual or serious physical assault matter can use CCTV (Australian Law Reform Commission [ALRC] & Human Rights and Equal Opportunities Commission [HREOC], 1997, para. 14.103).

The Effect on the Child

Reports from children who have been involved as witnesses in court proceedings consistently indicate that their greatest concern or fear is having to face the accused (Goodman et al., 1992; Whitcomb, Shapiro, & Stellwagen, 1985). In two evaluations in Australia and one in Scotland, children who testified using CCTV generally reported that they preferred testifying from outside the courtroom than in open court in front of the accused. Some Scottish children, however, said they found the television set-up 'strange' (Murray, 1995) and a small number of adolescents in the two Australian studies chose to go into court, primarily to show the accused they were not afraid (Cashmore, 1992; O'Grady, 1996). Although there are no figures available from actual court studies to indicate whether CCTV reduced the likelihood of children refusing to testify, an extensive court simulation study found that children were less likely to refuse if they could testify via CCTV than in the courtroom (Goodman et al., 1998).

The Effect on the Quality of Evidence: the Link Between Stress, Confrontation, and the Evidence

The traditional legal view is that requiring witnesses to confront the person they are accusing makes it more likely that the witness will tell the truth and that the fact-finder will be able to detect whether the witness is telling the truth or not (Montoya, 1995; Spencer & Flin, 1993). There is little, if any, evidence, however, to support either assumption. Indeed, it seems that jurors have considerable difficulty discerning accurate from inaccurate testimony from children whether it is presented live in court, via CCTV, or by videotape (Leippe, Manion, & Romanczyk, 1993; Tobey, Goodman, Batterman-Faunce, Orcutt, & Sachsenmaier, 1995; Westcott, Davies & Clifford, 1991). Experimental and court simulation studies have also shown that errors of omission are increased and the quality and completeness of children's testimony are compromised when children are required to confront the accused.

Experimental and Court Simulation Studies

Several experimental studies have found that asking children to say what happened in front of the alleged offender reduced both the accuracy and the completeness of children's reports about witnessed events. The staged events in these studies were relatively trivial (involving the theft of a book from a room [Peters, 1990] and a glass being broken [Bussey, Lee, & Grimbeek, 1993]), the children were not victims of the crime and the perpetrator was not known to the child; even so, children were significantly more reluctant to reveal what had happened when the perpetrator was present.

Several court simulation studies confirmed and extended these findings, with children in the courtroom condition showing more signs of anxiety, providing less complete and less accurate information, and being less resistant to leading questions than children giving evidence in a small separate room (Hill & Hill, 1987; Saywitz & Nathanson, 1993). Saywitz and Nathanson (1993) also found that objective physiological measures of stress were significantly higher for the children in the courtroom, indicating a link between the level of stress children experience and the completeness and accuracy of the information they provide.

The most sophisticated and extensive court simulation study involved 88 simulated trials with six and eight-year-old child witnesses and over 1200 mock jurors (Goodman et al., 1998). In this study, children testified either in the normal courtroom or via CCTV from a separate small room about what had happened in several play sessions with a male confederate. The play sessions involved making a movie during which the confederate asked the child to place stickers on their own exposed body parts or on their clothes. Before the children were questioned, they were told that the babysitter was 'perhaps not supposed to make the movie and might be in trouble because of it' (original emphasis, p. 178). Not only, as reported earlier, did CCTV affect children's willingness to testify, it also affected the completeness of the evidence given by the younger children. Younger children testifying in the separate room made fewer errors of omission than their age-mates in the open court condition. There was also a trend for fewer errors of commission, especially in relation to misleading questions.

In these studies, it was possible to have some reasonably objective measure of the accuracy and completeness of the child's evidence about an experimentally controlled event which the children either witnessed or participated in. The finding was consistent: children who were more stressed by the presence of the perpetrator or by the courtroom environment were both less willing to say what happened and less accurate and complete in their reports.

Court Observation and Evaluation Studies

When children are giving evidence in court in real-life cases, there is rarely any objective measure of the accuracy of their testimony because in the cases in which children are most often called upon to testify—in relation to child sexual assault—the child and the perpetrator are generally the only witnesses. (On rare occasions, a videotape of the assault made by the perpetrator may be available to substantiate the child's account of events.) It is possible, however, for researchers to rate both the observed distress and emotional reactions of children in court and their capacity to answer questions, provide detail and resist leading questions. Two studies involving actual child witnesses (in Denver and Glasgow) have done just that and found that the children who were rated as being more distressed (crying, looking very unhappy or tense, faltering speech) had more difficulty answering the questions and provided less detail than those who showed fewer signs of distress (Flin, Bull, Boon, & Knox, 1993; Goodman et al., 1992).

Both of these court studies used rating scales devised by or adapted from Goodman's work, as did three evaluation studies of the use of CCTV in England and Wales, Scotland, and Australia.[1] Again there was a relationship between children's emotional state and their ability to testify. Davies and Noon (1991) observed 100 live-link trials involving 154 child witnesses in England and Wales and compared their ratings with those obtained for 89 children testifying in open court in Scotland by Flin et al. (1993). They found that children using the live link were rated as 'significantly less unhappy, more audible and more forthcoming' than Scottish children testifying in open court (Davies, 1999, p. 250).

In a smaller study involving 37 child witnesses in Australia, Cashmore (1992) found significant correlations between ratings of children's emotional state and their performance as witnesses both in examination-in-chief and cross-examination. Significantly, however,

---

[1] In all three studies, children using CCTV testified from the separate room and the lawyers were in the courtroom (English version) whereas in the US, the usual arrangement is for the lawyers to be present in the separate room with the child (US version) (Davies, 1999). There are, however, no evaluation studies of the US method of using CCTV, apparently because it is not used very often.

children's observed emotional state and their performance as witnesses was found to have been influenced more by whether they were able to use CCTV when they wanted to than by whether or not they did or did not use CCTV.

Similarly, Murray's (1995) study of 65 child witnesses in Scotland found that children who showed more signs of stress were more likely to be inconsistent and to recant their evidence about the assault than children who were rated as being more relaxed. In contrast to the other two evaluations, the children using the live link were *not* judged to be 'less unhappy' or more effective witnesses, but they were younger and had to meet various criteria of vulnerability in order to use CCTV.

In summary, the experimental, court simulation, and court observation studies indicate that child witnesses who are less stressed are able to provide more complete and more accurate information, particularly when they are protected from the presence of the accused. It may, however, not just be the mode of giving evidence that is important for child witnesses but their feeling of having some control over the process when they are allowed to choose how they provide their evidence in court (Cashmore, 1992; Davies & Seymour, 1997).

The Effect of Closed-circuit Television on Jurors' Perceptions

While the accuracy *per se* of children's reports is of course very important, what is probably more important is the extent to which children are *perceived* by the fact-finder to be accurate and credible witnesses. There is little point in increasing children's access to the courts as witnesses and taking measures to accommodate their needs if those measures reduce their credibility and lessen the impact of their testimony.

Once again, the evidence comes from both experimental or simulated trial conditions and from actual court studies and relates to the perceived impact of the child witness and to the jurors' ability to detect deception.

Perceived Credibility and Impact

The findings of two trial-simulation studies indicate that there is no straightforward or consistent effect of the way children's testimony is presented (in court with or without a protective screen or via CCTV or videotaped deposition) on the trial verdict or on the perceived credibility of the child witness or of the defendant. While mock jurors in Swim, Borgida and McCoy's (1993) study remembered more of the testimony given by videotaped deposition, they tended to be more positive about the accuracy, consistency, and confidence of in-court testimony. The verdict and perceived credibility of the child and the defendant were, however, not affected. In Ross et al.'s (1994) study, there was little or no effect of the medium when the ratings were made after all the evidence was provided, but the likelihood of a conviction differed when the ratings were made after jurors had seen only the child's testimony.

In both studies, however, the in-court testimony was presented to mock jurors on videotape so the comparison did not provide a true test of the effect of televised versus in-court testimony (Davies, 1999). Goodman et al.'s (1992, 1998) extensive study (with children randomly assigned to testify live, either in open court or via CCTV) overcame this problem and found that the medium had no effect before or after deliberation on the likelihood of a guilty verdict. The means of presentation did, however, affect jurors' pre-deliberation ratings of children, with children using CCTV being rated less favourably than children in open court. In addition to this *direct* effect, however, there was a counteracting and stronger *indirect* effect with children testifying via CCTV being seen to be *more* accurate and believable because they were in fact more accurate.

In the only study involving actual jurors in real trials, O'Grady (1996) found that trials in which CCTV was used were less likely to result in a guilty verdict than those in which children testified in court with or without a screen. She concluded, however, that it was too early to establish the effect on outcome because a number of other changes came into effect at the same time and there were differences in age and vulnerability (and possibly ability to testify) between children granted permission by the court to use CCTV and those who were not.

Prejudicial Impact and Unfairness

Any innovations that try to accommodate the needs of child witnesses also need to be fair to the accused. One concern is that jurors might be prejudiced against the accused and more likely to presume guilt if special measures are deemed necessary to protect a child witness. Simulation and court observation and interview studies provide no evidence, however, that jurors either see these measures as unfair or are more likely to convict if they are used (Goodman et al., 1998; O'Grady, 1996; Ross et al., 1994). Although some jurors in O'Grady's (1996) study indicated that they would have liked to see the child (in court), they mostly understood why it was better for the child to be outside the courtroom and generally did not believe it would have made it easier to reach a verdict if they had testified in court.

AUDIO/VIDEOTAPED INTERVIEWS OR STATEMENTS

The aim of audio- or videotaping interviews with children is to preserve the child's early report of events after disclosure. These tapes may be made by the workers in various agencies but are commonly made by police or statutory child-protection workers. While no specific authority may be required to record the interview, the tapes are generally inadmissible as hearsay evidence without specific statutory provision. If they are available, however, they may be subpoenaed by the defence to show prior inconsistency without infringing the hearsay rule (Spencer & Flin, 1993). Increasingly, most common-law jurisdictions are making statutory provision to admit such evidence.

The effect on the child

The main child-focused reasons for videotaping a child's statement are to try to reduce the number of times children are interviewed to obtain evidence and to reduce the trauma of testifying. Reducing the number of interviews during the investigation does not require the tape to be admissible in court, however, and could be achieved by more effective case management and collaboration in multidisciplinary teams. Unfortunately, there is little research to indicate whether or not the availability of a taped interview reduces the number of interviews.

If the tape is admissible, depending on the jurisdiction and prosecutorial discretion, it can replace the child's examination-in-chief either in whole or in part. Where it replaces the examination-in-chief in full, there is some concern that this may not benefit child witnesses if they do not have the opportunity to settle down by being led through their evidence by someone they trust (the prosecutor) before being cross-examined (Davis, Hoyano, Keenan, Maitland, & Morgan, 1999). Whether or not children find this more difficult, however, needs to be tested empirically, taking particular account of children's view of the advantages and disadvantages.

Another possible benefit for children is the possibility that the accused may decide to plead guilty when faced with the child's allegations on tape, so averting the need for the child to give evidence in court. While there is some indication from the English evaluation of an increase in late guilty pleas, the evidence is not strong and needs to be tested systematically across several jurisdictions, taking account of other factors that influence the plea rate (Davies, Wilson, Mitchell, & Milsom, 1995).

The Effect on the Reliability of the Evidence

One of the main reasons for taping statements is to increase the accuracy and completeness of the statement by providing a verbatim account of both the questions and the answers and the emotional presentation of the child. Because children's use of language is more context-dependent and literal than that of adults, it is important to know what questions the child was asked and in what sequence. When interviewers rely on notes to reconstruct the question–answer process, sometimes days or weeks after the interview, without the benefit of a taped record to produce the child's statement of evidence, the accuracy and completeness of that record of interview is questionable and important details may be omitted or misinterpreted (NSW Children's Evidence Taskforce, 1997, para. 3.12). As a number of officers in New South Wales admitted in a survey of their methods, they found it very difficult to maintain rapport and to be child-focused while simultaneously trying to type or take notes during the interview.

The second advantage of *video*taping (rather than audiotaping) is that it preserves the child's statement and allows the fact-finder to see the child's age, appearance, and facial expressions at the time of the disclosure, often months or even years before the trial. Where there is consistency between the child's evidence on tape and testimony in court, the tape can also be used to rebut claims that the child's evidence has been contaminated by the questioning or influence of others. Where it indicates inconsistency, however, it provides the defence with a line of attack on the reliability of the child's evidence.

Third, the tape can be used to refresh the child's memory for events that occurred some time earlier. Because there is some evidence that children forget more quickly than adults (Brainerd, Reyna, Howe, & Kingma, 1990; Flin, Boon, Knox, & Bull, 1992), a visual record may be useful, especially when children are too young to read their statement. How defence lawyers react to this practice, and how children react to seeing themselves on tape some time after the event, again need to examined empirically.

Effects on the Process

The main disadvantages of taping interviews, and of videotaping in particular, concern the associated financial costs and the exposure of, and likely focus on, workers' (poor) interviewing techniques. The costs include the expense associated with transcribing and with storing and maintaining the tapes to ensure their confidentiality and integrity. While early evidence suggested that only a small proportion of the tapes (less than 10%) were finally used in court (Davies *et al.*, 1995), more recent research indicates less reason for concern. In a recent study in Yorkshire, England, for example, about three-quarters of the videotaped interviews over a four-year period were deemed to contain relevant evidence (Cherryman, King, & Bull, 1999). Although only about 20% were shown in court, guilty pleas, possibly encouraged by the evidence on the tape, were entered in just over half the cases.

In an attempt to manage the increased scrutiny of interviewer skills and the anxiety that that can engender among workers, many jurisdictions have introduced guidelines for interviewing and specific training to increase the skill of interviewers. While these attempts to improve poor practice are important, there are a number of questions about the inflexible use of the guidelines, the most appropriate timing of the interview, the effectiveness of short-term training in changing interviewing practice, and ultimately whether there are any benefits for child-victim witnesses (Aldridge & Cameron, 1999; Westcott & Jones, 1997).

Evaluation of Videotaped Interviews

The only large-scale evaluation to date of the use of videotapes (Davies *et al.*, 1995) found strong support for their introduction by child-protection workers but less support among lawyers and judges in the first two years. Some prosecutors were concerned that the tape had less impact on the jury than live testimony and preferred to lead the evidence live asking the questions themselves rather than relying on the tape. Some judges and lawyers were also concerned that replacing the child's examination-in-chief with the tape meant that the child was unprepared for cross-examination. Both problems, however, may be alleviated by greater flexibility in the way the tape can be used in court so that it supplements but does not replace the child's examination-in-chief. Empirical evidence is also needed to investigate children's perceptions of the process.

PRE-TRIAL DEPOSITIONS

Pre-trial depositions involve replacing the child's live testimony at the time of the trial with a videotape of their whole testimony (direct and cross-examination) recorded some months beforehand. This is technically possible in various jurisdictions when the child is unavailable as a witness, is permitted by specific statute in others, and was recommended for use in England by Justice Pigot (Spencer & Flin, 1993). Western Australia appears, however, to be the only common-law jurisdiction in which pre-trial depositions are routinely used.[2] In the two-year period from November 1997 to October 1999, the evidence of 150 children aged between 5 and 17 was recorded prior to trial and was available to replace their in-court testimony (information from the Ministry of Justice, Western Australia).

The Effect on the Child

The main benefit for children of taking and recording their testimony early is that it allows the child to get on with life sooner, allowing therapy to focus on the child's needs without concern about contamination. The delays and waiting time at court are also likely to be reduced because the hearing of the child's evidence can be more easily scheduled without concern about the time taken by other aspects of the trial process such as legal argument, adjournments, and empanelling the jury. In the event of a retrial or an appeal, the child's testimony can be replayed without the need for the child to be present. On the other hand, the benefit of pre-recording may be lost if the defence lawyer needs to cross-examine the child again to ask about new points of evidence. Although there has been no formal evaluation, reports from a number of judges and from court professionals in Western Australia indicate no significant problems with the process and little need for further cross-examination.

The Effect on the Reliability of the Evidence

A significant advantage of expediting the child's testimony is the likely increased reliability of the child's evidence because it is given earlier, when the events are fresher in the child's memory and the child's appearance and verbal expression are similar to those at the time of the alleged offence. In addition, the tape of the child's evidence may then be edited to remove any inadmissible material which may avert a mistrial and the need for a retrial.

---

[2] In 1989, an advisory committee in the UK headed by Justice Pigot recommended showing a trial both the videotaped interview of the child's evidence soon after disclosure and a video recording of a preliminary hearing during which the child is cross-examined before a judge in chambers. While videotaped interviews with children may now be admitted in England and Wales as the child's evidence-in-chief, and the Youth Justice and Criminal Evidence Act 1999 to allow pre-recorded cross-examination to be admitted as evidence has also been passed, the routine use of pre-trial depositions has not yet been implemented. In Scotland, pre-recorded hearings are legally allowed but are rarely used while videotaped interviews remain inadmissible (Davis et al., 1999).

The Effect on the Process

The advantage of pre-recording the child's testimony for both the prosecution and defence is that both know the content of that evidence before the trial. The prosecution knows whether or not the child has come up to proof and can decide not to proceed if the evidence is deemed unlikely to support a conviction. The defence lawyer knows the strength of the evidence against the accused from the primary witness and can give realistic advice about the prospects of a conviction, perhaps encouraging a guilty plea. Preliminary analysis from 48 trials involving 73 children in Western Australia (in which the Child Witness Assistance Service was involved) found that 42% of these children ($n = 31$), mostly under 14 ($n = 22$), had their testimony pre-recorded and did not need to appear at the trial itself; those over 14 were more likely to give evidence live at the trial using CCTV (16 children, all 13 or older). The conviction rate (about 70% of cases overall) was not affected either by the use of pre-recorded depositions (70% for pre-trial depositions and 61.9% without) or by the live-link (68.8% with the live-link and 66.7% without). The available evidence does not indicate whether the pre-recorded evidence encouraged a higher rate of guilty pleas.

The other considerations in relation to the impact on a jury of televised testimony are similar to those already outlined in relation to CCTV.

CONCLUSIONS

Video-technology offers one approach to alleviate some of the difficulties that child witnesses face as part of the court process, with the research suggesting that it can facilitate children's testimony and increase the reliability of their evidence. It is, however, not the panacea that some had hoped for and is not without problems, not the least of which are the attitudinal barriers of the professionals involved in the court process. When judges and lawyers are able to use their discretion about the use of CCTV and pre-trial depositions with little if any reference to the needs or wishes of child witnesses, such discretion tends to undermine the use of such approaches and may strengthen concerns about them (Westcott & Jones, 1997); for example, if CCTV is used only for the weakest cases where an acquittal is the more likely outcome with or without the use of special procedures, it is not surprising that this encourages the belief that it is more difficult to gain a conviction when these procedures are used. Similarly, it is not surprising that the conviction rate has decreased in cases involving children since some of the restrictions on their evidence have been eased, as these cases often rely heavily on the uncorroborated evidence of children who are now giving evidence at younger ages than previously.

What is needed, as long as children are required to testify in adversarial court proceedings, is not just a technological fix but a change in the way children are treated in the court process. They need to be asked questions they can understand and to be treated with respect. It is now well recognized that children's emotional state and the consistency and completeness of their testimony are affected by the way they are questioned (Brennan & Brennan, 1988; Davies & Noon, 1991; Davies & Seymour, 1998; Goodman et al., 1992; Perry et al., 1995). The need for lawyers to change their style and for judges to exercise greater control over inappropriate questioning is, however, less well accepted (Cashmore & Bussey, 1996; Davies et al., 1995; Davies & Seymour, 1998). While training for interviewers and court preparation for child witnesses are both useful and necessary (Sas et al., 1991; Saywitz, Snyder & Nathanson, 1999), such approaches need to be supplemented by education for the legal professionals in court so that they can recognize linguistic and power differences regarding child witnesses and thereby enhance the fact-finding function of the court.

REFERENCES

Aldridge, J., & Cameron, S. (1999). Interviewing child witnesses: Questioning techniques and the role of training. *Applied Developmental Science, 3*, 136–47.

Australian Law Reform Commission, & Human Rights and Equal Opportunity Commission (1997). *Seen and heard: Priority for children in the legal process.* Sydney: Australian Government Printing Service.

Brainerd, C.J., Reyna, V.F., Howe, M.L., & Kingma, J. (1990). The development of forgetting and reminiscence. *Monographs of the Society for Research in Child Development, 55*(3–4), Serial No. 222).

Brennan, M., & Brennan, R.E. (1988). *Strange language: Child victims under cross-examination* (3rd ed). Wagga Wagga, NSW: Charles Sturt University.

Bussey, L., Lee, K., & Grimbeek, E. (1993). Lies and secrets: Implications for children's reporting of sexual abuse. In: G.S. Goodman & B.L. Bottoms (Eds), *Child victims, child witnesses* (pp. 147–68). New York: Guilford Press.

Cashmore, J. (1995). The prosecution of child sexual assault: A survey of NSW DPP solicitors. *Australian and New Zealand Journal of Criminology, 28*, 32–54.

Cashmore, J., & Bussey, K. (1996). Judicial perceptions of child witness competence. *Law and Human Behavior, 20*, 313–34.

Cashmore, J. (with de Haas, N.). (1992). *The use of closed circuit television for child witnesses in the ACT.* Sydney: Australian Law Reform Commission.

Cashmore, J., & Horsky, M. (1988). The prosecution of child sexual assault. *Australian and New Zealand Journal of Criminology*, **21**, 241–52.

Cherryman, J., King, N., & Bull, R. (1999). Child witness investigative interviews: An analysis of the use of children's video-recorded evidence in North Yorkshire. *International Journal of Police Science and Management*, **2**, 50–6.

Davis, E., & Seymour, F. (1997). Child witnesses in the criminal courts: Furthering New Zealand's commitment to the United Nations Convention on the Rights of the Child. *Psychiatry, Psychology & Law*, **4**, 13–24.

Davies, E., & Seymour, F.W. (1998). Questioning child complainants of sexual abuse: Analysis of criminal court transcripts in New Zealand. *Psychiatry, Psychology and Law*, **5**, 47–61.

Davies, G. (1999). The impact of television on the presentation and reception of children's testimony. *International Journal of Law and Psychiatry*, **22**, 241–56.

Davies, G., & Noon, E. (1991). *An evaluation of the live link for child witnesses.* London: Home Office.

Davies, G., Wilson, C., Mitchell, R., & Milsom, J. (1995). *Videotaping children's evidence: An evaluation.* London: Home Office.

Davis, G., Hoyano, L., Keenan, C. Maitland, L., & Morgan, R. (1999). *An assessment of the admissibility and sufficiency of evidence in child abuse prosecutions.* London: Home Office Research Development and Statistics Directorate.

Flin, R., Boon, J., Knox, A., & Bull, R. (1992). The effects of a five-month delay on children's and adults' eyewitness memory. *British Journal of Psychology*, **83**, 323–36.

Flin, R., Bull, R., Boon, J., & Knox, A. (1993). Child witnesses in Scottish criminal trials. *International Review of Criminology*, **2**, 319–39.

Goodman, G., Taub, E., Jones, D., England, P., Port, P., Purdy, L., & Prado, L. (1992). Emotional effects of criminal court testimony on child sexual assault victims. *Monographs of the Society for Research on Child Development*, **57**(5, Serial No. 229).

Goodman, G.S., Tobey, A.E., Batterman-Faunce, J.M. Orcutt, H., Thomas, S., Shapiro, C., & Sachsenmaier, T. (1998). Face-to-face confrontation: Effects of closed-circuit technology on children's eyewitness testimony and jurors' decisions. *Law and Human Behavior*, **22**, 165–203.

Hill, P.E., & Hill, S.M. (1987). Videotaping children's testimony: An empirical view. *Michigan Law Review*, **85**, 809–33.

Leippe, M.R., Manion, A.P., & Romanczyk, A. (1993). Discernability or discrimination? Understanding jurors' reactions to accurate and inaccurate child and adult witnesses. In: G.S. Goodman & B.L. Bottoms (Eds), *Child victims, child witnesses.* New York: Guilford Press.

McGough, L. (1997). Stretching the blanket: Legal reforms affecting child witnesses. *Learning and Individual Differences*, **19**, 317–40.

Montoya, J. (1995). Lessons from Akiki and Michaels on shielding child witnesses. *Psychology, Public Policy and Law*, **1**, 340–69.

Murray, K. (1995). *Live television link: An evaluation of its use by child witnesses in Scottish criminal trials.* Edinburgh: The Scottish Office, HMSO.

Myers, J.E.B. (1996). A decade of international reform to accommodate child witnesses. *Criminal Justice and Behavior*, **23**, 402–22.

NSW Children's Evidence Taskforce. (1997). *Audio and videotaping of children's out-of-court statements.* Sydney: NSW Attorney-General's Department.

O'Grady, C. (1996). *Child witnesses and jury trials.* Perth: Western Australia Ministry of Justice.

Perry, N.W., McAuliff, B.D., Tam, P., Claycomb, L., Dostal, C., & Flanagan, C. (1995). When lawyers question children. *Law and Human Behavior,* **19,** 609–29.

Peters, D. (1990, March). Confrontational stress and children's testimony: Some experimental findings. In: S. Ceci (Chair), Do children lie? Narrowing the uncertainties. Symposium presented at the American Psychology and Law Society Meeting, Williamsburg, VA.

Ross, D.F., Hopkins, S., Hanson, E., Lindsay, S., Hazan, K., & Eslinger, T. (1994). The impact of protective shields and videotape testimony on conviction rates in a simulated trial of child sexual abuse. *Law and Human Behavior,* **18,** 553–66.

Sas, L., Hurley, P., Austin, G., & Wolfe, D. (1991). *Reducing the system-induced trauma for child sexual abuse victims through court preparation, assessment and follow-up.* London, Ontario: London Family Court Clinic.

Saywitz, K., & Nathanson, R. (1993). Children's testimony and their perceptions of stress in and out of the courtroom. *Child Abuse and Neglect,* **17,** 613–22.

Saywitz, K., Snyder, L., & Nathanson, R. (1999). Facilitating the communicative competence of the child witness. *Applied Developmental Science,* **3,** 58–68.

Spencer, J.R. & Flin, R.H. (1993). *The evidence of children: The law and the psychology* (2nd ed.). London: Blackstone.

Swim, J., Borgida, E., & McCoy, K. (1993). Videotaped versus in-court witness testimony: Does protecting the child witness jeopardize due process? *Journal of Applied Social Psychology,* **23,** 603–31.

Tobey, A.E., Goodman, G.S., Batterman-Faunce, J.M., Orcutt, H.K., & Sachsenmaier, T. (1995). Balancing the rights of children and defendants: Effects of closed-circuit television on children's accuracy and juror's perceptions. In: M.S. Zaragoza, J.R. Graham, G.C.N. Hall, R. Hirschman, & Y.S. Ben-Porath (Eds), *Memory and testimony in the child witness* (pp. 214–39). Thousand Oaks, CA: Sage.

Westcott, H., Davies, G., & Clifford, B. (1991). The credibility of child witnesses seen on closed-circuit television. *Adoption and Fostering,* **15,** 14–19.

Westcott, H., & Jones, J. (1997). *Perspectives on the Memorandum: Policy, practice and research in investigative interviewing.* Aldershot: Arena.

Whitcomb, D., Shapiro, E.R., & Stellwagen, L.D. (1985). *When the victim is a child: Issues for judges and prosecutors* (2nd ed., 1992). Washington, DC: National Institute of Justice.

CHAPTER 14

New Measures and New Challenges: Children's Experiences of the Court Process

AMANDA WADE

Department of Sociology and Social Policy, University of Leeds, UK

Between 1988 and 1991, there was a transformation in the position of the child witness within the criminal justice process in England and Wales. Rules of evidence which had placed barriers in the way of children's testimony being put before the courts were abolished and new procedures established to allow some of the more stressful features of a court appearance to be circumvented when children give evidence in criminal cases involving sexual or violent offences. Until this time, children had been viewed as inherently unreliable witnesses; their competence to act in this capacity had to be established before they could be permitted to testify, and any evidence then given became subject to child-specific corroboration rules. Yet, in all other respects, they were treated no differently to adults, being expected to cope with the demands of a court appearance without any special support or preparation. However, this dichotomy in the perception of children was subjected to a straightforward reversal by the reforms introduced by the Criminal Justice Acts of 1988 and 1991. Children's evidence should (theoretically) now be treated like that of an adult; all children with adequate language skills are assumed to be competent to testify, and

Children's Testimony. Edited by H.L. Westcott, G.M. Davies, and R.H.C. Bull.
© 2002 John Wiley & Sons, Ltd.

there is no longer any requirement that their evidence should be corroborated simply because it is that of a minor. At the same time, with the development of trial procedures specifically for use by child witnesses, a system has been created which is premised on children having special needs by virtue of their emotional, cognitive, and social immaturity.

The reforms introduced far-reaching changes in the law and legal procedure and radically altered the image of the child witness which informs the criminal justice process. The means by which the new measures were brought about provides a fascinating insight into the social, historical, and cultural location of law reform, for, while there was a significant body of research supporting the abolition of the rules of evidence which circumscribed children's testimony (Hedderman, 1987), there was no equivalent empirical support for the proposed procedural reforms. Evidence was becoming available which showed that many children found a court appearance stressful and that this had implications for the quality of the testimony they were able to provide (see Flin, Davies, & Tarrant, 1988; Goodman *et al.*, 1988), but no systematic evaluation was yet available of the proposed solutions to this problem—the introduction of video-links and pre-recorded evidence (Murray, 1988). Instead, advocates of the use of video relied largely on *assumptions* about its likely efficacy in protecting complainants in cases of child sexual abuse from the inhibiting effects of testifying in the presence of the defendant about distressing and abusive experiences. The widespread support which these proposals attracted among childcare professionals and the general public were an outcome of the concern attendant on the rediscovery of child sexual abuse during the 1980s, the reconceptualization of such abuse as a criminal justice rather than a welfare problem, and emotive arguments about the traumatic effects of a court appearance on child complainants, rather than the proven effectiveness of video-communicated testimony (Wade, 1997).

Once in place, the new procedural measures were evaluated (see Judy Cashmore, Chapter 13 in book). Conducting a formal evaluation of the live-link for the government's Home Office, Davies and Noon (1991) concluded that children testifying from a remote witness room were happier, more fluent, and less inconsistent in their testimony than those testifying conventionally in a courtroom. The positive note struck by this initial study was then somewhat tempered by the researchers' subsequent evaluation of the introduction of pre-recorded evidence (Davies, Wilson, Mitchell, & Milsom, 1995), which showed trial outcomes to be independent of whether evidence-in-chief was live or pre-recorded. Nevertheless, children whose evidence was pre-recorded were rated as displaying less anxiety than those offering live evidence, suggesting that the new procedures were effective in their primary aim of reducing the stress of a court appearance for children. A limitation, however, of both studies is the lack of feedback from child witnesses themselves. The researchers were not permitted to contact child witnesses directly in the first study and were limited to circulating children with a questionnaire in the second, to which only 17 responded. Given these restrictions on data collection, it is unsurprising that the study findings were less nuanced than those of an evaluation of the live-link conducted for the Scottish Office by Murray (1995), which drew both on observational ratings and interviews with child witnesses. Murray's report is rather more equivocal on the benefits of the new measures, indicating that, in comparison with testimony given by children in open court, that offered over a live-link was less detailed, less complete, less fluent, less effective, and less credible. Furthermore, while noting that link-users were significantly less likely to report feeling fear while they testified, she commented that more than half of the children had found the system 'strange', a minority had not liked it at all, and some would have preferred to be in open court.

RESEARCH OUTLINE

The questions which these formal evaluations of the procedural reforms were raising suggested there would be value in a qualitative study of the post-reform reality of children's experience of becoming a witness, as this would allow exploration of the complexities and divergences of their responses to, and perceptions of, the new procedures. I therefore carried out a small-scale study in one Crown Court Centre during 1994 and 1995. Over a seven-month period, all cases in which children were listed as witnesses were identified with the assistance of the Crown Prosecution Service (CPS), 16 cases being found. Eleven of these were eventually dealt with by way of a jury trial, the remaining five being resolved by a late guilty plea or discontinuance. Each trial was observed in full and a detailed transcript taken of the proceedings. All but one of these cases concerned sexual offences against children and a wide range of charges were involved, from single incidents of sexual assault or rape to long-term incest, buggery, or sexual intercourse with one or multiple complainants. The remaining case was one of murder which arose from a violent incident between pupils from two rival schools. Altogether, the full sample of cases listed 53 children as potential witnesses, of whom 40 were eventually required to testify at court.

Of the latter, 26 children were complainants and 14 bystander witnesses. Nineteen of the children in the trial subsample were aged between 7 and 12 years at the time of the trial and 21 were between 13 and 18 years.

Child witnesses and their carers were given information about the study at the time of the final hearing, and children were asked if they would be willing to be interviewed about their experiences of court once the trial was conclusively over. The CPS was able to provide addresses for only 42 of the 53 children, and in two cases children were found to have left the address supplied. However, 26 of the children contacted agreed to be interviewed and, in 7 cases, a parent or carer offered to be interviewed in the child's place. In-depth interview data was obtained for at least one child in all but one of the study cases.

FINDINGS

Preparation and Waiting at Court

Reflecting back on their experiences, more children identified lack of knowledge of the court process as a source of anxiety about their court appearance than any other subject, including the prospect of seeing the defendant or his[1] family at court. Despite the availability of the Child Witness Pack (National Society for the Prevention of Cruelty to Children & ChildLine, 1993), this was seen by children in only two of the study cases, and they received little in the way of other pre-trial preparation. All but 3 of the 22 complainants for whom interview data is available had been taken on a visit to the courthouse in the week before the trial began. However, this had primarily been an exercise in familiarization. Rather than providing them with information about their role as a witness, the focus of the visit was on showing the children the layout of the courthouse and the remote-witness room.[2] Few attempts appeared to have been made to create an opportunity for the children to ask questions or express any of their anxieties or to ensure that they had a clear understanding of what giving evidence involves. Many thus felt that the visit had done little to help them to

---

[1] All the defendants in cases which went to trial were men. One case, which involved two defendants, one of whom was a woman, was severed. The case against the woman was discontinued after the man's conviction.

[2] Six children commented on the fact that they had not been shown any of the courtrooms. The resident judge had ruled that this would be counterproductive. However, while two children said they were glad about this as thinking about the defendant would have made them nervous, three were critical and cited this as one of the reasons why they had not found the visit particularly helpful.

understand what would happen at court or to alleviate their fears, some seeing it in terms of 'just being shown round'. Bystander witnesses received even less preparation, being provided only with a leaflet distributed by Victim Support. Not surprisingly, many of the children based their expectations of court on what they had seen on television and felt this had given them a distorted picture of what would happen:

> It wasn't half as bad as we'd all expected, 'cos we all expected it to be like you see on telly, where they start shouting at you, and you know how they always get upset on telly? And start shouting and that? We all expected it to be like that. But it were nothing like that at all. *(Witness, Joanne: 15 years)*

> I keep watching *The Bill* and all these men witnesses, and all these ladies being really silly on it. . . . The real court is a lot different. *(Complainant, Kelly: 9 years)*

Once at court, the children were appreciative of the attention paid to them by ushers and volunteers attached to the recently established Witness Support Service, whose support offered an unexpected level of personal warmth and concern. Efforts had been made to provide separate waiting areas for complainants (and also witnesses in the murder trial), with games and videos usually being provided for the younger children. However, the emphasis was on providing *for* the children rather than finding out from them what assistance they would like. Some complainants described the arrangements at the courthouse as having heightened their anxiety, one 11-year-old saying, 'It were just frightening because everywhere we went, we had to have someone with us.' Another girl described her seclusion in a small room and dependence on volunteers to fetch any food or drinks she wanted as having emphasized her feelings of powerlessness in comparison with the defendant who 'had the run of the court'. As one adolescent commented:

> I think everyone understands . . . understood that what they were doing, they were doing for us own good, but I think if they'd asked us what we were worried about or . . . maybe even any sort of conversation really, it would have been better. *(Nicole, 16 years)*

The Video Facilities

Children whose evidence was given from the remote-witness room identified a number of benefits in this facility; the most frequently mentioned was the protection which the closed circuit system offers from direct confrontation with the defendant:

If I was standing in a [witness] box, knowing me, if I saw [the defendant] I'd probably faint. I'd probably do summat. Or tell a lie. *(Susie, 11 years)*

I didn't feel as nervous as I think I would have done if I went in the court. . . . All I could see was the people I was speaking to and a bit of behind them and in front of them. And that's all I could see. And that made me a lot better. I think if I saw [defendant], then I wouldn't be able to look. *(Kelly, 9 years)*

I wanted to give [my evidence] that way. I couldn't face him. I couldn't see him. If I'd have had to see him, that would have been that. I wouldn't have been able to go in. [But] I felt safe, not having to see him. *(Caitlin, 16 years)*

However, these feelings were not universal and some children found the thought of the defendant watching them, when they were unable to see him, a disturbing one:

It just felt horrible knowing he was watching that TV screen when I was saying [what he'd done to me]. He could be gloating over it and everything. *(Ivy, 14 years)*

When he saw me on the television it was really frightening thinking about [him seeing me] and I'm not seeing him. *(Gemma, 9 years)*

Where a video recording had taken the place of a child's evidence-in-chief, the main advantage from the children's perspective was that the recording helped them to remember what had happened:

It were like, ages ago I'd made the actual video. . . . It made it easier because then I remembered what . . . like some of things I'd told [the police]. And then when questions were asked [in cross-examination] I'd like, know what I'd said. *(Bonnie, 13 years)*

However, some became agitated or distressed watching the recording and found it revived unwelcome memories in a particularly vivid way. One girl, for instance, spoke of it arousing such intense feelings that she had to try to block out the sight and sound of the recording as much as she could—a strategy which was not helpful when it came to cross-examination.

The artificiality of the closed-circuit system was also found problematic by some children:

There were little microphones you had to clip on, and . . . instead of looking at screen to look at judge you've got to look at this red light, 'cos otherwise they couldn't see you. I were thinking, what do I look at? The telly or the light? So I were [*mimics looking from one to the other*] . . . And I just made answers up sometimes 'cos I couldn't hear him. Well, I could hear him but there were blubbering [*interference*] and things . . . and I couldn't hear. *(Chloe, 9 years)*

It were a bit funny . . . it weren't as if . . . people were talking to me straight face to face. It were . . . really funny. I couldn't hear them right. . . . It were loud enough. It's just that they had to keep repeating it over and over again because I couldn't understand. I couldn't hear them *right. (Lucy, 13 years)*

So, while some children felt they could not have testified if the link had not been available, the response of others was more equivocal. None of the children had been consulted about their mode of testifying and three said they would have preferred to give evidence in the courtroom. The youngest child concerned thought this would have enabled her to 'see' the defendant punished while for two adolescents issues of influence and control were involved. They spoke of wanting to see the responses of jurors to their testimony and one girl in particular had also wanted to see its effect on the defendant. For her, the trial represented a lost opportunity to 'tell' her father how she felt about what he had done; something which she had been unable to do as she had had no contact with him since making her allegations.

Testifying in the Courtroom

The bystander witnesses were among the older children in the sample, all being aged 13 years or above at the time of the trial. One of the younger girls attended court alone and found the experience extremely stressful:

> I were scared of going in 'cos, like, I've never seen [a court] and I've never been there and like, there were people looking at me and ... I'm like, in that box, and then there's big manager there or summat, and then there's some more stood down there. They were *pushing* me to say opposite thing ... and they shouldn't really do that. They should, like, ask you to say what happened and then ask you questions. But they didn't. They kept ... pushing me to say summat else. And as soon as I got out I started crying 'cos they pushed me and they scared me. *(Shannon, 13 years)*

The murder trial, in particular, aroused intense anxiety and fears of reprisals among those involved and was the one case in the sample which, for a short time, appeared unlikely to proceed due to the reluctance of the Crown's main witness to testify. However, despite their anxiety while waiting to go into court, all but one of the bystander witnesses said their nervousness diminished once they began answering questions. Invariably, they spoke of the presence of the defendant as being the worst aspect of testifying in the courtroom, but two commented that despite the discomfort this caused them, his presence also acted as an incentive to tell the court what they knew:

> I just felt so vulnerable. ... I was very aware [the defendant] was near me and he was there. Because even though [he] was behind, you could still see out of the corner of your eye. You know, I could feel him. I could feel him watching me. And I didn't like that at all. ... But if anything, I think

it helped ... because I thought, I'm not letting you get away with it, kind of thing. I'm going to say what I've got to say. *(Georgia, 17 years)*

Cross-examination

Cross-examination was anticipated with trepidation by many interviewees. Nevertheless, the actual experience differed for complainants and bystander witnesses, all but two of the latter group saying cross-examination was less of an ordeal than they had expected and many expressing surprise at the manner of the defence counsel which, contrary to their expectations, was courteous and non-confrontational:

> I thought it was going to be a lot worse than what it were. ... I was expecting [the defendant]'s barrister to, like, say [the complainant]'s told you this—you know, say it's not really happened. And for them to, like, try and make out I were a liar and all that. But ... it were alright actually. [It wasn't as bad as you'd expected?] It were a lot better. *(Jade, 14 years)*

> I expected [defence counsel] to be like they are on television. Like, really getting at you, to get answers out of you, and twist your answers round. And he didn't. He just wanted to make sure that what I'd said were what I meant. ... Compared to what I thought it would be like, it was a lot easier. *(Nicole, 16 years)*

> It was ... I don't know, I think that it were more psychological than anything. [Defence counsel] were nice, you know what I mean? He weren't horrible to me. But the things he were saying weren't nice. You know, they got me angry and upset. But it was the way he came across, were quite nice. ... He weren't aggressive or anything like that. ... I don't think it were as bad as what I'd expected it to be. *(Georgia, 17 years)*

The experience was, however, rather different for complainants. The accounts of these children highlight some specific cross-examination strategies which intensified the pressure they felt while their evidence was tested. Repeated questioning on individual topics, manipulative use of witnesses' responses, and tight control of the way in which the witness could respond, were the most frequently cited of these:

> [Defence counsel] didn't give me chance to finish any of the questions [he] asked. I couldn't answer them at all properly, and he was always confusing me. [He'd interrupt me] while I was trying to speak and come on to another question. I got very confused. I couldn't work out the proper dates and times when everything happened. *(Ivy, 14 years)*

> The person who was on my side wasn't as horrible as, wasn't as bad as the person who was on [the defendant]'s side. Like, he asked me a cartload of questions, person on my side, and the one on his side kept on asking me the same questions. Did it happen, Susie? I'm suggesting it never happened, Susie. I'm suggesting that you're telling lies, Susie, and you're doing this, Susie, and you're making it up, Susie. ... But I never had a

break. . . . 'Cos I thought if I had a break, I'd back down, I'd change me story. So I thought I'd go straight through it and I did. *(Susie, 11 years)*

[Defence counsel] wasn't very nice. . . . He'd question me over and over again. It was like, I went to answer a question . . . if I'd say summat, he'd say, just please answer the question, yes or no? I mean, he were shutting everything else out, he didn't want to know owt else. [He] just wanted *that* answer. . . . He were bugging me, so I told him straight! *(Marlene, 12 years)*

Two carers reported that children were acutely distressed by this aspect of the trial process, but some of the children were sanguine about the experience or felt they had been treated quite fairly:

Some of questions were really hard to answer, 'cos, like, I'd forgot most of stuff. But then, some of questions were easy as well. . . . They treated me fair. *(Marie, 13 years)*

[Defence counsel] just asked questions and that. He'd say things like . . . he only really tried to make it out once when . . . 'cos I didn't tell my mum until quite a long while afterwards. He said did I not tell mum straight away because I were lying, but I said no. And he asked did I have any particular friends . . . just in case I were ganging up and lying and things. And then he said, alright then, and switched back to judge. *(Chloe, 9 years)*

His solicitor *[sic]*, when he tried to make me out a liar, he looked at judge, and judge says summat to him, not quite sure what he said, but then [defence counsel] didn't make questions so hard, after judge said that. . . . I weren't really bothered [that he tried to make me out a liar.] I just told them what had happened and, like . . . I knew I were in right and I weren't lying. . . . I think [defence counsel] believed me, because he told him to say why he'd done it, like.[3] *(Lucy, 13 years)*

Even where cross-examination was experienced as difficult, children did not describe the experience in wholly negative terms when they looked back, but expressed a justifiable pride in themselves for having coped with a stressful and demanding task:

The person who was, like, talking for [the defendant] was, like, really strict . . . he looked grumpy . . . and he was, like, trying to get the truth and everything, and trying to get everything out of me. . . . It was really scary, and I didn't like that, but I could have done it again. *(Kelly, 9 years)*

I felt like just getting [defence counsel] by the neck and saying, 'I'm *not* telling a lie'. But every time I said 'Yes, [the defendant] *did* do that', 'Yes, he did do *that* as well', I kept on getting stronger and stronger. 'Cos I knew what I was saying was true. [What were you thinking of when that was happening?] A lot of things – if he gets out he'll do it to other people. And I don't want to let him get away with this. . . . It's something that— probably no one wants to do it, but you've got to. You've got to

---

[3] This girl was aware that defence counsel spoke to the defendant before the trial began, trying to persuade him to enter a late guilty plea.

kind of ... stand up for yourself. And stand up for other people. *(Susie, 11 years)*

All the children and young people interviewed had stood up well to cross-examination and most had some understanding of the role of defence counsel. Yet, as indicated above, their expectations were based on images of criminal justice purveyed in popular culture. These sometimes intensified their anxieties needlessly and, without exception, the children felt that their court experience would have been made easier by pre-trial information and preparation.

Evaluations

Seven of the 11 cases in the trial subsample resulted in a conviction, and this undoubtedly influenced the children's evaluations of their experiences. Nevertheless, the emotional repercussions of the trial were not resolved with the conclusion of the court case. Three children spoke of the trial having awakened memories which otherwise had begun to pre-occupy them less, and two briefly lived apart from their families, needing time to readjust and recover from the strains of the preceding months. For two, fears of reprisals proved a reality, a boy and a girl (involved in separate cases) being assaulted on the street by friends or relatives of the defendant. Yet, despite all of this, and contrary to the views of some carers (who described the court case as a waste of time because of the failure to secure a conviction or perceived leniency of the sentence), the children interviewed were invariably positive about the prosecution and their treatment at court. Their comments included:

> I thought we were treated alright. ... I think we were treated a lot better than what all other grown-ups would have been. *(Bonnie, 13 years)*

> Just—say it's good. And you want to lick the person who did it to you. And when you get [to court] there's lots to do. And judge is cheerful. *(Chloe, 9 years)*

> If I had to, I really would do it again, if I had to get somebody in jail for doing something bad, I would. *(Kelly, 9 years)*

> One good thing, [the defendant]'s in prison. The next good thing, he's got to stay away from kids. ... I think that the video link is the best thing that they've come up with so far. *(Susie, 11 years)*

> I feel relieved [now it's over]. It *is* worth going through it. *(Caitlin, 16 years)*.

These children felt a justifiable sense of pride in themselves as a result of surviving their abusive experiences and participating in the prosecution of their abuser. Similarly, it was clear that the court case had made a deep impression on those young people who had acted as bystander witnesses, many of whom voiced a heightened interest in the criminal justice process and feelings of enhanced self-esteem as a result of taking on a role which they saw as involving far-reaching responsibilities.

DISCUSSION

The children involved in this study viewed the criminal justice process with respect. The court case played a significant role in their lives over a period of many months (cases taking from 41 to 91 weeks from the investigation to the final hearing) and, for many, its effects were not concluded with the reaching of a verdict. As has been shown above, many of the children were impressed with the kindness they received from ancillary staff at the court and felt they were treated fairly by judges and counsel. Yet, it is clear from their accounts that far more could have been done to equip them for the demands which would be made of them as witnesses, thereby assisting not only the children themselves but also the trial process.

Much has changed since this study was completed. Attention drawn to the problem of delay in child witness cases (Plotnikoff and Woolfson, 1995a) has resulted in the development of protocols for close case management and the introduction of fast-tracking (see Criminal Justice Consultative Council, 1993; West Midlands and Warwickshire Criminal Justice Liason Committe, n.d.). Pre-court preparation has received attention (Plotnikoff and Woolfson, 1995b; Murray, 1997), and by early 1999 Witness Support schemes had become available at 86 Crown Court Centres (Hansard (Lords) 1.2.1999: 1324). Most significantly, the government has stated its commitment to ensuring that 'vulnerable children should ... be kept out of court altogether by finding other ways to put their evidence ... We intend ultimately that all such children will be cross-examined before trial and the proceedings recorded on video' (Howarth, 1999). With the Youth Justice and Criminal Evidence Act 1999, the process of achieving full implementation of the Pigot Committee recommendations (Home Office, 1989) has at last begun.

Does this mean that the problems which for so long beset child witnesses are finally being resolved? Even the most well-intentioned and liberal reforms have a habit of disappointing, at times resulting in unanticipated or ambiguous outcomes (Smart, 1995). I would suggest that the findings of my study, while small and localized, point to some potentially tricky areas.

The child-witness reforms introduced in 1988 and 1991 were framed in a prescriptive manner, implicit in the legislation being a presumption in favour of the use of video facilities. This presumption has now been made explicit in the Youth Justice and Criminal Evidence Act 1999 (YJ&CE Act). The Act creates three categories of child witness, the first of which—those giving evidence in cases involving sexual offences—are automatically deemed to require 'special protection' (YJ&CE Act, s. 21(1)(b)(i)). These children will always be cross-examined pre-trial and their evidence offered at court in recorded form unless they tell the court that they do not want to be cross-examined in this way (YJ&CE Act, s. 28). The remaining two groups of children—those testifying in cases of violence, neglect, abduction, or false imprisonment; and those testifying in all other cases—will, for the time being, normally have a video recording of their evidence-in-chief admitted and will be cross-examined over the live-link, although the strength of the presumption in favour of these measures is weaker for the latter of the two groups. The government has thus defined children's need for special measures on the basis of the type of case in which they appear. In many ways, of course, this offers a simple and elegant solution to the resource problems inherent in establishing a system for pre-recording cross-examination. However, while welcoming these measures, I believe there are disadvantages in categorizing children in this way and in making the legislation so prescriptive.

In 1988 and 1991, there was resistance to the introduction of new procedures for child witnesses among some sections of the legal profession and a powerful presumption in favour of their use was necessary to bring about the requisite changes in the culture of the criminal justice system. However, parliamentary debates on the 1999 Act indicate general support for special measures for vulnerable witnesses and a recognition that these do not invariably undermine the integrity of the justice system. The difficulty with continuing to maintain a doctrinaire stance towards special measures is that this risks the system becoming routinized, thereby ignoring the wishes of child witnesses themselves. My own study shows how difficult it is to represent children's needs in any simple and unified way. There was considerable diversity among the children I interviewed in their responses to the live-link and pre-recorded evidence. A majority favoured these measures, but there were children who found the artificiality of the link problematic, the use of pre-recorded evidence disturbing, or simply the provision of 'protective' procedures disempowering. Moreover, observation of the 11 trials showed that it cannot always be assumed that the issues involved in sexual offence cases are necessarily more traumatic than those in, for instance, some cases of violence. The study suggests that, rather than defining children's needs by creating prescriptive categories, a flexible system offering children a range of options for testifying and the opportunity to express an informed choice would better meet their needs.

At present, despite the diverse provisions now available, it is unclear what real choice child witnesses will have about their means of testifying. The 1999 Act states that children who advise the court that they do not want the special measures provided for them will not be obliged to use them. One wonders, however, how children will communicate their wishes and what weight will be accorded to them. Although legislation and practice guidelines invariably acknowledge the importance of ascertaining children's views on matters affecting them, in practice their expressed wishes (when sought) are usually rejected if they run counter to the views of the professionals concerned with what is in their best interests (Neale & Smart, 1999). Particularly where they are seen as victims, there is an understandable tendency for adults to want to avoid anything which may expose children to apparently needless distress, increasing the likelihood that they will be guided towards the perceived 'best' option. It may be, however, that such 'caring' subtly undermines the confidence and self-esteem of some children. Having created a system of new measures for child witnesses, might the next challenge be to allow the children concerned to participate in decisions about how and whether they are used?

The research was made possible by a grant from the Wingate Foundation, for whose support I am especially grateful.

REFERENCES

Criminal Justice Consultative Council. (1993). *Timetabling of criminal proceedings*, DL11/275/2, 8 November 1993.

Davies, G.M., & Noon, E. (1991). *An evaluation of the live link for child witnesses*. London: Home Office.

Davies, G., Wilson, C., Mitchell, R., & Milsom, J. (1995). *Videotaping children's evidence: An evaluation*. London: Home Office Publications Unit.

Flin, R.H., Davies, G.M., & Tarrant, A.B. (1988). *The Child Witness*. Final report to the Criminological Research Branch, Central Research Unit, The Scottish Office Home and Health Department, Grant 85/9290.

Goodman, G.S., Jones, D.P.H., Pyle, E.A., Prado-Estrada, L., Port, L.K., England, P., Mason, R., & Rudy, L. (1988). The emotional effects of criminal court testimony on child sexual assault victims: A preliminary report. In: G. Davies & J. Drinkwater (Eds), *The child witness: Do the courts abuse children?* (Issues in Criminological and Legal Psychology No. 13, pp. 46–54). Leicester: The British Psychological Society.

Hedderman, C. (1987). *Children's evidence: The need for corroboration*. (Home Office Research and Planning Unit, Paper No. 41. London: Home Office.

Home Office (1989). *Report of the Advisory Group on Video Evidence* (Chairman: Judge Thomas Pigot, QC). London: Home Office.

Howarth, G. (1999). Youth Justice and Criminal Evidence Bill (Lords), Standing Committee E, Tuesday 22 June 1999 (Morning); online at http.// www.parliament.the-stationery-of...9899/

Murray, K. (1988). *Alternatives to in-court testimony in criminal proceedings in the United States of America* (Research paper on evidence from children). Edinburgh: Scottish Law Commission.

Murray, K. (1995). *Live television link: An evaluation of its use by child witnesses in Scottish criminal trials*. Edinburgh: The Scottish Office Central Research Unit, HMSO.

Murray, K. (1997). *Preparing child witnesses for court: A review of literature and research*. Edinburgh: The Scottish Office Home Department Central Research Unit.

National Society for the Prevention of Cruelty to Children, & ChildLine. (1993). *The child witness pack*. London: NSPCC.

Neale, B, & Smart, C. (1999). *Agents or dependants? Struggling to listen to children in family law and family research* (Working paper No. 3). Leeds: Centre for Research on Family, Kinship & Childhood, University of Leeds.

Plotnikoff, J., & Woolfson, R. (1995a). *Prosecuting child abuse: An evaluation of the government's speedy progress policy*. London: Blackstone Press.

Plotnikoff, J., & Woolfson, R. (1995b). *Evaluation of the child witness pack: The support and preparation of children to give evidence*. Report to the Home Office Research and Planning Unit, May 1995.

Smart, C. (1995). Feminism and law: Some problems of analysis and strategy. In: C. Smart (Ed.), *Law, crime and sexuality: Essays in feminism* (pp. 146–7). London: Sage.

Wade, A. (1997). The child witness and the criminal justice process: A case study in law reform. Ph.D. thesis, University of Leeds.

West Midlands and Warwickshire Criminal Justice Liason Committee (n.d.). *Caring for the child witness*.

CHAPTER 15

A German Perspective on Children's Testimony

Günter Köhnken

Institut für Psychologie, University of Kiel, Germany

As most readers will know the inquisitorial system of criminal justice
(which is typical for German-speaking countries) differs in several
aspects from the adversarial system. Although in practice these differences are often less pronounced than in theory they do have significant
implications with regard to child witnesses.

THE COURTS

The most obvious difference between the adversarial and the inquisitorial system is the court itself. At the lowest level, the district court, a
German court comprises one professional judge and two lay judges.
The next level, the regional court, is either the entry level for more
serious crimes or the appeal court for cases which have been tried
before a district court in the first instance. A regional court comprises
three professional judges and two lay judges. All decisions, including
the final verdict, are made by the panel of professional and lay judges.
No juries are involved in a criminal trial.

If the defendant or the victim of an alleged crime is below the age of 18
years, the case is brought before a special juvenile court. The judges of
a juvenile court are supposed to have special education and particular
experience in dealing with children and juveniles. In cases of sexual
abuse, the victim of the alleged crime may appoint a lawyer who acts

Children's Testimony. Edited by H.L. Westcott, G.M. Davies, and R.H.C. Bull.
© 2002 John Wiley & Sons, Ltd.

on his or her behalf as a co-prosecutor. If a child is the only witness (as is usually the case in sexual-abuse cases) the court often (although not always) appoints an expert witness (usually a psychologist) to aid the court in judging the child's competency to testify and the credibility of the statement.

One of the professional judges chairs the panel of judges. This chairperson has a much more active role in the criminal trial than a judge in the adversarial system of justice. He or she always starts interviewing the defendant and the witnesses. When the defendant or witness has been interviewed by the chair, the right to ask questions is granted (in this order) to the other (professional and lay) judges, the prosecutor, the co-prosecutor, the defence lawyer and the expert witness.

Numerous studies have shown that giving evidence in court is often a stressful experience for children. In this respect, the results of German studies do not differ very much from experiences in countries which have adopted the adversarial system of criminal justice (Dannenberg, Mantwill, Stahlmann-Liebelt, & Köhnken, 1997; Busse, Volbert, & Steller, 1996; Volbert & Busse, 1995; Volbert & Pieters, 1993). Busse et. al. (1996) have reported that about one-third of the children in their sample suffered from, among other things, sleep disturbances, fever, and diarrhoea before going to court. This emotional distress which is experienced by children produces various negative consequences beyond a potential additional trauma for the victim of the crime. Parents, for example, who anticipate these effects may be more reluctant to report sexual abuse to the police. As a result, the perpetrator may attack other children as well. Furthermore, emotional strain and distress may have detrimental effects on the child's cognitive performance with the consequence of increased difficulties in interviewing the child, resulting in less complete statements, etc.

Since 1971, the code of criminal procedural in Germany has provided various measures in order to reduce the emotional strain and distress which children may suffer when they have to testify in court; for example, the court may decide to remove the defendant from the courtroom while a child witness under the age of 16 years is giving his or her statement. A survey conducted in northern Germany has shown that in about 60% of cases child witnesses were interviewed without the defendant being present (Dannenberg, Höfer, Köhnken, & Reutemann, 1997). This proportion was considerably lower (41%) in a sample of criminal trials in Berlin (Busse et al., 1996).

A number of studies have shown that the fear of meeting the defendant in court is the single most stress-inducing factor for child witnesses. Removing the defendant from the courtroom should, therefore, significantly reduce stress for the child. However, whether or not this positive effect does indeed occur depends to a large extent on additional circumstances. If, for example, the child witness does not know of this possibility prior to the trial, s/he will still fearfully anticipate the confrontation with the defendant. Furthermore, the potential positive effect of this measure may completely be destroyed if the defendant and the child meet outside the courtroom before the opening of the trial or during a break. In recent years, the courts have become more aware of these problems and try to avoid any encounter between child witnesses and defendants.

Criminal trials are, in principal, open to the general public. Not surprisingly, the presence of people who are not known to the child may put additional strain on the child witness. Consequently, the code of criminal procedure in Germany allows for the exclusion of the general public (including the media) from the courtroom while a witness under the age of 16 years gives his or her statement. In a Northern German sample of cases, the defendant was removed from the courtroom in about 60% of the cases. Busse et al. (1996) report a proportion of 41% for Berlin cases. This measure may indeed help to reduce strain and distress for the child witness. However, the beneficial effects are sometimes overestimated. Even if the public is excluded there still are (in a regional court) five judges, at least one prosecutor, perhaps a co-prosecutor, at least one defence lawyer, the court reporter, and perhaps an expert witness, all of them (except the expert witness) wearing black gowns (though no wig) and most of them being unknown to the child. On average, in the northern German sample, eight individuals were present in the courtroom while the child witness testified (Dannenberg, Höfer et al., 1997). In a sample drawn from criminal trials in Berlin, an average of 14 court officials were present (Busse et al., 1996), even though the general public had been excluded.

In order to protect the child witness from the stressful experience of cross-examination, children below the age of 16 years are exclusively interviewed by the chairing judge. The defence lawyer and the prosecutor are allowed to put questions to the child. However, they have to pass their question to the judge who then questions the child witness.

In 1998, a witness protection bill was introduced in Germany which now allows the use of video recorded statements as evidence. Furthermore, witnesses do not have to testify in the courtroom. Instead, their statements can be transmitted via closed circuit TV into the court. In both cases, the child witness would not have to appear in court. Compared to other countries (e.g. England and Wales, where video technology in the courtroom was introduced 10 years earlier), this legislation came rather late (see Judy Cashmore, Chapter 13 in this book).

Furthermore, it has been subject to harsh criticism, particularly from the side of child-protection organizations. From a child witnesses' point of view the reform is half-hearted because the use of video recorded interviews as evidence in a criminal trial is subject to restrictive conditions. Although police interviews of child witnesses are usually video recorded, only interviews conducted by a judge may be admitted as evidence if, and only if, the defendant and the defence lawyer had the opportunity to participate in the interview. Furthermore, even if this condition is met, the court may require an additional interview of the child witness either in the courtroom or through CCTV. As a consequence, this legislation is likely to result in an additional interview of the child witness who will still have to testify in court.

COURT PREPARATION PROGRAMMES

Although these measures may help to reduce a child witnesses' fears, their effects are limited if the child has no information about these options prior to the trial. S/he would still anticipate meeting the defendant, testifying about traumatic experiences in public, etc. Therefore, it appears to be necessary to pass on this information to child witnesses before they have to go to court.

In recent years, a variety of court preparation programmes for child witnesses have been introduced in different parts of Germany. The most advanced scheme was implemented in Schleswig-Holstein in 1996. It is based on the finding that a major fear- and distress-inducing factor is the lack of or incorrect information about a trial (Dannenberg, Mantwill et al., 1997; Wolf, 1997). Furthermore, children usually have only very limited knowledge about their role as witnesses, what they are expected to do and not to do and which coping behaviours are available to them in court. This lack of information may cause confusion and the feeling of a loss of control (Thompson, 1981). According to Thompson (1981), the limited predictability of aversive events, in combination with the belief of having no influence on the course of events, results in feelings of insecurity, fear, stress, and helplessness.

In Schleswig-Holstein, all children under the age of 16 years who are suspected victims of sexual or physical assault and who are required to testify in court are offered participation in a court preparation programme free of charge. The programme is carried out by psychologists and social workers (the supporters) who have received special training from psychologists and lawyers. During this training, it is particularly stressed that the supporters are not allowed, under any circumstances, to talk about the case or even rehearse the statement. The supporters receive no information about the case itself. This is done in order to prevent them from passing any case-relevant information to the witness. If the child witness participates in the programme, the court and defence lawyer are informed about this decision and about the contents and the procedure of the court preparation programme. This extensive transparency of the procedure appears to be crucial with regard to the acceptability of the programme in court.

The court preparation programme comprises activities before, during, and after the trial. The main emphasis before the trial is on the supply of information. The roles of the judges, prosecutors, and defence lawyers are explained to the child. The supporter also describes the trial procedure and particularly the procedure of a witness interview. S/he demonstrates and explains where the participants of the trial are seated. A wooden model consisting of schematic puppets and court furniture is used as an illustration. Furthermore, child witnesses receive an illustrated brochure which gives an idea about a criminal trial in a form suitable for a child (Eipper, Hille, & Dannenberg, 1997; Hille, Eipper, & Dannenberg, 1997). This brochure (available for two age groups) has been tested for its efficiency and suitability with regard to this task (Hille, 1997; Eipper, 1997). In two pre–post comparisons with first- and third-graders (six and nine years old), children demonstrated significant increases in court and trial relevant knowledge as well as significant decreases of incorrect expectations (a substantial number of children, for example, expected the judge to wear a wig and use a hammer; this is most likely a consequence of having seen American or English court series on German TV).

In order to provide the feeling of at least partial control, the child witness is told, for example, that s/he may ask for a break or ask the judge for additional information if a question is unclear. The child also learns that crying or blushing are not a problem and that nobody will blame him or her for the tears. Child witnesses are often worried because they do not know acceptable words, particularly for sexual details. To cope with these worries the child is told that the judge has talked with a great number of other children about these things and that s/he will understand whatever expression the child witness may use.

Furthermore, the supporter visits the waiting room in the courthouse and the courtroom itself together with the child and again explains where the trial participants are seated. They also pay a visit to the chairing judge provided that s/he agrees. A few judges reject such visits because they fear that their neutrality may suffer. However, the great majority of judges are quite happy with this procedure. They indicate that it helps them to get into contact with the child which in turn makes it much easier to interview the child witness in the courtroom.

On the day of the trial, the supporter picks up the child witness at home and accompanies him or her to the courthouse. Together they wait in a special waiting room and play games until the witness is called in to testify. During the witness interview, the supporter is seated right beside the child. When the child witness is dismissed, the supporter takes him or her home. The experiences are discussed and, if known at the time, the verdict is explained. Sometimes children suffer from emotional or behavioural disturbances. If this is the case, the supporter will arrange suitable therapy for the child.

The effects of this court preparation programme have been evaluated over a period of one year (Dannenberg, Höfer et al., 1997; Köhnken, 1999). During this time, child witnesses with and without court preparation were observed in the courtroom and questionnaires were completed by parents, supporters, judges, prosecutors, and defence lawyers. In a survey among judges, prosecutors, and defence lawyers prior to the implementation of the court preparation programme, almost 95% of participants indicated that they had experienced child witnesses suffering in court when they had to testify in cases of sexual or physical abuse. Against this background, the expectations for the court preparation programme were high. Almost 90% of the participants (regardless of the professional group) expected positive effects of the programme. Interestingly, the anticipated positive effects were not limited to a decrease in fear and distress on the side of the children. Eighty-one per cent of the lawyers expected that it would be easier to interview the child in court if they had participated in the programme. Furthermore, 87% pointed out that they themselves would be relieved if they knew that someone would care for the child witness before and after testifying in the courtroom. Overall, the results of this survey revealed a high acceptance of the programme by all professional groups.

In a second survey which was conducted 18 months after the program had been implemented, the positive assessment was even higher. All participants now indicated that the programme was useful (compared with 92% in the first survey). Two-thirds of the participants said that, according to their own experience, those child witnesses who had been in the programme were indeed less distressed. A majority also indicated that interviewing these children was easier, that their statements were more fluent and coherent, and that, altogether, it was more useful as evidence. Interestingly, the proportion of lawyers who, in the first survey, had indicated their concern that the children's statements might be influenced in the course of the programme substantially decreased in the second survey.

Systematic observations of the child witnesses' verbal and nonverbal behaviour in the courtroom revealed that children who had participated in the programme were significantly less distressed, insecure, nervous, and upset than those who had not been in the programme. Furthermore, their accounts were clearer and more intelligible if they had participated in the court preparation programme.

Altogether, the evaluation of the court preparation programme has revealed exceptionally positive effects. As a consequence, it has received unanimous support from parents, lawyers, authorities, and child-protection institutions. Based on these positive and encouraging experiences, a number of initiatives in various parts of Germany have now been implemented or are currently in the process of being implemented.

THE EXPERT WITNESS

The court may also decide to appoint an expert witness, usually a psychologist, to give evidence on the cognitive abilities of a child witness and/or the credibility of his or her statement. Although the usually necessary psychological examination and the additional interview by the expert witness may put further strain on the child, in the long run the availability of psychological expertise often takes pressure off the child witness. If, for example, the expert witness comes to the conclusion that the statement is credible, it would usually be a rather fruitless strategy for the defence to challenge the child's credibility directly. Instead, the defence would attack the expert witness and dispute the quality of his or her expertise. As a consequence, the child witness is taken out of the line of fire.

The expert witness acts as an aid to the court rather than as a 'hired gun' of the defence or the prosecution. He or she, therefore, has to be strictly neutral. Also, the expert witness has no right to silence. Every information, without exception, that may be relevant with regard to the expert opinion has to be disclosed to the court. On the other hand, the expert witness has to treat as confidential everything that comes to his knowledge as an expert. Serving as an expert witness is a public duty. This means that, if a court has appointed someone as expert witness, he or she is obliged to produce the expert opinion. Exceptions are only made if the person has convincing reasons for withdrawing (e.g. lack of competence with regard to the required opinion, appointments by other courts).

Although the expert witness eventually is appointed by the court, in practice s/he is often asked by the prosecution to prepare an expert opinion. There are two reasons for this procedure: the prosecution usually wants to assess the child witness's competence and credibility before the case is brought to court. This avoids exposing the witness to the stress of testifying in court when it is unlikely that the defendant will be found guilty. The second reason is primarily a pragmatic one. In controversial cases, without a confession from the defendant, the defence often applies for an expert opinion on the credibility of the child witness's statement anyway. Therefore, anticipating the application of an expert opinion during the trial, the prosecution prefers to ask for an opinion in an early stage of the investigation. This, however, does not mean that the expert witness acts as an expert for the prosecution. Usually, s/he will be appointed by the court later. This implies the legal obligation to be neutral and give the opinion to the best of his or her knowledge. The defence would normally not object to the appointment of this expert witness by the court, although there are exceptions from this general rule.

A CASE EXAMPLE

A brief description of a case example may help to give an overview of the work of an expert witness in a sexual-abuse case. The case involved a 17-year-old female who allegedly had been repeatedly sexually abused by her teacher at the age of 14 and 15. She had disclosed the alleged abuse after a delay. A further delay was caused by the duration of the criminal investigation.

As usual, the prosecution sent the expert the complete case file and asked for an expert opinion regarding the credibility of the statement. After a careful evaluation of the case file, the witness and her mother were invited for a psychological examination. First, the witness's mother was interviewed. This is usually done because the mother can provide useful information about the child's personality, fears, expectations, etc. This information can later be used for planning the interview of the witness. The mother was asked to describe her daughter's physical and psychological development. From her account, it became clear that the girl had a very difficult childhood. The father, an alcoholic, had left the family shortly after her birth. During the following years, the mother had worked as a lorry driver while the girl lived with her grand parents and in three different children's homes. The mother also described her daughter as insecure and socially isolated.

While the mother was interviewed, the girl completed a personality questionnaire and an intelligence test. The results of these tests indicated average general intelligence. With regard to personality, the questionnaire results showed high scores in introversion, emotionality, physical complaints, and inhibition.

The interview of the witness started with a prolonged rapport-building phase in order to cope with the witness's insecurities and fears. Slowly she started to describe the events in question. She mentioned that her teacher had touched her genitals on several occasions (in school, in a car while driving her home from school, on an overnight trip on a sailing yacht, and on a school journey to Greece). The account was fairly detailed. The witness was able to describe times and locations as well as the sexual activities. What was most important in this case, however, was the very detailed account of her emotional responses and the strategies that she used in order to cope with these events. She described her helplessness and her complete incompetence to deal with the assaults. What made it particularly difficult for her was the fact that the teacher did not use any violence. Instead, he told her that he loved her and that he would marry her when she would be old enough for a marriage. Furthermore, she described how he very gradually increased the intensity of his sexual activities. Eventually, she tried just to do nothing, hoping that the assaults would end some way or another. Altogether, the sexual assaults continued for a period of almost six months. The witness also described how her relationship with the teacher changed during this period. Initially, she had positive feelings towards him and regarded him as a substitute for the father she never had. When the first sexual activities started, she felt increasingly insecure about the relationship. At this point, the meaning of his behaviour was not clear to her. Later, she realized that his activities, which had become more and more sexually explicit, were illegal and she tried to avoid contacts. Even during this stage, however, she had not thought of involving the police or anyone else. All that she wanted was to be left in peace, to avoid any form of excitement.

After she had moved to another school at the age of 15, contact with the teacher ceased completely until her 16th birthday. Then, the teacher phoned her supposedly to wish her a happy birthday. However, he also mentioned that she had now reached legal age for marriage and that he would contact her again soon. At this point, the young woman panicked. She developed strong fears and eventually spoke to a friend about her experiences with the teacher. The friend informed her parents who convinced the witness to contact the police.

From a psychological point of view, this account was very interesting. First, it became clear that suggestive influence could not be a sufficient explanation for the report. Furthermore, the witness apparently had no particular motivation to harm the teacher. On the contrary, she had initially avoided any public allegation. Only after he had phoned her on her birthday and, in her view, threatened to revive the sexual relationship did the young woman see no other way out than to disclose her experiences to a friend.

The witness account was tape recorded and later transcribed for criteria-based content analysis of the statement (CBCA, see Steller & Köhnken, 1989). The basic question underlying this technique is: would this witness, with her cognitive abilities, be able to fabricate a statement with the content qualities which are defined in the so called reality criteria of CBCA? The statement was rather detailed, although forgetting due to the long time delay had to be taken into account. The witness had described the sexual interactions between her and her teacher in great detail. However, these descriptions were not particularly discriminative because at her age she had fairly detailed sexual knowledge and, based on this knowledge, probably would have been able to fabricate the account. Much more interesting from a diagnostic point of view were her descriptions of her emotional responses, the development of the relationship between her and her teacher, and her unsuccessful attempts to cope with the situation. What she described was consistent with what would have been expected from her personality (emotional lability, high introversion, deficits in social behaviour, inhibition). To fabricate these psychologically consistent and coherent details would have been much more difficult, even for a 17-year-old juvenile, than fabricating some sexual activities.

Based on this analysis, a preliminary expert opinion was sent to the prosecution service who eventually brought the case to court. The court appointed an expert witness and summoned him to participate at the court sessions. During the court sessions, he had the opportunity to put questions to all witnesses and to the defendant. After having heard all witnesses, he orally presented his opinion to the court. The defendant finally confessed and was convicted.

SUMMARY AND CONCLUSION

This brief overview of the German's perspective of children's testimony has shown some remarkable differences between the inquisitorial system of justice in Germany and the adversarial system in England and Wales. German procedural law provided several ways to reduce the stress that a child witness is experiencing in court (e.g. trial before special youth courts, questioning of the child witness exclusively by the chairing judge, removal of the defendant from the courtroom while the child witness gives evidence) many years before countries which have adopted the adversarial system of justice introduced legislation to protect children in the court. As a consequence, however, there was considerably less pressure to introduce further reforms for the benefit of child witnesses. Therefore, it took much longer to introduce video technology than, for example, in England and Wales. Furthermore, the German approach to video in the courtroom appears to be less advanced than the British one.

Contrary to widespread beliefs, the involvement of an expert witness (as is common practise in German courts when a child is a main witness) often reduces the pressure that a child will experience in court. Not only does an expert witness assist the court in the evaluation of a particular piece of evidence. The presence of an expert witness also takes the child witness out of the line of fire.

REFERENCES

Busse, D., Volbert, R., & Steller, M. (1996). *Belastungserleben von Kindern in Hauptverhandlungen* (Abschlußbericht eines Forschungsprojekts im Auftrag des Bundesministeriums der Justiz) [*Children's distress in the courtroom* (final research report)]. Bonn: Federal Ministry of Justice.

Dannenberg, U., Höfer, E., Köhnken, G., & Reutemann, M. (1997). *Abschluß- bericht zum Modellprojekt Zeugenbegleitprogramm für Kinder* [*Court prepara- tion programme for child witnesses*] (Final report to the Government of Schleswig-Holstein). Kiel: University of Kiel.

Dannenberg, U, Mantwill, M., Stahlmann-Liebelt, U., & Köhnken, G. (1997). Reduzierung von Informationsdefiziten und Ängsten kindlicher Zeugen [Compensating misinformation and fear in child witnesses]. In: L. Greuel, Th. Fabian, & M. Stadler (Eds), *Psychologie der Zeugenaussage* [*Psychology of witness statements*]. Weinheim: Beltz.

Eipper, S. (1997). Entwicklung und Evaluation einer Spiel- und Lernbroschüre für Kinder, die als Zeugen zu Gericht gehen [Development and evaluation of a primer for child witnesses]. Unpublished thesis, University of Kiel.

Eipper, S., Hille, P., & Dannenberg, U. (1997). *Rasmus Rabe ermittelt: Was passiert eigentlich vor Gericht* [*Rasmus Rabe investigates: What happens in court?*]. Neumünster: Rathmann Druck und Verlag.

Hille, P. (1997). Verbesserung der Situation kindlicher Zeugen vor Gericht: Entwicklung und Evaluation von Informationsmaterial für Kinder [Improving child witnesses' situation in court: Development and evaluation of an information package for children]. Unpublished thesis, University of Kiel.

Hille, P., Eipper, P., & Dannenberg, U. (1997). *Klara und der kleine Zwerg. Ein Buch für Kinder, die bei Gericht sind* [*Klara and the midget. A book for children who have to go to court*]. Neumünster: Rathmann Druck und Verlag.

Köhnken, G. (1999). Der Schutz kindlicher Zeugen vor Gericht [Protecting child witnesses in court]. In: R. Lempp, G. Schütze, & G. Köhnken (Eds),

Forensische Psychiatrie und Psychologie des Kindes- und Jugendalters [*Forensic Psychiatry and Psychology of Children and Juveniles*]. Darmstadt: Steinkopff.

Steller, M., & Köhnken, G. (1989). Statement analysis. In: D.C. Raskin (Ed.), *Psychological techniques in law enforcement*. New York: Springer Verlag.

Thompson, S.C. (1981). Will it hurt less if I can control it? A complex answer to a simple question. *Psychological Bulletin*, **90**, 326–45.

Volbert, R., & Pieters, V. (1993). *Zur Situation kindlicher Zeugen vor Gericht. Empirische Befunde zu Belastungen durch Strafverfahren und zu möglichen Reformmaßnahmen* [*On the situation of child witnesses in court: Empirical findings on distress caused by criminal trials and on potential reforms*]. Bonn: Forum-Verlag Godesberg.

Volbert, R., & Busse, D. (1995). Belastungen von Kindern in Strafverfahren wegen sexuellen Mißbrauchs [Children's distress in court cases on sexual abuse]. In: L. Salgo (Ed.), *Vom Umgang der Justiz mit Minderjährigen* [*On the treatment of children by the legal authorities*]. Neuwied: Luchterhand.

Wolf, P. (1997). *Was wissen Kinder und Jugendliche über Gerichtsverhandlungen?* [*What do children and juveniles know on criminal proceedings?*] Regensburg: S. Roederer.

CHAPTER 16

Child Witnesses and the Oath

Thomas D. Lyon

University of Southern California Law School, Los Angeles, California, USA

Despite the liberalization of competency requirements for child witnesses in many countries (Spencer & Flin, 1993; Youth Justice and
Criminal Evidence Act, 1999, s. 53 [Engl.]), a substantial number of
courts in the United States and other countries require that every
witness take the oath or make some sort of affirmation that s/he will
tell the truth (Federal Rules of Evidence 602, 2001; Shrimpton, Oates,
& Hayes, 1996). In order to guarantee that an oath or affirmation is understood by child witnesses, courts routinely inquire into children's
understanding of the difference between the truth and lies and their
obligation to tell the truth (Myers, 1997). Even when unsworn testimony
is allowed, many jurisdictions require child witnesses to demonstrate an appreciation of their duty to tell the truth (Flin, Kearney,
Murray, 1996; Fla. Stat. Ch. 90.605, 1999 (US); Ho, 1996; Pipe &
Henaghan, 1996). Moreover, many courts continue to conduct oath-
taking competency hearings in spite of legislatively enacted presumptions of competency (Gold, 1992; Cashmore, 1995). Regardless of a jurisdiction's competency requirements, investigators and attorneys
routinely ask child witnesses about the truth and lies under the theory
that children's understanding is evidence of veracity (Spencer & Flin,
1993).

Neither the legislatures nor the courts have specified the questions
that must be asked in order to ascertain oath-taking competence. In a
review of oath-taking competency questions in court, Cashmore
and Bussey (1996) found that some judges ask questions that appear

Children's Testimony. Edited by H.L. Westcott, G.M. Davies, and R.H.C. Bull.
© 2002 John Wiley & Sons, Ltd.

too difficult, whereas others essentially lead children through the competency evaluation (Pipe & Henaghan, 1996; Walker, 1999).

Developmental psychologists ought to provide guidance to courts seeking the most appropriate means by which young children's oath-taking competency can be assessed. A large developmental literature exists on children's understanding of the meaning and wrongfulness of lying (see Aldert Vrij, Chapter 12 in this book) and provides some guidance in establishing age trends in oath-taking competency (Burton & Strichartz, 1991; Myers, 1997). However, the research is limited in two respects. On the one hand, virtually all the research examined non-maltreated children from middle-class homes. The results of such research may overestimate the competence of children actually appearing in court. On the other hand, researchers examining children's understanding of lying have frequently used tasks that are unsuitable for testing children in court, because they assess children's understanding of distinctions that are legally irrelevant; for example, much attention has been paid to children's understanding of the distinctions between lies and jokes or lies and mistakes (Strichartz & Burton, 1990; Wimmer, Gruber, & Perner, 1984). Although some have asserted that children must understand these distinctions in order to be competent witnesses (Perner, 1997), children who conflate lies, jokes, and mistakes can nevertheless appreciate the importance of truthfulness when testifying. The resulting complexities of the tasks may underestimate the age at which children are competent to take the oath. In this chapter, I review research that I have conducted (largely in collaboration with Karen Saywitz, Joyce Dorado, and Debra Kaplan) examining maltreated children's oath-taking competency, with the goal of prescribing sensitive measures by which child-witness competency can be assessed in court.

THE MEANING OF TRUTH AND LIES: QUESTION COMPLEXITY

The courts assess children's understanding of the meaning of truth and lies in various ways. They ask children to describe the difference between the truth and lies, define the terms, or identify statements as the truth or lies. Defining and describing require an abstract understanding of the proper use of a word across different contexts and necessitate that one generate rather than merely recognize the proper use of a word. Identifying ought to be easier than defining the terms or describing how they differ (Piaget, [1932] 1962). However, most research has failed to compare performance across different tasks, and studies examining children's understanding of lying have usually found that even the youngest children understand that lies are false statements, regardless of whether they are asked to define lying or to identify lies (Saywitz, Jaenicke, & Camparo, 1990 [defining 'lie']; Haugaard, Reppucci, Laird, & Nauful, 1991 [identifying lies]). Pipe and Wilson (1994) found that 6- and 10-year-olds were much better at identifying a statement as a lie than defining a lie. However, children were only asked one forced-choice identification question, so that guessing or a response bias could have inflated performance.

Saywitz and I (Lyon & Saywitz, 1999) compared different means of assessing children's understanding of the basic difference between the truth and lies with 96 four- to seven-year-old children awaiting a court appearance due to allegations of parental abuse and/or neglect. We gave each child three tasks: (a) an identification task, (b) a difference task, and (c) a definition task. In the identification task, the interviewer told the child that the interviewer would sometimes tell the truth and sometimes tell a lie and then asked the child to choose whether statements about pictures of objects were the truth or lies. In the difference task, we asked the child to explain the difference between objects, both to assess the child's understanding of the word 'difference' and to warm the child up to the key question regarding the truth and lies. We then asked whether telling the truth and telling a lie are 'different' or 'the same' and how they were 'different' (or 'the same'). In the definition task, we first asked the child to define some common terms ('cat' and 'taking a nap'), in part in order to orient the child to the task of defining words. We then asked the child whether she knew what it meant to tell the truth and to tell a lie, and we asked her to define the terms.

In order to provide a stringent test of our prediction that children would find it easier to identify statements as the truth and lies than to define the terms (or explain the difference between the terms), we adopted a liberal criterion for assessing children's definitions or explanations of difference: a child was counted a success if in describing either word she referred to whether a statement corresponded with reality (e.g. 'The truth is what really happened'), gave an example of a truthful statement or a lie, or defined one term as the negation of the other ('a lie is not the truth').

Our prediction that children would perform best on the identification task was confirmed, and the magnitude of the difference was striking. We defined success on the identification task as four out of four trials correct, which means that a child who responds randomly has only a 6% chance of succeeding. Over 60% of the children who succeeded on the identification task failed on the definition task. Nearly 70% of the children who succeeded on the identification task could not explain the difference between the terms.

Even the youngest children were above chance on the identification task (though the results for the four-year-olds will be qualified below); by five years of age, most children were answering four out of four identification questions correctly. It was not until seven years of age that most children could provide a definition of either 'telling the truth' or 'telling a lie,' and less than half of the seven-year-olds could explain the difference between the terms.

We also gave children a test of receptive vocabulary (the Peabody Picture Vocabulary Test-Revised), and found that the average child was a year behind the age norm. Indicative of children's linguistic difficulties was our finding that most of the four-year-olds could not correctly identify objects as 'the same' or 'different' and that neither the four-year-olds nor the five-year-olds performed above chance when asked if telling the truth and telling a lie were the 'same' or 'different'.

Our results suggest that by five years of age, most maltreated children have a good understanding of the meaning of the truth and lies, despite serious delays in vocabulary. However, young children ought not to be asked to define the truth and lies or asked to explain the difference as a prerequisite to taking the oath. Large numbers of children who have a good understanding of the distinction between truthful and untruthful statements will fail such tasks.

THE MEANING OF TRUTH AND LIES: MOTIVATIONAL DIFFICULTIES

The difficulties posed by defining and describing terms largely implicates cognitive and linguistic limitations. However, there are also reasons to believe that children have motivational difficulties in talking about lies. In the definition task of the study described in the previous section, participants were asked whether they knew what it meant to tell the truth and to tell a lie. Although most children claimed to know both terms, twice as many children denied knowing about lies as about the truth. The findings are reminiscent of young children's denials that they have ever told a lie (Peterson, Peterson, & Seeto, 1983). On the identification task, children were better at identifying truthful statements than lies. This pattern was particularly notable among the younger children. Although the four year olds performed above chance on the task overall, closer examination revealed that although they were 80% correct in labelling truthful statements, they were no better than chance (50%) in identifying lies. Such a pattern suggests a bias toward labelling every statement as the 'truth'. Indeed, of the 11 children who exhibited a bias toward labelling every statement as the 'truth' or a 'lie', 10 labelled every statement the 'truth'.

We suspected that children were inhibited from labelling statements as lies in the identification task because they were afraid to call the interviewer a liar. They may have denied knowing what a lie was because it might make the interviewer suspect that they would tell a lie. In our second study (Lyon & Saywitz, 1999), with 96 maltreated four- and five-year-olds, we designed a task that we hoped would overcome children's reluctance to identify lies. We presented each child with pictures that depicted an object and two story-children accompanied by 'speech bubbles' depicting what each story-child said about the object. One story-child correctly identified the object (i.e. the picture in the speech bubble was identical to the object) and the other story-child incorrectly identified the object (i.e. the picture in the speech bubble was of a different object), and we asked the child to choose which story-child told the truth (or told a lie) (see Figure 16.1). We believed that the task would reduce motivational difficulties because the child did not have to identify the interviewer as a liar. Moreover, the pictures made it clear that *someone* was a liar, and the child merely had to identify which one.

The results suggested that we were successful in overcoming motivational difficulties. Both the four- and five-year-olds performed above

Figure 16.1. Stimuli for assessing understanding of 'truth' and 'lie' in second study (Lyon & Saywitz, 1999).

chance, and both age groups were as proficient at identifying liars as at identifying truth-tellers. Using our stringent criterion of success as six out of six trials correct, a majority of the five-year-olds answered all trials correctly. However, most four-year-olds did not perform at ceiling (100% accurate), suggesting that even with motivational barriers removed, many maltreated children this young do not understand the meaning of 'truth' and 'lie'.

Another possibility is that our task was insensitive to young children's understanding. However, use of the task with a non-maltreated group from middle-class homes (whose receptive vocabulary is much more advanced than our maltreated sample) has uncovered good understanding among children as young as three years of age (Lyon & Saywitz, in preparation), in contrast to previous research finding no comprehension among three-year-olds (Strichartz & Burton, 1990).

Recently, we directly tested the hypothesis that children's oath-taking competence is underestimated if the interviewer asks the child to evaluate the interviewer's statements, which requires the child to call the interviewer a liar. A native Spanish-speaker interviewed 115 low-income four- to six-year-old Spanish-speaking children (Lyon, in preparation). One-half of the children were asked questions about whether the interviewer's statements were the truth or lies and whether it would be good or bad for the interviewer to lie, whereas the other half were asked whether a story-child's statements were the truth or lies and whether it would be good or bad for the story-child to lie. Consistent with our prediction, children performed better when asked about the story-child than when asked about the interviewer. Clearly, asking children to evaluate the questioner's statements leads to underestimation of children's competency.

THE CONSEQUENCES OF LYING: QUESTION COMPLEXITY

In addition to understanding the difference between the truth and lies, children must also understand the importance of telling the truth in order to qualify as competent to take the oath. Usually, the child is found competent if she understands that lying leads to punishment of some sort; she need not be aware of the specific punishment for perjury (e.g. *State v. Irey*, 1998).

In the two studies we conducted assessing maltreated children's understanding of the meaning of lying, we also asked children about the wrongfulness of lying (Lyon & Saywitz, 1999). In the first study, we showed four- to seven-year-old children scenarios of story-children talking to various authority figures (a judge, a social worker, a grandmother, and a doctor) and asked whether telling the truth (or telling a lie) was good or bad, why it was good or bad, and whether it would make an authority figure happy or mad. Even the four-year-olds were above chance in labelling lying as bad and as making authority figures mad, and a majority of the four-year-olds were at ceiling (100% accurate) in labelling the authority figures as happy or mad depending on whether the story child told the truth or lied. In the second study, we showed four- and five-year-olds scenarios of two story-children speaking to one professional, explained that one child told the truth and the other told a lie, and asked which child would 'get in trouble' or 'said something bad'. Consistent with the first study, even the youngest children were above chance in correctly identifying the liar as the troublemaker. When we gave the same tasks to our non-maltreated sample, we found that three-year-olds were over 80% accurate (Lyon & Saywitz, in preparation).

Children's ability to identify lies as wrong or as leading to punishment contrasted with their difficulty in explaining why lies are wrong. In the first study, most four-year-olds were unable to give a minimally sufficient explanation of why it was bad to lie (e.g. 'you'll get in trouble'). As with defining the terms 'truth' and 'lie', children often understood what they could not explain.

THE CONSEQUENCES OF LYING: MOTIVATIONAL DIFFICULTIES

When children in court are asked about the consequences of lying, they are frequently asked to describe what would happen to them if they lied. However, the child who fails to answer a question such as 'What would happen if you lied in court' might be fully aware of the consequences of lying, but afraid to discuss those consequences. Several researchers have found that pre-school children often perform poorly when asked to reason with premises they find implausible or undesirable (e.g. Reilly, 1986). Young children's hypothetical reasoning performance improves when adults encourage them to pretend or when reasoning with fantasy content (e.g. Dias & Harris, 1990). Hence, young children may misinterpret hypothetical questions as suggestions and thus resist responding when they find the premises unpleasant.

One possible means for reducing the implausibility or undesirability of lying in court is to ask the child about consequences to other children, rather than to herself. For this reason, we asked participants about the morality and consequences of other children's lies in the tasks we described above. However, because the courts routinely ask children to discuss what would happen to themselves, we directly tested the proposition that children find it easier to talk about other children. We asked 64 five- and six-year-old maltreated children to describe the consequences of lying to three professionals (a judge, a social worker, and a doctor) (Lyon, Saywitz, Kaplan, & Dorado, 2001). Participants in the 'self' condition were asked what would happen to themselves if they lied, whereas participants in the 'other' condition were asked to describe what would happen to a story-child if s/he lied. The questions concerned the potential actions of the professional, the child's mother, and God. Children, asked about themselves rather than another child, were more likely to refuse to respond to the questions or to respond 'I don't know'. A subset of children were particularly reticent during the procedure and they were all in the 'self' condition.

One might object to questions about other children on the grounds that children might believe themselves uniquely invulnerable to punishment from lying. Children believe that they are less likely to experience negative events than other children (Whalen *et al.*, 1994). Such children would be fully capable of describing the negative consequences when other children lie but would not be truly competent to take the oath, because they would not endorse such negative consequences for themselves.

To test this possibility, we further examined the responses of the participants in the two conditions. If children believe themselves invulnerable, then responsive children in the self condition ought to be less likely to endorse negative consequences than responsive children in the other condition. However, the data did not bear this out, thus giving no support to the invulnerability hypothesis; that is, children were more likely to say 'I don't know' in the self condition but, if they *did* respond, were no less likely to mention negative consequences than children in the 'other' condition. In sum, the study demonstrated that asking children about themselves suppresses their responsiveness, making them appear to understand less than they really do.

THE FORM OF THE OATH: 'PROMISE' V. 'WILL'

Few courts require children to take a formal version of the oath; some explicitly allow for children to simply promise to tell the truth (Cal. Evidence Code Section 710, 2001 (US); Pipe & Henaghan, 1996). This is a step in the right direction, given the likelihood that children will not understand what it means to 'solemnly swear'. However, whether children understand the word 'promise' is itself subject to question.

Some researchers have argued that young children do not understand the obligations imposed by promising, which raises concerns regarding their appreciation of even simplified versions of the oath. Astington (1988b) found that, when asked to explain why actors should perform various actions, six-year-olds (in contrast to eight- and ten-year-olds) described the virtues of the actions themselves rather than the importance of keeping one's promises (see also Rotenberg, 1980). Although this might reflect a failure to distinguish between promises and the actions promised, as Astington has argued, an alternative possibility is that the salience of actions masks children's understanding of the obligations imposed by promising. This possibility is suggested by Astington's (1988b) finding that children were more likely to mention a promise as a reason for performing an action when there was a 'less compelling external reason' to keep the promise.

Children may understand 'I will' better than 'I promise', which would support the use of an affirmation that one 'will tell the truth'. 'Will' appears in children's speech by two and a half years of age (Astington, 1988a). Whether children understand the certainty implied by 'will', however, is unknown. Moreover, 'I promise' is a stronger guarantee of performance than 'I will,' because one has explicitly undertaken the responsibility to act in accordance with one's words. Using the words 'I will' may constitute a promise, but using the words 'I promise' almost always does.

It thus remains unclear whether and at what age children understand the relative significance of stating that they 'will' or 'promise to' perform some action. In order to test children's understanding of 'promise' and 'will', we adapted a procedure used by Moore and colleagues to examine children's developing understanding of relative certainty as expressed through words such as 'know', 'think', 'must', and 'might' (e.g. Moore, Pure, & Furrow, 1990). We tested children's understanding that one who 'promises' or says s/he 'will' perform some action is more likely to act than one who says s/he 'might' or 'won't' perform. The task was structured as a game in which the participant heard contrasting statements regarding which story-child was going to put a toy in his or her box and chose which box would contain a toy. The task was sensitive to understanding in several respects. Children did not have to produce the terms, only recognize their meaning. The forced-choice procedure over repeated trials could detect incipient understanding. Because children were presented with words alone, there is no opportunity for their focus on deeds to mask their understanding of the importance of words.

We questioned 96 maltreated children from four to seven years of age (Lyon, Saywitz, & Kaplan, in preparation). We predicted that children would exhibit better understanding of the word 'will' than the word 'promise', and that preference for 'promise' over 'will' would increase with age. Our predictions were confirmed. Whereas about half of the seven-year-olds consistently chose the character who said 'I promise' over the character who said 'I will', about half of the four-year-olds exhibited the opposite pattern, consistently choosing the character who said 'I will'. Younger maltreated children do not appear to understand that 'promise' increases the likelihood of performance over saying 'I will', six-year-olds appear to view 'promise' as synonymous with 'will', and even the seven-year-olds were ambivalent regarding the relative certainty of promising. Using the same procedure with 96 three- to six-year-old non-maltreated children, we found similar patterns, but with understanding accelerated by one to two years. 'Promise' implied greater certainty than 'will' for the six-year-olds but was less well understood than 'will' by the younger children.

The results advise caution in using the word 'promise' in administering an oath to young children. On the other hand, children at all ages in our research understood that 'will' predicts performance, and some children at older ages understand that 'promise' increases the likelihood of performance. In order to communicate the importance of telling the truth to children at all ages, we suggest that children be asked if they can 'promise' that they 'will' tell the truth and that they 'won't' tell any lies.

THE EFFECTS OF A CHILD-FRIENDLY OATH ON HONESTY

The primary function of the oath-taking competency questions is to determine if an oath or affirmation will be meaningful to the child. Ultimately, the legal system hopes that the oath or affirmation will increase honesty. Whether it does so is an important empirical question. Although researchers have explored the relation between oath-taking competency and children's eyewitness memory (Clarke-Stewart, Thompson, & Lepore, 1989, cited in Goodman & Clarke-Stewart, 1991; Feben, 1985; Goodman, Aman, & Hirschman, 1987; Huffman, Warren, & Larson, 1999; Larson, 1999; Pipe & Wilson, 1994), the research is of limited relevance in assessing the potential significance of the oath.

First, children were asked questions about the meaning and morality of lying but were not asked to promise to tell the truth. In court, the purpose of the competency questions is to determine whether the oath is meaningful to the child, and it is the oath itself, rather than the competency questions, that is expected to correlate with sincerity. Although not formally eliciting a promise to tell the truth, Huffman,

Warren, and Larson (1999) examined whether an extended discussion of the meaning and morality of truth-telling improved children's perform- ance and found that it did; however, Larson (1999) was unable to repli- cate this finding. Second, in most of the research, children had no motive to lie, and the measure of accuracy did not isolate deliberate errors (Feben, 1985; Goodman, Aman, & Hirschman, 1987; Huffman, Warren, & Larson, 1999; Larson, 1999). An understanding of the impor- tance of telling the truth may be unrelated to memory errors but never- theless predictive of honesty. In Pipe and Wilson (1994), children were motivated to lie about one detail of the to-be-remembered event (an ink-spill), but only one of the subsequent questions asked about the ink-spill. The researchers found that whether children *spontaneously* mentioned the ink-spill did correlate with good performance on the competency questions but they discounted this finding as confounded by the fact that both factors were positively related to the age of the child. In Clarke-Stewart, Thompson, & Lepore (1989, cited in Goodman & Clarke-Stewart, 1991), a janitor performed a number of activities and asked five- to six-year-old children to keep them a secret. In an inter- view that focused on those activities, children who were less knowl- edgeable about the meaning of a lie were more likely to keep the janitor's secret and fail to disclose his behaviour. There is thus limited evidence that oath-taking competency affects honesty and no evidence exploring the effects of an oath or affirmation on honesty.

Building on our research developing a sensitive measure of children's oath-taking competence and a child-friendly version of the oath, Dorado and I have explored the effects of the oath on children's willing- ness to disclose minor transgressions in two studies (Lyon & Dorado, 1999). In each study, the experimenter first assessed the child's under- standing of the meaning and wrongfulness of lying. The experimenter then showed the child a large multicoloured 'Lego house' that had a number of 'surprise doors' behind which miniature toys were hidden and told them that they would play a guessing game with the 'Lego house'. Looking through her papers, the experimenter told the child that she had to go to her office but that she would be back in a few minutes.

In each study, we placed children into one of three conditions. In the control condition, we did not give children any instructions regarding telling the truth. In the oath condition, we elicited from each child a promise that s/he 'will tell the truth' and 'will not tell any lies', in line with our recommendations regarding a child-friendly version of the oath. In the reassurance condition, we told the child that it was impor- tant to tell the truth and stressed that lots of children transgressed, did not know it was wrong, and that the child would not get in trouble if s/he had done so. The transgression involved playing with a 'forbidden toy', similar to a number of other studies examining children's tendency to lie (e.g. Polak & Harris, 1999).

In the first study, with 109 maltreated five- and six-year-olds, the experimenter told the child when she returned with her papers that she hoped the child hadn't looked at or touched any of the surprise toys. After no instructions (control), administration of the promise (oath), or reassurance, the experimenter asked the child whether she had looked at, touched, or taken out any of the toys. Children's performance on the oath-taking competency test did not predict sincerity. Children were significantly more likely to admit a transgression in the reassurance condition (83%) than in the control (47%) or the oath condition (31%), and the latter two conditions were not significantly different.

We suspected that the oath may have been rendered ineffective by the experimenter's statement to the child that she hoped the child had not looked in the doors. If the experimenter's desires regarding what the 'truth' is are clear, asking the child to tell the truth may be ineffective. In contrast, in the reassurance condition, the experimenter coupled her desire that the child state the truth with the explicit assurance that looking in the doors was 'OK'. In our second study with 109 maltreated six- and seven-year-olds, a confederate played with the child and the toy and then informed the child that playing might be wrong, making it unnecessary for the interviewer to do so. In order to provide a fairer test of the oath, we excluded children who did not succeed on the competency tasks. While the experimenter was away getting her papers, a confederate entered the room and engaged the child in play with the Lego house. As she left, the confederate told the child, 'We might get in trouble if anyone found out we played with the toys.' Shortly thereafter the experimenter returned and administered the same instructions in the oath and reassurance conditions as in the previous study. The experimenter then asked about the child's actions and about the actions of the confederate (if the child acknowledged that someone had come into the room).

Children in both the reassurance condition and the oath condition were more forthcoming about their actions than children given no instructions. Across the six questions regarding their actions and those of the confederate, over 80% of the children in the oath and reassurance admitted some type of transgression, compared to about half of the children in the control condition. The results supported our prediction that the oath would have an effect on children's willingness to disclose a minor transgression if the request for the truth was not coloured by the interviewer's desire that the child had refrained from playing with the toy. This suggests that an interviewer's bias—at least if clearly communicated to the child—may override the beneficial effects of eliciting a promise to tell the truth.

These are the first studies to examine the effects of the oath on child witnesses. They provide some support for the utility of the oath in encouraging young children to reveal information (see also Talwar & Lee, 2000). We view these conclusions as tentative, however, both because of the limited research available on the effect of the oath and the obvious difficulties in applying our research to child-abuse victims, who surely have stronger motives to both conceal and to reveal abuse. Moreover, we do not know the effects of the oath or reassurance on children who have *not* been involved in any wrongdoing. We are currently conducting a study in which the confederate does *not* engage the child in play with the toy, and the interviewer then returns and asks both direct and suggestive questions about the confederate's actions.

CONCLUSION

Based on our research, we can make several recommendations regarding oath-taking competency. First, young children should not be asked to define the truth and lies or explain the difference between the concepts. Young children are much better at choosing whether statements are the truth or lies and can be asked multiple questions to ensure that good performance is not attributable to chance. Second, when asked to identify lies as such, children should be asked about statements made by others rather than by the interviewer, given their reluctance to call the interviewer's statements lies. Although we did not directly test it, we would also recommend against asking children to generate examples of lies as a means of testing their understanding; children will likely find such a task difficult and unpleasant.

Second, young children should not be asked to describe the consequences of lying, particularly what would happen to them if they lied. Forced-choice questions about other children regarding the goodness or badness of lying or the negative consequences of lying are more sensitive to early understanding. We have created a version of our tasks that can be used by forensic interviewers and interested readers may request a copy from the author (tlyon@law.usc.edu).

Third, it is fair to presume that most children are competent to take the oath by five years of age, because even maltreated children with serious delays in receptive vocabulary perform well on our tasks by that age. Higher functioning non-maltreated children as young as three years of age have demonstrated good understanding of the meaning and wrongfulness of lying.

Fourth, children should be asked if they 'promise' that they 'will tell the truth' and that they 'won't tell any lies', because of younger children's difficulty in understanding the meaning of 'promise'.

Fifth, we recommend that researchers explore the potential efficacy of the oath and other devices (such as reassurance) in encouraging honesty among young children, as a possible means of reducing false denials and false allegations.

The research reviewed in this chapter highlights how minor changes in the oath-taking competency questions may dramatically affect young children's performance. The finding that children's apparent understanding is highly dependent on the structure of the task is nothing new to developmental psychology. Its practical significance, however, has yet to be fully realized by legal practitioners and other professionals who work with child victims. Moreover, simplification of the competency inquiry is just one step toward making the receipt of children's testimony sensitive to young children's special vulnerabilities.

Most of the original research described here was conducted in collaboration with Karen J. Saywitz, Associate Professor in Psychiatry at Harbor-UCLA Medical Center, Joyce Dorado, and Debra Kaplan, and with the assistance of Tina Goodman-Brown, Suma Mathai, Cecelia Kim, Kimberly Schock, Robin Higashi, Christina Oyster, Michelle Dominguez, Shameka Stewart, Candis Watson, Tim Dixon, Tara Fallon, Kristina Golesorkhi, Susan Lui, Nkia Patterson, and Verinder Shaw. The research was supported in part by National Center on Child Abuse and Neglect grant 90-CA-1553, and in part by a grant from the Zumberge Foundation.

REFERENCES

Astington, J.W. (1988a). Children's production of commissive speech acts. *Journal of Child Language*, **15**, 411–23.

Astington, J.W. (1988b). Promises: Words or deeds? *First Language*, 8, 259–70.

Burton, R.V., & Strichartz, A.F. (1991). Children on the stand: The obligation to speak the truth. *Developmental and Behavioral Pediatrics*, **12**, 121–8.

Cashmore, J. (1995). The prosecution of child sexual assault: A survey of NSW DPP solicitors. *The Australian and New Zealand Journal of Criminology*, **28**, 32–54.

Cashmore, J., & Bussey, K. (1996). Judicial perceptions of child witness competence. *Law & Human Behaviour*, **20**, 313–34.

Clarke-Stewart, A., Thompson, W., & Lepore, S. (1989, April). Manipulating childrens' interpretations through interrogation. Paper presented at the biennial meeting of the Society for Research in Child Development, Kansas City, MO.

Dias, M.G., & Harris, P.L. (1990). The influence of the imagination on reasoning by young children. *British Journal of Developmental Psychology*, **8**, 305–18.

Feben, D.J. (1985). *Age of witness competency: Cognitive correlates.* Unpublished Honours Thesis, Monash University.

Flin, R., Kearney, B., & Murray, K. (1996). Children's evidence: Scottish research and law. In: B.L. Bottoms & G.S. Goodman (Eds), *International perspectives on child abuse and children's testimony: Psychological research and law* (pp. 114–31). Thousand Oaks, CA: Sage.

Gold, V.J. (1992). Do the federal rules of evidence matter? *Loyola of Los Angeles Law Review*, **25**, 909–23.

Goodman, G.S., Aman, C.J., & Hirschman, J. (1987). Child sexual and physical abuse: Children's testimony. In: S.J. Ceci, M.P. Toglia, & D.F. Ross (Eds), *Children's eyewitness memory* (pp. 1–23). New York: Springer-Verlag.

Goodman, G., & Clarke-Stewart, A. (1991). Suggestibility in children's testimony: Implications for sexual abuse investigations. In: J. Doris (Ed.), *The suggestibility of children's recollections* (pp. 92–105). Washington, DC: American Psychological Association.

Haugaard, J.J., Reppucci, N.D., Laird, J., & Nauful, T. (1991). Children's definition of the truth and their competency as witnesses in legal proceedings. *Law & Human Behavior*, **15**, 253–71.

Ho, T.-P. (1996). Children's evidence: Mandating change in the legal system of Hong Kong. In: B.L. Bottoms & G.S. Goodman (Eds), *International perspectives on child abuse and children's testimony: Psychological research and law* (pp. 182–200). Thousand Oaks, CA: Sage.

Huffman, M.L., Warren, A.R., & Larson, S.M. (1999). Discussing truth and lies in interviews with children: Whether, why, and how? *Applied Developmental Science*, **1**, 6–15.

Larson, S.M. (June, 1999). Another look at truth/lie discussions: Do they improve preschoolers' testimony? Paper presented at the annual meeting of the American Psychological Society, Denver, CO.

Lyon, T.D. (in preparation). Reducing young Spanish-speaking children's difficulty in identifying and evaluating lies.

Lyon, T.D., & Dorado, J.S. (June, 1999). Does the oath matter? Motivating maltreated children to tell the truth. Paper presented at the annual meeting of the American Psychological Society, Denver, CO.

Lyon, T.D., & Saywitz, K.J. (1999). Young maltreated children's competence to take the oath. *Applied Developmental Science*, **3**, 16–27.

Lyon, T.D., & Saywitz, K.S. (in preparation). Young children's understanding of the meaning and wrongfulness of lying.

Lyon, T.D. Saywitz, K.S. & Kaplan, D.L. (in preparation). Young children's understanding that promising predicts performance.

Lyon, T.D. Saywitz, K.S., Kaplan, D.L., & Dorado, J.S. (2001). Reducing maltreated children's reluctance to answer hypothetical oath-taking competency questions. *Law and Human Behavior*, **25**, 81–92.

Moore, C. Pure, K. & Furrow, D. (1990). Children's understanding of the modal expression of certainty and uncertainty and its relation to the development of a representational theory of mind. *Child Development*, **61**, 722–30.

Myers, J.E.B. (1997). *Evidence in child abuse and neglect cases* (Vol. 1, 3rd ed.). New York: Wiley.

Perner, J. (1997). Children's competency in understanding the role of a witness: Truth, lies, and moral ties. *Applied Cognitive Psychology*, **11**, S21–S35.

Peterson, C.C., Peterson, J.L., & Seeto, D. (1983). Developmental changes in ideas about lying. *Child Development*, **54**, 1529–35.

Piaget, J. ([1932] 1962). *The moral judgement of the child* (M. Gabain, trans.). New York: Collier.

Pipe, M., & Wilson, J.C. (1994). Cues and secrets: Influences on children's event reports. *Developmental Psychology*, **30**, 515–25.

Pipe, M.-E., & Henaghan, M. (1996). Accommodating children's testimony: Legal reforms in New Zealand. In: B.L. Bottoms & G.S. Goodman (Eds), *International perspectives on child abuse and children's testimony: Psychological research and law* (pp. 145–67). Thousand Oaks, CA: Sage.

Polak, A., & Harris, P.L. (1999). Deception by young children following non-compliance. *Developmental Psychology*, **35**, 561–8.

Reilly, J.S. (1986). The acquisition of temporals and conditionals. In: E.C. Traugott, A. ter Meulen, J.S. Reilly, & C.A. Ferguson (Eds), *On conditionals* (pp. 309–31). Cambridge: Cambridge University Press.

Rotenberg, K.J. (1980). 'A promise kept, a promise broken': Developmental bases of trust. *Child Development*, **51**, 614–7.

Saywitz, K.J., Jaenicke, C., & Camparo, L. (1990). Children's knowledge of legal terminology. *Law & Human Behavior*, **14**, 523–35.

Shrimpton, S., Oates, K., & Hayes, S. (1996). The child witness and legal reforms in Australia. In: B.L. Bottoms & G.S. Goodman (Eds), *International perspectives on child abuse and children's testimony: Psychological research and law* (pp. 132–44). Thousand Oaks, CA: Sage.

Spencer, J.R., & Flin, R.H. (1993). *The evidence of children: The law and the psychology*. London: Blackstone.

State v. Irey, 1998 WL 193491 (Ohio App. Ct. 1998).

Strichartz, A.F., & Burton, R.V. (1990). Lies and truth: A study of the development of the concept. *Child Development*, **61**, 211–20.

Talwar, V., & Lee, K. (March, 2000). The relation between children's moral understanding of lying and their truth telling behavior. Paper presented at the biennial meeting of the American Psychology-Law Society, New Orleans, LA.

Walker, A.G. (1999). *Handbook on questioning children: A linguistic perspective* (2nd ed.). Washington, DC: ABA Center on Children and the Law.

Whalen, C.K., Henker, B., O'Neil, R., Hollingshead, J., Holman, A., & Moore, B. (1994). Optimism in children's judgments of health and environmental risks. *Health Psychology*, **13**, 319–25.

Wimmer. H., Gruber, S., & Perner, J. (1984). Young children's conception of lying: Lexical realism-moral subjectivism. *Journal of Experimental Child Psychology*, **37**, 1–30.

CHAPTER 17

Child Witnesses' Experiences Post-Court: Effects of Legal Involvement

Robin S. Edelstein,* Gail S. Goodman,* Simona Ghetti,*
Kristen Weede Alexander,* Jodi A. Quas,† Allison D. Redlich,‡
Jennifer M. Schaaf,¶ and Ingrid M. Cordon*

*Department of Psychology, University of California, Davis,
California, USA
†Department of Psychology and Social Behavior, University of
California, Irvine, California, USA
‡Department of Psychiatry, Stanford University, Stanford,
California, USA
¶Frank Porter Graham Child Development Center, University of North
Carolina, Chapel Hill, North Carolina, USA

In past decades, researchers have become increasingly interested in children's reactions to legal involvement, especially when children are victims of sexual abuse. A pervasive concern is that involvement in prosecution may further exacerbate the distress of children already traumatized by abuse experiences. Consistent with this concern, several researchers and legal professionals have suggested that stressful legal experiences, such as being repeatedly interviewed and testifying in criminal court, can retraumatize children and further stigmatize the victim and his or her family (e.g. Goodman, 1984; Newberger, 1987; Sas, Wolfe, & Gowdey, 1996; Tedesco & Schnell, 1987). In contrast, others have argued that some components of legal involvement (e.g. testifying

Children's Testimony. Edited by H.L. Westcott, G.M. Davies, and R.H.C. Bull.
© 2002 John Wiley & Sons, Ltd.

in juvenile court), can be beneficial for children (Melton, 1984; Runyan, Everson, Edelsohn, Hunter, & Coulter, 1988). These two tenets are not necessarily opposed. A more nuanced picture of children's legal involvement may reveal both positive and negative effects, or negative effects under some conditions and positive effects under others.

Despite growing interest in this topic, relatively few studies have actually examined children's reactions to legal involvement. Even fewer have investigated children's reactions over long time periods. Nevertheless, evidence that legal involvement can be an added source of distress for children has motivated legal change worldwide. Many countries, focusing on the unique needs of child victims, have adopted procedures designed to protect children in the legal system. In the United States, for instance, Child Advocacy Centers (also called Multidisciplinary Interview Centers) have been established in many communities to control the format and number of forensic interviews children receive. In the United Kingdom, the *Memorandum of Good Practice* (Home Office & Department of Health, 1992) has been implemented to promote high-quality forensic interviewing. Moreover, in the United Kingdom, when children's evidence is needed in criminal proceedings, children's statements are first presented in court via videotaped forensic interviews followed by testimony via 'live-link' (i.e. closed-circuit television, Westcott, Davies, & Spencer, 1999).

Although these modifications have been implemented in consideration of children's best interests, relatively little is known from scientific study about the efficacy of these modifications (see Judy Cashmore, Chapter 13 in this book; Amanda Wade, Chapter 14 in this book). Moreover, without adequate knowledge of children's reactions under conventional conditions, it is difficult to judge whether or not modified procedures are more beneficial.

It is important to understand how the effects of traditional or innovative legal procedures unfold over time: Are the benefits primarily short-term or do they persist several years after children's legal involvement? Research has indicated that the effects of child sexual abuse (CSA) may persist into adulthood (Browne & Finkelhor, 1986; Kendall-Tackett, Williams, & Finkelhor, 1993). The effects of legal participation may do so as well. The impact of legal involvement on children may be attenuated as children grow older and as the legal experience grows more remote. Alternatively, it is possible that effects of the legal system would not fully emerge until adulthood, because children may lack the knowledge and experience to understand the implications of their legal involvement. Finally, it is important to understand long-term outcomes before evaluating innovations designed to assuage the potentially negative effects of legal participation. If such negative effects do persist over time, modified legal procedures may be even more important and necessary for children's well-being.

EFFECTS OF LEGAL INVOLVEMENT

Relatively few studies have examined children's short-term reactions to legal involvement. Extant studies focused on child victims of sexual abuse and their experiences during the progression of their legal cases. In general, these studies suggest that the short-term effects of involvement in CSA prosecutions include, for at least a subset of children, heightened anxiety, behavioral problems, and emotional distress (Goodman et al., 1992; Whitcomb et al., 1991). Unfortunately, very few studies have examined long-term effects more than three years after children's legal involvement. These studies suggest that the negative effects on children of court attendance may persist over several years (Oates & Tong, 1987; Sas, 1993).

We now review studies concerning general court involvement and psychological adjustment. However, because particular features of legal involvement, such as multiple interviews, testifying in court, and prolonged legal process, have been specifically identified as contributing to negative short- and possibly long-term effects, these factors are discussed in greater detail in following sections. As the research base permits, a few other key influences (maternal support, legal knowledge, case outcomes) are also discussed.

Court Involvement and Psychological Adjustment

One of the first studies to examine effects of legal involvement was conducted in Australia by Oates and Tong (1987). In this study, the non-offending caregivers of 46 children who had been sexually abused were interviewed, approximately two and a half years after their children's referral to a hospital for evaluation. Twenty-one of the 46 cases went to court, and children were required to testify in six of those cases. Parents were asked about their child's reactions to the legal system. Of children whose cases went to court: 86% (18) were rated by their parents as being very upset immediately after the hearing; 57% (12) were reported by their parents still to be upset about the legal case two and a half years after the prosecution and/or to have persisting behavioral problems; compared to only 12% (3) of those whose cases did not go to court.

This suggests that court involvement may continue to be a source of distress for children, even several years after the case has ended.

However, only 20% of the original sample of 229 could be contacted for the follow-up, limiting inferences about the generalizability of these results. Moreover, there may have been pre-existing differences between the children whose cases went to court and those whose cases did not; these differences may have confounded the children's distress with factors associated with the abuse experience itself. It is also unclear from Oates and Tong's results which specific features of the court experience caused most distress. Subsequent studies have often sought to determine more specific aspects of legal and court involvement that are distressing to children. Testifying in court has been one important focus of study.

Testifying in Court

Particularly in cases of sexual abuse, when there is little or no physical evidence, the testimony of the victim is often essential to successful prosecution. However, many have argued that testifying in court, particularly the experience of facing the defendant, may further traumatize already victimized children (Goodman, 1984; Goodman et al., 1992; Sas, 1993). The majority of research on children's testimony has indicated that testimony in criminal court is associated with short-term distress in some children (Goodman et al., 1992; Whitcomb et al., 1991). Additionally, certain factors associated with testifying, including testifying multiple times, harsh courtroom treatment, and lack of maternal support, have been related to children's short-term emotional distress (Berliner & Conte, 1995; Goodman et al., 1992; Whitcomb et al., 1991). Short-term distress in these studies generally refers to distress that can still be measured around the time the legal case was resolved, that is, at the end of the prosecution or trial, or shortly thereafter. However, one caveat is in order: a methodological confound may exist to the extent that children testify in particularly serious cases, making it difficult to attribute negative effects to court involvement *per se*, unless abuse severity is statistically controlled.

Goodman and colleagues (1992) compared 60 children who testified in criminal court with a matched group of children who did not (e.g. matched in terms of age, pre-court behavioral adjustment, abuse severity). Throughout the legal case, the predominant fear expressed by children who testified concerned having to face the defendant. After seven months, children who testified exhibited more behavioral problems than non-testifiers. This pattern was especially robust among children who had testified multiple times, lacked maternal support, and whose claims were uncorroborated. Such children may have had fewer emotional resources to cope with the stress of testifying, particularly when called on to do so several times. They may also have felt conflicted about testifying in the absence of maternal support or greater pressure regarding the importance of their testimony when their cases lacked corroboration.

Goodman et al.'s (1992) results are consistent with those reported by Whitcomb et al. (1991), who found that lack of maternal support and testifying more than once were associated with children's increased distress. Moreover, long and harsh cross-examinations predicted distress, at least for older children (Whitcomb et al., 1991). For children in the Goodman et al. (1992) study, however, the short-term effects of testifying appeared to diminish after the prosecution ended, suggesting that perhaps the adverse consequences of testifying may be predominantly short term. (Interestingly, Runyan et al., 1988 found that short-term effects of testifying in juvenile court may not be negative, but for several reasons, such as small sample sizes and possible regression to the mean, further research is warranted.)

Although testifying in criminal court has been associated with more immediate, short-term distress in children, how do child testifiers fare in the long term? Sas (1993) found that children's psychological adjustment, as rated by clinicians three years after criminal case closure, was unrelated to whether or not children testified. Consistent with findings of Goodman et al. (1992), Sas (1993) suggests that testifying in court may have the most negative emotional effects on children in the short term and may diminish several years after legal involvement.

However, Runyan (cited by Whitcomb et al., 1991) also followed a sample of children who had been involved in abuse prosecutions, finding that testifying more than once was associated with negative long-term outcomes. Children who have testified multiple times had more problems as adolescents, such as teenage pregnancy, dropping out of school, and suicide attempts.

To address the paucity of research on children's long-term reactions to legal involvement, especially testifying in court, Goodman and colleagues are currently conducting a follow-up study of children involved in the legal system. Close to 200 CSA victims and their caregivers, who participated in research on the short-term effects of legal involvement in the 1980s (Goodman et al., 1992), are being re-interviewed to assess their mental health, legal attitudes, memory, and criminality. Furthermore, these children's mental health is being compared to that of children with no known history of CSA. Importantly, most of the former child victims are now adults, making it possible to understand the relationship between legal experiences in childhood and mental-health outcomes in adulthood.

Preliminary analyses from this follow-up study indicate that, 12–14 years after legal involvement, 'testifiers' and 'non-testifiers' do not significantly differ on measures of mental health (Quas, Redlich, Goodman, Ghetti, & Alexander, 1999). Thus, although testifiers originally evidenced greater levels of distress, this difference diminished in the long term. However, as adults, testifiers, compared to non-testifiers, self-reported significantly more aggressive acts, were more likely to commit crimes against persons, and were more likely to have engaged in serious delinquent acts before turning 18 (Redlich *et al.*, 2000).

Anticipation of Testifying

Even the anticipation of testifying in criminal court has been associated with increased distress and anxiety in children. Berliner and Conte (1995) interviewed 82 children and families approximately three and a half years after they had been seen at the Harborview Sexual Assault Center. About half the children, at some point in the legal process, believed that they would have to testify in court, although only 15% actually did testify. Whereas testifying was not related to children's reports of increased distress, the anticipation of testifying was. The uncertainty of waiting to testify may result in feelings of helplessness and anxiety, particularly as the duration of the case increases. Consistent with the hypothesis that anticipation of testifying may often be more stressful than testifying itself, Goodman *et al.* (1992) reported that, although many children expressed strong fears about testifying, after their testimony was over, they reported feeling better about the experience than they had expected.

Multiple Interviews and Multiple Interviewers

Under traditional procedures in the United States, as a legal case proceeds toward trial, children are likely to be interviewed many times by many people (Goodman *et al.*, 1992; Tedesco & Schnell, 1987). In fact, participants in one study reported being interviewed up to 40 times, by an average of seven people (Tedesco & Schnell, 1987). The mean number of child interviews by authorities in abuse prosecutions in another study was five (Goodman *et al.*, 1992). A common concern is that interviewing children multiple times can be detrimental to their emotional well-being, because intense and repeated questioning about the abuse experience may force them to re-experience the trauma. It has also been suggested that questioning children may intensify their feelings of self-blame and guilt about the abuse experience (Runyan *et al.*, 1988). Moreover, concerns have been raised that repeated interviewing, if it is suggestive and misleading, could promote inaccuracies in children's reports of abuse (Ceci & Bruck, 1995), although repeated interviewing can also help consolidate accurate memory (Brainerd & Ornstein, 1991; Goodman, Bottoms, Schwartz-Kenney, & Rudy, 1991).

Studies examining the emotional effects on children of repeated interviews and multiple interviewers have yielded mixed results; for example, in a retrospective study, Tedesco and Schnell (1987) obtained information on 48 sexually abused children who had testified in a criminal prosecution. A greater number of forensic interviewers was associated with lower ratings of perceived helpfulness of the legal system. Similarly, Henry (1997) studied 90 nine- to nineteen-year-olds who had been involved in CSA investigations and interviewed between two and five times. The number of investigatory interviews children experienced, even when abuse characteristics were statistically controlled, significantly predicted children's scores on the Trauma Symptoms Checklist.

Goodman *et al.* (1992) reported that the number of times children were interviewed was not associated with increased emotional or behavioral distress. However, more recent analyses from this dataset reveal that children who were interviewed eight or more times rated the effect of the investigation on their life more negatively than did children who were interviewed fewer than 8 times. It is possible that these negative perceptions could persist as children approach adulthood. However, to date, researchers have not examined the long-term effects of multiple interviews on children.

Length of the Legal Process

Like the anticipation of testifying, the uncertainty and lack of resolution associated with a drawn-out legal case may exacerbate children's feelings of powerlessness as the case continues. Sas (1993) argued that lengthy delays in the prosecution of CSA cases may be unbearable for children. Although a delay in resolution was not associated with increased distressed in Goodman *et al.*'s (1992) sample, Runyan and colleagues (1988) found that, after five months, children whose cases were still unresolved showed the least improvement on measures of depression, regardless of whether they had testified or not, their age, or abuse characteristics. The waiting and lack of resolution in these cases appeared to have had an adverse effect on the children, more so than any individual aspect of the court proceedings. Runyan *et al.* (1988) suggest that the length of these cases may have prevented the children from resolving the negative effects related to their abuse experience, possibly even exacerbating those adverse effects. Whether these effects persist over time has not been examined. Moreover, although some countries (e.g. Israel) take seriously the need to expedite cases involving child victim/witnesses, other countries still tend to draw out such prosecutions, although often for understandable reasons (e.g. to give attorneys the chance to prepare their cases, to provide time for a plea bargain).

Maternal Support

As mentioned previously, maternal support can be an important moderator of the effects of children's legal involvement. Goodman *et al.* (1992) reported that children who testified without the benefit of maternal support were less likely to improve on measures of behavioral adjustment. Additionally, lack of maternal support was associated with children's negative ratings of the effects of testifying and of the legal involvement on their lives (Goodman *et al.*, 1992). These findings are consistent with previous research indicating that maternal support is an important predictor of outcomes for children following disclosure of CSA (Everson, Hunter, Runyan, Edelsohn, & Coulter, 1989; Sas, 1993); for example, Sas (1993) assessed CSA victims who had been referred, prior to their legal involvement, to the Child Witness Project in Canada. Her findings indicate that children who received maternal support following their disclosure of abuse, compared to those whose mothers were ambivalent or unsupportive, were initially less depressed at referral to the project (Sas, 1993).

Three years after the verdict, and consistent with her short-term finding, Sas (1993) found that the strongest predictor of clinicians' ratings of children's adjustment was a supportive maternal caregiver following disclosure and during legal involvement. Thus, maternal support appears to be an important moderator of children's adjustment in both the short and long term.

Knowledge of Legal Procedures

A great deal of research suggests that children's knowledge of legal procedures and terminology is limited, potentially leading to misunderstandings and confusion (e.g. Flin, Stevenson, & Davies, 1989; Saywitz, Jaenicke, & Camparo, 1990; Warren-Leubecker, Tate, Hinton, & Ozbek, 1989). Furthermore, lack of knowledge has been associated with increased distress for children in a legal context (Sas, Austin, Wolfe, & Hurley, 1991). Goodman *et al.* (1998) found that children who were more knowledgeable about the legal system were less anxious about taking the stand in a mock trial. In addition, court-related anxiety may adversely affect children's memory. Saywitz and Nathanson (1993) report that children who were interviewed in a mock courtroom were more anxious and performed more poorly on memory assessments than did children interviewed in a more familiar school setting. Taken as a whole, this research suggests that children's lack of legal knowledge can lead to increased anxiety.

Case Outcome

Although Sas (1993) found that testifying was unrelated to children's psychological adjustment at three-year follow-up, the outcome of the case did matter. Children whose cases resulted in a guilty verdict were rated as better adjusted socially and emotionally by clinicians, compared to those whose cases did not result in an adjudication of guilt. Case outcome was also related to clinical symptoms consistent with Post-Traumatic Stress Disorder (PTSD); children whose cases had not resulted in a guilty verdict reported significantly more intrusive thoughts compared to children whose cases ended with an adjudication of guilt.

Similarly, Ghetti et al. (2000) found that case outcome was an important predictor of children's satisfaction with their legal case. Specifically, children whose cases resulted in a guilty verdict or were plea-bargained reported being more satisfied. Case outcome was also a consistent predictor of children's current satisfaction with the legal system 12–14 years after legal involvement and was, in fact, an even stronger predictor than level of legal involvement (e.g. interviewed by police v. testified in court) or characteristics of the abuse that led to the legal involvement.

Summary

In general, research on children's reactions to the legal system suggests that forensic interviewing, court involvement generally, and testifying and/or its anticipation specifically may be stressful experiences for children. Although the effects of a few interviews or one experience of testifying may be less robust, excessive interviewing and repeated testimony are especially distressing, at least in the short term. Even after several years (up to 3 years and possibly even 12–14 years), experiences with the criminal justice system may continue as a source of upset. The length of the legal process and children's lack of knowledge of legal procedures have also been related to increased anxiety, while maternal support has been found to be an important moderator of both short- and long-term effects of legal involvement. In the end, however, case outcome may prove to be the most important determinant of children's reactions to the legal system.

REDUCING THE IMPACT OF LEGAL STRESSORS

Consistent with research findings, reducing the number of times children are interviewed and lessening or eliminating the need for them to testify have been prominent goals of current legal innovations, as has been familiarizing children with the legal process. In the following sections, several legal changes relevant to these three potential stressors will be discussed, followed by a description of existing research intended to evaluate these innovations.

Videotaping Forensic Interviews

Videotaping forensic interviews may be one way to prevent further distress to children involved in the legal system (see Judy Cashmore, Chapter 13 in this book). If interviews are videotaped the first time they are conducted, additional interviews may no longer be required. In addition, videotaping, if performed early in the investigation, has the advantage of capturing accounts of events closer in time to the child's disclosure, possibly before forgetting, misinformation, and successive interviews jeopardize children's accuracy. It is believed that videotaping of interviews helps promote a non-leading interview style, because interviewers will be obligated to use more open-ended questions, knowing that fact-finders (e.g. jurors) will see exactly how a child was interviewed. Another advantage is that a convincing child disclosure captured on videotape can help elicit perpetrator confessions. Videotaping of interviews is a common practice in Child Advocacy Centers in the United States and in criminal investigations in the United Kingdom.

Another important advantage of videotaped interviews is that they are a potential substitute for children's testimony in court. With the belief that testifying in court can be damaging to children, several countries allow the admission of videotaped interviews at trial. England and Wales, for example, passed the 1991 Criminal Justice Act, which established that videotapes of forensic interviews could be considered admissible in criminal cases for children less than 14 years of age. Canada and New Zealand have similarly resolved that videotaped interviews are a viable substitute for children's live testimony.

At least one study exists on the effects of videotaped forensic interviews on children's legal experiences. Davies, Wilson, Mitchell, and Milsom (1995) in England found that trained court observers rated children who testified via videotaped interview as less anxious than children who testified live and rated interviewers who questioned children on videotape as more accommodating and more supportive towards the children than attorneys who questioned children live in court. Davies *et al.* (1995) reported no significant difference in the number of guilty verdicts when jurors in actual trials were presented with videotaped versus live testimony. An ongoing national study in the United States examining Child Advocacy Centers may reveal additional important information on the effects of videotaped interviews (Finkelhor, Cross, & Jones, 2000; see also Myers *et al.*, 1994).

Despite the potential advantages to children of videotaping forensic interviews, several obstacles limit its widespread use. First, there is evidence that this technique is not always used due to difficulty of implementation and because prosecutors are often reluctant to introduce videotaped testimony (Bull & Davies, 1996; Goodman, Quas, Bulkley, & Shapiro, 1999; Sas, Wolfe, & Gowdey, 1996). Second, in the United States, the introduction of videotaped evidence at trial in place of the child's live testimony can be considered a restriction of a defendant's right to face his or her accuser, because, technically, introduction of children's out-of-court statements through a videotaped interview constitutes hearsay (Myers, Redlich, Goodman, Prizmich, & Imwinkelreid, 1999). Third, some research suggests that jurors are more likely to find children credible and to vote guilty when children testify live in court compared to when videotapes of their testimony are presented, and there is a hint in the empirical literature that jurors may dwell on the forensic interview if they are permitted to replay it during deliberations (Redlich, Goodman, Myers, & Qin, 1996; Swim, Borgida, & McCoy, 1993). If the outcome of the case is more likely to be an acquittal when a videotaped interview is presented in court, then this procedural reform may in the end adversely affect children. Further research is clearly needed to establish whether videotaping forensic interviews is beneficial in the long term for children's emotional well-being, so that these potential benefits may be weighed against the potential costs of the introduction of videotaped interviews at trial.

Alternatives to Testifying in Court

As mentioned previously, among the most common fears expressed by children involved in prosecutions concerns testifying and facing the defendant. Because of this, current efforts to protect children in the legal system have focused on minimizing the negative impact of taking the stand by eliminating, or at least reducing, the need for them to testify. Or, instead, several countries have established that children can be treated differently than adults while on the witness stand; for instance, alternative methods for obtaining children's testimony have been developed, such as testifying behind a screen or partition and testifying via closed-circuit television (CCTV, see Judy Cashmore, Chapter 13 in this book). Years ago, the Israeli Legislation recognized the potential harm to children of testifying and passed the Law of Evidence Revision-Protection of Children (LER-PC). This law established that children should be protected from cross-examination and that specified professionals could testify in place of children and evaluate the veracity of their allegations. Sternberg, Lamb, and Hershkowitz (1996) report that, although the LER-PC has successfully protected children from potential harm associated with testifying, it has been an impediment to CSA prosecutions due to dismissals. Because of the stringent criteria for allowing children to testify, less than 10% of children are permitted to testify in court, and, without a live appearance, the number of cases that can be successfully prosecuted is affected (Sternberg *et al.*, 1996). The current trend in Israel is a return to having children testify live in court (Hershkowitz, pers. comm., 2000).

Court Preparation

As discussed earlier, lack of legal knowledge may be related to children's increased anxiety when faced with testifying (Flin *et al.*, 1989; Goodman *et al.*, 1998; Sas, 1993; Saywitz *et al.*, 1990). Several court-preparation programs provide children with knowledge, thus reducing anxiety, when they are required to testify in CSA prosecutions (Sas, 1993). Important goals of such programs are to help children gain self-confidence and familiarity with the legal process.

At the London Family Court Clinic in Ontario, Sas (1993; Sas *et al.*, 1996) addressed the problem of children's limited legal knowledge through court preparation. Preparation activities included simulations of legal procedures, role-playing, and courthouse tours. After the preparation, children were in fact more knowledgeable about the legal system, and, when their psychological and social adjustment was measured, results suggested that children's court preparation was associated with less anxiety and greater confidence (Sas *et al.*, 1996).

In addition to the benefit of decreasing children's short-term distress in legal contexts, court preparation seems to be viewed positively by prosecutors in CSA cases. According to a recent survey, prosecutors appreciate the importance of increasing children's familiarity with the criminal process and report that preparation is helpful in decreasing children's distress while testifying (Goodman *et al.*, 1999).

However, to examine how effects observed in the short term might change over time, Sas (1993) followed 126 of the children in her program. Results of the three-year follow-up study indicated that, although many of the children were distressed at referral, 66% of those re-interviewed had improved on measures of depression. Additionally, the children showed significant improvement on the Intrusive Thoughts Scale, indicating that they were less distressed by recurrent thoughts of the abuse at the three-year follow-up. Children's scores on the Personal Vulnerability Scale, however, had increased significantly. Thus, despite general improvement, there was evidence of continued distress three years after the preparation program and the legal involvement ended.

Summary

Concern for children involved in the legal system has inspired both research and procedural reform. Reducing the number of times a child is interviewed, and reducing or even eliminating children's need to testify, may be particularly helpful in assuaging children's legal anxiety. However, modifications of children's testimony may have legal ramifications, in that they preclude a defendant's right to face his or her accuser in court and may affect jurors' perceptions of children's credibility. One way of reducing children's level of distress, at least in the short term, without affecting the legal process directly is through programs that provide them with knowledge of the legal system before they enter the courtroom. In this way, children may be more confident and less anxious when they are required to testify. Nevertheless, if the outcome of the case is indeed the most important predictor of children's reactions to legal involvement, the effects of procedural reform on case outcome must be carefully considered.

CONCLUSION AND IMPLICATIONS

Despite growing knowledge of the effects of child maltreatment, surprisingly little is known about the consequences of intervention and legal involvement for abused children. Because children are at times required to take part in criminal prosecutions, it is imperative to understand the differential effects of abuse and legal involvement: What parts of the legal process may be particularly harmful, or possibly even beneficial, for children? Not only do children's short-term reactions need to be considered but the long-term consequences need to be determined as well, because the effects of legal involvement may persist over long periods of time or not emerge for several years.

At present, only a small number of studies have examined children's reactions to legal involvement. In general, this area of research suggests that children involved in the legal system as victims of CSA may experience heightened emotional and behavioral distress, particularly during and (at least for some children) very soon after the legal case. The long-term effects of legal involvement are less clear, but the overall impression that emerges is that distress associated with legal involvement can persist over periods of several years, an effect that can be moderated by maternal support.

Although several alterations have been made to traditional legal procedures, much less attention has been paid to evaluation of these changes, with some exceptions (Doueck, Weston, Filbert, Beekhuis, & Redlich, 1997; Jenson, Jacobson, Unrau, & Robinson, 1996). The efficacy of these modifications and preparation programs is an important factor that must be considered in future research. Particularly, in light of the resources involved in many of these programs as well as the potential infringement on the truth-seeking function of a trial, it is imperative to understand if and how these innovations may affect prosecution outcomes and children's well-being.

Future researchers should be careful to avoid the limitations of some of the research conducted in the past. Importantly, researchers should control for potentially confounding factors that may create preexisting differences between groups of children whose cases go to court and those whose cases do not. This is an important consideration if the consequences of child maltreatment are to be distinguished from those that may be associated with legal involvement. This distinction is crucial if children's reactions to legal involvement are to be fully understood and, consequently, if informed decisions about children's welfare are to be made.

Preparation of this chapter was supported in part by a grant from the National Science Foundation to Drs Gail Goodman and Jodi Quas. Correspondence concerning this chapter should be addressed to: Gail S. Goodman, Department of Psychology, University of California, 1 Shields Avenue, Davis, CA 95616-8686, USA.

REFERENCES

Berliner, L., & Conte, J.R. (1995). The effects of disclosure and intervention on sexually abused children. *Child Abuse and Neglect*, **19**, 371–84.

Brainerd, C., & Ornstein, P. (1991). Children's memory for witnessed events: The developmental back drop. In: J. Doris (Ed.), *The suggestibility of children's recollections* (pp. 10–20). Washington, DC: American Psychological Association.

Browne, A., & Finkelhor, D. (1986). Impact of child sexual abuse: A review of the research. *Psychological Bulletin,* **99,** 66–77.

Bull, R., & Davies, G. (1996). The effect of child witness research on legislation in Great Britain. In: B.L. Bottoms & G.S. Goodman (Eds), *International perspectives on child abuse and children's testimony.* Newbury Park, CA: Sage.

Ceci, S.J., & Bruck, M. (1995). *Jeopardy in the courtroom: A scientific analysis of children's testimony.* Washington, DC: American Psychological Association.

Davies, G., Wilson, C., Mitchell, R., & Milsom, J. (1995). *Videotaping children's evidence: An evaluation.* London: Home Office.

Doueck, H.J., Weston, E.A., Filbert, L., Beekhuis, R., & Redlich, H.F. (1997). The child witness advocacy program: Caretakers' and professionals' views. *Journal of Child Sexual Abuse,* **6,** 113–32.

Everson, M.D., Hunter, W.M., Runyan, D.K., Edelsohn, G.A., & Coulter, M.L. (1989). Maternal support following disclosure of incest. *American Journal of Orthopsychiatry,* **59,** 197–227.

Finkelhor, D., Cross, T.P., & Jones, L.M. (2000). *National evaluation of Children's Advocacy Centers.* Washington, DC: Office of Juvenile Justice and Delinquency Prevention.

Flin, R.H., Stevenson, Y., & Davies, G.M. (1989). Children's knowledge of court proceedings. *British Journal of Psychology,* **80,** 285–97.

Ghetti, S., Goodman, G.S., Quas, J.A., Redlich, A.D., Alexander, K.W., Edelstein, R.S., & Jones, D. (2000, March). *Child sexual abuse victims' experiences and perceptions of the legal system years after legal involvement.* Paper presented at the 2000 American Psychology-Law Society Biennial Conference, New Orleans, LA.

Goodman, G.S. (1984). The child witness: Conclusions and future directions for research and legal practice. *Journal of Social Issues,* **40,** 157–75.

Goodman, G.S., Bottoms, B.L., Schwartz-Kenney, B., & Rudy, L. (1991). Children's memory for a stressful event: Improving children's reports. *Journal of Narrative and Life History,* **1,** 69–99.

Goodman, G.S., Pyle-Taub, E.P., Jones, D.P.H., England, P., Port, L.K., Rudy, L., & Prado, L. (1992). Testifying in criminal court: Emotional effects of criminal court testimony on child sexual assault victims. *Monographs of the Society for Research on Child Development,* **57** (Serial No. 229).

Goodman, G.S., Quas, J.A., Bulkley, J., & Shapiro, C. (1999). Innovations for child witnesses: A national survey. *Psychology, Public Policy, and Law,* **5,** 255–81.

Goodman, G.S., Tobey, A.E., Batterman-Faunce, J.M., Orcutt, H., Thomas, S., Shapiro, C., & Sachsenmaier, T. (1998). Face-to-face confrontation: Effects of closed-circuit technology on children's eyewitness testimony and jurors' decisions. *Law and Human Behavior,* **22,** 165–203.

Henry, J. (1997). System intervention trauma to child sexual abuse victims following disclosure. *Journal of Interpersonal Violence,* **12,** 499–512.

Home Office, & Department of Health. (1992). *Memorandum of good practice for video recorded interviews with child witnesses for criminal proceedings.* London: Her Majesty's Stationery Office.

Jenson, J.M., Jacobson, M., Unrau, Y., & Robinson, R.L. (1996). Intervention for victims of child sexual abuse: An evaluation of the Children's Advocacy Model. *Child and Adolescent Social Work Journal*, **13**, 139–56.

Kendall-Tackett, K.A., Williams, L.M, & Finkelhor, D. (1993). Impact of sexual abuse on children: A review and synthesis of recent empirical studies. *Psychological Bulletin*, **113**, 164–80.

Melton, G. (1984). Child witnesses and the First Amendment: A psycholegal dilemma. *Journal of Social Issues*, **40**, 109–38.

Myers, J.E.B., Gordon, S.M., Pizzini, S., Saywitz, K., Stewart, D.C., & Walton, T. (1994). *Child victim witnesses investigative pilot projects: Research and evaluation final report*. Sacramento, CA: Office of the Attorney General.

Myers, J.E.B., Redlich, A.D., Goodman, G.S., Prizmich, L., & Imwinkelreid, E. (1999). Jurors' perceptions of hearsay in child sexual abuse cases. *Psychology, Public Policy, and the Law*, **5**, 388–419.

Newberger, E. (1987). Prosecution: A problematic approach to child abuse. *Journal of Interpersonal Violence*, **2**, 112–17.

Oates, R.K., & Tong, L. (1987). Sexual abuse of children: An area with room for professional reforms. *The Medical Journal of Australia*, **147**, 544–8.

Quas, J.A., Redlich, A.D., Goodman, G.S., Ghetti, S., & Alexander, K.W. (1999, April). Long-term consequences on child sexual abuse victims of testifying in criminal court: Mental health and revictimization. Paper presented at the Society for Research in Child Development Biennial Conference, Albuquerque, NM.

Redlich, A.D., Alexander, K.W., Goodman, G.S., Quas, J.Q., Ghetti, S., & Edelstein, R.S. (2000, March). Relations between child sexual abuse and juvenile delinquency: Findings from a prospective study of children and adolescents involved in the legal system. Paper presented at the American Psychology-Law Society Biennial Conference, New Orleans, LA.

Redlich, A.D., Goodman, G.S., Myers, J.E.B., & Qin, J. (1996, June). Juror's perceptions of children's evidence in child sexual abuse cases: Effects of videotaped testimony and hearsay. Paper presented at the Conference of the American Psychological Society, San Francisco, CA.

Runyan, D.K., Everson, M.D., Edelsohn, G.A., Hunter, W.M., & Coulter, M.L. (1988). Impact of legal intervention on sexually abused children. *Journal of Pediatrics*, **113**, 647–53.

Sas, L. (1993). *Three years after the verdict*. Ontario, Canada: London Family Court Clinic Inc.

Sas, L.D., Austin, G., Wolfe, D.A., & Hurley, P. (1991). *Reducing the system-induced trauma for child sexual abuse victims through court preparation, assessment, and follow-up*. Ottawa: Health and Welfare Canada, National Welfare Grants Division.

Sas, L.D., Wolfe, D.A., & Gowdey, K. (1996). Children and the courts in Canada. In: B.L. Bottoms & G.S. Goodman (Eds), *International perspectives on child abuse and children's testimony* (pp. 77–95). Newbury Park, CA: Sage.

Saywitz, K., Jaenicke, C., & Camparo, L. (1990). Children's knowledge of legal terminology. *Law and Human Behavior*, **14**, 523–35.

Saywitz, K.J., & Nathanson, R. (1993). Children's testimony and their perceptions of stress in and out of the courtroom. *Child Abuse and Neglect*, **17**, 613–22.

Sternberg, K.J., Lamb, M.E., & Hershkowitz, I. (1996). Child sexual abuse investigations in Israel: Evaluating innovative practices. In: B.L. Bottoms & G.S. Goodman (Eds), *International perspectives on child abuse and children's testimony* (pp. 62–76). Newbury Park, CA: Sage.

Swim, J.K., Borgida, E., & McCoy, K. (1993). Videotaped versus in-court witness testimony: Does protecting the child witness jeopardize due process? *Journal of Applied Social Psychology,* **23**, 603–31.

Tedesco, J.F., & Schnell, S.V. (1987). Children's reactions to sex abuse investigation and litigation. *Child Abuse and Neglect,* **11**, 267–72.

Warren-Leubecker, A., Tate, C.S., Hinton, I.D., & Ozbek, I.N. (1989). What do children know about the legal system and when do they know it? In: S.J. Ceci, D.F. Ross, & M.P. Toglia (Eds), *Perspectives on children's testimony* (pp. 131–57). New York: Springer-Verlag.

Whitcomb, D., Runyan, D.K., De Vos, E., Hunter, W.M., Cross, T.P., Everson, M.D., Peeler, N.A., Porter, C.Q., Toth, P.A., & Cropper, C. (1991). *Child victim as witness project: Final report.* Washington, DC: Office of Juvenile Justice and Delinquency Prevention.

CHAPTER 18

Persuading and Controlling: The Theory of Cross-examination in Relation to Children

EMILY HENDERSON

University of Cambridge, UK

Research has identified that many of the cross-examination tactics lawyers use to question children are suggestive and evidentially unsafe (Brennan & Brennan, 1988; Dent & Flin, 1992; Goodman & Bottoms, 1993; Kranat & Westcott, 1994). The average cross-examination of a child is a virtual 'how not to' guide to investigative interviewing: The characteristics of a typical interview conducted during cross-examination appear to violate all the principles of best practice, with the predicted outcome of maximizing the risk of contaminating the evidence (Spencer & Flin, 1993).

This chapter is a lawyer's attempt to explain the legal profession's behaviour by arguing that the theory of interviewing which underpins cross-examination is aimed not at accuracy but at persuasion and, accordingly, tactics deemed unsafe by non-lawyers are widely acceptable to lawyers. The hope is that this analysis might suggest new directions for research and ways of tailoring reforms of court practice to better meet the needs of the child and the community.

The chapter draws on the author's two qualitative studies of experienced lawyers' theories of cross-examination: a study of fourteen New

Children's Testimony. Edited by H.L. Westcott, G.M. Davies, and R.H.C. Bull.
© 2002 John Wiley & Sons, Ltd.

Zealand and five English barristers' beliefs about cross-examining children in sexual assault trials ('the Child Witness Study', Henderson, 1997) and a second study of eight New Zealand and ten English barristers' theories of the function of cross-examination in the criminal trial generally ('the General Study', Henderson, 2000). Interviews followed a semi-structured format, so that respondents could develop themes according to their experiences. Interviews took between one and three hours and were audiotaped. The interview transcripts were analysed using a grounded theory methodology (Glaser & Strauss, 1967). The chapter also refers to advocacy manuals giving practical advice on trial management and cross-examination techniques. It uses as examples two typical and well-regarded manuals; for New Zealand, Eichelbaum's *Mauet* (1989) and, for England, Stone (1985).

The starting point for this analysis is that, overall, the lawyers in the studies appeared to believe children were capable of remembering events accurately and of being reliable witnesses, although having difficulties with peripheral details and dates, etc. Similarly, the lawyers generally believed that false allegations of sexual abuse are rare, although they had unrealistic views about likely causes of false allegations; for example, seven New Zealand and four English Child Witness study respondents believed that fantasy was a plausible although unusual defence to child sex abuse and, furthermore, all held inflated views of what constituted dangerous suggestion, often citing the 'friendly atmosphere' in the evidential interviewer's office. This aside, overall, it seems that the respondents personally were not particularly sceptical of child witnesses.

IGNORANCE V. INTENTION

Lawyers' ignorance of the dynamics of suggestion suggests that their use of unsafe and suggestive questioning tactics might also result from ignorance. Both my interviews and the manuals indicate lawyers were unaware of the dangers of some techniques; for example, almost all the Child Witness Study respondents were anxious to use age-appropriate language. However, their understanding of it extended to 'keeping sentences short and words simple', which research suggests underestimates the care required (MacFarlane *et al.*, 1986; Spencer & Flin, 1993). Furthermore, virtually all believed that children very rarely misunderstand cross-examination questions and that any misunderstandings are immediately corrected, whereas research suggests that children misunderstand a high proportion of cross-examination questions, which are rarely corrected

(Brennan & Brennan, 1988; Davies, 1998; Flin, Bull, Boon & Knox, 1992). Nonetheless, the lawyers apparently truly believed that their language was exemplary and, more generally, all believed in the power of cross-examination as a method of investigation.

However, ignorance does not provide a complete defence for lawyers' unsafe questioning tactics. Outside cross-examination, lawyers demonstrate a thorough understanding of the dangers of suggestive questions to children's accuracy, mounting sustained criticisms of evidential interviewers' techniques (Myers, 1987). The Child Witness Study respondents were universally critical of evidential interviewers, despite often describing examples of their own questioning that appeared highly suggestive. Furthermore, the same manuals that advise cross-examiners to change subjects rapidly to confuse dishonest witnesses (Eichelbaum, 1989; Levy, 1994; Myers, 1987; Stone, 1985) invariably advise that examiners cover topics with their own witnesses in 'chronological and logical order' because it 'helps the comprehension and retention of evidence' (Hyam, 1995; Stone, 1985).

The issue is as much the intention behind cross-examination as any lack of awareness of its effects. Lawyers use suggestive techniques because current cross-examination theory puts presentation and persuasion above investigation and perceives witnesses as tools to construct that presentation. Accordingly, current cross-examination theory emphasizes the need to control witnesses' disclosures or alternatively to minimize unfavourable disclosures escaping the lawyers' control, asking 'questions which will discredit the witness or his or her evidence so that the jury will minimise or even disregard them' (Eichelbaum, 1989, p. 202).

Children are treated little differently from adult witnesses (Ellison, 1998, on cross-examination of adult rape complainants). The only differences in technique seem to be slight linguistic adaptations and some presentational adaptations, standard practice for any witness deemed sympathetic. As one New Zealander stated of cross-examining children:

> I lean forward and look all nice and parental. ... The questions are basically the sort of questions I would ask any witness.

The intent to control, direct, and/or discredit aparent in ordinary cross-examination remains the same for child cross-examination.

THE THEORY OF WITNESSES IN ADVERSARIAL TRIALS

The methodological premise behind the adversarial trial is radically different from that of social science. Adversarial philosophy assumes that the best investigation separates argument from assessment. The assessor (judge and/or jury) remains neutral while the debate is delegated to partisan competitors (lawyers representing clients), each motivated to advance every possible point favouring their clients and every possible critique of the opposition's arguments, provided that they do not assert as facts things they actually know are false.[1] Lawyers see themselves as responsible for maintaining this process but not as having any direct responsibility for its outcome.[2] Under this theory, advocacy is essentially an exercise in competitive story-telling, persuading the fact-finders to accept the lawyer's client's, rather than the opposition's, story. In Stone's words, 'Belief or disbelief in a story is the ultimate test for most practical purposes' (Stone, 1985, pp. 120–1).

The adversarial system profoundly affects the character of witness examinations conducted within it. First, witness examination is also divided into two, with one lawyer in direct examination eliciting evidence favourable to the case while the other in cross-examination attempts to discredit that same evidence or to obtain further information favouring the contrary position (Eichelbaum, 1989). Non-legal commentators often criticize cross-examination for being 'destructive' whereas lawyers regard discrediting adverse witnesses as entirely proper. Direct examination builds up the lawyer's case, while cross-examination breaks it down. That witnesses must also be broken down is viewed as unfortunate but necessary.

Second, although lawyers also believe them to be investigative, examinations have been co-opted into the story-telling process, becoming an integral part of the presentation. Stone (1985, pp. 120–1) states 'for an advocate, his witnesses are the principal medium by which he tells his story.' The respondents in the General Study regarded cross-examination as, in the words of one New Zealander 'part of your advocacy. In a trial I have three speeches: my opening, my cross-examination, and my closing.' All the General Study respondents sought to make examinations persuasive, all listing persuading the jury as a major function of cross-examination.[3] One New Zealander, asked 'what it is to cross-examine', stated 'you're a salesman'. Similarly, two English respondents described cross-examination as 'selling' and 'spin-doctoring'.

Accordingly, courtroom examinations are significantly different

---

[1] Knowledge interpreted as actual not constructive.
[2] The issue of lawyers' ethical responsibility for the truth of the outcome of the trial, overall, is a major issue outside the ambit of this article, which focuses merely on the theory underpinning one aspect of the trial, the interrogation of adverse witnesses. Interested readers are referred to Luban (1988, 1994).
[3] The manuals agree (e.g. Stone, 1985, pp. 120–1).

from other investigative interviews. Unlike investigative interviews, ideally conducted with an open mind and no preconceived agenda, in-court examinations are really demonstrations of pre-selected information illustrating a pre-conceived hypothesis (Eichelbaum, 1989). It is as if the lawyer had already conducted an investigative interview and now, before the jury, replays the tape to display the findings, fast-forwarding to the critical points supporting the interpretation. Counsel organizes the fragments into an intelligible structure, making inferences plain and reinforcing them with judicious comment.[4] As such, examinations focus on controlling the witness's speech in order to reach the major goal of demonstrating the desired evidence and per-suading the jury.

The Theory of Adversarial Cross-examination

The twin factors of examination as part of the competition and as part of the argument create a style of cross-examination dominated by the need to disrupt the witness's testimony and the need to control the witness. The need to control in cross-examination outstrips that in direct examination, because the witness may resist the questioning and damage the lawyer's presentation. Stone makes the link between persuasion and control explicit:

> Janus-faced, a cross-examiner has to look in two directions—at the witness and at the Court. He seeks to induce the witness to give certain testimony, and he wishes to persuade the Court that a certain version of the facts is true. (Stone, 1985, p. 121)

One American manual even heads a chapter 'Controlling Responses' (Haydock & Sonsteng, 1994). Similarly, all the General Study respondents emphasized its importance.

It is the need to control a potentially subversive witness and the fact that lawyers view cross-examination as essentially demonstrative that encourages suggestive questioning in cross-examination. In this context, tactics that heighten the witness's suggestibility appear appropriate and desirable. Challenged that the tactics he described were 'sheer manipulation', a senior New Zealand barrister replied: 'Well, it is. I wouldn't defend myself.' To manipulate the witness is, in a very real sense, very close to the purpose of cross-examination.

This intention does not change just because the witness is a child or has a greater susceptibility to suggestion; for example, Myers's

---

[4] Comment is in fact illegal under the rules of cross-examination but lawyers admit using it extensively (see below).

American manual explicitly advises cross-examiners to exploit children's suggestibility:

> undermine the [child's] credibility ... by demonstrating that the child is highly suggestive. ... Some suggestible children can be led to alter their direct testimony through skilful use of suggestive questions during cross-examination. (Myers, 1987, p. 204).

The following sections consider the impact of the objectives and theory described above on three aspects of cross-examination practice: commonly advised cross-examination techniques explicitly designed to increase the potential for suggestion, tactics advised to enable lawyers to avoid or minimize unwelcome disclosures, and, third, tactics to obtain the jury's sympathy.

THE IMPACT OF THEORY ON PRACTICE

Suggestive questioning

The first technique avoided by other professions because of its suggestive potential but adopted by lawyers for the same reason is the leading question (Home Office, 1992; Spencer & Flin, 1993). Stone calls leading questions the 'normal form of cross-examination' (Stone, 1985, p. 128). Leading questions are used to both elicit specific information and to avoid other unfavourable disclosures. One respondent commented:

> I control my cross-examinations by not giving the opportunity to make a speech to the witness. And the best way to do that is of course to ask direct questions, leading questions.

Non-legal interviewers regard repeating questions as bad practice. Several studies demonstrate that repetition can generate inaccurate reports because children believe repetition signals that their original answer was wrong (Ceci & Bruck, 1995; Hughes & Grieve, 1980; Spencer & Flin, 1993). Manuals, however, advise repeating questions to control recalcitrant witnesses. *Mauet* suggests:

> repeating the question the witness answered unresponsively. It lets the witness know you cannot be put off with a non-responsive answer. The Court will also understand that the witness is evading a hard question. (Eichelbaum, 1989, p. 204)

Manuals also routinely advise using emotional reinforcement to induce compliance:

> how you ask the questions is as important as the question itself. Projecting humour, incredulity, and sarcasm are all a proper part of cross-

examination. . . . Above all, make sure that the witness understands and
feels your attitude about the facts of the case and your expectations in
your questioning. If you project that attitude it will usually have a significant impact in obtaining the answers you want. (Eichelbaum, 1989, p. 209)

These techniques are not aimed at eliciting accurate testimony but at
inducing agreement. Their potential to mislead the Court as to the
child's evidence is troubling.

Avoiding Disclosures

Cross-examiners use their control to avoid disclosures as much as to
elicit them. Avoiding certain evidence is an accepted aspect of cross-
examination. Again leading questions are the main method by which
this is done. Cross-examiners should 'lead the witness forcefully on one
point after another, keeping maximum control over him and his testimony with a view to excluding harmful statements' (Stone, 1985, p. 128).

One classic piece of advice is to avoid asking 'one too many questions'
or questions which, when the lawyer has set up an apparent inconsistency in the witness's testimony, give the witness 'a chance to qualify
or retract what he said. . . . [because he] may succeed in explaining or improving his position,' thereby 'ruining the whole result' (Stone, 1985,
pp. 118–19). Instead, 'leave the point and . . . exploit the inconsistency
in the closing speech' (Stone, 1985, pp. 118–19). The respondents
endorsed this warmly:

> If you think you have a witness who will run away at the mouth and bury
> you, you might decide, 'well I can get from that witness one point, but . . .
> I'm not prepared to . . . run that risk.' That's how I try to run my trials,
> I try to minimise the risk. I had one recently where the mother of the
> girl . . . was very hostile, so I asked her nothing apart from one thing.

Legally, lawyers must confront witnesses with allegations against them
and give an opportunity to reply, or the Courts assume they accept any
unchallenged testimony.[5] However, 'opportunity' is defined very
loosely. Lawyers need merely show they reject the witness's evidence,[6]
and need not confront at all if the point of rejection is 'obvious'.[7] Stone
advises:

> One or two leading questions, provided they are comprehensive enough,
> should cover both legal and tactical requirements completely. They
> should be framed in such a way as to call for a 'Yes' or 'No' answer. This

---

[5] *Browne v. Dunn* (1898) 6 LR 67.
[6] *Hart* (1932) 23 Cr. App R 202.
[7] *Browne v. Dunn* (1898) 6 LR 67.

will minimise the harm which an adverse witness can do. (Stone, 1985, p. 141)

It is difficult to see how witnesses can give meaningful explanations to broad, closed questions, let alone ones left unasked.

Another way of avoiding unwelcome testimony is to obstruct witnesses' ability to communicate. *Mauet*, referring to the witness's ability to describe events in terms of exact measurements or times, states:

> Another method of discrediting evidence is to examine the witness's ability to communicate. The observations are only as good as is the witness's ability to tell the Judge and jury what actually happened. (Eichelbaum, 1989, p. 216).

Children are sometimes targets of the deliberate use of age-inappropriate language and questioning in order to obstruct their communication. Although 11 of 14 New Zealand Child Witness Study respondents stressed the importance of age-appropriate language, 3 stated that some counsel deliberately confuse children with age-inappropriate language:

> The difference [between adult and child witnesses] is in being able to consistently communicate that in a public forum. ... You're looking ... to make sure they make mistakes. [...] Some counsel ... give double negatives to kids. And the kids get it wrong. ... But that is a valid technique that is used by very senior counsel and very successfully.

Similarly, seven New Zealand Child Witness respondents volunteered that stress obstructed children's ability to testify. Three advocated deliberately increasing their stress:

> You want to get them to sweat a bit ... My technique is to ... extend the time for cross-examination. ... you're deliberately making it as long as possible. [...] Tactically you want to put them under as much pressure as possible. I want them to crack.

Interestingly, the English lawyers denied using either technique. Although relatively small numbers of respondents reported this highly exploitative conduct, its inclusion in standard practice manuals suggests it may be widely accepted.

Jury Sympathy

The jury's perceived reaction to the witness is the guiding principle in choosing cross-examination techniques. Lawyers must control witnesses in order to persuade the Court but cannot be too obvious in doing it.

There is no point in eliciting testimony on which the Court is unwilling to rely because of the way in which it was obtained. To persuade the Court to accept or reject what the witness was led to say is the essential and ultimate aim. For this, the focus must be on the Court, and this must qualify the tactics used with the witness. Consequently, a cross-examiner's strategy must maintain a balance between manipulating the witness and presenting the case to the Court (Stone, 1985).

All the respondents stressed this factor in different ways. They particularly emphasized the need to avoid alienating juries. An English respondent remarked:

> I should have thought I would have no trouble in making any child witness cry within about five minutes of asking him or her questions. Bloody stupid thing to do. If you go at children the same way ... as at a crooked Detective Sergeant ... it will backfire spectacularly.

The need for caution varies depending on how sympathetic the particular witness is. Lawyers are especially concerned about juries' reactions to children, although research suggests this concern is misplaced.[8] Almost all the New Zealand defence counsel believed juries exhibit 'overwhelming, overwhelming sympathy' towards children:

> I have had jury trials with child witnesses and the jurors are crying. ... it is one situation where I believe the defence has to prove the case and not the other way around. ... the onus of proof ... is really a very nominal safeguard.

Conversely, the English respondents stated juries were sympathetic but still fair. Two suggested this was a recent development:

> They are kicking back against it [allegations of child sex abuse]. They've seen it ... in the media, and they are up to saturation point with it. And you don't have to push them ... hard ... to make them nod in agreement with you: 'well, there's a lot of it about, isn't there, ladies and gentleman?'

They still believed, however, that hostility towards children alienated juries:

> You are terrified of upsetting the child because of what the jury would think, never mind the effect on the child.

Differences in perceptions of jury bias appeared to cause different choices between possible defences. The respondents identified four

---

[8] Studies (Dziech & Schudson, 1991; Yarmey & Jones, 1983; Lieppe & Romanczyk, 1987, 1989; Lieppe, Brigham, Cousins, & Romanczyk, 1989; Lieppe, Manion, & Romanczyk, 1993; Luus & Wells, 1992) suggest juries are either neutral or biased against children. Similarly, research (Plotnikoff & Woolfson, 1995; Cross, Whitcomb, & De Vos, 1995; Martone, Jaudes, & Cavins, 1996) suggests child sex offences receive fewer convictions than other offences (see also Home Office, 1993–96).

common defences to child sex assault: suggestion, coaching, fantasy, and deliberate lying. The New Zealanders, believing juries favour children strongly, avoided alleging lies because it blames the child for the allegations. They preferred suggestion (twelve endorsements) or even fantasy (seven endorsements), blaming adults or an unconscious process outside the child's control. The English, although they endorsed all four defences, had different preferences:

> Suggestion, ... is raised in maybe a quarter [of cases]. You've got the lies: fifty percent. In maybe a quarter (and some ... overlapping with the lies), you're getting it suggested that it's really the mum's agenda or someone else's agenda ... fed into the child.

The English barristers' greater complacency regarding jury attitudes and greater preparedness to use defences blaming children suggest that English juries may be less supportive of children than their New Zealand counterparts.

Both groups responded to the perceived risk of alienating the jury by avoiding making outright accusations against children. All the English and seven of ten New Zealand defence counsel in the Child Witness Study advocated this strategy:

> There is a saying ... 'never do a movie with animals or children', because the implicit emotional sympathy is with the children. Tactically I am conscious of ensuring that I don't alienate the ... triers of fact ... You can't attack [children's] credibility because you will just be seen as a fascist, offensive prick.

They advised adopting a softer manner and using euphemisms for unpleasant allegations. 'You never say they are lying. You are always "suggesting that they might be wrong."' They also avoided putting allegations directly, leaving unfavourable conclusions to the jury:

> You try to cross-examine them just to bring out the possibility [of fantasy] and ask them 'do you make things up? Do you play with dolls?' ... and then from that you can lay the seed without being direct about it because you can offend a jury by being too direct. ... Imply it, basically.

However, it is a mistake to interpret this gentleness as evidence that cross-examination has become safer for children. It does not change cross-examination's underlying theory. The gentle approach is not child-specific but a long-established technique to deflect criticism.[9] The issue is delivery, not content. The intention is not to relieve

---

[9] Eichelbaum (1989, p. 221) advises cross-examining a defendant's mother similarly: 'Carefully suggest the partially bit by bit during your cross-examination, then stop. If you zealously cross-examine you run the risk of offending the jury. Be subtle ... the jury will respect your good taste and reach the proper conclusion on its own.'

pressure on children but to suggest arguments without offending jurors. 'What you want ... is always look like you have got the ... child at heart yourself. You want to look like the truth is at issue even if it is not.' As one respondent quipped 'softly-softly catchy monkey'. Another New Zealander stated:

> The best cross-examination ... is the impeccably polite approach: ... 'I'm not bullying at all, I'm just allowing the witness to give their own account'. And the witness finds they go from there [mimes one point] to there [mimes distant point]. They're subtly harsh ... you don't need all the ... public bar-room stuff.

This respondent was apparently using a gentle manner as a smoke-screen for manipulative tactics.

It is obviously preferable that child witnesses are not treated aggressively. However, it is questionable whether the soft technique represents a net gain to children without a corresponding change to the intention to use suggestive questioning tactics. This point was reinforced when the respondents advocating a gentle approach simultaneously argued that the pro-child bias disadvantaged defendants so badly that it necessitated more aggressive defence overall (differentiated from cross-examination manner). Six New Zealand Defence Counsel emphasized that in child sex abuse trials raising reasonable doubt is insufficient. Counsel must convince the jury the allegations are false:

> In sexual abuse cases there's almost a presumption of guilt against the accused person, and unless you can say to the judge or the jury ... 'Look: here is a reasonable motive for this complaint to be false', and make the facts of the case work around that, you are really struggling to defend it.

That they believe in this disadvantage reinforces the improbability that lawyers have softened their intentions in cross-examination. Furthermore, if, as the research suggests, the respondents are mistaken and juries are not biased in favour of children, this style of defending could be overzealous, going beyond ensuring a fair trial and instead create false doubt.

Finally, one prosecutor in the Child Witness Study and three New Zealanders and three English respondents in the General Study stated that they avoided intervening to prevent confusing cross-examination because they feared alienating jurors:

> If I object as prosecutor [even] to outrageously leading questions the jury might think I've got something to hide.

This echoes findings in Davies' survey of prosecutors' attitudes to child sex abuse trials (Davies, 1996) and Davies and Seymour's (1998) analysis of 26 child cross-examination transcripts, throughout which prosecutors only intervened four times, despite many instances of unsafe questioning. This cannot be attributed to superfluity: Judges intervened only six times, three assisting the defence. All four prosecution objections supported teenagers.

Comment

So important is the need to use cross-examination to influence the jury that if the witness could not be brought under control, the lawyers resorted to direct comment to communicate messages about the witness or evidence to the jury. It is prohibited to use comments to the jury during cross-examination because it entails the lawyer giving evidence of his or her opinions, which are supposedly irrelevant to the debate. However, all the General Study lawyers admitted using comment regularly. They avoided the rule disallowing comment by using gesture and tone and especially by rephrasing statements as questions.

> You could phrase it [the comment] as a question 'well, do you think you can ask the members of the jury to believe in the convenience of that?' There's nothing wrong with that and it's really just the same thing in a different way.

Rephrasing comment as a question is not a justifiable solution, except on the most technical grounds. Such 'questions' are virtually unanswerable, as the lawyers acknowledged. With a well-turned comment 'it doesn't matter what you say: you're dead in the water.' A child is likely to have even more difficulty formulating a meaningful response to comment than do adults.

CONCLUSION

The essential issue is the intention underlying cross-examination. While lawyers continue to regard cross-examination as an extension of their argument aimed at persuasion, rather than an investigation aimed at reliability, lawyers will continue to use manipulative techniques, provided they can avoid alienating the jury.

This argument has implications for the direction of future reform. First, any reform initiatives relying on re-educating lawyers about children's capacities or suggestive questioning is likely to be only partly successful because lawyers will not be prepared to make any adjustments reducing their ability to control witnesses or present the case.

Education may even backfire if it enables lawyers to design more sophisticated and discrete methods of controlling witnesses; for example, Myers's American manual advises using children's tendency to be perseverate to obtain favourable (but unintended) answers, a classic instance of developmental knowledge being used against children (Myers, 1987, p. 198).

Nor is it necessarily the case that creating a rule against a practice will prevent it. Even when a technique is expressly prohibited, lawyers will seek ways around the rule while the basic intent behind cross-examination remains intact. One example of this is the rule against comment (Murphy, 1997, para. F7.8).

The technical reasoning the lawyers used to avoid the rule against comment is one of the major problems which has to be faced in designing cross-examination reforms. A longer term solution to the problems of misuse of cross-examination requires not only the scientific research on specific techniques which has previously been the focus of the child witness reform movement but also an evaluation of cross-examination theory, challenging lawyers' assumptions that adversarial methodology justifies using cross-examination primarily as an extension of their argument rather than a genuine investigative technique.

Without such a theoretical re-evaluation, the essential elements of cross-examination—the control, the suggestion, the destructive intent—will remain and our only recourse will be to enlarge the current initiatives (such as have already been undertaken in New Zealand[10] and which are now in place in Britain, Home Office, 1998) to introduce intermediaries to cross-examine in the lawyers' stead. Even then, some children will fall outside the parameters of the legislation, as will many other vulnerable witnesses, who are equally affected by the current practice of cross-examination.

A theoretical analysis of cross-examination offers the potential to identify the structures and beliefs supporting the use of evidentially unsafe techniques, enabling reforms to be tailored accordingly (e.g. identifying practices amenable to education and those requiring another approach).

The legal profession as a whole is likely to resist any reassessment. The overwhelming majority of the respondents regarded their tactics as ethical. Very few in either study criticized each others' techniques or recognized problems with their own. Pressure to re-evaluate cross-examination therefore needs to come from outside as well as inside the profession. The intention behind this chapter is to begin the process of

---

[10] Twice used, to my knowledge.

reassessment by providing an insider's map of the structures underlying cross-examination, in the hope that it will prove helpful in the development of future initiatives.

REFERENCES

Brennan, M., & Brennan, R. (1988). *Strange language: Child victims under cross-examination.* Riverina, NSW: Riverina Institute of Higher Education.

Ceci, S., & Bruck, M. (1995). *Jeopardy in the courtroom: A scientific analysis of children's testimony.* Washington, DC: American Psychological Association.

Cross, T., Whitcomb, D., & De Vos, E. (1995). Criminal justice outcomes of prosecution of child sexual abuse: A case flow analysis. *Child Abuse and Neglect,* **19**, 1431.

Davies, E. (1996, given in Davies & Seymour, 1998). *Report to the Working Party on Child Witnesses.* New Zealand January.

Davies, E., & Seymour, F. (1998). Questioning child complainants of sexual abuse: Analysis of criminal court transcripts in New Zealand. *Journal of Psychiatry, Psychology and the Law,* 276.

Davies, G. (1998). The impact of television on the presentation and reception of children's testimony'. *International Journal of Law and Psychiatry,* **22**, 241.

Dent, H., & Flin, R. (Eds) (1992). *Children as witnesses.* Chichester, UK: Wiley.

Dziech, B., & Schudson, C. (1991). *On trial: America's courts and their treatment of sexually abused children* (2nd ed.). Boston: Beacon Press.

Eichelbaum, T. (Editor-in-chief) (1989). *Mauet's fundamentals of trial technique* (New Zealand edition). Auckland: Oxford University Press.

Ellison, L. (1998). Cross-examination in rape trials. *Criminal Law Review,* **605**.

Flin, R., Bull, R., Boon, J., & Knox, A. (1992). Children in the Witness Box. In: H. Dent & R. Flin (Eds), Children as witnesses (p. 167). Chichester, UK: Wiley.

Glaser, B., & Strauss, A. (1967). *The discovery of grounded theory: Strategies for qualitative research.* Chicago: Aldine.

Goodman, G., & Bottoms, B. (Eds) (1993). *Child victims, child witnesses: Understanding and improving testimony.* New York: Guilford Press.

Haydock, R., & Sonsteng, J. (1994). *Examining witnesses: Direct, cross and expert Examination.* St Pauls: West Publishing.

Henderson, E. (1997). *Reckless disregard: Cross-examining child witnesses in sexual abuse trials.* Unpublished Masters thesis, Auckland University.

Henderson, E. (2000). *Cross-examination: A critical examination.* PhD thesis submitted for examination, Cambridge University.

Home Office (1993–96) *Criminal Statistics: England and Wales: Supplementary Tables* (Vols. 1 and 2) London: Her Majesty's Stationery Office.

Home Office (June 1998). *Speaking up for justice: Report of the Interdepartmental Working Group on the Treatment of Vulnerable or Intimidated Witnesses in the Criminal Justice System.* London: Her Majesty's Stationery Office.

Home Office, & Department of Health (1992). *Memorandum of good practice on video recorded interviews with child witnesses for criminal proceedings.* London: Her Majesty's Stationery Office.

Hughes, M., & Grieve, R. (1980). On asking children bizarre questions. *First Language,* **1**, 149.

Hyam, M. (1995). *Advocacy skills* (3rd ed.). London: Blackstone Press.

Kranat, V., & Westcott, H. (1994). Under fire: Lawyers questioning children in criminal courts. *Expert Evidence*, **3**, 16.

Levy, E. (1994). *Examination of witnesses in criminal cases*. Ontario: Carswell.

Lieppe, M., Brigham, J., Cousins, C., & Romanczyk, A. (1989). The opinions and practices of criminal attorneys regarding child eyewitnesses: A survey. In: S. Ceci, D. Ross & M. Toglia (Eds), *Perspectives on children's testimony*. New York: Springer-Verlag.

Lieppe, M., Manion, A., & Romanczyk, A. (1993). *Discernability or discrimination?: Understanding juror's reactions to accurate and inaccurate child and adult eyewitnesses*. In: G. Goodman & B. Bottoms (Eds), *Child victims, child witnesses: Understanding and improving testimony*. New York: Guilford Press.

Lieppe, M., & Romanczyk, A. (1987). *Children on the witness stand: A communication/persuasion analysis of juror's reactions to child witnesses*. In: S. Ceci, M. Toglia, & D. Ross (Eds), *Children's eyewitness memory*. New York: Springer-Verlag.

Lieppe, M., & Romanczyk, A. (1989). Reactions to child (versus adult) eyewitnesses: The influence of juror's preconceptions and witness behaviour. *Law and Human Behaviour*, **13**, 103.

Luban, D. (1994). *The ethics of lawyers* (2nd ed.). Boston: Beacon Press.

Luban, D. (1988). *Lawyers and justice: An ethical study*. Princeton, NJ: Princeton University Press.

Luus, J., & Wells, G. (1992). The perceived credibility of child eyewitnesses. In: H. Dent & R. Flin (Eds), *Children as witnesses*. Chichester, UK: Wiley.

Martone, M., Jaudes, P., & Cavins, M. (1996). Criminal prosecution of child sexual abuse cases. *Child Abuse and Neglect*, **20**, 457.

MacFarlane, K., Waterman, J., Connerly, S., Damon, L., Durfee, M., & Long, S. (1986). *Sexual abuse of children: Evaluation and treatment*. London: Holt Rinehart and Winston.

Murphy, P. (Ed.). (1998). *Blackstone's criminal practice* (8th ed.). London: Blackstone Press.

Myers, J. (1997). *Child witness law and practice*. New York: Wiley.

Plotnikoff, J., & Woolfson, R. (1995). *Prosecuting child abuse: an evaluation of the government's speedy progress policy*. London: Blackstone Press.

Spencer, J., & Flin, R. (1993). *The evidence of children: The law and the psychology* (2nd ed.). London: Blackstone Press.

Stone, M. (1985). *Cross-examination in criminal trials* (2nd ed.). London: Butterworths.

Yarmey, A.D., & Jones, H.P.T. (1983). Is the psychology of eyewitness identification a matter of common sense? In: S.M.A. Lloyd-Bostock & B.R. Clifford (Eds), *Evaluating eyewitness evidence*. Chichester, UK: Wiley.

CHAPTER 19

What Do Judges Know about Young Witnesses?

JOYCE PLOTNIKOFF AND RICHARD WOOLFSON

Independent Consultants, UK

What do judges *need* to know about young witnesses? In this chapter, we look at problems in communicating with judges about children on a case-by-case basis and in relation to judicial training. We have drawn on our research in Scotland on behalf of the Lord Advocate (Scottish Executive, 2001) and on our projects in England and Wales (Plotnikoff & Woolfson, 1993, 1995a, 1995b, 1995c, 1996, 1997) to explore some of the barriers to judicial knowledge and suggest ways in which it could be improved.

Articles 12 and 13 of the 1989 UN Convention on the Rights of the Child create obligations 'not only to hear a child witness but to free the child from any constraints or fear, anxiety or distress which might inhibit his evidence [and] to create the optimum circumstances in which a child as witness is freed to give his or her account of events' (Cleland & Sutherland, 1996). The UN Convention is binding in international law on the United Kingdom in common with all other Member States of the Council of Europe. When taking decisions concerning children's evidence, judges should be guided by these principles.

In Scotland, children are expected to testify in open court 'without suffering undue trauma or stress' provided that they receive pre-trial preparation coupled with 'sensitive handling ... from the moment of arrival at the court house' (Scottish Law Commission, 1990, para. 2.8). In England and Wales, in contrast, children are recognized as

Children's Testimony. Edited by H.L. Westcott, G.M. Davies, and R.H.C. Bull.
© 2002 John Wiley & Sons, Ltd.

'a particular group of vulnerable witnesses ... in need of special protection' (Home Office, 1998, para. 10.1). Increasing numbers give evidence-in-chief by means of a videotaped interview and are cross-examined over a live TV link outside the courtroom.

Despite these differences, criminal policy in England, Wales, and Scotland is predicated on the understanding that judges and other criminal justice system personnel will be given information about the needs of young witnesses to enable children to testify as effectively as possible. All too frequently, however, neither jurisdiction meets the standards set by the UN Convention. Communication with judges about the needs of young witnesses is often poor, undermining legislative intent and the quality of children's evidence.

In one English case, for example, a boy of six was brought to court at 9.15 a.m. but was not shown his 50 minute videotaped interview (his evidence-in-chief) until 3. p.m. During subsequent cross-examination by live TV link, he said that could not remember what he had said in the video. The prosecution concluded that the case could not proceed. His mother said no child of six should have been expected to wait all day and give evidence in the late afternoon; no one had told the judge that he was tired and unfit to give evidence. Following the court case, the boy began wetting the bed and had trouble sleeping. He told his mother that he could not understand the question at the court and said 'Why wouldn't they let me tell the truth?' (Plotnikoff & Woolfson, 1996).

In one Scottish case, a seven-year-old witness with cerebral palsy used a wheelchair, but no arrangement was made for the family to use court parking. The child arrived at 9.45 a.m. but was not called until the afternoon. She testified in open court. During her evidence, her mother offered her a drink of water and was admonished by the judge. The girl was asked to point out the accused but had not brought her glasses. She was wheeled round the court and then made the identification. During cross-examination, she broke down in tears, without intervention by the judge or procurator fiscal (prosecutor). Neither of these cases resulted in a conviction. In both, partial plea offers had been rejected by the prosecution.

INADEQUATE MECHANISMS FOR RECORDING AND PASSING ON INFORMATION BEFORE THE TRIAL

The police are the primary source of information about the needs of young witnesses. However, flagging up these cases by the police is erratic, and recording and transmission of non-evidential information about children is not systematic. In England and Wales, the police use a confidential form to transmit witness information to the Crown Prosecution Service (CPS), including police opinions about witness strengths, weaknesses, and vulnerability. In our 1995 study, the police provided an assessment of the child's capabilities in 57% of cases and passed on the child's wishes about giving evidence in 45% of cases (Plotnikoff & Woolfson, 1995b). Guidance issued in 1996 encouraged the police to give the CPS more detailed information about children. However, by 1998 communication in these categories had dropped to 26% and 29% respectively (Crown Prosecution Service Inspectorate, 1998).

In Scotland, applications for screens, live TV links, or evidence on commission (i.e. where the child's evidence-in-chief and cross-examination is recorded pre-trial) are appropriate only in 'exceptional circumstances'.[1] The police need not provide information to the procurator fiscal about all young witnesses or transmit witness information according to a prescribed format. Police reports rarely include an assessment of the child's abilities or wishes, even though the child's view about giving evidence is one of the statutory criteria for use of special measures.[2] Prosecutors in both jurisdictions are expected to seek information about young witnesses if it is not supplied by the police but, in practice, few take remedial action. As one procurator fiscal put it: 'We already delay to remedy evidential deficiencies. We have not got time to get "nice-to-know" information.'

POOR COMMUNICATION WITH THE COURT

A key concern for young witnesses is to know with certainty before the trial how they will give their evidence. In England and Wales, a pre-trial hearing is held in all Crown Court cases. A young witness checklist for completion by the advocates was introduced in 1999; the pre-trial hearing judge adds any pre-trial orders and includes the questionnaire in the trial judge's papers. However, pre-trial decisions are not yet binding on the trial judge.

Pre-trial hearings in Scotland, except to rule on live TV link and screens applications, are not routinely held in High Court cases. In the Sheriff Court, such hearings should be used to plan how child witnesses are dealt with at trial but, in practice, this seldom happens (Macphail, 1997). (Most criminal cases in Scotland are dealt within the Sheriff Court, where sentences of up to three years can be imposed.) Judges

---

[1] *Crown Office Book of Regulations*. Evidence on commission has not yet been used.
[2] Criminal Procedure (Scotland) Act 1995, section 271.

and sheriffs are often assigned to cases at the last minute, without prior notice that a young witness is involved. The age of the child is not necessarily on their papers or provided by the prosecution.

For the small proportion of children in Scotland who are the subject of applications for live TV links or screens, procurators fiscal obtain reports from teachers, social workers, or others who know the child. These reports (not required in England and Wales) often contain information potentially useful in planning the child's court attendance; for example: 'His level of concentration and patience is limited ... Asking him to wait five minutes is like asking him to wait for three hours ... Waiting time should be kept to a minimum ... He requires a high level of support in stressful situations.' However, there are obstacles to such reports reaching the trial judge. Some applications are not pursued by prosecution counsel, and the reports are then dispensed with. Even when applications proceed, reports are often only read by the pre-trial hearing judge who rules on the application. Sheriffs acknowledge that a report submitted in advance was liable to be mislaid or overlooked by the time of the trial. Authors of reports expect their information about the child's views, needs, and abilities to be taken into consideration by the trial judge and may be unaware that reports are not always passed on. Trial judges may then be unaware why a particular child needs to give evidence with screens or by live TV link.

Neither jurisdiction in the UK systematically updates information about young witnesses during the pre-trial period. Despite their 'priority' status, many young-witness cases take a year or more to come to trial. Prosecutors and judges may be unaware, for example, of the child's growing reluctance to give evidence, rejection of the child by family members, exclusion from school, or attempts at self-harm.

THE LACK OF CONSISTENCY IN THE EXERCISE OF JUDICIAL DISCRETION

The exercise of wide-ranging judicial discretion, leading to uncertainty and inconsistency, can actually increase rather than reduce witness trauma (Sanders, Creaton, Bird, & Weber, 1997). Some judges have cloaked with blanket restrictions provisions intended to be implemented on a case-by-case basis; for example, declining to admit videotaped evidence for children over the age of 12 but otherwise within the age group to which the legislation applies. However, judges in England and Wales were unaware of the divergence of their practices until the first child abuse seminars run by the Judicial Studies Board began in

1996. The judge who was course director said 'It became immediately apparent how much practice varied at different courts. That surprised both those organising the seminars and those attending' (Crane, 1999, p. 19).

The Scottish Law Commission (1990) acknowledged the problem of inconsistency: 'Where attempts are made ... to prepare a child for the experience of giving evidence, it may be difficult to do so accurately and effectively where certain practices and procedures are merely discretionary' (para. 2.2). Without removing judicial discretion, the Commission hoped that the issuing of judicial guidance would promote 'some desirable uniformity of approach'. The Lord Justice General issued a Memorandum in 1990 suggesting several discretionary measures, with the objective of ensuring that testimony by those under 16 'causes as little anxiety and distress to the child as possible in the circumstances', while ensuring that the accused receives a fair trial.

This Memorandum invites judges to take each child's circumstances into account before deciding what steps, if any, should be taken. However, it does not set out formal procedures for communicating this information to the trial judge. Despite the Memorandum's clear intentions, judicial attitudes differ as to whether it is appropriate for sheriffs and judges to receive child-centred information, from 'I want to be informed about anything taking the child out of the ordinary run' to 'I don't like directions telling me what to do'; 'We don't need to know anything about the child, unless the child is terrified—but I would want to be convinced'; and 'It is better not to know, though I would take a break if necessary' (Scottish Executive, 2001).

One sheriff puts the approach of the judiciary in Scotland as follows: 'there is, quite deliberately, an absence of formal mechanisms for the transfer of *any* information to the trial judge prior to the trial. The position is quite different in England, where the trial judge knows far more than his Scottish counterpart about the case before he goes into court. [Scottish practice] has the advantage that it enables the judge to preside at the trial with a mind unaffected by any prior information about the accused or the witnesses. One would therefore expect a Scottish judge to be circumspect about receiving information about a child witness prior to the trial' (Macphail, 1997).

The Lord Advocate's Working Group on Child Witness Support, reporting in 1999, found that the 'sensitive handling' and 'desirable uniformity of approach' to child witnesses advocated by the Scottish Law Commission in 1990 had not materialized and recommended that judges be given standard categories of information about young witnesses at a pre-trial hearing. A group representing sheriffs responded that there were 'very many cases' when it would be unnecessary to make enquiries about the child's circumstances.[3] In 'exceptional circumstances' (e.g. where the child had a health problem), a note could be passed up by the procurator fiscal with the consent of the defence just before the child entered the courtroom. The Lord Advocate's Working Group did not consider this to be an adequate approach in planning to assess and accommodate the child's needs.

THE PRESENCE OF A SUPPORTER WHEN THE CHILD GIVES EVIDENCE

Judges have discretion as to whether a supporter may accompany children giving evidence. Research indicates that children not only derive emotional support from the presence of a supporter whom they trust, but the consequent reduction in anxiety may improve the accuracy of their evidence (e.g. Moston, 1992). The Scottish Law Commission acknowledged these benefits and the presence of a supporter was one measure to alleviate stress suggested by the Lord Justice General's Memorandum. In a study of the live TV link in Scotland, all but one of 49 children gave evidence with a supporter present; 84% of supporters were well known to the child (Murray, 1995).

Prior to implementation of the live TV link in England and Wales, the government left open whether a supporter should accompany the child (Home Office, 1987), and, in 1990, a Home Office report endorsed the presence of 'a parent or supporter' (Pigot, 1989). However, judicial guidelines issued in 1991 without consultation or reference to research stated that other than in 'very exceptional cases' only an usher should accompany the child in the TV link room (Watkins, 1991). Around 80% of children giving evidence by TV link in England in Wales have been accompanied only by the usher (Chandler & Lait, 1996). The 1991 guidance now conflicts with the 1996 Victim's Charter, which advises that 'if you have to give evidence you can ask to have a friend or supporter in court. Someone from the Witness Service can accompany you if you wish.'

WHO IS RESPONSIBLE FOR CHILDREN'S WELFARE WHILE THEY ARE GIVING EVIDENCE?

In England and Wales, no one has specific responsibility for the welfare of the child giving evidence. The Court of Appeal has reiterated

---

[3] Sheriffs' Association, letters 31.8.98 and 5.9.98.

judges' powers to intervene in inappropriate cross-examination,[4] but these powers are rarely exercised (Davis, Hoyano, Keenan, Maitland, & Morgan, 1999). In 1993, the Royal Commission on Criminal Justice recommended that judges take a more interventionist role and 'should be particularly vigilant to check unfair and intimidatory cross-examination' (recommendation 201). Similar recommendations have been made in Scotland (Scottish Office, 1998). Research has demonstrated that lawyers need training in age-appropriate questioning (Davies & Noon, 1991; Flin, Bull, Boon, & Knox, 1993; Kranat & Westcott, 1994). Judges need to be able to recognize inappropriate questioning and ensure they do not compound the problem by asking confusing questions themselves.

Research reveals many instances where judges fail to control what is perceived as oppressive or confusing cross-examination. But what if it is the judge who acts inappropriately? The Lord Advocate's Working Group on Child Witness Support was told of one sheriff who called a 15-year-old girl 'a lying little bitch' and another who asked a seven-year-old to put her hand down her pants and show where the man touched her. Lawyers and social workers in the courtroom failed to intervene on either occasion: 'We can't object—it's the sheriff's court'; 'When the sheriff behaves inappropriately, pragmatism may demand that we do nothing'; 'When the sheriff behaves inappropriately, pragmatism may demand that we do nothing'; 'I used to say to children "It's my job to keep you safe"—I soon gave that up!'; and 'I don't know if we can intervene. I wouldn't dare with a senior sheriff' (Scottish Executive, 2001).

JUDICIAL TRAINING

In Scotland, judges and sheriffs are generalists and do not receive any special designation for serious sexual assault or child witness cases; most have relatively little experience with children's evidence. However, a Judicial Studies Committee established in 1997 has incorporated some child welfare issues in its materials and seminars. The Lord Advocate's Working Group made several recommendations to augment judicial training.

Recommendations concerning judicial training on child witness issues in England and Wales have been made since at least 1989 (Pigot,

---

[4] For example, Press Release from the Criminal Division of the Court of Appeal, 6 May 1998.

1989, para. 7.9). During 1996–1998, the Judicial Studies Board held the first seminars for judges authorized to try child abuse cases. Judges were shown *A case for balance*, a video produced in 1997 by a consortium of government departments, children's charities, the Bar, and Law Society.[5] It aimed to raise awareness of good practice in young witness cases and to stimulate judicial discussion about differences in approach. Judges at Judicial Studies Board seminars were also shown the video *Out of the mouths of babes* which claims to 'raise big questions about the testimony of children'.[6] This excerpt from an American TV programme, about the work of Professor Stephen Ceci of Cornell University, appears to be a convincing demonstration of the unreliability of children's evidence. It shows interviews with pre-school children who, after suggestive questioning, provide details about completely fictitious events. Defendants are interviewed who claim they were wrongly convicted of child abuse. It ends with Ceci's co-researcher, Maggie Bruck, agreeing that there are 'dozens of people in jail [convicted on children's evidence] who are totally innocent.'

One commentator has observed that Ceci and Bruck's work gives 'the impression that many, if not most, interviews are conducted improperly and that children's accounts of abuse are often false. The authors' occasional references to children's strengths and to proper interviewing are lost like the proverbial needle in a haystack ... it is important to draw attention to their "spin" and to emphasise its potential to damage legitimate efforts to protect children' (Myers, 1995, pp. 392, 396; Westcott, 1998). Their questions often '*tell* rather than *ask* the child what has occurred' (Lyon, 1995, p. 434), and their perspective has been described as of 'questionable authoritativeness' in relation to criminal investigations (Mansel, 1996, pp. 751).[7] Since making *Out of the mouths of babes*, Ceci has conceded that 'We pursued kids repeatedly ... We "grew a narrative" over long periods of time, with repeated false suggestions by an interviewer ... Not only do I believe that children can be reliable in sexual abuse cases, I believe the vast majority of them are reliable witnesses.'[8]

The importance of balance and objectivity in judicial training is crucial. Several judges who were shown *Out of the mouths of babes* commented to us that it 'proved you can't believe what children say.' This video was not the subject of a peer review process before being

---

[5] Available from National Society for the Prevention of Cruelty to Children, 42 Curtain Road, London EC2A 3NH.
[6] Part of the television programme *20/20*, broadcast in the USA in October 1993.
[7] L. Mansel describes one of their publications as having 'sparked an outcry due to alleged factual distortions, omissions, and mis-characterisations.'
[8] Interview in ABC *Nightline* TV programme 'A child's word'.

included in judicial seminars. Some child psychiatrists and psychologists have expressed concern privately about its use, but there is no avenue for expert groups to comment on the content of judicial training. In England and Wales, the 1998 report of the Interdepartmental Working Group on the treatment of Vulnerable and Intimidated Witnesses (Home Office, 1998), and, in Scotland, the report of the Lord Advocate's Working Group on Child Witness Support (Scottish Executive, 2001), recommended that judicial training be informed through consultation with groups with specialist knowledge. However, although a criminal justice training-needs analysis was set up following the English report, this does not include the judiciary. In Scotland, Sheriff Macphail, QC described the provision of guidance to the judiciary as 'a difficult matter' (1997). While agreeing that 'there is everything to be said for lawyers keeping themselves well-informed' he took the view that 'it would be objectionable if a judge were to reach a conclusion by supplementing the evidence and submissions before him with his private knowledge of some relevant topic.'[9]

THE FUTURE

In Scotland, the report of the Lord Advocate's Working Group on Child Witness Support (Scottish Executive, 2001) has been the subject of a consultation exercise. Its recommendations include the assignment of child witness cases to a designated group of trained sheriffs,[10] introducing mechanisms for communicating the needs and wishes of young witnesses to judges and other criminal justice system personnel along with proposals concerning judicial guidance (including updating the Lord Justice General's Memorandum) and training.

Judges in both jurisdictions and elsewhere would benefit from information based on a consensus of expert advice representing the most up-to-date research and best practice. Written guidance on the management of young witness cases (e.g. Matthews & Saywitz, 1992) updated regularly, should be available to all judges, not only those attending seminars. Such consultation need not impinge on judicial independence. The content would address, for example, child development; the importance of exercising judicial discretion with input about the needs of the child in question and the need to request such information

---

[9] In *B v. Ruxton* 1998 (*Green's Weekly Digest* 24–1191), Lord Sutherland dismissed an appeal on the grounds that the sheriff, in assessing the witness, took into account his private research into sexual abuse.

[10] This was the only one of 43 recommendations rejected by the Lord Advocate.

if not provided; and recognition of some of the more subtle reasons why certain questioning may not be developmentally appropriate. It would draw on research to illustrate the effect of pre-trial delay on the child and ways in which case management to expedite these cases can be improved (Davis *et al.*, 1999, p. 84).[11] Common but unfounded beliefs would be confronted, such as the view that teenagers generally need less protection than younger children when giving evidence; that child victims of non-sexual or 'less serious' offences are likely to be less traumatised; and that juries are less likely to convict when videotaped evidence or the TV link are used. It is promising that a section on children was included in the *Equal treatment bench book* for judges in England and Wales in 2000.

The forthcoming revision of the *Memorandum of good practice on video recorded interviews with child witnesses for criminal proceedings* (Home Office & Department of Health, 1992) will extend its scope from the investigative interview into the pre-trial period and preparation for court. The new guidance will reinforce the need to obtain information about individual children in order to enable them to give evidence most effectively. The new *Memorandum*, entitled *Achieving best evidence in criminal proceedings*, needs to be the subject of judicial consultation and training, something which did not occur with the original version in 1992.

While the police have primary responsibility to provide information about the child to the CPS, supporters preparing children for court also have a responsibility to pass on relevant information on a case-by-case basis (Plotnikoff & Woolfson, 1998). There are, however, no independent preparation schemes for young witnesses in Scotland, and the Lord Advocate's Working Group on Child Witness Support (Scottish Executive, 2001) called for the funding of an integrated support service. The Association of Chief Police Officers has expressed serious dissatisfaction with current arrangements in England and Wales which vary widely and has called for a national body of accredited supporters that is properly funded and managed (Murray, 1997). The unevenness of support service provision means that many judges do not receive periodic feedback about the experience of young witnesses at court and are unaware of the extent of some of the problems they encounter.

A clear policy decision is needed to make judges aware of the benefit to young witnesses giving evidence of the presence of a trusted supporter. Judges should be consulted in developing guidance on the support

---

[11] Young witness cases may be listed more quickly if placed under the supervision of a designated judge on receipt at the Crown Court.

role, to ensure that the rights of the defendant are not affected. At present, many supporters complain about the uncertainty; for example: 'We don't know how to act. Can I touch her if she's upset or say "There, there"? It's hopeless'.[12] Trained supporters should be entitled to alert the judge if problems arise for the child while s/he gives evidence (Murray, 1995). In the USA, 16 States allow independent representation of the child witness by a guardian *ad litem* in criminal cases. A similar proposal was considered in England and Wales by the Children Act Advisory Committee (1993) and may be re-visited in light of the Children and Family Court Advisory Service announced by the Lord Chancellor in July 1999. Set up to look after the welfare of children in family proceedings, 'its remit may be extended ... to take on additional functions.'

In 1997, in the Report of the Review of Safeguards for Children Living Away from Home, Sir William Utting described the treatment of child witnesses in England and Wales as 'systems abuse of a very harmful kind' (Utting, Baines, Stuart, Rowlands & Vialva, 1997). Further criticisms of the process were made by Sir Stephen Brown (1999), then President of the Family Division, and Lord Williams of Mostyn (1999), then Home Office minister, who also criticised the scope of judicial training. The Youth Justice and Criminal Evidence Act 1999 introduces the most ambitious reforms thus far designed to assist young witnesses in England and Wales including, for certain categories of witness, the pre-trial videotaping of cross-examination and the use of intermediaries. Such measures will not achieve the objective of reducing children's stress and improving the quality of their testimony unless court culture and attitudes are also tackled. Judicial sensitivity to the child's needs and abilities will remain crucial: oppressive cross-examination will be just as devastating at a pre-trial hearing as at trial. The experience of intermediaries in South Africa has demonstrated the continued importance of judicial intervention to ensure appropriate questioning. Lord Williams of Mostyn (1999) also emphasized that 'the key' to the new provisions is 'finding out what child witnesses need. The State has no business in further increasing their trauma.'

If best use is to be made of the 1999 Act in England and Wales, and the principles of the UN Convention are to be fulfilled there and in Scotland, more rigorous systems are essential for communicating

---

[12] Ushers, likely to be strangers to the child, can 'make comforting gestures to ease the child's distress'. Ushers accompanying child witnesses. *TV links* (A guide to live TV links in the Crown Court). London: Lord Chancellor's Department. (1994).

information to judges and lawyers and for raising judicial awareness about young witnesses' concerns.

REFERENCES

Brown, Sir Stephen. (1999). Court ordeal as bad as abuse. *The Lawyer*, 28 June 1999.

Chandler, J., & Lait, D. (1996). An analysis of children as witnesses in the Crown Court. In: Victim Support (Ed.), *Children in court*. London: Victim Support.

Children Act Advisory Committee. (1993). *Second annual report* (p. 16). London: Lord Chancellor's Department.

Cleland, A., & Sutherland, E. (1996). *Children's rights in Scotland*. Edinburgh: W. Green/Sweet & Maxwell.

Crane, P. (1999). Child abuse procedures in practice. *Judicial Studies Board Journal*, 7.

Crown Prosecution Inspectorate. (1998). *Report on cases involving child witnesses*. London: Crown Prosecution Inspectorate.

Davies, G., & Noon, E. (1991). *An evaluation of the live link for child witnesses*. London: Home Office.

Davis, G., Hoyano, L., Keenan, C., Maitland, L., & Morgan, R. (1999). *An assessment of the admissibility and sufficiency of evidence in child abuse prosecutions*. London: Home Office.

Flin, R., Bull, R., Boon, J., & Knox, A. (1993). Child witnesses in Scottish criminal trials. *International Review of Victimology*, **2**, 319–39.

Home Office. (1987, May). *Use of video technology at trials of alleged child abusers*. London: Home Office.

Home Office. (1998). Speaking up for justice (Report of the Interdepartmental Working Group on the Treatment of Vulnerable and Intimidated Witnesses in the Criminal Justice System). London: Home Office.

Home Office, & Department of Health. (1992). *Memorandum of good practice on video recorded interviews with child witnesses for criminal proceedings*. London: Her Majesty's Stationery Office.

Judicial Studies Board. (2000). *Equal treatment bench book* (Chapter 11).

Kranat, V.K., & Westcott, H.L. (1994). Under fire: Lawyers questioning children in criminal courts. *Expert Evidence*, **3**, 21–3.

Lyon, T. (1995). False allegations and false denials in child sexual abuse. *Psychology, Public Policy and Law*, **1**, 429–37.

Macphail, I. (1997). Child witness support initiative: A response. *Socio-legal research in the Scottish courts* (Vol. 4). Edinburgh: Scottish Office Central Research Unit.

Mansel, L. (1996). The child witness and the presumption of authenticity after *State v. Michaels*. *Seton Hall Law Review*, **26**, 685–763.

Matthews, E., & Saywitz, K. (1992). *Child victim witness manual*. California Center for Judicial Education and Research.

Moston, S. (1992). Social support and the quality of children's eyewitness testimony. In: H. Dent & R. Flin (Eds), *Children as witnesses*. Chichester, UK: Wiley.

Murray, K. (1995). *Live TV link: An evaluation of its use by child witnesses in Scottish criminal trials.* Edinburgh: Her Majesty's Stationery Office.

Murray, K. (1997). *Preparing child witnesses for court.* Edinburgh: Her Majesty's Stationery Office.

Myers, J. (1995). New era of skepticism regarding children's credibility. *Psychology, Public Policy and Law,* 1, 387–98.

Pigot, T. (1989) *Report of the Advisory Group on Video Evidence.* London: Home Office.

Plotnikoff, J., & Woolfson, R. (1993). *The Child Witness Pack.* London: National Society for the Prevention of Cruelty to Children/ChildLine.

Plotnikoff, J., & Woolfson, R. (1995a) *Prosecuting child abuse: An evaluation of the government's speedy progress policy.* London: Blackstone.

Plotnikoff, J., & Woolfson, R. (1995b). *The pace of child abuse prosecutions: Follow-up study.* London: Department of Health.

Plotnikoff, J., & Woolfson, R. (1995c). *Evaluation of the Child Witness Pack.* London: Home Office.

Plotnikoff, J., & Woolfson, R. (1996). Evaluation of witness service support for child witnesses. In: Victim Support (Ed.), *Children in court.* London: Victim Support.

Plotnikoff, J., & Woolfson, R. (1997). *A case for balance* (video). London: National Society for the Prevention of Cruelty to Children.

Plotnikoff, J., & Woolfson, R. (1998). *Preparing young witnesses for court.* London: National Society for the Prevention of Cruelty to Children.

Royal Commission on Criminal Justice. (1993). *Report CM2263.* London: Her Majesty's Stationery Office.

Sanders, A., Creaton, J., Bird, S., & Weber, L. (1997). *Victims with learning disabilities: Negotiating the criminal justice system.* Oxford: University of Oxford Centre for Criminological Research.

Scottish Law Commission. (1990). *Report of the evidence of children and other potentially vulnerable witnesses* (SLC No. 125). Edinburgh: Scottish Law Commission.

Scottish Office. (1998). Towards a just conclusion: Vulnerable and intimidated witnesses in Scottish Criminal and Civil Cases (Recommendation 14). Edinburgh: Scottish Office.

Scottish Executive Central Research Unit (2001). *An evaluation of child witness support.* Edinburgh: Scottish Executive.

Utting, W., Baines, C., Stuart, M. Rowlands, J., & Vialva, R. (1997). *People like us* (The report of the safeguards for children living away from home). London: Her Majesty's Stationery Office.

Watkins, T. (1991). Live TV link cases: Person to accompany the child in the video room. *Deputy Chief Justice Guidelines.* London: Lord Chancellor's Department.

Westcott, H.L. (1998). Jeopardy in the courtroom. *British Journal of Psychology,* 89, 525–7.

Williams of Mostyn, Lord. (1999). Keynote speech at Lucy Faithfull Foundation/NOTA conference, 19 July 1999.

CHAPTER 20

Young Witnesses: Still No Justice

BARBARA ESAM

National Society for the Prevention of Cruelty to Children, London

Mary's Experience as a Young Witness in a Criminal Prosecution

I am 12 years old. The man next door, Uncle Bob, he and his wife were good friends of our family, he did sex things to me for about three years. All our family liked him and I did too. He was always very kind to me and used to babysit for us. He used to give me sweets and presents and take me to the park to the swings. I can't remember when it all began but he started doing things to me I didn't like. At first I didn't understand what was happening and kept thinking I must be imagining things. I couldn't get him to stop although I asked him to. He made me feel like it was my fault and he told me nobody would believe me if I did say anything. He told me it was our secret and if I told anybody my mum would get into trouble and I would be sent to foster parents and wouldn't see my family any more. I was just too frightened and confused to say anything about it to anybody.

I couldn't stop thinking about it and one day when the teacher at school asked me what was the matter, it just all came out. She said she would tell my mum and then everything would be alright. My mum was really upset but she believed me. A policeman and, I think it was a social worker, came to see me and we went to a room with a video camera in and I told them some of what had happened to me. They were alright and they kept saying it would be okay in the end. I had to see a doctor. I was told not to talk to my mum or my sister about what had happened. I tried not to think about going to court but one day my mum told me it was going to be next week.

We waited and then somebody came to tell me that I couldn't go into the television link room because it was being used by somebody else. They

---

Children's Testimony. Edited by H.L. Westcott, G.M. Davies, and R.H.C. Bull.
© 2002 John Wiley & Sons, Ltd.

said I could give my evidence behind a screen but that meant I had to go into the courtroom. They said that if I wanted to wait for the television link we'd have to come back another day. I knew my mum didn't want to go home and come back again another time. I felt I had to go ahead with it that day. I don't think I would have ever gone through with it if I hadn't done it then.

The first barrister was okay but he didn't ask me much and I didn't always understand what he was saying. He helped me tell some of what had happened. It was really embarrassing to say the details. I didn't tell them everything. I just couldn't. When the next barrister questioned me. She had a smiley face and made jokes with me. I began to think it wasn't going to be so bad. Then she seemed to change. She kept asking me about dates and times and I couldn't remember them exactly. I told her I could remember what had happened to me but not when. I didn't understand some of the long words she used. Sometimes, she asked three or four questions at once and I didn't know which one I was answering. She called me a liar. I still don't understand half of what went on. I felt dirty. They made me feel like I didn't exist. (Le Roy, n.d.)

This case illustrates just how iniquitous the process can be when children and young people are called upon to be witnesses in criminal prosecutions in England and Wales. It is one of the more extreme examples but it is not atypical, and it is based on a real-life case. The examples of bad practice within it are repeated either individually or in combination with depressing regularity for young witnesses throughout the criminal courts.

There are examples of good practice as well. Indeed, the video for judges and lawyers dealing with child witnesses (National Society for the Prevention of Cruelty to Children [NSPCC], 1997) represents good practice which is drawn from around England and Wales. However, there is no reassurance that can confidently be given to children and young people about what they will experience as witnesses because there is no consistency regarding the way young witnesses are dealt with within each court, let alone across the country. All too often, young witnesses have the same reaction to their experience as Mary had:

If I had known how it was going to be at court, I never would have gone through with it.

SOME OF THE PROBLEMS

The Lack of Consistency

Where a case involves a young witness, it should be possible to get firm answers to these important questions:

- Will the case be allocated a trial for a fixed date with all due speed (in a court equipped with a TV link and video facilities if needed)?
- Will the child meet the judge and/or the barristers before the hearing? Will the court have information about the particular needs of the child witness (e.g. regarding their attention span or language difficulties)?
- Will issues that could prevent the trial going ahead be sorted out on a pre-trial basis (e.g. requests for third-party disclosure or editing of the video evidence)?
- Will the judge take an active role in managing the case to ensure that the proceedings, generally, and any questions put to the child, in particular, enable the child to participate in the proceedings at a level that is consistent with that child's level of development?

The answer to these and other questions about policies and procedures will not be consistent and certain. The answers will instead depend on which area of the country the trial will take place in and, more particularly, which judge will be hearing the case. The treatment a young witness can expect comes down to a lottery.

In order to establish consistency in the way children and young people are treated as witnesses, there is a need for one government department to oversee the impact of the criminal justice system on young witnesses and to assess what improvements are needed to meet their needs.

In England and Wales, three government departments are involved, namely the Home Office, the Crown Prosecution Service, and the Department of Health. The Home Office statement of Purpose and Aims contains as its Aim 2: 'Delivery of justice through effective and efficient investigation, prosecution, trial and sentencing, and through support for victims.' The Home Office funds the witness service which is based in the Crown Courts and Magistrates Courts and offers assistance to witnesses and their families. The Crown Prosecution Service is responsible for prosecuting people in England and Wales who have been charged by the police with a criminal offence. They have as one of their objectives: 'To meet the needs of victims and witnesses in the Criminal Justice System, in co-operation with other criminal justice agencies.' The Department of Health states that 'it is the duty of the State, through local authority social services departments to both safeguard and promote the welfare of vulnerable children' (Department of Health, 2000). There can be no doubt that children who are alleged to have been abused, and who are required to give evidence in criminal proceedings, are vulnerable children who are in need of someone to safeguard and promote their welfare. Equally, children who are victims, of crimes other than abuse (sexual or physical) and children who are not victims, but have witnessed a crime, will need to have their welfare safeguarded and promoted before, during, and after they go through the process of giving evidence.

Much well-intentioned work has gone on and significant progress has been made in England and Wales, including passing new legislation in the form of the Youth Justice and Criminal Evidence Act 1999 (see below). And yet, the uncertainty and inconsistency of treatment continues. The result is a failure to protect the welfare of children and young people who are asked to be witnesses in criminal proceedings and a failure to satisfy the interests of justice. The Department of Health would seem to be the most appropriate department to take on the overall responsibility for the welfare of young witnesses, in cooperation with the Home Office and the Crown Prosecution Service.

Why No Statistics?

In order to tackle the issues relating to child witnesses, we need to know the nature and extent of the problems. We need to know:

- How many child witness cases are prosecuted each year?
- What are the ages of the child witnesses?
- How many cases result in convictions and how does this relate to the conviction rate for prosecutions generally?
- How many cases fail to get to court because the child witness does not feel able to give evidence (or because a parent/carer considers that it would not be in the child's interests to give evidence)?
- How many cases do not go to court because the police decide not to proceed and what are the reasons for these decisions?
- How many cases do not go to court because the Crown Prosecution Service decides not to proceed and what are the reasons for these decisions?
- How many cases involve retrials?
- How many cases accept reduced pleas?
- How many cases fail due to technical problems with the video equipment?
- How many cases fail because of inadequate/poor-quality video evidence?
- What is the success of local service level agreements?
- What is the effectiveness of Plea and Directions Hearings?
- What is the effectiveness of the Supplementary Pre-Trial Checklist (see below)?
- How long are these cases taking to come to trial?

It is only the government departments who have access to this information. If one government department were to take responsibility for young witnesses, they could coordinate the development of a research or management information programme and obtain this information and keep it updated.

Listing Problems

There is legislation and a number of policy documents in England and Wales to support the expedition of these cases. The legislation allows cases to be transferred directly from the Magistrates Court to the Crown Court without the need for committal proceedings. The Lord Chancellor's Department (1993) has issued guidelines which spell out the need for child witness cases to be given the earliest possible fixed date for a trial and make it clear that these dates can only be changed in exceptional circumstances. The Court Service (1995) has produced a Charter for court users which highlights the need to assign the earliest possible date for a trial involving a child witness. The Home Office (1996) have produced a Victims Charter which also contains a commitment to assign a high priority to child abuse cases.

Despite all this stated policy and guidance, there is an all too frequent practice of fixing a number of trials at one Crown Court which all involve young witnesses requiring a television link. This is done with a certain knowledge that there will not be enough courtrooms connected to television link rooms to accommodate the number of trials listed. Having created this problem of overbooking (presumably to ensure that no judge time or court time is lost), the courts 'resolve' the problem by transferring cases to other Crown Courts at the last minute. No apparent consideration is give to the impact this might have on the young witness. Worse still, a recent practice has been developing in the Central Criminal Court in London whereby young-witness cases are listed as 'floaters' (i.e. with no fixed date) so that young-witnesses are warned that their case may possibly be heard some time during a particular week. This is in clear contravention of the Lord Chancellor's Guidelines and puts children and their families under a degree of pressure that is utterly unreasonable.

The following real-life examples illustrate the impact from the young person's point of view:

1   The Crown Court listed four fixed trials involving young witnesses for the same date despite the fact there were only two television-link courts. Other witnesses were warned that their cases would begin on a particular Monday. A decision was taken on the Friday

before the court hearing that one case would be transferred to another court. The young witness involved in that case was an alleged rape victim who had just been discharged from a psychiatric unit following treatment for suicidal feelings associated with the rape. She was living in a bedsit (aged 17) with no family support. She was not informed of the transfer until the day of the trial. A second trial involved the rape and indecent assault of a 12-year-old girl. The alleged victim was told on Monday that the trial would not be going ahead and that she should return the following day. At the end of that day, Tuesday, she was told that the trial could not be heard at all because there was no judge available. This was the second time the trial had been cancelled, the first time being five months prior to this court date. A new trial date was not set for a further six months. Two remaining cases proceeded on the date as planned, one of those cases had been listed for a previous date which had fallen through.

2   In another example, two 10-year-old girls and one 11-year-old girl were all the alleged victims of indecent assault by one defendant. The case was listed for trial at Crown Court A on 21 April. Two weeks prior to the trial, the witnesses learned that the case would be transferred to Crown Court B. On the day of the trial, 21 April, the witnesses were told that the trial was again being transferred to another Crown Court C, 75 miles away, and would not start until the following day, 22 April. On 22 April, the first young witness attended court at 12.30 p.m. as arranged and was told to wait at the police station as the court building did not have suitable waiting facilities. Legal arguments had taken place throughout the morning, and the witnesses were told at 1.00 p.m. that the trial was being transferred back to Crown Court B to be heard on 28 April. The reasons given were that the judge did not have sufficient time to hear the trial; the location was not con-venient to the defence barristers; and the defendant would not agree to a change in barrister. Subsequently, the witnesses were told that the case could not be heard on 28 April after all. A new date was eventually fixed for 5 May at Crown Court A. The defence then applied to Crown Court B for a change of date as 5 May was not convenient for the defence barrister. The trial was finally heard on 19 May.

Two separate independent young-witness supporters have made the following comments:

> In our experience, listing problems are more likely to happen than not. The
> child never is a central focus of the planning, and information about the

reason for delay is rarely relayed by the court to the child and their family. Many of the problems that arise could be dealt with at the Plea and Directions Hearing. (Frances Le Roy)

'I did some work with the children after the court to talk about their feelings, how they felt the court had gone for them, etc., and one thing that kept on being repeated by all the children was that they did not like being sent away. They each in turn had psyched themselves up for the day to give their evidence and were suddenly finding themselves being told, yet again, to leave the court. One of the problems was that there were endless legal arguments and the QC for the defence openly stated in court that he was looking at the papers on a day-to-day basis and at one point stated that he had not seen the whole of one of the children's videos. This, of course, meant that he couldn't raise any legal arguments until each morning, having prepared that day's work the night before. (Kate Rosevear)

Pre-trial Therapy

When children and young people have been the victims and/or the witnesses to a crime, especially a serious crime, it is common sense to expect that they will be able to receive appropriate therapy as soon as possible to help them deal with the trauma that they have experienced. It often comes as a shock to parents and carers to learn that there is not a straightforward answer to the question of whether or not their child can get therapy in advance of the trial. The concern is that the child's evidence could be said to have been tainted by the therapy if it takes place prior to the criminal trial and that, as a result, the prosecution will be lost.

There is some written guidance on this issue already. The Home Office and Department of Health *Memorandum of Good Practice* (1992) states that once a video recorded interview has been made 'it should be possible for appropriate counselling and therapy to take place' (para. 2.44). There is also guidance in *Working Together under the Children Act* (Department of Health, 1991, para. 5.26.9) which says that 'there will be occasions when the child's need for immediate therapy overrides the need for the child to appear as a credible witness in a criminal case.' The Crown Prosecution Service also has written guidance which states that the question of whether a child should receive pre-trial therapy is not a decision for the police or the Crown Prosecution Service. These decisions can only be taken by the appropriate agencies and professionals responsible for the welfare of the child, in consultation with the carers of the child.

Despite all this guidance, many young witnesses are told time and again locally that they should not get therapy in advance of the trial because it will prejudice the outcome of the trial. It would appear that many local branches of the Crown Prosecution Service either have not heard of the policy or do not agree with it. Even where children and young people are told that it is alright to go ahead with therapy in advance of the trial, they and their parents/carers are left with a strong message that pre-trial therapy could destroy the case and they are therefore left in a double bind. Further good-practice guidance is anticipated from the Crown Prosecution Service.

Refreshing Memory

Child witnesses do need to view their videotaped interview during the trial.[1] This is important because cross-examination usually follows almost immediately and the contents of the video will be fresh in the child's memory. However, children should also have the opportunity to view the videotaped interview prior to the trial for the following reasons:

- All witnesses have a right to refresh their memories prior to being called to give evidence. Child witnesses should not be denied this basic right.
- The child needs to refresh his/her memory prior to experiencing the courtroom pressures of viewing the video during the trial. They should be able to view the video in more informal/relaxed surroundings.
- The child is more likely to concentrate on the contents prior to the trial. The videotaped interview may be the first time the child has seen him/herself on video. They are likely at first to concentrate more on their appearance/dress, mannerisms or accent, rather than the content of their statement.

Decisions regarding the admissibility of video evidence should be made pre-trial. If all or part of the video is ruled inadmissible, other arrangements for refreshing the child's memory will need to be made in good time before the trial. Considerations need to be made as to when and where the child views the video pre-trial and who can accompany them (not a defence representative or the child's independent supporter).

The practice of viewing the video twice on the day of the trial (i.e. once before the trial begins and secondly with the court) is not helpful. Experience has shown that children find it difficult to concentrate through two viewings.

---

[1] In England and Wales, the videotape of the child's investigative interview, conducted according to guidance in the *Memorandum of Good Practice*, can replace the child's live evidence-in-chief at court.

All children have different needs and it is important that they are given the correct information to make informed decisions as to whether they wish to view the videotaped interview before the trial. It is important to give children all relevant information and to listen to what they feel would be best for them.

Independent Young-Witness Supporter

Most adults find it hard to stand up in a courtroom to give evidence and, for young people, the experience can be even more threatening. When the subject matter of the evidence involves giving details of sexual abuse they have suffered, the stakes rise even higher.

Regrettably, it is not possible under our present system to take all the stress away. However, so much of the stress caused by the system is unnecessary stress. It is the roots of the unnecessary stress that need to be tackled, and preparing children for their role as a witness can help them to cope and thus enable them to give more complete and more accurate testimony.

A significant proportion of young witnesses do not receive this crucial preparation and support work. Home Office commissioned research reported in 1995 that 30% of young witnesses in Crown Court cases received no preparation at all for court (Davies, Wilson, Mitchell, & Milsom, 1995). In 1996, a study conducted by Victim Support reported that 65% of young witnesses in non-sex offence cases and 25% of young witnesses in sex offence cases did not have the benefit of a pre-trial familiarization visit to court (Chandler & Lait, 1996). This is another area where the treatment which a young witness can expect is left to chance depending on where they live. If there were one government department taking clear responsibility for young witnesses, this would have to include the development of a national body of accredited young-witness supporters with proper funding and management.

The key components for a court preparation programme are (NSPCC/ChildLine 1998):

- assessing the child's needs in relation to a court appearance;
- helping children to understand the court process and their role in it;
- taking the child to visit the court before the trial;
- providing the child with stress reduction and anxiety management techniques;
- involving the child's parent or carer;
- communicating information (including the child's wishes) to the police, Crown Prosecution Service, and courts; keeping the child,

parent, or carer informed; and ensuring that practical arrangements are made concerning the child;
- the possibility of accompanying the child while giving evidence;
- debriefing the child witness and parent or carer when the case is over.

It is essential that an independent young-witness supporter has not been involved in the investigative interview and does not discuss the prosecution case or the child's evidence. If the young person begins to talk about their evidence, the supporter must notify the police so that the child can speak to those conducting the investigation properly. A list of competencies for independent young-witness support work has been developed by the NSPCC, in London.[2]

The court preparation programme includes only the possibility of someone other than an usher being able to accompany the young witness when they give their evidence even though this is often the most stressful point of the whole procedure. This is yet another area of uncertainty where practice varies from court to court.

SOME SOLUTIONS? THE YOUTH JUSTICE AND CRIMINAL EVIDENCE ACT 1999 IN ENGLAND AND WALES

Part II: Giving of Evidence or Information for Purposes of Criminal Proceedings

This Act is divided into two main parts. Part I deals with reform to the youth justice system. Part II of the Act provides a variety of special measures which are aimed at young, disabled, vulnerable, or intimidated witnesses and which are intended to help these witnesses give evidence in criminal prosecutions. Here, I concentrate on Part II of the Act and, more particularly, on the impact which the Act will have on children and young people who are called upon to be witnesses in criminal proceedings.

Throughout the consideration of this legislation, the legitimate interests of the defendant have been kept at the forefront of the minds of all those concerned with drafting and amending the new legislation. Section 32 of the Act requires the trial judge to give the jury such warning (if any) as s/he considers necessary to ensure that any special measures direction given in relation to the witness does not prejudice the accused. The case law in relation to the need to protect the

---

[2] Public Policy Department, NSPCC National Centre, 42 Curtain Road, London EC4A 3NH.

defendant's right to a fair trial would seem to support the view that the provisions within the Act, which aim to help young witnesses to give their evidence, do not contravene the European Convention on Human Rights and in particular Article 6, which enshrines the defendant's right to a fair trial.

The range of measures included in the Act are:

- physical measures to reduce the stress of giving evidence at trial;
- additional restrictions on the admissibility of evidence about an alleged victim's sexual behaviour in sexual offence trials;
- additional restrictions on publishing information which might identify the witness;
- an expansion to the definition of who is competent to give evidence.

Physical Measures to Reduce the Stress of Giving Evidence at Trial

The Act expands the range of special measures and puts them all into a statutory framework. The menu of special measures is:

- Screens, to ensure that the witness does not see the defendant (previously available as a matter of practice in some courts).
- Allowing an interview with the witness, which has been videotaped pre-trial to be shown at the trial as the witness's evidence-in-chief (previously admissible under the Criminal Justice Act 1988).
- Allowing the witness to give evidence from outside the court by live TV link (previously admissible under the Criminal Justice Act 1988).
- Clearing members of the press and public from the court so that evidence can be given in private (previously available in the Children and Young Persons Act 1933).
- Not wearing the court dress of wigs and gowns (court dress previously dispensed with as a matter of practice in some courts).
- Allowing the witness to be cross-examined before the trial about their evidence and the video recording of that cross-examination to be shown at trial instead of calling the witness (this has never been available previously either by statute or as a matter of practice).
- Allowing an approved intermediary to help the witness communicate with legal representatives and the court (this has exceptionally been available in some courts). This special measure is restricted to witnesses under 17 and witnesses who are considered to be vulnerable because of their mental condition or disability (i.e. it will not be available on grounds of fear or distress about testifying).

- Allowing the witness to use communication aids (this has previously been available in some courts). This special measure is subject to the same restrictions as apply to intermediaries above.

All witnesses under the age of 17 at the time of the hearing are automatically eligible for any of these special measures (except a person under 17 who is charged in criminal proceedings). Children who have attained the age of 17 will be treated as adults rather than as children under the Act. This is not in accordance with the meaning of the term 'child' as defined by Article 1 of the United Nations Convention on the Rights of the Child (1989). The Convention defines children as being below the age of 18 years as does the Children Act 1989 (s. 105(1)). Attempts were made to amend the 1999 Act to raise the age to 18 so that it would be consistent with the Children Act and the Convention, but these attempts failed.

The Presumption in Favour of a Special Measures Direction in Relation to Child Witnesses

There will be a presumption under the new provisions in favour of all children under 17 years of age giving their evidence-in-chief by video. This is a new presumption, which will take most of the uncertainty out of this aspect of the system. What happens next depends upon the crime that is alleged:

- Child witnesses in sex offence cases will receive the most protection and most of them will not have to appear in court at all. Instead, they will give both their examination-in-chief evidence and their cross-examination evidence on video, which will be recorded in advance of the trial.
- Child witnesses in cases involving violence, neglect, abduction, or false imprisonment will be subject to a presumption which states that the child's evidence-in-chief will be given by pre-recorded video and their cross-examination will be given on the day of the trial by live TV link. Both presumptions will apply unless the court takes the view that they would not be in the interests of justice.
- Child witnesses in all other cases will have a presumption that their evidence-in-chief will be given pre-recorded on video and their cross-examination will be given on the day of the trial via live TV link. The presumptions apply unless the court takes the view that the measures would not maximize the quality of the child's evidence.

Competence

Previously, child witnesses below the age of 14 could give unsworn evidence.[3] That meant that these children did not have to take an oath. However, in order for their evidence to be received by the court, they had to be capable of giving 'intelligible testimony'.[4]

The Youth Justice and Criminal Evidence Act 1999 extends the ability to give unsworn evidence to witnesses of any age in criminal proceedings if they can understand the questions put to them and can answer the questions in a way that can be understood by the court. The effect of this is that witnesses under the age of 14 will continue always to give their evidence unsworn, as long as they can be understood. Where children have attained the age of 14, the court will determine whether their evidence is to be given sworn or unsworn. The child may not be sworn unless he can understand the solemnity of the occasion and the particular responsibility to tell the truth. The defendant is never competent to give evidence for the prosecution in his own trial.

Will the New Legislation Help?

The new Act represents an important step towards a legal system which takes account of some of the needs of young witnesses and which eliminates some of the unnecessary stress they have been put through under the previous system. However, the need to reduce delay in these cases remains a serious concern and one can find little in the Act that addresses this problem. The Pigot Report (Pigot, 1989) recommended that no child should be required to appear in public as a witness in court unless they positively chose to do so. The Act falls far short of meeting this goal. It does not offer any help to young defendants who no doubt find the experience of court very intimidating in most instances. Nor does the Act address the failures within the system which have their roots in issues such as a lack of understanding of child development or a lack of understanding of the process of grooming used by child abusers. These issues are too complex to be dealt with properly in this chapter but they deserve further consideration.

SOME SOLUTIONS? THE PRE-TRIAL CHECKLIST

A new Supplementary Pre-trial Checklist for Cases Involving Young Witnesses was introduced in the Autumn of 1999 to all Crown Court

---

[3] Criminal Justice Act 1988 s. 33A (inserted by s. 52 of the Criminal Justice Act 1991).
[4] Inserted by the Criminal Justice and Public Order Act 1994.

centres in England and Wales by the Lord Chancellor's office. The Checklist is for use at the Plea and Directions hearings. Its aims and objectives are:[5]

- to improve the experience of children who are required to come to court as witnesses;
- to recognize the specific needs and requirements that children have in this environment;
- to set a minimum national standard for courts in preparing young witnesses to give evidence in criminal trials;
- to enable the trial to proceed smoothly by giving early attention to matters raised.

The Lord Chief Justice has endorsed the use of the Checklist, which gives consideration to the following areas:

- videotaped evidence;
- television links;
- screens;
- memory refreshing;
- the child's preparation for court;
- court dress;
- scheduling;
- the requirement for breaks during the trial;
- special circumstances;
- disclosure of third-party records.

CONCLUSION

There are a number of problems and gaps within the system which remain. I have referred to the confusion over pre-trial therapy; the problem of delays; inappropriate questioning which leaves young witnesses feeling intimidated and confused; the lack of certainty in almost every aspect of the process; problems with listing cases; the varying levels of preparation for court which are available; and the lack of a consistent procedure for identifying an individual child's particular needs.

In addition, there is a need for adequate specialist training for judges and for prosecution and defence lawyers dealing with cases involving young witnesses. There are problems with juries who do not understand child abuse (e.g. how paedophiles groom children) and who, therefore, are not able to consider these cases effectively. It is a problem that the

---

[5] Lord Chancellor's Department website.

defendant's history of previous convictions/evidence of previous misconduct cannot be revealed, even where similar offences have been committed.

There remains a big question mark over whether our current system in England and Wales, even as amended by the new legislation, will adequately meet the needs of young witnesses and justices. It may well be that we need to start again 'with a blank sheet of paper'.

REFERENCES

Chandler, J., & Lait, D. (1996). An analysis of children as witness in the Crown Court. In: Victim Support (Ed.), *Children in court.* London: Victim Support.

The Court Service (1995). *Charter for court users.* London: The Court Service.

Davies, G.M., Wilson, J.C., Mitchell, R., & Milsom, J. (1995). *Videotaping children's evidence: an Evaluation.* London: Home Office.

Department of Health. (1991). *Working together under the Children Act 1989: A guide to arrangements for inter-agency cooperation for the protection of children from abuse.* London: Her Majesty's Stationery Office.

Department of Health (2000). *Framework for the assessment of children in need and their families.* London: Her Majesty's Stationery Office.

Home Office. (1996). *Victims charter.* London: Her Majesty's Stationery Office.

Home Office, & Department of Health. (1992). *Memorandum of good practice on video recorded interviews with child witnesses for criminal proceedings.* London: Her Majesty's Stationery Office.

Le Roy, F. (n.d.). *Young witness project.* London: National Society for the Prevention of Cruelty to Children.

Lord Chancellor's Department. (1993). Guidelines for Crown Court listing. Unpublished.

National Society for the Prevention of Cruelty to Children [NSPCC] (1997). *A case for balance* (video). London: NSPCC.

National Society for the Prevention of Cruelty to Children [NSPCC]/ChildLine. (1998). *Preparing young witnesses for court.* London: NSPCC.

Pigot, T. (1989). *Report of the Advisory Group on Video Evidence.* London: Home Office.

Review of Part III

Contributors to Part III again have covered a wide range of issues related to facilitating children's testimony. At times, this makes rather depressing reading, as reforms psychologists have striven to implement seem to have fallen short of their goals. At other times, it is easy to feel disheartened by the apparent impunity of the criminal justice system and its personnel to the needs of children. What can we learn from the review of investigative policy, practice, and research contained in Part III?

One of the striking features is perhaps the differences in practice that have arisen from goals shared by reformers. Taking just one example—closed circuit television (CCTV)—Judy Cashmore's chapter demonstrates just how differently various cultural and legal frameworks have accommodated the new technology; for example, who stays inside or who stays outside the courtroom. Günter Köhnken reminds us also, in his comparison of adversarial and inquisitorial systems, that innovations can have unexpected outcomes; for example, expert witnesses can deflect some of the pressure from child witnesses when used in a non-adversarial setting. We can make no easy assumptions when considering the reception of children's testimony by the courts, or the impact of further refinements.

Another lesson to emerge is the importance of listening and responding to the wishes of children and young people. It may be surprising to realize how many of the legal and procedural innovations to date have occurred in the absence of feedback from children themselves, as well as in the absence of prior evaluation. Through all stages of the investigation, it is imperative that children are given as much choice and control as possible; even well-intentioned reforms can feel oppressive in the absence of choice. Amanda Wade comments, 'a flexible system offering children a range of options for testifying and the opportunity

Children's Testimony. Edited by H.L. Westcott, G.M. Davies, and R.H.C. Bull.
© 2002 John Wiley & Sons, Ltd.

to express an informed choice, would better meet their needs.' How do children and young people communicate their wishes in practice, and what weight do professionals at all stages of the investigative process accord to their wishes?

Thomas Lyon's work on children's understanding of the oath is a clear example of the need to evaluate all our practice from the perspective of children, and to remember that children often understand what they cannot—or are not enabled to—explain. His work indicates that, even at the age of seven, substantial difficulties are experienced by children in trying to explain the difference between 'truth' and 'lies'. Young children should not be asked to define truth or lies, nor asked to explain the difference as a prerequisite to taking the oath; rather, he suggests, they should be asked to choose from prepared statements. If this seems obvious in the light of developmental psychology, other aspects highlighted by Lyon's work seem unappreciated; for example, that children find in inherently unpleasant to generate examples of lies or to discuss the consequences of lying. In addition, children are less likely to respond if discussions of truth and lies include examples of wrongdoing which require them to challenge their own behaviour or that of an adult authority figure. This research is applicable not only at court but also to children's videotaped investigative interviews for use as evidence-in-chief, which usually contain some type of 'truth and lies ceremony' arbitrated by the interviewer. Furthermore, Lyon's chapter provides another, more simple example, of methodological improvement, through the involvement of maltreated children as research participants rather than their non-abused peers.

The attitudinal barriers of court professionals continue to require considered and sustained attention. In the United Kingdom, Barbara Esam, Joyce Plotnikoff, and Richard Woolfson have been at the forefront of moves to 'tackle court culture and attitudes', and their contributions to this volume underscore the need for vigilance against ignorance and complacency. Judicial discretion, and the inevitable prioritizing of courtroom personnel's needs above those of the witness(es), can seem insurmountable barriers. Emily Henderson's chapter is explicit about the limits of psychological knowledge and influence regarding the accuracy of children's statements when compared to defence barristers' need for absolute control. Even against this backdrop, however, limited positive interventions can be made; for example, the eradication of procedural inconsistency and uncertainty in relation to children's evidence, the thorough preparation of children for all aspects of their court appearance, and the identification of named persons responsible for children's welfare throughout different stages of an investigation, court appearance, and afterwards.

The greatest hope for change is for psychologists and lawyers to work together. In England and Wales, a recent example towards this aim is the current revision of the government's *Memorandum of Good Practice* (Home Office & Department of Health, 1992) on interviewing child witnesses. The revised guidance has a much wider remit, including vulnerable and intimidated adult witnesses, *and* the court appearance itself. The drafting of the original *Memorandum* and revised guidance has involved psychologists and lawyers.

Several contributions to this part of our book have emphasized how little we know about long-term outcomes for children involved in criminal investigations and highlight the benefits of continued evaluations. Psychologists have had surprisingly little to say about the importance of long-term support and resources for children and their families, and yet it seems testifying may affect child witnesses in unpredictable ways, such as a tendency towards aggression and delinquency noted among testifiers by Robin Edelstein and colleagues. This represents but one area where psychologists are developing more skilled and sophisticated methodologies to meet the challenge of empowering children in the adult world of the courtroom. Child witnesses and victims have rights, and we must continue efforts to reduce the abuse they suffer from judicial procedures.

REFERENCE

Home Office, & Department of Health. (1992). *Memorandum of good practice on video recorded interviews with child witnesses for criminal proceedings.* London: Her Majesty's Stationery Office.

PART IV

Alternative Perspectives on Children's Testimony

CHAPTER 21

Methodological Issues in the Study of Children's Testimony

BRIAN R. CLIFFORD

School of Psychology, University of East London, London

In the last 15 years, child witnesses have been receiving more favourable evaluations from both the legal and the psychological community. No longer do the courts require competency hearings before a child of tender age can proffer testimony. And psychologists who write textbooks, in which they discuss the memory status of different age groups, now have to document carefully where children and adults are comparable as well as deficient, rather than routinely trotting out the shibboleth that adults are better than children on any memory task one would like to consider.

What has caused this reappraisal of the quality of children's memory? Is it simply another manifestation of the sociology of knowledge (Clifford, 1993), or is it that more sensitive, more relevant methodological investigations have evolved which have served to uncover the ability that young children have always had? As with most things human, the answer is not straightforward. The zeitgeist is certainly flowing in the child's favour. But the aim of this chapter is to show that the rhetoric is in danger of racing ahead of the reality and that much remains to be done on the methodological front in order to ensure that the child is not, perversely, disadvantaged in the criminal justice system.

Children's Testimony. Edited by H.L. Westcott, G.M. Davies, and R.H.C. Bull.
© 2002 John Wiley & Sons, Ltd.

FROM LAB. TO LIFE

One answer to the revised status of the child as witness is that the methodology used to test their memory in the eyewitness domain has been expanded and refined. As a result of this revision and elaboration, it is now clear that previous research has seriously underestimated the quality and quantity of the information that children can retain following exposure to a criminal episode or an analogue of it, either as an innocent bystander or as an engaged 'victim'.

Progressively, research that looks at children's testimony ability is eschewing the laboratory or, more specifically and accurately, its sterile methods of presenting stimuli. Gone are the days when children were compared to adults in terms of testimony, or more precisely visual memory, by comparing them on ability to memorize numerous faces or scenes presented as pictures within a forced-choice paradigm. Currently, slide and video presentations are being superseded by a real-life staged event methodology or the utilization of naturally occurring events.

But this more ecologically valid development in presentation of the to-be-remembered material is only part of the story. Child witness research has increasingly been conducted within the framework of what has become known as 'everyday memory' rather than 'laboratory memory' (Banaji & Crowder, 1989). This means that, in the last two decades, children's eyewitness ability has been judged against a background of fundamental questioning concerning *what* memory phenomena should be studied, *how* they should be studied, and *where* they should be studied and has been characterized by eclectic and innovative methodology. The *what* focus of children's memory research has been led by considerations of relevance to legal issues and practical applications. The *how* focus of the research tradition has meant that, wherever and whenever possible, research has been mindful of ecological validity, mundane realism, legal verisimilitude, and external validity, while being at pains to ensure as much experimental control and generalizability as possible. Lastly, the *where* emphasis of child witness research has given full scope to considerations of the social–functional context of remembering. But these eclectic and innovative methodologies are themselves reflective of something yet deeper.

Koriat and Goldsmith (1996) argue that eyewitness testimony research has been at the forefront of a fundamental change in how memory is conceptualized. They argue that eyewitness testimony research represents a prime example of a shift from a storehouse conceptual model or metaphor of memory to that of a correspondence metaphor. The storehouse metaphor conceptualizes memory as a mental space in which memories are stored and then retrieved by a search process. These memories are discrete, elementary units, whose essential characteristic is that they can be counted. Thus, forgetting is defined in terms of item loss. Furthermore, these items are interchangeable or equivalent in terms of the eventual, calculated, percentage correct output. The storehouse metaphor of memory, therefore, engenders a quantity-orientated approach to memory.

The correspondence metaphor of memory is very different. In this metaphor, the basic criterion is not the quantity of items remaining in store but rather the correspondence between what the person reports happened and what actually happened. Under this metaphor, reliability, accuracy, and faithfulness of memory become important, because memory is about past events and states of affairs. Forgetting is conceived of as a loss of correspondence between the memory report and the actual event being reported: a deviation from veridicality rather than as a simple loss of items. This naturally leads on to a consideration of various types of memory distortions such as confabulation, which are more qualitative than quantitative, and were not countenanced in traditional laboratory-type memory experiments. These characteristics lead Koriat and Goldsmith to argue that the correspondence metaphor of memory is accuracy-orientated.

Now this shift from quantity to accuracy in the evaluation of memory is precisely what underlies and has powered the shift in the perception of children's memory: from very poor, vis-à-vis adults, to comparable in many respects to adults. If memory is conceptualized as a storage space which is then searched during retrieval, then it is natural to assume the space will increase in size with age or development, and that search and retrieval strategies will also increase in number and quality as age increases. If not these, then what is left to develop?

However, under the correspondence metaphor, where accuracy is the dependent variable and the input stimuli are meaningful real-life events, then the prediction of massive age differences is more difficult to make because 'meaningfulness' is something that shows little development, as opposed to change, after the self has been established, and accuracy is something the participant has control over (i.e. it is an output-bound measure reflecting the likelihood that each reported item is correct).

Thus, as the perennial question of the reliability and credibility of children's memory relative to that of adults has moved from the laboratory to the everyday memory paradigm, with its liberalization of the 'what', 'where', and 'how' constraints, underpinned by the meta-theoretical switch from a quantity-orientated storehouse metaphor to an accuracy-orientated correspondence one, so children's relative standing *vis-a-vis* adults has 'improved'. However, we must not be complacent. There is still much to do and many questions to be addressed.

It is still the case that children develop into adults, with the presupposition that with development comes improvement. In the socio-political drive to get children's voices heard in court, there may have been an overplaying of the quality of children's testimony. Are there not still areas of testimony where children are poorer in terms of accuracy or completeness than adults?

Just as expert witnesses are predominantly called by the defence rather than the prosecution because they are seen to be saying adult witnesses are always mistaken, so in the near future psychologists may be called, in cases involving children, because their narrative is perceived as always stating that children are good witnesses. The evolving current paradox between adult witnesses being challenged (while historically the law held them to be reliable) and child witnesses being supported (while historically the law held them to be unreliable) is interesting and instructive.

It is instructive because it tells us not to oversell the case of the reliable child witness. It instructs us to be cautious, contrite, and circumspect in our proclamations and protestations lest the child be disadvantaged and lose advantages already gained: such as live-link and video-based evidence-in-chief—two innovations that do not sit easily with the legal system but which were allowed because of the child's espoused vulnerability, fragility, and 'different-from-adult' status.

But there is another reason why the 'child-as-good-as-adult' card should not be overplayed. Are the findings of children's memory, even under the new everyday memory paradigm, as grounded as some would like us to believe? Are the findings consistent and consensual? A careful reading of this book would suggest they are not, and this is reflective of the wider published data in children's eyewitness testimony research. We must not let our rhetoric run ahead of our results.

This chapter will try to show that, despite the rhetoric, consistency in findings is not always present, illustrating this in the fields of stress and arousal, suggestibility, and misleading information, and that there is scope for methodological developments which could serve to further empower the child within the criminal justice system. This will be illustrated by recent line-up research, questioning methodology, and, finally, the need for portfolio research.

STRESS AND AROUSAL

The areas of stress and arousal, that have proved most difficult experimentally and theoretically with adults, have, somewhat paradoxically, proved an apparently fertile site for some of the most positively valenced evidence for the quality of children's testimony abilities. While it is impossible to simulate the experiences of an actual rape or sexual abuse victim, investigations of memory for traumatic events have progressed apace, by utilizing naturalistic invasive procedures such as bladder catheterization (Goodman, Quas, Batterman-Faunce, Riddlesberger, & Kuhn, 1997; Merritt, Ornstein, & Spicker, 1994; Principe, Myers, Furtado, & Merritt, 1996); medical examinations, injections, and invasive radiological procedures (Ornstein, 1995); and dental visits (Peters, 1991a). It has been argued that these situations qualify as valid constructs of stressful, highly emotional events.

Utilizing these situations, the weight of evidence suggests that children have good memories under these most trying of situations and that they do not make mistakes on questions concerning bodily touching or undressing—issues that are central to sexual abuse cases (Goodman et al., 1997). And yet, the evidence may not be as conclusive as is portrayed.

How do we measure and what do we mean by stress and/or arousal? How stressful is stressful? It is clear that as one moves to naturally occurring stressful incidents which happened sometime in the past, so the quality of data one gets is dependent upon veridical perception and memory by the child of his or her reaction to the incident at the time. Where caregivers' estimates or recollections (rather than the child's) are relied upon, then the quality of the data becomes, inevitably, more questionable still. When research which uses subjective estimates of arousal is compared with comparable studies that use objective measures the results are not always congruent.

The exchange between Goodman (1991) and Peters (1991b)—two researchers who work in this area, but come to different conclusions concerning whether stress decreases witnessing ability (Peters) or leaves it unaffected (Goodman)—is instructive. Peters (1991b) accuses Goodman of unbalanced high- and low-stress groups and questionable control groups. Furthermore, Peters questions the use of single ratings or measures of anxiety/stress and asks what they actually measure—a dispositional/trait characteristic or a situational, event-produced arousal.

Goodman (1991), in her turn, points out that Peters's standard finding of decreased eyewitness accuracy with increased stress or arousal is questionable because it is doubtful if stress was actually present. In the specific case of a visit to the dentist, Goodman points out that only 1 child out of 71 investigated by Peters actually had a filling. In addition, she points out that the self-report scales Peters uses would predispose to ratings of anxiety, even if no anxiety actually existed.

Both attack each other for small cell sizes, resulting in low statistical power. What about the correlation of stress with age? To the extent that age is not factored out, or statistically controlled for, then any finding of a decrease in memory with increase in arousal could be due to an age effect. Note—an *age* effect. Thus, we cannot treat all children as an undifferentiated, homogenous non-adult population.

In addition to these conceptual, methodological, statistical, and measurement problems in this particular area, it is the case that inconsistencies do occur within the same research laboratory; for example, while Goodman usually finds no reduction in eyewitness accuracy for her high-arousal subjects, this is not always the case, nor is it always the case that children never make errors when asked about personally meaningful events involving their bodies. In fact, Goodman *et al.* (1997) reported that children did make errors about touching of their bodies and this has also been found by Steward *et al.* (1996). Thus, even in this most apparently consensual area of research—reporting or not reporting bodily touching—the research is not consistent.

Taking the above spat as typical of exchanges that could be engaged in concerning nearly all child eyewitness testimony domains, the point being made is that any premature closure concerning the status of children in this domain, far less their status *vis-à-vis* adults, is premature and detrimental to the well-being of the child in the criminal justice system. The effect of heightened arousal on children's recall and recognition performance is frequently an issue of debate in court—at the moment, the direction of resolution is still without solid empirical guidance. As always, more and better controlled and conceptualized research is needed before firm conclusions can be drawn on this issue.

SUGGESTIBILITY

Another area where apparent tranquillity exists, born of declared consensus and consistency of findings, is in the area of suggestibility. The rhetoric seeks to offset the legal view, long held, that children are inherently more suggestible than adults and thus should be accorded less credibility in courts of law (Heydon, 1984).

The 'new wave' of child witness research seems to suggest that children are much less suggestible than was originally thought, especially about personally relevant details. There is, however, a whole body of evidence showing that, just like adults, children are susceptible to suggestion. Indeed, Ceci and Bruck (1995, pp. 234–5) suggest 'one can safely conclude that, compared to older children, younger children and specifically pre-schoolers, are at greater risk for suggestion about a wide variety of topics, including those containing potentially sexual themes.' Once again, it should be noted that 'children' are being disaggregated, and when this is done *general* statements about 'children' are seen to lack validity and reliability.

A study that confirms this view and raises additional issues intimately connected to suggestibility is White, Leichtman, and Ceci's (1997). They had three- to five-year-olds engage in a 'Simon Says'-type game involving two children and one adult researcher. For half the time, one child performed the actions specified by the researcher while the other child observed. For the remainder of the time, the two children reversed roles, the observer became the doer and the performer became the observer. The events involved being physically touched or not and carrying out usual or unusual actions. One and two months after the 'game', each child was interviewed twice by two separate adults who had been briefed with either correct or incorrect information about each event. It was found that younger children acquiesced more than older children to questions based on inaccurate information, and their reports became more inaccurate over time (interviews) than did the older children's.

This study also contradicted the suggestion (Goodman, Rudy, Bottoms, & Aman, 1990) that children are less suggestible for events where they experience physical touching than for events that they merely observe. In addition, the results suggest that pre-schoolers' reports about these bodily experiences are not immune to adult's schema-generated misleading questions.

Clearly, then, the suggestibility of children of different ages is far from settled, despite what the 'headline rhetoric' may imply or state explicitly. White *et al.*'s (1997) study shows that suggestibility is not just a question of the age of the child being investigated, nor the type of question being asked, nor the subject matter being interrogated, but also of repeated questioning by people who may have non-veridical understandings of what did or did not take place. This shows the complexity of methodology that must be employed to begin to approximate the complexity of the issues involved in suggestibility and credibility, and possible ways of exploring the strong motives, threats and inducements that are often part of the aftermath of abuse, an area of concern all but ignored by existing research.

MISLEADING INFORMATION

Research is very clear that children can be misled by post-event information (Lee & Bussey, 1999), and such information can come from numerous sources. On the other hand, it has been argued that children are not as susceptible as research might suggest because the standard paradigm has been to (a) mislead on incidental or peripheral details and (b) on information that was viewed or presented only once. Do single-exposure findings generalize to children's memories for recurring and well-learned information or experiences? If the misinformation effect is due, at least in part, to the strength of the target memory (Payne, Toglia, & Anastasi, 1994), then it is argued that suggestibility findings from single-exposure procedures should not be generalized to children's memory for recurring information or experiences. Thus, it is argued, children are not as suggestible as the laboratory-based literature might suggest.

However, such may not be the case. Lee and Bussey (1999) had seven-year-olds learn a game to criterion (i.e. they over-learned relationships between rooms, clothing, and fruit to the extent that they could demonstrate perfect memory for these objects and their relationships on several occasions). They then introduced either misleading or inconsistent information and eventually tested for misleading/suggestion effects in the over-learned game.

Clear effects for misleading information were observed—despite the learning to criterion of the target memory. Obviously then, children are not immune to misinformation effects even when they are tested on material they have experienced several times and for which they are known to have a good memory.

While deficient in ecological validity, this study suggests that the issue of child susceptibility to misleading information on repeated or frequently experienced events is not closed but rather stands in need of much more research, perhaps buttressed by stronger theoretical understanding of the structure and function of children's memories.

LINE-UP PERFORMANCE OF CHILDREN

Research has shown that children can be as good as adults in identification of perpetrators from a target-present array (Pozzulo & Lindsay, 1998). Shown a target-absent line-up, however, children consistently produce more false positives than do adults: 83% vs. 58% (Parker & Ryan, 1993) or 70% vs. 34% (Lindsay, Pozzulo, Craig, Lee, & Corber, 1997). For adult witnesses, however, the presentation of sequential, as opposed to simultaneous, line-ups reduces false positive responding (Cutler & Penrod, 1988; Lindsay, Lee, & Fulford, 1991; Lindsay et al., 1997). Unfortunately, children do not respond to sequential line-ups in the same way. Their false positive responses do not decrease (Lindsay *et al.*, 1997; Parker & Ryan, 1993; Pozzulo & Lindsay, 1998). When show-ups (a single photograph shown to a witness) are used children's responses are even more prone to be false positives than with simultaneous or sequential line-ups.

Clearly then, if police or courts were to become aware of these findings they may well be discouraged from seeking or using the identification evidence of child witnesses. This would be a retrogressive step.

Are there, therefore, any methodologies available that should be researched in order to seek to reduce this known fallibility of the child witness? One promising line of advance is offered by Pozzulo and Lindsay (1999). They have tested a method of line-up identification with children that appears to reduce their proclivity to pick out someone (anyone) from a line-up. This technique is referred to as an elimination line-up. In such line-ups, the child is required to eliminate all but one line-up member before being asked if that remaining line-up member was the actual perpetrator. Elimination of foils can be done one by one (slow elimination) or all at once (fast elimination). Pozzulo and Lindsay found that elimination line-ups decreased false positive responding in children without significantly reducing correct identification. Fast-elimination line-ups, together with modified instructions emphasizing the negative consequences of identifying an innocent person and explaining how to make an absolute judgement (as opposed to a relative judgement), significantly decreased false positive rates to a level comparable to adults shown a simultaneous line-up.

Self-evidently then, here we have a methodology that could benefit from further research and which has direct implications for children as 'partners in the pursuit of justice' (Melton, 1992).

QUESTIONING

While it is true that even very young children can free-recall material accurately (Fivush, Haden, & Adams, 1995: Peterson, 1996), it is the case that they do not spontaneously provide much information in either free recall or in response to open questions (Ceci & Bruck, 1995; Fivush, 1993). As a result, interviewers have to resort to specific questions in order to elicit information. In fact, McGough and Warren (1994) have suggested up to 90% of all questions asked of suspected child abuse victims by US investigators were highly specific, mostly yes/no questions, and in the UK, Davies, Westcott, and Horan (2000) found, in a sample of *Memorandum* interviews, 55% of all questions were specific/non-leading and 40% were closed. Now, the problem about yes/no questions is that they can be highly suggestive or misleading. Is there any way out of this impasse?

It seems as if there is. An alternative type of specific question is the so-called 'wh-' question, in which the child is asked to specify a specific detail by being asked, for example: '*Who* was there?' '*What* did the man wear?' While both yes/no and wh- questions are specific questions, wh-format questions require the child to supply the sought-after information, whereas in the yes/no question the interviewer proposes the information and the child has to assent to or demur from it. Thus, these question types have different potentiality in terms of both misleadingness and the potential for veracity.

This differential potentiality has been looked at recently by Peterson, Dowden, and Tobin (1999). Three- to five-year-olds were engaged in a craft activity during which a staged event occurred, an adult spilling cereal all over the floor. One week later, the children were asked questions about actions, persons, and environments associated with the staged event. The questions could either be framed in a yes/no format or in a wh- question format.

One very important finding was that the frequency of 'I don't know' responses were given in 40% of cases of wh- questions but in only 5% of yes/no questions. Thus, clearly, children were discriminating about their knowledge when asked a wh- question, but not when they were asked a yes/no question. In terms of errors, collapsing across person, action and environment content, fewer errors followed the wh-questions than the yes/no questions. In terms of accuracy (excluding 'I don't know' responses), wh- questions' and yes questions (yes being the veridical, correct answer) were equivalent. However, when it is noted that the probability of being right on a yes/no question is 50% by chance, whereas the probability of being right on a wh- format question must be considerably less than 50% by chance, it can be concluded that wh- questions eventuate in greater accuracy.

This research offers a salutary lesson. With the *Memorandum of Good Practice* (Home Office, 1992) well established in England and Wales, its phased interviewing approach, which ends in specific questioning, still needs careful further attention. Peterson *et al.*'s (1999) research shows the issue of child questioning is far from closed and is in need of further research (see Michael Lamb, Yael Orbach, Kathleen Sternberg, Phillip Esplin, & Irit Hershkowitz, Chapter 9 in this book and Amanda Waterman & Mark Blades, Chapter 10 in this book for additional perspectives). We know from Hughes and Grieve (1980) and Waterman and Blades (Chapter 10 in this book) that young children will often respond yes to a yes/no nonsensical question. The current study shows they will also exhibit a response bias to answer yes to a sensible yes/no question—which is an error.

Peterson *et al.*'s (1999) error rates, together with the high proportion of 'I don't know' responses to wh- questions, suggests strongly that further research into this type of question should be pursued under more forensically relevant situations than were present in their study. Would the same clear findings of wh- question superiority over yes/no questions hold up under longer questioning sessions, concerning personally distressing content? We just don't know, but clearly this is an empirical question the answer to which we still don't have.

A PORTFOLIO OF RESEARCH IS NEEDED

While the quality and quantity of research into child witnesses is impressive, it has one basic flaw: almost none of it has been conducted with forensic child witnesses; that is, with witnesses or victims of actual crimes (but see Thomas Lyon, Chapter 16 in this book). To establish our knowledge base concerning child witnesses, such witnesses must be an integral part of our research. As Yuille (1993) points out, the critical question is whether eyewitness testimony, both recall and identification, is context dependent or independent. If the latter, then controlled laboratory methodology will suffice to generalize to real-life criminal situations. However, if the former, then emotional, environmental, and consequential context considerations become critical in making statements about child witness performance.

There are sufficient studies around in the adult witnessing literature to suggest that eyewitnessing is far from being context independent (Cutshall & Yuille, 1989; Yuille & Cutshall, 1986, 1989). In the light of these findings, there can be little doubt that controlled laboratory work must be supplemented by both archival and case study research. For earlier statements of this need, see Clifford (1978) and Clifford and Lloyd-Bostock (1984). This may be unpalatable because such research is both time consuming and difficult to analyse. But only when a combination of research methodologies all point in the same direction can we be certain of the knowledge base to which we make recourse when that prosecution or defence lawyer requests our services in the course of justice. I would contend that, at the moment, we just do not have sufficient evidence, of the right type, on the performance of child witnesses to draw any broad—far less narrow and focused—conclusions about their abilities in real criminal situations. This deficit must be rectified.

CONCLUSION

Boring (1963) argues that '. . . scientific truth . . . must come about by controversy . . . without fighting you get science nowhere . . .' (p. 68). I have taken the opportunity to raise a questioning voice concerning the development of opinion that is concerned to state that children's testimony is non-contentious and that their memories are every bit as good as adults. Hopefully, I have made the point that this is not unequivocally the case and that much work remains to be done at the methodological, procedural, complexity, and conceptual level if results are to become more consistent, consensual, and convincing. This may be seen as a controversial position in the current climate but it is a required position if the child who appears in the court is to remain protected and perceived properly.

REFERENCES

Banaji, M.R., & Crowder, R.G. (1989). The bankruptcy of everyday memory. *American Psychologist*, 44(9), 1185–93.

Boring, E. (1963). *The psychology of controversy*. New York: Academic Press.

Ceci, S.J., & Bruck, M. (1995). *Jeopardy in the courtroom: A scientific analysis of children's testimony*. Washington, DC: American Psychological Association.

Clifford, B.R. (1978). A critique of eyewitness research. In: M. Gruneberg, P. Morris, & R. Sykes (Eds), *Practical aspects of memory* (pp. 199–209). London: Academic Press.

Clifford, B.R. (1993). Witnessing: A comparison of adults and children. In: N. Clark & G. Stephenson (Eds), *Children, evidence and procedure issues in criminological and legal psychology* (No. 20, pp. 15–21). British Psychological Society (BPS) for the Division of Criminological and Legal Psychology (DCLP).

Clifford, B.R., & Lloyd-Bostock, S. (1984). Witness evidence: Conclusion and prospect. In: S. Lloyd-Bostock & B.R. Clifford (Eds), *Evaluating witness evidence* (pp. 285–90). Chichester, UK: Wiley.

Cutler, B.L., & Penrod, S. (1988). Improving the reliability of eyewitness identification: Line-up construction and presentation. *Journal of Applied Psychology*, 72, 629–37.

Cutshall, B.L., & Yuille, J.C. (1989). Field studies of eyewitness memory of actual crimes. In: D.C. Raskin (Ed.), *Psychological methods in criminal investigation and evidence* (pp. 97–124). New York: Springer-Verlag.

Davies, G.M., Westcott, H., & Horan, N. (2000). The impact of questioning style on the content of investigative interviews with suspected child sexual abuse victims. *Psychology, Crime and Law*, 6, 81–97.

Fivush, R. (1993). Developmental perspectives on autobiographical recall. In: G.S. Goodman & J. Hudson (Eds), *Understanding and improving children's testimony* (pp. 1–24). New York: Cambridge University Press.

Fivush, R., Haden, C., & Adams, S. (1995). Structure and coherence of pre-schoolers' personal narratives over time: Implications for childhood amnesia. *Journal of Experimental Child Psychology*, **60**, 32–56.

Goodman, G.S. (1991). On stress and accuracy in research on children's testimony: Commentary on Peters. In: J. Dorris (Ed.), *The suggestibility of children's recollections: Implications for eyewitness testimony* (pp. 77–82). Washington, DC: American Psychological Association.

Goodman, G.S., Quas, J.A., Batterman-Faunce, J.M., Riddlesberger, M., and Kuhn, J. (1997). Children's reactions to and memory for a stressful experience: Influences of age, knowledge, anatomical dolls, and parental attachment. *Applied Developmental Sciences*, **1**, 54–75.

Goodman, G.S., Rudy, L., Bottoms, B.L., & Aman, C. (1990). Children's concerns and memory: Issues of ecological validity in children's memory. In: R. Fivush & J. Hudson (Eds), *Knowing and remembering in young children* (pp. 249–84). New York: Cambridge University Press.

Heydon, J. (1984). *Evidence: Cases and materials* (2nd ed.). London: Butterworths. Home Office, & Department of Health. (1992). *Memorandum of good practice on video recorded interviews with child witnesses for criminal proceedings*. London: Her Majesty's Stationery Office.

Hughes, M., & Grieve, R. (1980). On asking children bizarre questions. *First Language*, **1**, 149–60.

Koriat, A., & Goldsmith, M. (1996). Memory metaphors and the real-life/laboratory controversy: Correspondence versus storehouse conceptions of memory. *Behavioural and Brain Sciences*, **19**, 167–228.

Lee, K., & Bussey, K. (1999). The effects of misleading and inconsistent post event information on children's recollections of criterion-learned information. *Journal of Experimental Child Psychology*, **73**, 161–82.

Lindsay, R.C.L., Lee, J.A., & Fulford, J.A. (1991). Sequential line up technique matters. *Journal of Applied Psychology*, **76**, 741–5.

Lindsay, R.C.L., Pozzulo, J.D., Craig, W., Lee, K., & Corber, S. (1997). Simultaneous line-ups, sequential line-ups and show-ups: Eyewitness identification decisions of adults and children. *Law and Human Behaviour*, **21**, 391–404.

McGough, L.S., & Warren, A.R. (1994). The all-important investigative interview. *Juvenile and Family Court Journal*, **45**, 13–29.

Melton, G.B. (1992). Commentary: Children as partners for justice: Next Steps for Developmentalists. In: G.S. Goodman, E.P. Taub, D.P.H. Jones, P. England, L.K. Port, L. Rudy, & L. Prado (Eds), *Testifying in criminal court: Monographs of the Society for Research in Child Development*, **57**, 5, (pp. 153–9).

Merritt, K.A., Ornstein, P.A., & Spicker, B. (1994). Children's memory for a salient medical procedure: Implications for testimony. *Pediatrics*, **94**, 17–23.

Ornstein, P.A. (1995). Children's long term retention of salient personal experiences. *Journal of Traumatic Stress*, **8**, 581–605.

Parker, J.F., & Ryan, V. (1993). An attempt to reduce guessing behaviour in children's and adult's eyewitness identifications. *Law and Human Behaviour*, **17**, 1–26.

Payne, D.C., Toglia, M.P., & Anastasi, J.S. (1994). Recognition performance level and the magnitude of the misinformation effect in eyewitness memory. *Psychonomic Bulletin & Review*, **1**, 376–82.

Peters, D.P. (1991a). The influence of stress and arousal on the child witness. In: J. Dorris (Ed.), *The suggestibility of children's recollections: Implications for eyewitness testimony* (pp. 60–70). Washington, DC: American Psychological Association.

Peters, D.P. (1991b). Commentary: Response to Goodman. In: J. Dorris (Ed.), *The suggestibility of children's recollections: Implications for eyewitness testimony* (pp. 86–91). Washington, DC: American Psychological Association.

Peterson, C. (1996). The pre-school child witness: Errors in accounts of traumatic injury. *Canadian Journal of Behavioural Science*, 28, 36–42.

Peterson, C., Dowden, C., & Tobin, J. (1999). Interviewing pre-schoolers: Comparisons of yes/no and wh- questions. *Law and Human Behaviour*, 23(5), 539–55.

Pozzulo, J.D., & Lindsay, R.C.L. (1998). Identification accuracy of children versus adults. A meta analysis. *Law and Human Behaviour*, 22, 549–70.

Pozzulo, J.D., & Lindsay, R.C.L. (1999). Elimination line-ups: An improved identification procedure for child witnesses. *Journal of Applied Psychology*, 84(2), 167–76.

Principe, G.F., Myers, J.T., Furtado, E.A., & Merritt, K.A. (1996). The relation between procedural information and young children's recall of an invasive medical procedure. Symposium presented at the Biennial Meeting of the Conference on Human Development, Birmingham, Alabama.

Steward, M.S., Steward, D.S., Farquhar, L., Myers, J.E., Reinhart, M., Welker, J., Joye, N., Driskill, J., & Morgan, J. (1996). Interviewing young children about body touch and handling. *Monograph of the Society for Research in Child Development*, 61, (4, Serial No. 248).

White, T.L., Leichtman, M.D., & Ceci, S.J. (1997). The good, the bad, and the ugly: Accuracy, inaccuracy, and elaboration in pre-schoolers' reports about a past event. *Applied Cognitive Psychology*, 11, S37–54.

Yuille, J.C., (1993). We must study forensic eyewitnesses to know about them. *American Psychologist*, 48(5), 572–3.

Yuille, J.C. & Cutshall, J.L. (1986). A case study of eyewitness memory of a crime. *Journal of Applied Psychology*, 71, 291–301.

Yuille, J.C. & Cutshall, J.L. (1989). Analysis of statements of victims, witnesses and suspects. In: J. C. Yuille (Ed.), *Credibility assessment* (pp. 175–91). Dordrecht, The Netherlands: Kluwer Academic.

CHAPTER 22

A Sociological Approach to Child Witness Research

CORINNE WATTAM

Department of Social Work, University of Central Lancashire,
Preston, UK

All knowledge, being an orderly vision, a vision of order, contains an interpretation of the world. It does not, as we often believe, reflect things as they are by themselves; things are, rather, called into being by the knowledge we have. (Bauman, 1990, p. 227)

In an area so predominantly charged with psychological experiment and the importance of recall, the rules of evidence, and legal texts, one could be forgiven for examining what sociology has got to do with witnessing at all. The purpose of this chapter is to demonstrate that a sociological perspective does have a role in the child witness field and to suggest that it is one which psychologists and lawyers may find relevant to their own work. Sociology in its more traditional guise can provide information on the context within which legal questions might be considered. However, I believe it can go further than that. Sociology is, as Bauman (1990) points out, also interested in interpretations of the world. Both law and psychology, as it is applied in legal settings, are also concerned with interpretation. The sociological perspective taken here treats interpretation as achieved through interaction, as situated and co-produced. This has consequences for all involved in the legal process and also for those involved in research which purports to be relevant to it.

Children's Testimony. Edited by H.L. Westcott, G.M. Davies, and R.H.C. Bull.
© 2002 John Wiley & Sons, Ltd.

SOCIOLOGY AS CONTEXT

Sociology is a broad discipline and there are a multitude of approaches within it, but, it has to be said, very little sociological attention has been paid to child witnesses. Even in the criminological literature, there has been a reluctance to address witnesses in general and child witnesses in particular. Criminological attention has been directed more at deviance, offending behaviour, sentencing, and prisons than to the child witness. There is an emerging interest in 'victims', particularly in relation to offences against the person, but this rarely stretches to the issue of witnessing (though see Rock, 1993).

Traditionally, the applied side of sociology has followed the path of mapping patterns and trends. Home Office statistics are available for analysis, although they are rarely interrogated in relation to child witnesses. Owing to the way that crime is recorded, it is very difficult to gain accurate data on how many offences are actually reported as perpetrated against children, how many are taken to court, and how many involve a child being considered as a potential witness or being a witness at trial. In general, we know that the bulk of reported offences are not cases involving children; for example, the Metropolitan Police Borough Based Crime Statistics for the third quarter of the financial year 1998/1999 show that of a total of 224,471 notifiable offences, 31,120 (14%) involved violence against the person and 1,890 were sexual offences (less than 1%). A proportion of these would have involved adults. Some research studies (Plotnikoff & Woolfson, 1995; 1996; Wattam, 1997) suggest that many child witnesses are victim witnesses involved in cases with sexual charges, others that they may be also be a bystander witness to a variety of other crimes (Flin, Bull, Boon, & Knox, 1993). Although relating to a different year, indications of the volume of *potential* child victim witness cases can be drawn from the Metropolitan Police Child Protection Team. In 1996, the CPT investigated 5,692 allegations of physical abuse, 3,536 allegations of sexual abuse, and 4,360 other allegations involving child abuse, a total of 13,588 allegations. Of these allegations, the person believed responsible was charged or summonsed in 991 cases, 289 were cautioned, and 3,703 cleared up in other ways. A general trend emerges so that cases involving child witnesses are in a minority among the range of crimes dealt with by the police and only a minority of those will end up in court.

THE SOCIAL CONSTRUCTION OF CHILD ABUSE

It is generally accepted that child abuse is a 'social construction' (Department of Health, 1995). In sociological terms, however, this assertion is also almost meaningless, since from one perspective it could be asserted that all that is known, or made sense of, is socially constructed. Thus, this is hardly a discovery. What is of interest, sociologically, are the ramifications of the social construction of the concept of child abuse in particular contexts (Parton, 1985, 1991; Parton, Thorpe, & Wattam, 1997; Wattam, 1996). The topic is far too large for this chapter. Here, I will summarize what I consider to be relevant to the child witness field.

In a book which focuses on False Memory Syndrome, Hacking (1995) attempts to tease out the difference between the concept of 'cruelty' to children which was customary language in Victorian times and 'child abuse', the modern manifestation of 'cruelty'. He proposes that cruelty is distinct from abuse in four different ways: class, evil, sex, and medicine.

In its English form, the anti-cruelty movement was founded on individual philanthropy and charity. Cruelty to children was seen primarily as a vice of the lower classes from which children required saving, and from which the rest of (middle-class) society should be protected. Child abuse, however, in its modern form is seen as a largely classless problem. While certain forms of child abuse are associated with the lower classes (e.g. severe neglect and perhaps some physical abuse), we are now more open to considering, particularly, sexual abuse as behaviour which occurs across all socio-economic groups. Once classless, child abuse becomes a problem that could be happening anywhere to any child. This is another context that jurors and professionals will bring to their interpretation of testimony.

The second difference has to do with evil. Hacking notes that cruelty to children was seen as a bad thing, even wicked, or despicable. In contrast, child abuse has become almost the greatest evil in private life. Its perpetrators are 'monsters', exiled from communities. This shift, from badness that can be decried but understood to evil which is inexplicable, is likely to be due to the association with sexual abuse, which was not an explicit element of child cruelty. Incest provokes feelings of revulsion and horror in a great many societies, a revulsion which has somehow spread to the general term of child abuse. Sexual abuse has, for many, become the very prototype of child abuse—certainly in Europe. The concept of evil, now reinforced by public outrage, is a further factor which people involved in the court process will bring to their judgement of testimony, however detached they may wish to be. The unfolding of testimony in child abuse cases brings with it an anticipation of worst-case scenarios that have become so familiar in the press.

Others, such as Parton (1985), have written about the medicalization of child abuse, particularly the way in which child abuse came to be constructed as a medical, individual, disease-like problem with the discovery of the 'battered baby syndrome'. The important point which Hacking draws out in addition to these observations is that medicalization and the scientific paradigm which came with it turned child abuse and the children who experience it into an object of knowledge. An object to be researched, studied, predicted, and so forth. It created certain types of persons, child abusers, 'abusing families', and child abuse became a cause of illness and harm.

This was a significant shift in understanding. What it did was demand that child abuse had consequences and that these should be measured. As a result, those who were interested in child abuse became what Hacking describes as 'consequentialists'; forever trying to discover and establish the negative results of such acts. It was not enough, as it was with cruelty, to say these acts are morally wrong. The current position is one which states it is only child abuse if it causes significant harm. This provides a further context in which testimony is judged. The child's testimony is enhanced by evidence of consequence, preferably medical consequences but most certainly some consequence—an emotional or relationship effect, a lack of educational attainment, low scores on a self-esteem test to name but a few. In short, if hearing about abuse, the jury expect to see a victim with all the signs that being a victim entails (see Blagg, 1989 for an account of the effects of the 'ideal victim' on intervention). If no signs are apparent, the jury may wonder whether abuse did occur. Thus, the way in which the concept of child abuse is operationalized in the language of public discourse, media, research, and policy provides a context which jurors and legal personnel bring to the court and have available as one resource for deciding on the truth in a child's testimony.

THE SOCIAL CONSTRUCTION OF CHILDHOOD

In the late 1980s, a renewed interest emerged in the concept of 'childhood' itself, perhaps best articulated by James and Prout (1990) as a new 'paradigm'. This paradigm argued against the dominant paradigm with its 'conceptual pair' of socialization and development representing childhood in a particular way: as 'natural, passive, incompetent and incomplete' (James & Prout, 1997). Children in sociology were practically non-existent except as subjects of socialization processes or in relation to their parents in statistical research (Qvortrup, 1997); passive receivers of culture or appendages to the adult world. James and Prout argued for an approach which took account of the agency of children, which reviewed children as people and childhood as a social category as being conceptually distinct. This important move stimulated a research agenda which has reached into children's health behaviour, school work, risk taking, and much more (e.g. see the projects funded under the United Kingdom's Economic and Social Research Council Childhood Programme). What is important for consideration of child witnesses is this emphasis on agency with its acceptance that children are not merely passive recipients of information or operating in a stimulus response-type manner, but rather are active, thinking, sense *making* inter-actors who co-produce the social world.

In addition to agency, the 'new paradigm' recognized the production of childhood as a social concept by the adult world. Historical analyses (Aries, 1973; Pollock, 1983; Hendrick, 1998) chart childhood as a differently perceived category over time. In particular, the length of childhood has increased considerably over the last century. One hundred years ago, for example, a 15-year-old girl complaining of sexual abuse in court would not have been viewed in quite the same way as it is in contemporary English-speaking countries, unless it was incestuous abuse. Others have turned their attention to the production of childhood in the present. Beck (1992), for example, considers that in a 'risk society' childhood is more valued than ever. This is because, in a time of change, discontinuity, relationship breakdown, and risk, children represent the future and a relationship that parents can depend on. Jenks (1996) suggests that childhood may also represent visions of nostalgia, more to do with romantic notions of the past. Whatever the case, generally it would be agreed that childhood is a social category which has a consistency and meaning over and above the individual children who pass through it. This socially constituted childhood contains expectations, ideal types, of how children 'should' be. Child witnesses cannot therefore be judged in isolation as if detached from childhood. The concept of childhood, rather, is drawn upon as a further resource for the assessment of validity and the co-production of 'truth'.

The co-production of childhood has implications for psychological research. Some of these have been pointed out in relation to universality. Critiques of orthodox developmental views are now almost orthodoxy themselves, particularly in relation to ethnocentrism. However, the co-production of childhood in witnessing research has not been challenged. Children are researched in age cohorts and compared to adult cohorts for certain characteristics such as recall ability, suggestibility, and reliability. Age cohort research assumes a developmental paradigm to the exclusion of all others. It does not take account of the agency and capacity of children and young people to master skills such as giving testimony. More importantly, it does not take into account the way in which childhood is co-produced by both adults and children.

Kitzinger (1997) considered the co-production of childhood in relation to child sexual abuse arguing that dominant expectations of childhood which view children as innocent, ignorant, and passive serve to make them attractive to abusers, to undermine the legitimacy of their natural responses (artful strategies of avoidance and coping) as deviance, and also to maintain 'adult-centric' constructions of childhood. Sexual violence to children is viewed as the 'the decay of childhood' (Seabrook, 1987) and 'childhood is treated rather like a rare animal threatened with extinction' (Kitzinger, 1997, p. 175). Those who must judge children's testimony are doing so in the context of such hopes, fears, and expectations that ideologies of childhood engender.

THE PLACE OF THE 'SOCIAL' IN LAW

Much of this section is drawn from the work of King and colleagues who have written on the place of child welfare in the legal process (King, 1990; King & Piper, 1995; King & Trowell, 1992; King, 1997). King himself begins from the work of the German social theorist, Nikolas Luhmann (1985), who makes a distinction between people (conscious systems) and society (social systems). The defining feature of social systems are their communications (this includes statements, theories, texts, explanations, decisions, and so forth, in effect everything that can be communicated by words). People are conceptualized as conscious systems, which may include thoughts, beliefs, ideas, streams of consciousness, conscience, and attitudes which exist and remain in an uncommunicated state. The concept of relevance, here, for the judgement of testimony is that of the system within which communications are heard and interpreted:

> Where consciousness is communicated, whether by words, gestures or actions, these communications and the meanings attributed to them will depend upon their interpretations within systems. (King, 1997, p. 27)

Both law and science are identifiable as contemporary, authorized systems which have their own ways of communicating. Before a communication can be recognized by a system, it has to be reproduced in the system's own terms. Systems and their discourses are autopoetic. This term, borrowed from biology, defines a way of communicating and understanding which is self-referential, translating everything into itself. The law has an autopoetic discourse and all other systems become 'enslaved' by it (when adopted into it). Thus, the social welfare discourse becomes interpreted by law, in legal terms, in the way the law 'thinks' (King & Piper, 1995).

Over the last three decades, the professional response to child sexual abuse has changed from a therapeutic/denial response to a criminalized/aware response (Wattam, 1992). In the UK and the USA (though less so in Europe), child sexual abuse is treated as a criminal issue. In order to be able to adjudicate on sexual offences against children, the laws needed 'clear evidence'. The primary source of evidence turns out to be, in the majority of cases, the child victim herself. Thus, following King's line, the laws looked to science (medicine and psychology) since these are the closest referents to its own way of thinking in order to determine rules and procedures for understanding the communications of children. In Britain, some may argue that it did produce a hybrid— the *Memorandum of good practice* (Home Office & Department of Health, 1992), a strange document for psychologists and lawyers alike, and one which has a different meaning again for social workers, families of victims, and victims themselves. Psychology has been very successful in establishing legal communication about child witnesses. This is, I suggest, because psychology has a parallel process (though not the same) for screening out the 'noise', reducing the complexity which is offered by experimental methodology. Indeed, that is what experiments are about, isolating dependent and independent variables, to produce scientifically validated proof. This is language that the law can understand.

SOCIOLOGICAL 'THINKING'

Despite centuries of philosophical debate, lawyers, juries, judges, and members of the public have little doubt about their ability to get to the truth of the matter. Sometimes, they may be wrong, but they would never maintain that the truth could not be 'got'. The problem to be resolved has less to do with what is truth and more to do with enhancing, developing, and improving the methods by which the truth might be sought; methods such as DNA testing, expert evidence, use of video techniques, medical examinations, and so forth. These 'practices of truth-finding' (Scheppele, 1994) provide a means of glossing over the moral or social issues in law. At the heart of the legal process are competing versions of events, which must be resolved one way or another (Pollner, 1975). The law cannot cope with two, or three or four or more 'truths'. It must adjudicate on one truth: the facts.

While there are legal rules of evidence which circumscribe questioning and appropriate behaviour in court, these do not wholly cover the issue of truth formation or presentation. Atkinson and Drew (1979) propose that witnesses are approached in ways which build up their credibility or in ways which are designed to discredit their testimony, which, while structured by the conventions of courtroom practices, depend on considerably more for their interpretative value. The examples they give, through a conversation analysis approach, are: the way in which silences can be interpreted depending on the place in the sequence of questioning, the management of accusations, denials, and blame; the way in which these can be prospectively managed by both counsel and witnesses, the use of expected response types to infer motive or culpability (such as where accusations may expectedly precede denials, justifications, and the like); and the way in which other activities (such as accusation and blame) are accomplished through accepted questioning techniques. These features are the 'locally managed', rather than procedurally given, aspects of testimony, which underpin its co-production.

RELEVANT EVIDENCE FOR PRACTICAL PURPOSES

There are legal definitions about evidence and what is considered relevant evidence. To understand what is relevant in a strictly legal sense is a matter of applying the legal 'rules'. What I want to direct attention to here is something of how the 'rules' are applied in practice; for example, consider the following extract from a case file:

> The only piece of corroborative evidence we have is when the mother administers cream because of damage to the complainant's private parts, although the mother's statement gives no detail of what injury the child has.

The only way this works as 'corroborative evidence' is by proposing that mothers can be expected to tend to their children when ill—put cream where it hurts. This is not the application of rules in its formal sense, such that we might say in every case where a child is hurt the mother might be expected to tend to the child. That is inexhaustable and clearly not the case (Suchman, 1987). This has to be a case-by-case, situation-specific matter—in another case, the reverse may be argued depending on the circumstances. Relevant facts must attain a status of relevance, and they do so by the application of what could be termed the day-to-day rules of human conduct. As such, they amount to a number of peculiar, idiosyncratic, relevant-on-this-occasion matters.

Underpinning the evidence in the majority of child witness cases is the fact that the complainant is a child. Thus, the usual rules about admissibility of evidence concerning a complaint apply, but in addition the 'reliability' of the child as complainant becomes an issue. There is an extensive amount of research literature on the reliability of children, most of which seeks to show how reliable children are in relation to adults (Spencer & Flin, 1993). Very little rigorous research attention has hitherto been paid, however, to the way in which the reliability of children is used as a topic and resource in the construction of evidence concerning them.

Judging reliability is a practical problem in everyday life. It becomes particularly relevant to all cases where the main evidence is the testimony (the account, the words and *how* they are spoken, by whom) of the alleged 'victim'. Such cases also include adult sexual offences, racial harassment, and others, and, while my concern here is solely with offences against children, the practical 'troubles' are generic. A question central to the task of assessing witness reliability is also central to judging reliability in other contexts. How is it known in a practical, everyday sense, that information given to us comes from a reliable source? One way in which this is done is through the activity of categorization and category incumbent behaviours (Sacks, 1992). For an account of an event, for example, the category of 'people who were there' might be considered relevant. Something would also need to be known about particular persons' viewpoints; are they going to give a biased version of events? Thus, it would be important to know other identity descriptions such as age, gender, ethnicity, or occupation; descriptions which could give information about a possible way of interpreting and recounting the event. This is not to say that any of these descriptions necessarily bias statements one way or another, but merely to suggest that in practice they can operate as criteria for assessing the judgements of others in relation to our own. There are other identity descriptions, such as degree of interrelationship—a different account might be expected from a friend, for example, rather than from a reporter—all of which might influence the interpretation of reliability attributed to the account. Reliability will be achieved, in part, by this kind of categorization of information source. Thus, an assessment of source reliability is a resource for interpretation and co-production of 'truth'.

The following is an extract from a trial which exemplifies this process in action:

B2:   You have been giving your mum a terrible time lately. Swearing, shouting, staying out late.

C: I don't swear

B2: Just so the judge knows what your answers are, have you been swearing at your mum?

C: No.

B2: Have you been staying out late?

C: *Yes.*

B2: Have you got into trouble with your mum for staying out late?

C: Yes.

B2: Has your mum smacked you?

C: Yes.

B2: Have you said to her that you'll have her put away? You see what I have to suggest *C* is that it's all lies.

C: It's not.

Here, *B2* is the barrister for the defence and *C* is the child witness. In this trial transcript, the barrister is asking questions which directly pertain to the child's way of behaving, in general. Does she swear, get into trouble, stay out late, and act in a way which warrants a smack. If she does all these things, her reliability is immediately called into question, in front of a jury. The barrister explains the relevance of his questioning by using the words 'you see', as in I see it and I expect you to see it and any other relevant person to see it, that, in the context of these kinds of behaviours, lying might also be expectable. It is not the reliability of children that is at issue, not even this individual child, but the reliability of *this* child, for *this* time, about *these* charges, on *this* occasion. Something which could not, for all possible cases, be subject to research or legislation. This should not simply be interpreted as a complaint, or moral indictment on our legal system—or even this lawyer. It is but one small example of a routinely recurring process, which must occur where the testimony of a person is the main or central evidence in a case—not because of the 'legal system', 'bad practice', or personal financial gain ('we're only doing our job') but because these are some of the specific, occasioned, and locally situated practices for judging reliability in any place and no other method has been, or could be, developed to meet the requirement of doing this work.[1] The extract is a clear example of the way in which the accusations and blame that Atkinson and Drew (1979) describe are co-produced through accepted questioning techniques.

---

[1] I have a number of reservations about Statement Validity Analysis and have written about them elsewhere (Wattam, 1992). The proposition that 'real time' locally situated and occasioned practices can be mathematicized and formulated as 'scientific' criteria is one which, while achievable, and achieved if the research and literature around SVA or CBCA is taken as an instance of it, is necessarily a gloss on practical reasoning. For a review of the history and development of SVA and CBCA, see Vrij (2000).

How reliable a child will be becomes a topic for consideration, talking about, giving evidence of. The child's reliability is not only a resource for interpreting the evidence, it becomes part of the evidence itself. Reliability can be achieved through certain attributes which are looked for in witness assessments; for example, consider this description from a legal letter:

> In this particular case the girls are unlikely to be impressive witnesses. Firstly there are inconsistencies in their own accounts both inherently and when compared with each other. That inconsistency probably reflects the fact that the girls are probably unwilling to tell the entire truth which is that they were content to permit indecencies for money and were prepared to return for such indecencies to continue.

The criteria in this example is 'consistency'. It is used both as a resource—to assess whether the girls are telling the truth—and a topic—as evidence of a potential truth that they were 'content to permit indecencies for money'. In legal-case files, the testing out of reliability is accounted for as a routine matter formulated as a request for a witness assessment. While much of the research literature examines the reliability of children in terms of age-related typical abilities or characteristics, the examples in my research materials suggested (as in the case above) that much has to do with the impression given by the child (Wattam, 1992). Again, it is not about children, in general, being reliable or not. What is being considered is impression formation; how the impression of being reliable is co-produced and locally managed. In the extract above, however, this co-production is not acknowledged; accounts were generally read as given and judged as (one-sided) versions of events.

In the event of assessed unreliability and the lack of other evidence, the allegation, the claim, will not be publicly put or adjudicated. Any intrinsic or 'real' reliability (if such a thing could ever be established) of a child is less central than the way in which relevant features of a case combine to give a sense of reliability or not. This is particularly disadvantageous for disabled children who may be prejudged as unreliable on the basis of their disability alone (Westcott & Cross, 1996)

A further trouble is that of competing versions of 'reality'. Effectively, if a case is going to court it means that there are at least two competing versions of reality to be presented: that of the defendant and that of the witness. Ultimately, one of these must be decided on. There are many situations in everyday life where people might claim competing versions of reality (Pollner, 1975). In some situations, this is of little consequence, the upshot may just be some informal agreement to see the world differently. There are situations where such 'reality disjunctures' can be, and are, left in abeyance; for example, watching a film and wondering whether it was a true story. However, the import of deciding on versions in legal settings, including videotaped interviews with children, is that they must be available to be decided—they must be presented in a way which makes them decidable; that is, for each specific occasion upon which it becomes relevant to decide: for this case, in this place, at this time. For the (legal) world's practical purposes, there is a compelling need to explicitly specify 'what really happened'.

Child testimony is open to choice and a choice must be made. Each side supports their evidence by drawing on empirically correct conclusions. However, Pollner suggests this creates further difficulties:

> Competitive versions equally satisfy (and, with respect to one another, fail to satisfy) the demands for empirical validation and empirically correct conclusions. Thus, a choice between them cannot be made compelling in empirical or logical terms alone for the choice is between empirically and logically self-validating and self-sustaining systems. (Pollner, 1975, p. 419)

Because there is often very little other evidence, children's (co-produced) accounts become the object of the choice which must be made. Those presenting the testimony do not have to make this choice—for them the choice is already made. Rather, it is the jury that must do so. Once deciding to accept one version over another, the juror becomes 'converted' to a particular way of thinking (about this particular case). Just as where reality disjunctures are resolved in other settings by a 'conversion of commitments', here the juror becomes 'converted':

> He is now their experiential colleague. He is collegial in his subscription to their version of 'what really happened' and in **its use for exposing and characterizing the subjective, specious or otherwise faulted methods upon which his previous claims and experiences were presumptively predicated**. (Pollner, 1975, pp. 419–20, my emphasis)

An element of legal work is to achieve this conversion, and the methods for working towards this achievement are very similar to those outlined by Pollner as methods used routinely in everyday and other settings to discredit one version over another. What can be seen in the earlier trial transcript is an attempt to characterize subjective, specious, or otherwise faulted methods which may be presented as methods employed by, or which characterize, the giver of the version to be discredited. The work of compiling acceptable child witness testimony, including, importantly, assessments of witness potential performance, characteristics, and 'impression formation', is the work of probing whether such 'subjective', 'specious', or 'faulted' methods will be made in court.

CONCLUSION

A tacit acknowledgement of the importance of the co-production of accounts is provided by research which examines interviewer reliability as well as child reliability. It continues to employ the same experimental methods, however, detached from situated local settings, to discover the generalizable and typical features of reliability in relation to children and, now, interviewing style. This is without consideration of how the problems of interpretation of testimony may be situated within the process of giving testimony rather than a priori within specific events or characteristics and behaviour of either the interviewer or the witness.

One fundamental starting point for the appropriation of psychological research into the law is the 'typical case': what can be typically known about children's abilities in relation to talking reliably about events in which they have been involved. This typicality is generated through numbers and replicability. Law can then contrast this to the circumstances of the individual children it has to deal with: Would a normal child under these circumstances do X? No amount of research on the typical child will, however, cover what Garfinkel (1967, 1992) referred to as the 'this's and that's'. These are the situated and specific features of testimony which occur on a case-by-case basis. Not unique, but uniquely played out in each case.

Research which examines the typicality of children's 'true' statements and the general level of memory reliability in recalling events ignores the central principles of the co-production of accounts and the situated achievement of meaning for each and every occasion. In making children ever more available to the criminal justice system, children are made ever more available to the resolution of what is a lawyer's trouble—providing for the sufficiency of evidence for practical purposes on each occasion of relevance—which may, incidentally, have quite damaging effects, particularly where the child as a source of reliability suffers such things as 'character assassination', accusation of lying, and disbelief in a public legal setting (Keep, 1996). These are not matters to be resolved by the use of video, or video link, the use of interlocuters, or even pre-trial hearings. They are features inherent to the social organization of evidence giving and yet relatively little of this is made overt, studied, or reflected upon in relation to child witnesses.

REFERENCES

Aries, P. (1973). *Centuries of childhood*. Harmondsworth, UK: Penguin.
Atkinson, J.M., & Drew, P. (1979), *Order in Court: the organisation of verbal interaction in judicial settings*. Basingstoke, UK: Macmillan.

Bauman, Z. (1990). *Thinking sociologically*. Oxford: Blackwell.

Beck, U. (1992). *Risk society: Towards a new modernity*. London: Sage.

Blagg, H. (1989). Fighting the sterotypes—'ideal' victims in the inquiry process. In: C. Wattam, J. Hughes, & H. Blagg (Eds), *Child sexual abuse: Listening, hearing and validating the experiences of children*. Chichester, UK: Wiley.

Department of Health. (1995). *Child protection: Messages from research*. London: Her Majesty's Stationery Office.

Flin, R., Bull, R., Boon, J., & Knox, A. (1993). Child witnesses in Scottish criminal trials. *International Review of Victimology*, **2**, 309–29.

Garfinkel, H. (1967 [1974]). Suicide for all practical purposes. In: R. Turner (Ed.), *Ethnomethodology* (pp. 96–101). Harmondsworth, UK: Penguin.

Garfinkel, H. (1992). *Studies in ethnomethodology* (2nd ed.). Cambridge: Polity Press.

Hacking, I. (1995). *Rewriting the soul. Multiple personality and the sciences of memory*. Princeton, NJ: University Press.

Hendrick, H. (1998). *Children, childhood and English society, 1880–1990*. Cambridge University Press.

Home Office, & Department of Health. (1992). *Memorandum of good practice on video recorded interviews with child witnesses for criminal proceedings*. London: Her Majesty's Stationery Office.

James, A., & Prout, A. (1990). *Constructing and reconstructing childhood*. London: Falmer Press.

James, A., & Prout, A. (1997). *Constructing and reconstructing childhood* (2nd ed.). London: Falmer Press.

Jenks, C. (1996). *Childhood*. London: Routledge.

Keep, G. (1996). *Going to Court: Child witnesses in their own words*. London: ChildLine.

King, M. (1990). Child welfare within law: The emergence of a hybrid discourse. *Journal of Law and Society*, **18**(3).

King, M., & Piper, C. (1995). *How the law thinks about children* (2nd ed.). Aldershot, UK: Arena.

King, M., & Trowell, J. (1992). *Children's welfare and the law: The limits of legal intervention*. London: Sage.

King, M. (1997). *A better world for children? Explorations in morality and authority*. London: Routledge.

Kitzinger, J. (1997). Who are you kidding? Children, power and the struggle against sexual abuse. In: A. James, & A. Prout (Eds), *Constructing and reconstructing childhood* (2nd ed.). London: Falmer Press.

Luhmann, N. (1985). *A sociological theory of law*. London: Routledge.

Parton, N. (1985). *The politics of child abuse*. Basingstoke, UK: Macmillan.

Parton, N. (1991). *Governing the family*. London: Routledge.

Parton, N., Thorpe, D., & Wattam, C. (1997). *Child protection: Risk and the moral order*. Basingstoke, UK: Macmillan.

Plotnikoff, J., & Woolfson, R. (1995). *Prosecuting child abuse: An evaluation of the government's speedy progress policy*. London: Blackstone Press.

Plotnikoff, J., & Woolfson, R. (1996). *Evaluation of witness service support for child witnesses*. London: Victim Support.

Pollner, M. (1975) 'The very coinage of your brain': The anatomy of reality disjunctures. *Philosophy of Social Science*, **5**, 411–30.

Pollock, L.A. (1983). *Forgotten children*. Cambridge University Press.

Qvortrup, J. (1997). A voice for children in statistical and social accounting: A plea for children's right to be heard. In: A. James, & A. Prout (Eds), *Constructing and reconstructing childhood* (2nd ed.). London: Falmer Press.

Rock, P. (1993). *The social world of an English Crown Court*. Oxford: Clarendon.

Sacks, H. (1992). *Lectures on conversation* (Vols I and II). Oxford: Blackwell.

Scheppele, K.L. (1994). Practices of truth-finding in a court of law: The case of revised stories. In: J.I. Kitsuse & T.R. Sarbin (Eds), *Constructing the social*. Thousand Oaks: Sage.

Seabrook, J. (1987). The decay of childhood. *New Statesman*, 10 July 1987, pp. 14–15.

Spencer, J., & Flin, R. (1993). *The evidence of children: The law and the psychology* (2nd ed.). London: Blackstone Press.

Suchman, L. (1987). *Plans and situated actions: The problem of human–machine communication*. Cambridge University Press.

Vrij, A. (2000). *Detecting lies and deceit. The psychology of lying and the implications for professional practice*. Chichester, UK: Wiley.

Wattam, C. (1992). *Making a case in child protection*. Chichester, UK: Wiley.

Wattam, C. (1996). Child abuse troubles. PhD thesis, Lancaster University.

Wattam, C. (1997). Is the criminalisation of child harm and injury in the interests of children? *Children and Society*, **11**, 97–107.

Westcott, H., & Cross, M. (1996). *This far and no further: Towards ending the abuse of disabled children*. Birmingham, UK: Venture Press.

CHAPTER 23

Remembering the Point: A Feminist Perspective on Children's Evidence

LIZ KELLY

Child and Woman Abuse Studies Unit, University of North London, London, UK

This chapter is a development of musings on what precisely a feminist critique or perspective on children's evidence might be. It is an expansion of a paper delivered at a seminar[1] for which each participant had to list their three main areas of interest, mine were: the historical and continuing questioning of children and women's credibility as witnesses with respect to sexual crime; the abject failure of policy to effectively prosecute abusers; and the focus in much of the literature and research on technicalities, rather than power and ideology. These three themes form the backbone of this chapter. At the outset though, it is necessary both to clarify certain terms and perspectives, and to recall and reflect on the critical moments which have informed contemporary discussions about children's evidence.

---

[1] The first version of this chapter was presented in October 1998 in Milton Keynes at the Research Seminar series *Understanding and Improving Children's Eyewitness Testimony*, supported by the British Psychological Society.

Children's Testimony. Edited by H.L. Westcott, G.M. Davies, and R.H.C. Bull.
© 2002 John Wiley & Sons, Ltd.

WHAT HAS FEMINISM GOT TO DO WITH IT?

It is not necessarily obvious, especially to those who neither use a feminist perspective nor have access to an accurate account of feminist contributions to understandings of sexual abuse, what a feminist critique/perspective might have to offer. The simplest response would be that feminism has something to say about every and any issue: in the words of a feminist cliché from the 1970s 'every issue is a women's issue'. But over the last three decades, feminism has become an increasingly complex and varied body of intellectual thought (Bell & Klein, 1996; Humm, 1992) as well as an arena of innovation with respect to policy and practice. In the UK and internationally, it has been feminist work—intellectual and practical—which has placed violence against women and also, to a significant extent, against children back at the centre of public policy and debate (Kelly, 1999).

Women's lives and experiences have always been a central focus for feminists, but it is important to note that early Women's Liberation writings in the 1970s contained impassioned pieces about children's liberation (Firestone, 1972), and much of the personal practice of feminists has involved exploring how childhoods, for girls and boys, could be lived differently. This interest in, and concern for, children also translated into more public actions, such as shared childcare nurseries which began from a set of assumptions about treating children with respect, promoting anti-sexism and anti-racism (Comer, 1974). It is easy, at the start of the new millennium, to forget just how visionary and challenging early feminist thinking and actions were, and how many of the ideas, which were regarded with derision and hostility 30 years ago, are now accepted mainstream policy and practice. It is not an exaggeration to claim that feminist thinking and practice with respect to children pre-figured shifts in thinking about children's rights and provision for children.

Certain currents within feminism have, therefore, consistently worked with the concepts of gender and generation.[2] Within this, there has always been a tension between the necessity in the 1970s to disaggregate women's interests, conceptually and in terms of practical social policy, from those of children and the family (Barrett & MacIntosh, 1982) while recognizing the continuing reality that women's and children's fates are inextricably connected. The challenge

---

[2] This is of necessity an oversimplified account. There were, and remain, tensions and debates between feminists about the position and role of children. Some of the early writings and activities drew more on a concern to free women from responsibility for children and childcare, whereas others had deeper analysis of children's social positioning.

both in theory and in practice continues to be how to simultaneously recognize that women and children's lives are currently intertwined, at the same time as avoiding conflating women and children's interests.

The re-discovery of sexual abuse in childhood can be dated from the 1970s. It was returned to the public and professional agendas through a potent combination of survivors' testimonies, feminist writing, service provision, and social research (Finkelhor, 1979; Kelly, 1988). 'Re-discovery' is the appropriate concept here, since sexual abuse of children was a matter of intense scrutiny in the late 19th century. Then, as more recently, it was feminists who were among the first to dare to hear, and publicly testify to, the brutal ways in which some children were treated. Linda Gordon, in *Heroes of their own lives* (1988), argues that sexual abuse emerges into the public arena at times where there is both a strong women's movement and strategic alliances between feminists and child welfare organizations. Judith Herman, a feminist clinician, comments on her involvement in this process in the America:

> Because of my involvement with the women's movement, I was able to speak out about the denial of women's real experiences in my own profession and testify to what I had witnessed. My first paper on incest, written with Lisa Hirschman in 1976, circulated 'underground' in manuscript, for a year before it was published. We began to receive letters from all over the country from women who had never before told their stories. Through them, we realised the power of speaking the unspeakable and witnessed first hand the creative energy that is released when the barriers of denial and repression are lifted. (Herman, 1994, p. 2)

Feminists did not, however, limit their activity to breaking the silence but also developed new and innovative forms of provision. The starting point was consciousness-raising groups in which women not only shared accounts of their lives, but also analysed them and took action to create change in their own and other women's lives. These actions included, among other things, 'speak-outs' where survivors gave public voice to their violation and local support services including telephone helplines and self-help support groups—each is a precursor of forms of response and provision which are now considered essential elements of support for child and adult survivors of sexual abuse.

Many of the adult survivors of sexual abuse who were encouraged and enabled to speak out through a variety of feminist activities were motivated by at least two ambitions: to break a silence which had consigned them to isolation and self-blame and to challenge the silence which created a context of impunity for abusers. These early personal testimonies contain calls to listen to today's children, to find ways to enable them to tell sooner rather than later, and for abusers to be called to account (Armstrong, 1978).

As practice developed through the 1970s, a set of principles for support work emerged, which still inform feminist practice in institutions like refuges (shelters) and rape crisis lines. These can be summarized as: belief; respect; prioritizing safety; returning as much choice and control as possible to the individual who has been victimized; offering both practical and emotional support; and challenging self-blame through placing responsibility on the perpetrator.

The principle of believing women and children was profoundly radical and challenging in the early 1970s. The notion that women and children routinely lie about sexual violence was endemic at this point, to the extent that it was encoded in law in the UK (and many other common-law jurisdictions) through the corroboration warning—that it was dangerous to convict a man of rape on the uncorroborated word of a woman or child (see Edwards, 1996 for more detailed discussion). While at a formal level, the denial of credibility to women and children as victim witnesses is no longer so explicit, residues remain and have been the fertile ground on which the concept of 'false memory syndrome'[3] has been developed and promoted.

The fundamental contention of this chapter is that the history of denying credibility to women and children lies at the heart of the debates and issues concerning children's evidence. One of the implications of this argument is that there can be no scientific or technical approach which will provide a resolution of debates which are at root political and ideological. The reason children's evidence is so deeply contested is not due to fundamental (or even smaller) differences in the capabilities and understandings of children as compared to adults, rather these arguments serve to deflect direct attention to, while also making more palatable, the continued resonances of centuries of disbelief and suspicion of children who accused adults (usually men) of sexual crimes. If this were not the case, then the concerns about children's evidence would have extended to every and all contexts in which children appear as witnesses in legal contexts. But the international literature is replete with discussions on children's evidence *about* sexual crime (as this book also demonstrates).

Remembering the Point

The initial professional response to the re-discovery of sexual abuse was to stress the importance of listening to and believing children, and an

---

[3] This is not a recognized diagnostic syndrome, but rather an invention of a group of accused parents in the USA (see Cossins, 1999 for a detailed discussion).

ambition to create a 'child centred practice' emerged (MacLeod & Saraga, 1988). This simple and obvious message (a reflection of already established feminist practice) was communicated much more widely in the UK through the Childwatch programmes in the mid-1980s which were to be followed by the establishment of ChildLine in 1986. At the time, few professionals or activists had the prescience to imagine just how much of a challenge listening to children, and believing their accounts of sexual victimization, would be to the status quo, or the multitude of ways in which this practice principle would be resisted and challenged.

For almost two decades, an unresolved tension in jurisdictions with adversarial legal systems has been whether criminal prosecutions or civil child protection processes are the most effective and/or appropriate legal route for child sexual abuse cases. The debate has many elements to it, but in the context of this discussion both require some form of evidence and often some form of account from the child before any legal process can be undertaken. Whether the primary concern of practitioners was child protection or justice, all have had to develop methods for enabling children to tell about their experiences.

The initial discussions about children's evidence were, therefore, framed within two connected concerns: understanding how children tell and the contexts which encouraged disclosure; and how to gather evidence which would enable legal processes to be instituted. At this point, there was an implicit presumption that where cases could enter the legal system, the truths which children were struggling to tell would be self-evident. This optimism, some might say with hindsight naivety, was rapidly undermined as it became clear how ill suited legal practices and procedures were to listening to children, and how far they systematically disadvantaged children who told about crimes committed against them (Droisen & Driver, 1989). Children were expected to cope with a formalized adult world which many adults find confusing and intimidating.

While the implications of these discoveries were being absorbed, a successive series of events and crises in the UK were to foreshorten the exploration and set the terms of the debate for more than a decade. Beginning with Cleveland in 1987 and moving through Nottingham in 1991/1992 and Orkney 1993/1994 (with additional less publicized cases in between), the professional and public policy agenda was determined not by how children tell and whether children had been abused—in Cleveland and Nottingham at least this was not disputed in at least some (and in Nottingham all) cases—but by a 'moral panic' about the powers and competencies of professionals to intervene in children's lives (Campbell, 1988). The discovery and creation of new forms of investigation,[4] alternative methods of hearing children's testimony and adapting procedural rules, and the reform processes initiated in many countries in the 1980s were rapidly overshadowed by a return to questions about the accuracy and credibility of children's evidence, albeit via concerns about the actions of professionals.

Children's accounts and ways of telling have never 'fitted' easily into adversarial legal frameworks, and as the framework for child protection investigations became increasingly legalistic this was even more evident.[5] Some commentators understood at the time that these were profound challenges to the status quo within the legal system and to the permissions which had existed for centuries which allowed the majority of child sex abusers to act with impunity (Armstrong, 1994). Many, however, embarked upon a search for quick fixes—technological and procedural changes which would resolve (or sidestep) the issue of credibility. As a direct consequence, a new research agenda emerged within psychology that had children's capacity for truthfulness, the accuracy of their memory and recall as its point of departure. It is also worth noting that many of the methods which purported to offer solutions were developed by psychologists.

The search by lawyers and other professionals for methods which could make 'scientific' assessments of the veracity of statements shows how quickly the discourse moved from listening to and believing children to listening to and (possibly) believing adults who claimed to be able to assess credible from incredible accounts.[6]

But what is an 'incredible' account? Every practitioner and researcher in this field has at least one story of how their credibility has been stretched and challenged by accounts of children and/or adult survivors. We did not want to believe that babies were raped—but now

---

[4] It is interesting to note that the first joint investigation process between police and social workers in the UK in Bexley had its origins in divergences of approach between the two agencies. Social work had moved towards a listening and believing framework, whereas the police were still operating from a position of scepticism (Kelly & Regan, 1990). This incompatibility of approach between police and other professionals was also a key factor in the Cleveland and Nottingham cases (Campbell, 1988).

[5] It has always been our contention (see Kelly & Regan, 1990) that the problem was never multiple interviews as such—such a process might in fact be helpful for small children and children with disabilities who find concentrating for long periods difficult—but rather the content and style of interviewing. One interview in which the child is badgered and undermined is likely to be far more damaging than a series of three or four short interviews which are designed to create conditions in which they are enabled to tell their story.

[6] I am aware that there are a variety of methods available and that some make less grandiose claims than others. The point here is not the relative claims of each, or even the methods used, but rather the speed at which the voices of adult 'experts' came to drown out the voices of children.

know there are cases where the medical evidence is incontrovertible. We did not want to believe that children were repeatedly and sadistically sexually abused—but there have been convictions for precisely this (e.g. in the Nottingham case, see Cook & Kelly, 1997; Nelson, 1998). We did not want to believe that there was a thriving, if small-scale, market and industry for child pornography—but it is increasingly there for all to see on the Internet (Hughes, 1999). We did not want to believe that two generations of children were systematically abused in countless children's homes—but this reality is now inescapable (Utting, Baines, Stuart, Rowlands, & Vialva, 1997). We did not want to believe stories of sexual slavery, sexual torture, murder—but how else do we describe the West and Dutroux cases (Kelly, 1998)? While there were arguably compelling reasons for academics, practitioners, and lawyers to seek scientific support for children's accounts, the issues and debates appear to have become separated from the indisputable evidence of confirmed cases which have moved the boundaries of credibility.

There is also another story which could be told here—a story of research and advocacy done in bad faith, whose sole intention has been to undermine the voices of children and adult survivors who have dared to question 'the rule of the fathers' (Armstrong, 1994; Breckenridge & Laing, 1999). The most telling example here has been the promotion of the concept of 'false memory', as if it were an established clinical category. In fact, it has no such status or recognition (Cossins, 1999), but the rapidity with which it became ubiquitous in media discussions of, and legal cases about, child sexual abuse from the early 1990s is yet further evidence of the continued legacy of the denial of credibility to children who accuse adults of sexual victimization.

It has always been a key theme in feminist practice to treat women and children with respect. Unfortunately, this principle does not hold true inside adversarial criminal processes, indeed the opposite is often the case. The tone and content of the examination of children's evidence is seldom respectful, and too few lawyers—including the prosecution—have adjusted their language and demeanour to take account of the age and abilities of individual children (Westcott, 1995). Rather, they still choose to use their adult and professional status to intimidate and attempt to confuse the child.

The centrality of safety has informed feminist work from the outset, through creating contexts in which women and children were able to speak out—such as helplines and institutions like refuges/shelters/safe houses. Alongside this has been the development of a perspective that women (and children) cannot be expected to report and pursue prosecution if they are not protected: in most interpersonal violence cases, be they rape, domestic violence or child sexual abuse, the victim–witness is having to give evidence against someone who knows them, sometimes intimately. This is further compounded by the intimidatory context of having to give evidence in court. The lack of fit between the criminal and civil law systems in the UK ensures that protection is often not assured for children, and the extent to which children have access to court preparation varies hugely. Arrangements for children to give evidence behind screens or via video-link have been attempts to create more security and safety for children. The defendant was prevented from cross-examining the child in person in England and Wales in 1988, in the Criminal Justice Act.[7] But with the exception of the last example, the provision of these protections has been variable (Westcott, 1995), and, more importantly, barristers frequently decide on the day that they would prefer the child to give evidence in open court (Plotnikoff & Woolfson, 1995). Thus, assurances which may have been given to the child about how they will give evidence are undermined by the personal preferences of powerful lawyers.

Procedural changes in the Youth Justice and Criminal Evidence Act 1999 will, hopefully, ensure more consistency in how children are treated.[8]

Extending the Focus

It is revealing, but not surprising, that only two of the contributions in this book focus exclusively on children's experiences/perspectives. It has always been a core principle of feminist research and practice to respect the voices and experiences of women and children. The case examples outlined below demonstrate that, despite two decades of reform, the experiences of children in court are all too frequently lessons in injustice, in inhumanity, and disrespect. These cases have

---

[7] Cross-examination by the accused was still allowed in the case of adult rape victims, and a number of high profile cases in the mid-1990s prompted widespread outrage. Commitments were given from the then Conservative government and the Labour Party election manifesto in 1997 that this would be rapidly corrected. The provision was not, however, introduced until the 1999 Youth Justice and Criminal Evidence Act.

[8] The Act introduces a raft of measures to enable 'vulnerable and intimidated' witnesses to give their best evidence (Home Office, 1998); these are being introduced in an incremental way following extensive legal training (Home Office, 2000). Children are specified within the legislation and the expectation is that they will automatically benefit from many of the possible protections. But the letter, intention, and implementation of law do not always correspond.

been chosen to extend the discussion to other contexts in which children may have to give evidence about violence and abuse which they have witnessed, rather than been the direct victim of.

This child was 12 and she had reported sexual abuse. There was strong corroborative evidence and she was a good witness. The jury had paid close attention to the evidence. The defence then played their trump card—a 20 minute clip from a morning UK TV programme *The Big Breakfast*. The family had been selected some time previously as 'house of the week'. The defence barrister asked the jury repeatedly 'would this child be smiling if she had been sexually abused.' The jury found the defendant not guilty.

This case took place in Sweden in 1998. A three-year-old girl was the key witness against her father, a doctor. She had witnessed him cutting up a woman he had murdered. Much of the child's evidence centred on a very explicit picture she had drawn while under the supervision of a respected professional. The case was undermined when the defence produced a picture book, established that the child had been read this book by its mother, and suggested that the picture was connected to the storybook. This strategy was allowed even though the connection between the drawing and the book was spurious.

Margaret Kennedy (1992) tells of the experience of a boy with multiple disabilities who had been enabled to give evidence of sexual abuse by one of his carers. During cross-examination, the defence barrister asked 'Who would want to touch an ugly smelly boy like you?'

In October 1998, a woman was on trial in the Midlands for killing her abusive husband. She had three sons, all of whom witnessed the abuse she was subjected to. Her eldest son, from a previous relationship, was targeted for secret physical and emotional abuse by his stepfather, the middle son was selected for 'special' treatment, and invited to collude in the abuse of his mother. This child was called as a witness for the prosecution, and, as the court case approached, his behaviour caused concern at home and at school. Yet no support could be found in the statutory or voluntary sector for this child, despite the fact that he lived in a large urban conurbation.

Source: All are cases known to author, or to colleagues.

Each of the cases involving sexual violence demonstrate that children's credibility was at issue. It may be less acceptable to say that children lie in everyday discourse, but there are no such limits in the courtroom and nor do there seem to be any limits to the underhand tactics which defence lawyers will use to undermine children's evidence and testimony. Why was a video of a television programme which had nothing but tangential relevance to the case acceptable as evidence while still in the UK, videotapes of children's testimony are often disallowed? How can a barrister be permitted to emotionally abuse a disabled child in open court and this be accepted as legitimate legal argument? Some of the accepted practices in adversarial legal systems are unlikely to stand the test of the UN Convention on the Rights of the Child with respect to preserving children's rights and dignity when they appear in court.

It has already been noted that the focus of work on children's evidence, and their experience as witnesses, has become almost entirely a concern about child sexual abuse. Why sexual abuse has become the fulcrum around which these debates have coalesced bears further investigation. The usual response to this question is that cases of physical abuse and neglect invariably involve other forms of evidence, so the case does not stand or fall on the child's testimony. With extreme neglect this may well be the case, but with physical abuse, while the evidence on a child's body may be indisputable with respect to harm, there is still the question of who did it. And, in at least some cases, children's testimony will be the only, or at least a crucial, aspect of establishing this key legal fact. And, even where it is not, the evidence of professionals who proffer opinion as to the cause of injury and harm has not been subject to the kinds of scrutiny and challenge in courts or the literature that it has for sexual abuse.[9]

The lack of attention, interest, and care concerning how children give evidence in other contexts is also revealing, especially when looked at from the perspective of those organizations which purport to be advocates for children. Why has there been so little interest and concern for children as witnesses in domestic homicide and domestic violence cases? Here, protective parents—invariably the mother—are placed in impossible situations where they are asked to exercise the judgement of Solomon. Agreeing for a child/children to give evidence may support their case (and this will be especially acute where the woman is facing a murder charge), but this has to be weighed against the potential damage that may be done to the child in the process. The experience

---

[9] This is not to say that there are no debates in relation to other forms of child abuse, but that they are less extensive and do not carry the emotive burden which sexual abuse has.

of Justice for Women[10] attests to the fact that most women in this situation choose not to have their children as witnesses for the defence, even to the detriment of their own case. But this does not prevent them being called by the prosecution. And where is the principle of 'the best interests of the child' in this context, where the tensions created between mother and child which were central to the abuse are exacerbated rather than ameliorated by the legal system, and there is no support provided to endeavour to ensure that this intervention does not compound the traumatic history of this family.

Impunity Hardly Disturbed

The intention to challenge the impunity with which perpetrators were able to sexually abuse children has already been outlined, as has a reform process which endeavoured to provide some protection and support for children giving evidence. This section explores the failure—to date—of these projects, drawing on research and official statistics.

The London (Ontario) Family Court Clinic evaluated a programme designed to prepare children for court in the early 1990s (Child Witness Project, 1991). The findings reveal how the prospect of giving evidence is an additional pressure for children when they are already vulnerable and their capacities to cope overstretched. The sample was 675 reported cases, in almost two-thirds (63%) no charge was laid, so only a third of cases entered the criminal prosecution system, and the proportion falls to 14% where the child was aged between two and eight (Child Witness Project, 1991, p. 90). These figures are, however, higher than for the UK where between 2 and 5% of reported/suspected sexual abuse cases result in criminal prosecution (Gallagher, 1998). Of the 71 cases which went to trial, there was a conviction rate of 50%.

The stressors for children included delays; public exposure; having to face the accused; understanding the procedures; having a change of lawyers; cross-examination; the outcome; and lack of preparation. The project also recorded what children who gave evidence found stressful. Defence lawyers were experienced as: standing too close; using sharp loud intimidating voice; purposefully confusing children through language use and sentence construction; forcing children to face the

---

[10] Justice for Women is a campaign network in England established to support women who had killed their abusers. The network has supported over 40 women both pre-trial and through the appeal process and, with other women's organizations, especially Southall Black Sisters, is seen as responsible for a shift in judicial and legal thinking on the defences of provocation and self-defence in the context of domestic violence (Bindel, Cook, & Kelly, 1997).

accused by standing close to them during cross examination; arguing over points of law while the child was in the witness box; implying that the child enjoyed the abuse or that it didn't happen because they did not tell immediately; emphasizing the importance of dates and times when it has already been established that the child cannot confirm these. Prosecutors also used difficult language and asked confusing questions. They failed to intervene to protect children during cross-examination and neglected to apply for provisions which might have enabled children to give better evidence. Judges might deny access to protections and not protect children from inappropriate questions as well as asking unusually difficult questions to assess competence and failing to make eye contact with children. What is revealing about these findings is how many of them are the outcome of the theatre, per-formance, and presumptions underpinning adversarial legal systems. No amount of court preparation or care in how children's evidence is collected prior to trial can protect children from the worst excesses of adversarial court systems. The study includes statements from lawyers to illustrate the 'open season' which many take for granted with respect to child witnesses.

A study by NCH Action for Children (1994) confirms the continuing failure of the Criminal Justice System in the UK with respect to child sexual abuse. Files on 202 cases where professionals agreed abuse had occurred were the base sample and 35 of the children involved were interviewed. One in three cases were prosecuted, and one in four resulted in a conviction. Of the 35 children interviewed, 15 prosecutions had occurred, nine guilty verdicts resulted, seven of which involved guilty pleas.[11] Six children gave evidence in court, which resulted in two convictions. As disturbing was the fact that five children did not know if there had been a prosecution and four thought there had been one when there had not. Most of the children interviewed wanted justice, they sought public vindication; many were disappointed when their abusers were not prosecuted, and even stronger feelings were evoked by prosecutions which did not result in convictions.[12]

---

[11] The London Ontario study (Child Witness Project, 1991) make an interesting point about guilty pleas being used as mitigation with respect to sentencing, since it prevents the stress on children of giving evidence. They note that the timing of the plea is not considered, and many are only proffered the day the case comes to court; thus, the child has experienced the stress of believing they will have to give evidence for many months.

[12] This group of children also had challenging things to say about the support they were of-fered. They experienced one-to-one therapy as attempts to make them talk repeatedly about the abuse; for the children this was neither 'comfortable or helpful' (NCH Action for Children, 1994, p. 44). The most difficult form of therapy for children was family work, whereas group work with other children was the most popular; unfortunately, it was also the least common form of support provided for children.

Table 23.1. Attrition in reported rape cases, England and Wales 1977–1997.

Year	Number recorded	Convictions	Conviction rate (%)
1977	1,015	324	32
1987	2,471	453	18
1993	4,584	482	10
1996	5,754	573	10
1997	6,281	599	9

It is virtually impossible to track reporting and conviction rates for child sexual abuse in the UK, since many cases are prosecuted under offences which also apply to adults. There is, however, very recent work on rape which adds to our understanding. Table 23.1, drawn from Home Office yearly official crime figures, shows that while reporting rates have increased over the last 20 years the number of convictions has hardly risen at all: as a consequence, while a third of reported rapes resulted in conviction in 1977, this had fallen to less than a tenth in 1997.

A recent Home Office study into attrition in rape cases (Harris & Grace, 1999) reveals that a quarter of their sample of almost 500 cases involved under-16-year-olds. While cases involving children were more likely to proceed to court than those with adult complainants, attrition for child sexual abuse cases was also significant.

For many these data would lead to a conclusion that the criminal justice system—especially in its adversarial form—is simply not able to respond appropriately to children. And, indeed, it appears that in many reported cases in the UK civil child protection routes are much more commonly used than criminal prosecutions. But this amounts to a counsel of despair, leaving the culture of impunity virtually undisturbed. It also represents a failure under our obligations in the UN Convention of the Rights of the Child to ensure access to justice for children.

To my knowledge, there are no studies which look at survivors' perspectives on prosecution policy. A short series of questions in a prevalence study conducted by the author and colleagues (Kelly, Regan, & Burton, 1991) provides some baseline data. Over 1,200 young people at further education colleges completed a self-report questionnaire. Table 23.2 records the responses of 273 who reported sexual victimization to a short series of questions on public policy.

The overwhelming majority of these young people (aged 16–21) wanted their abusers prosecuted, even if they were family members. Those who were abused by a family member were, in fact, more likely

Table 23.2. Young survivors perspectives on prosecution policy.

Question	Yes		No/Not sure*	
	N	%	N	%
Should abusers be prosecuted?	260	95	13	05
Would your answer be the same if they were a member of your family?	231	87	36	13
Would you feel safe living with a familial abuser?	17	06	245	94
Would you feel safe having contact with a familial abuser?	23	09	237	91

* *Note:* The majority responded not sure to the first two questions, between 10 and 15 responded not sure to the third and fourth.

to support prosecution. When asked what the response to child sexual abuse should be, their priorities were: protection (63% mentioned removing abusers, and a further 15% removing the child); intervention which did not blame children; and for offenders to bear the consequences of their actions. These responses emphasize the critical importance of creating mechanisms which provide greater access to justice for both children who have been sexually abused and adult survivors.

Different questions, different answers

Under-reporting and under-prosecution of child sexual abuse cases continue to be intractable problems. Little research to date has explored what makes it more possible for children to tell about abuse, although the experience of ChildLine provides some important lessons. While more children are telling than did previously, most incidents remain unreported to official agencies. Children's accounts make clear how far the legal system has to go to accommodate their needs and perspectives (Keep, 1996; NCH Action for Children, 1994; Westcott, 1995; Wade & Westcott, 1997). The reforms which have been introduced in substantive law and procedure have clearly not yet been effective in creating either protection or justice for children. The priority remains to create investigation and prosecution processes which make an appreciable difference to the conviction rate and the short- and long-term protection of children.

It is my contention that no amount of psychological research on children's capacities for comprehension and recall, no amount of care in how interviews are conducted, and no 'scientific method' will resolve the central problem. And that in criminal cases in an adversarial system the defence's strongest tactic will be to attempt to undermine children's credibility. Moreover, the extent to which academics and practitioners have accommodated to the questioning of children's testimony has provided ammunition which is now frequently used in investigative systems, which might arguably have discovered more effective ways of enabling children to have access to justice.

REFERENCES

Armstrong, L. (1978). *Kiss Daddy Goodnight: A speak out about incest.* New York: Pocket Books.

Armstrong, L. (1994). *Rocking the cradle of sexual politics: What happened when women said incest.* New York, Addison Wesley.

Barrett, M., & McIntosh, M. (1982). *The anti-social family.* London: Verso.

Bell, D., & Klein, R. (Eds). (1996). *Radically speaking: Feminism reclaimed.* London: Zed Press.

Bifulco, A., & Moran, P. (1998). *Wednesday's Child: Research into women's experience of neglect and abuse in childhood, and adult depression.* London: Routledge.

Bindel, J., Cook, K., & Kelly, L. (1996). Justice for women: A feminist campaign for the 1990s. In: G. Griffin (Ed.), *Feminist activism in the 1990s.* London: Taylor & Francis.

Breckenridge, J., & Laing, L. (Eds). (1999). *Challenging silence: Innovative responses to sexual and domestic violence.* London: Allen & Unwin.

Campbell, B. (1988). *Unofficial secrets: Child sexual abuse—the Cleveland case.* London: Virago.

Child Witness Project. (1991). *Reducing the system-induced trauma for child sexual abuse victims through court preparation, assessment and follow-up.* London, Ontario: Family Court Clinic.

Comer, L. (1974). *Wedlocked women.* Leeds: Corner Books.

Cook, K., & Kelly, L. (1997). The abduction of credibility: A reply to John Paley. *British Journal of Social Work,* **27**, 71–84.

Cossins, A. (1999). Recovered memories of child sexual abuse: The science and the ideology. In: J. Breckenridge, & L. Laing (Eds), *Challenging silence: Innovative responses for sexual and domestic violence* (pp. 103–36). London: Allen & Unwin.

Droisen, A., & Driver, E. (1989). *Child sexual abuse: Feminist perspectives.* London: Macmillan.

Edwards, S. (1996). *Sex and gender in the legal process.* London: Blackstone Press.

Finkelhor, D. (1979). *Sexually victimized children.* New York: Free Press.

Firestone, S. (1972). *The dialectic of sex: The case for feminist revolution.* London: Paladin.

Gallagher, B. (1998). Attrition of child abuse cases in the criminal justice system. Paper presented to the BPS Research Seminar 1998, Understanding and Improving Children's Eyewitness Testimony, 19 October 1998. Milton Keynes: The Open University.

Gordon, L. (1988). *Heroes of their own lives: The history and politics of family violence.* New York: Viking Press.

Harris, J., & Grace, S. (1999). *A question of evidence?* London: Home Office.

Herman, L. (1994). *Trauma and recovery: From domestic abuse to political terror.* London, Pandora.

Home Office. (1998). *Speaking up for justice.* London: Home Office.

Home Office. (2000). *Implementation plan for vulnerable and intimidated witness measures.* London: Home Office.

Hughes, D. (1999). *Pimps and predators on the Internet: Globalizing the sexual exploitation of women and children.* Rhode Island: Coalition Against Trafficking in Women.

Humm, M. (Ed.). (1992). *Feminisms: A reader.* London, Wheatsheaf/Harvester.

Keep, G. (1996). *Going to court: Child witnesses in their own words.* London: ChildLine.

Kelly, L. (1988). *Surviving sexual violence.* Cambridge: Polity Press.

Kelly, L. (1998). Confronting an atrocity: The Dutroux case. *Trouble and Strife,* **36,** 16–22.

Kelly, L. (1999). *Violence against women: A briefing,* Manchester. The British Council.

Kelly, L., & Regan, L. (1990). Flawed protection. *Social Work Today,* 19 April 1990.

Kelly, L., Regan, L., & Burton, S. (1991). *An exploratory study of the prevalence of sexual abuse in a sample of 16–21 year olds* (Final report to the ESRC). London: Child Abuse Studies Unit, University of North London.

Kennedy, M. (1992). Special issue on disability and abuse. *Child Abuse Review,* **1**(3).

MacLeod, M. (1996). *Talking with children about child abuse.* London: ChildLine.

MacLeod, M., & Saraga, E. (1988). Challenging the orthodoxy: Towards a feminist theory and practice. *Feminist Review,* **28,** 16–56.

NCH Action for Children. (1994). *Messages from children: Children's evaluations of the professional response to child sexual abuse.* London: NCH Action for Children.

Nelson, S. (1998). Time to break professional silences. *Child Abuse Review,* **7**(3), 144–53.

Plotnikoff, J., & Woolfson, R. (1995). *Prosecuting child abuse: An evaluation of the government's speedy progress policy.* London: Blackstone Press.

Utting, W., Baines, L., Stuart, M., Rowlands, J., & Vialva, R. (1997). *People like us: The report of the review of the safeguards for children living away from home.* London: Her Majesty's Stationery Office.

Wade, A., & Westcott, H. (1997). No easy answers: Children's perspectives on investigative interviews. In: H.L. Westcott & J. Jones (Eds), *Perspectives on the Memorandum. Policy, practice and research in investigative interviewing.* Aldershot, UK: Arena.

Westcott, H. (1995). Children's experiences of being examined and cross-examined: The opportunity to be heard. *Expert Evidence,* **4**(1), 13–19.

Review of Part IV

Our three contributors in this final part of the book were invited specifically to offer challenging and provocative dimensions to the debate about children's testimony. Interestingly, a single theme does emerge from all three, albeit from radically different perspectives: the theme of 'credibility'.

Brian Clifford, from his position as 'sceptical psychologist' believes that the 'zeitgeist is really flowing in children's favour' and that, in brief, children's capabilities and credibility as witnesses are in danger of being overstated. He highlights a number of conceptual, methodological, statistical, and measurement problems which he sees as bedevilling psychological research on children's evidence, to the extent that child witnesses' credibility may be overestimated as a result. Clifford urges psychologists to stop treating all children as 'an undifferentiated, homogenous non-adult population' and to stop ignoring the 'strong motives, threats, and inducements that are often part of the aftermath of abuse'. Direct involvement with, and feedback from, child witnesses facilitates an understanding of the importance of these unstudied issues (see Wade & Westcott, 1997 for a review)

Corinne Wattam, from a sociologist's perspective, examines issues of social constructionism, impression formation, and the credibility of children as witnesses in court. She notes that the social organization of evidence is not studied or reflected upon by psychologists in relation to child witnesses, so that very little attention is paid to the way in which 'the reliability of children is used as a topic and resource in the construction of evidence concerning them'. Wattam stresses the agency of children who are 'active, thinking, sense-making interactors who co-produce the social world', thus highlighting the way in which children as research participants, or as witnesses, are typically marginalized by psychological discourse. Previous contributions in

Children's Testimony. Edited by H.L. Westcott, G.M. Davies, and R.H.C. Bull.
© 2002 John Wiley & Sons, Ltd.

this book have provided examples of this marginalization in the development and consequences of reforms aimed at child witnesses.

As a feminist, Liz Kelly asserts that 'the history of denying credibility to women and children lies at the heart of debates and issues concerning children's evidence.' Furthermore, there 'can be no scientific or technical approach which will provide a resolution of debates which are at root political and ideological' (and which sidestep issues of credibility). Many of the contributions to Part III, especially those concerned with the practicalities of getting children's evidence heard at court, would go some way to supporting such a view. Kelly stresses the importance of listening to survivors of abuse—and the court process—and of 'calling abusers to account'. When considering access to justice for children, and the protection of children, Kelly's chapter poses the question 'On what measure do we judge child witness reforms a success?'

In contrast to our attempts in previous reviews to draw together implications for practitioners from various authors, we simply present our Part IV summaries here for readers to consider. This is not a reflection on the value we ascribe to the contributions of Clifford, Wattam, and Kelly. Such diverse and challenging perspectives are essential if psychological research, and forensic practice, in the field of children's testimony are to develop in meaningful and sensitive ways.

REFERENCE

Wade, A., & Westcott, H.L. (1997). No easy answers: Children's perspectives on investigative interviews. In: H.L. Westcott & J. Jones (Eds), *Perspectives on the Memorandum. Policy practice and research in investigative interviewing.* Aldershot, UK: Arena.

Epilogue

Much—and varied—ground has been covered in the four parts of this book. Psychological theory, practice, and research as it applies to children's testimony has been reviewed, contested, and critiqued by contributors. A multitude of implications for practitioners and researchers have been suggested. As editors, it is difficult to know where to begin an appropriate ending!

Perhaps the very range of topics covered in this volume is one of its most striking features and testament to the steadfast interest and commitment psychologists have shown in progressing the rights of child witnesses and victims. The wealth of knowledge accumulated and shared is extensive. As knowledge has extended, however, so the complexities and challenges have become more apparent. What are the possibilities for further research and practice in this area?

PSYCHOLOGICAL RESEARCH

Several authors have suggested methodological improvements, and there is undoubtedly room for refinements in both experimental and applied approaches to research on children's testimony. It is perhaps worth reflecting again on the nature of sexual abuse, since so much psychological research has been prompted by sexual crimes against children. Although aspects of sexual abuse can be mimicked in experimental designs, it is the constellation of all these aspects—stress, fear, repeated attacks, abuse of authority and intimacy, secrecy—that makes sexual abuse so painful for its victims (Finkelhor & Browne, 1985). One challenge is to develop approaches to research which can consider this constellation of experiences in a more holistic fashion. In addition, psychologists must guard against overstating the ecological

Children's Testimony. Edited by H.L. Westcott, G.M. Davies, and R.H.C. Bull.
© 2002 John Wiley & Sons, Ltd.

realism of their research and also must monitor any misrepresentation of their findings in courts, in media, and in training of practitioners. Translating lessons from group data to applications regarding an individual child witness are but one example.

Another challenge facing researchers is that of evaluation—in all its guises. The need for more attention to—and evaluation of—methodology and realism has already been emphasized, and we have noted in our earlier reviews the need to evaluate what factors psychological research on child witnesses typically fails to address. These include issues of motivation, emotion, cultural diversity, disability, and other individual differences. Other evaluative strands have been suggested by contributors:

- evaluation of the interviewer's role, behaviour, and influence;
- evaluation of the child's strengths, requirements, and specific needs;
- evaluation of the communicative context within which the adult and child meet.

The need for more information about the long-term consequences of interventions for children has also been highlighted.

Some of the biggest questions surround evaluation of training concerning interviewing practice. Why do interviewers fail to do what they are trained to do? What can psychologists do to ensure that the lessons of their research are fully translated into practice? Is it simply a matter of resources? Part III emphasizes that the broader systemic influences, particularly the pressures created by the expectations of courtroom personnel, must also be recognized and taken into account.

PSYCHOLOGICAL PRACTICE

The importance of listening to children, young people, and adult survivors has been stressed in this book. Psychologists must respond to children's needs and requirements, and must help society avoid the marginalization of children and young people that has occurred in the past. If reforms already implemented, and those yet to be desired, are to work, then children and young people must be fully consulted and involved in their implementation. Strangely, for a profession based on understanding human behaviour, rather little understanding has been extended to the child's point of view in psychological research and practice relating to children's testimony. Instead, children have been portrayed as passive and voiceless. The child's own perspective is but another of the complexities waiting to be fully addressed.

A multitude of implications for interviewers have been raised. The onus is on the adult interviewer to take account of these implications and take steps to incorporate them into practice as far as possible; adults must take back the responsibility for investigating allegations rather than placing impossible expectations and responsibility upon children and young people. In this respect, if no other, we would do well to benefit from the range of perspectives that is represented in this book. The similarities and differences in international practice reported here offers the opportunity for new reviews of interviewing, as well as the possibility of exploring new approaches.

The fundamental difficulties in reconciling the different objectives of psychologists and lawyers in the courtroom remain and forensic practice must acknowledge these in order for reforms to progress at all. The attitudinal barriers of court professionals will persist, and must be addressed by multidisciplinary initiatives at many levels. Another challenge is to tackle the iniquities caused by discretionary measures in the system, without unintentionally removing flexibility which may be to the child witness's advantage. The decision about how to receive a child's evidence (live or via videotaped interview) is one example.

The United Nations Convention on the Rights of the Child (Article 12) unequivocally states children's rights to be heard in judicial proceedings that affect them. Inevitably, this position has proved problematic for adversarial systems of justice more concerned with any apparent imbalance in favour of the prosecution case. However, those adults whose work relates to children's testimony—in psychological research or forensic practice—have a responsibility to promote this right and must endeavour to remember what it is like to be a child.

REFERENCE

Finkelhor, D., & Browne, A. (1985). The traumatic impact of child sexual abuse: A conceptualization. *American Journal of Orthopsychiatry*, **55**, 530–41.

Glossary

Analogue study   A piece of experimental research which has parallels with an event or experience in the real world in major respects without being identical to it (e.g. studies into children's memory for non-abusive but unpleasant events, such as certain medical treatments, may be considered as analogous to memory for abusive events). Analogue studies are of particular value in situations where it would be unethical to evoke or create certain memories purely for experimental purposes.

ANOVA (analysis of variance)   A commonly used statistical procedure used to assess whether several groups of scores differ from each other by amounts which are unlikely to be due to **chance** (see below).

Ceiling (*see also* Floor)   If a test measure contains too many easy terms, this will result in most scores lying at the top (ceiling) level, so that the measure cannot discriminate between individuals. The opposite effect (uniformly low scores) is known as a **floor** effect.

Cell size   A cell is the smallest element in overall design of an experiment. Cell size refers to the number of individuals who underwent a particular experimental procedure.

Chance   The probability that the results obtained in an experiment are due to chance rather than to the experimental variable(s) manipulated by the investigator. Statistical tests enable the experimenter to determine whether the latter is plausible or not.

Cognitive   Term referring to higher mental processes. Examples of such processes include memory, attention, perception, thinking, and reasoning.

Children's Testimony. Edited by H.L. Westcott, G.M. Davies, and R.H.C. Bull.
© 2002 John Wiley & Sons, Ltd.

Condition   Way in which an independent variable may be experimentally varied. The variable being manipulated may have several conditions (or levels); for example, the experimental variable 'recall delays' might have three conditions: (1) ten minutes, (2) two days, (3) six months. *Control condition/group* is used in an experiment for comparison with the experimental condition. The control shares the characteristics of the experimental condition except in respect of one or more of the variables being tested (the Independent Variable or IV). *Baseline condition/group* is used to determine the level at which a function is operating before any experimental procedures have started. Baseline measures taken before an intervention is started may be used to predict what the level of function would have been without that intervention. *Experimental condition/group* is used in an experiment which receives the treatment under investigation.

Conformity demands   Where participants in an experiment feel obliged to change their behaviour/stated beliefs in response to real or imagined social pressure from the experimenter or experimental situation.

Confounding variable/s (*see also* Variable)   Aspects of an experimental study which are left uncontrolled by the experimenter and which may unduly affect the results and thereby have a 'confounding' (confusing) effect on interpreting the findings; for example, two tests conducted at different times of the day might produce differing results, but the difference could be due to an effect of time of day on the participant, rather than a real difference between tests.

Connectionist model of memory   One type of theoretical model of the mental processes involved in learning and remembering. It uses computer modelling techniques which allow the simulation and prediction of the effects of different conditions.

Demand characteristics   Those features of an experimental setting which suggest to participants that certain kinds of behaviour are expected in response to the task.

Dependent Variables (*see also* Variables)   The variable that is measured in an experiment to see if the manipulation of the Independent Variable has caused any changes is known as the Dependent Variable—it is an outcome measure which is *dependent* on the variables being manipulated.

Distractors/distractor items   New items added to previously studied items in an experiment to 'distract' participants and enable the experimenter to determine how well they can recognize the original items.

Ecological validity   (A concern with) whether the results obtained within the artificial environment of a laboratory can be considered to represent what might occur in a natural, real-life setting.

Emotional lability (*see* Lability)

Empirical Deriving from the philosophical view that experience is the basis of all knowledge, this term is used to indicate evidence which is derived from observation, experience, and measurement as opposed to pure theory, and which is capable of being objectively assessed by others.

Encoding Term used to refer to the taking in of information so that it can be represented internally in the memory's 'storage system'.

Experimental condition (*see* Condition)

Floor level (*see also* Ceiling) When a measure/test is too difficult for the participants involved, most items will tend to score at the bottom (floor) level, which means that the measure cannot discriminate usefully between individuals in different conditions. The opposite effect is called the **ceiling** level.

Factor/Factorial design (*see also* Variable) A research design which uses more than one independent variable (IV). Each IV is known as a factor in this kind of design (*see also* ANOVA).

Generalizability of results The extent to which the results obtained by a study may be considered representative of much wider situations outside the experimental setting (*see also* Ecological validity).

Grounded theory A non-statistical, qualitative approach to research which specifies that the information collected (e.g. through interviews) is 'grounded' in real-life observations rather than influenced in advance by theoretical assumptions. The information gathered (data) is explored in detail until recurrent themes or issues emerge.

Hierarchical linear modelling techniques Statistical procedures for analysing the effects of (independent) variables in a study in a systematic and ordered way.

Heuristics Problem-solving strategies which involve taking the most probable or likely option from a possible set of options, as opposed to working systematically through all possible options.

Hypothetical–deductive reasoning Technique of investigation/ form of reasoning proposed by the philosopher Karl Popper as being central to the scientific method.

Independent Variable (*see also* Variable) The variable(s) which is manipulated in an experiment in order to assess what, if any, effect it has on other variables.

Interaction A term used when reporting results from a study using ANOVA (analysis of variance), to indicate that each condition of

an independent variable has a different effect on each condition of
another independent variable.

Lability   Tendency to change rapidly, especially used with respect to
emotional states.

Line-up   An identification procedure used in criminal investigations
where the eye witness in case views a 'line-up' containing the
suspect plus a number of other individuals ('foils') who resemble
the suspect. The witness is invited to select the person they saw.
Simultaneous line-up is the traditional procedure in which the
witness is presented with all members of the line-up (i.e. the
suspect plus foils) at the same time. *Sequential line-up* is modification of the procedure in which the witness only sees one person at
a time, sequentially. As each person is presented, the witness has
to say whether or not the person is the suspect.

Main effect   Term used when reporting the results of a factorial study
to indicate the overall relationship between one class of Independent Variable and the Dependent Variable (the outcome measure).

Mean   The arithmetical average. One of three 'measures of central
tendency' used in statistics, the others being the mode and the
median. Written as M, $\bar{x}$ or μ.

Memory trace   Term associated with theories of *forgetting*. A trace is
a hypothetical representation of input material which is stored in
memory. It is assumed that forgetting occurs due to memory traces
fading away over time (trace decay) unless they are strengthened
by rehearsal.

Misinformation (*see also* Post-event information   Term associated with eye-witness memory for events. If witnesses are
exposed to misinformation/misleading information between witnessing an event and recalling it later (e.g. if they are inappropriately
questioned by an interviewer), the misleading information can
have the effect of supplementing or modifying the original memory.

Paradigm   The framework of assumptions or set of beliefs which are
shared by a scientific community and which are used to interpret
factual information.

Path analysis   Statistical method that aims to estimate the relationships between a number of variables. The relationships are
graphically portrayed as a diagram, with arrows representing
either causal relationships or correlations.

Positively related   Term used to denote the kind of relationship that
exists between pairs of values obtained from two different variables.
The variables are said to be positively related if, as the values of
one increase on a scale of measurement, so do those of the other

(e.g. as the temperature rises so does the number of ice-creams sold).

Post-event information (*see also* **Misinformation**) Term associated with eye-witness memory research. If witnesses are exposed to new information between witnessing an event and recalling it (i.e. post-event), that information may combine with the original memory to the extent of supplementing or modifying it.

Qualitative study Research which is informed by the assumption that the *meaning* of the information is the most important thing (cf. quantitative studies, which are concerned with obtaining numerical information that can be analysed using statistics).

Recall A form of remembering. Refers to the deliberate summoning up of item/s stored in memory and bringing them into consciousness. *Cued recall* is triggered by cues or prompts (verbal or non-verbal) which assist the process of retrieval. *Free recall* retrieves items from memory without the use of specific prompts or cues.

Receptive vocabulary Term used by professionals investigating children's language competence. The term refers to the vocabulary that a child can recognize (e.g. by pointing to a picture of something when told its name) but may not yet be able to use in expressive speech.

Regression to the mean The tendency for individuals who score at the extremes (high or low) of any measure to score less extremely on being retested; their scores will tend to move towards the mean (average) score.

Reliability How consistent a given measure is and how likely it is to produce the same results if used again in the same circumstances.

Representation The form that knowledge about the world takes when internalized and represented in the mind in a particular way. Language is one form of representation.

Response bias Tendency of participants in an experiment to produce responses that they feel are socially desirable or that they think the experimenter expects to find.

Retention interval The period of time that items are held in memory.

Retrieve/Retrieval Term used to refer to the process of remembering an event in which the relevant information is seen as being 'retrieved' from some kind of memory storage system.

Retrieval cues/Strategies Cues or strategies which facilitate the retrieval of information from memory.

Sample (size) (*see also* **Significance**) A part of any population of interest (e.g. a group of people) which is studied so that researchers can generalize from these results to the wider population. Samples

$(\mu_{\bar{x}})$ need to be of a reasonable size in order to yield statistically significant results.

Schema (*plural* Schemata/Schemas)   Schemas are hypothesized to be 'clusters' of knowledge about all kinds of things, simple and complex, derived from experience of the world. *Schema theory* claims that what we remember is influenced by what we already know (pre-existing schemas).

Script   A form of schema, a script is a general-knowledge structure which represents the information abstracted from a class of similar events rather than one *specific* event. People have 'scripts' for familiar, everyday experiences such as visiting a restaurant or seeing the doctor, whereby certain events/actions and their sequence will be common to each occasion.

Semantic   Concerned with meaning; semantics explore the intended meaning which underlies any utterance or signal.

Semi-structured interview   An interviewing approach whereby the interviewer has an idea of the general topics s/he wants to cover but does not wish to constrain the participants' responses unduly. It falls between the extremes of the totally unstructured interview (where there is no pre-set agenda) and the highly structured interview, where the questions are exactly the same for every respondent.

Show-up   An identification procedure sometimes used in cases where police believe they know the identity of the perpetrator and require confirmation. A witness is allowed to see the suspect (either live or as a photograph) and is simply asked whether the suspect is or is not the perpetrator.

Significance (*see also* Substantive)   As it is never possible to say with absolute certainty that a result is due to experimental manipulation, levels of statistical probability as to whether results should be accepted as *not* purely due to chance are set in advance. The accepted levels are usually equal to or less than 0.01 (1 in 100 or 1%) and 0.05 (5 in 100 or 5%) and, if either of these are met, a researcher may claim to have 'significant' results.

Source monitoring (*see also* Misinformation)   Memory can be a composite based on different sources of information so that memory for an event derived from one source (e.g. witnessing it) becomes confused over time with information derived from other sources (e.g. being told about it), and people may eventually have difficulty in distinguishing which information came from what source.

Stimulus   Any external event which is detected by the senses of a living organism (human, animal, plant) and responded to.

Substantive (significance) Researchers may obtain a result which is technically significant without being strong or important in real terms. 'Substantive' is a term which, when applied to the findings of research studies, suggests that findings are of *real* theoretical/ scientific importance and not purely of a 'statistical' significance.

Suggestibility Susceptibility to being unduly biased by inappropriate/suggestive questioning techniques (e.g. use of leading questions). Very young children can be particularly susceptible in this respect.

Validity (*see also* Ecological validity) Refers to how far any measure can really assess what it is intended to measure (e.g. is an IQ test really a valid measure of a person's intelligence?).

Variable (*see also* Independent Variable, Dependent Variable) Anything that can come in different forms (i.e. varies) (e.g. age, sex, test scores). In experiments, variables are 'manipulated' in order to see what effect this will have on other variables (i.e. which variables cause changes in other variables).

Index